RESEARCH DEVELOPMENTS IN DRUG AND ALCOHOL USE

ANNALS OF THE NEW YORK ACADEMY OF SCIENCES

Volume 362

RESEARCH DEVELOPMENTS IN DRUG AND ALCOHOL USE

Edited by Robert B. Millman, Paul Cushman, Jr.
and Joyce H. Lowinson

The New York Academy of Sciences
New York, New York
1981

Library of Congress Cataloging In Publication Data

Main entry under title:

Research developments in drug and alcohol use.
(Annals of the New York Academy of Sciences; v. 362)
Includes index.
1. Drug abuse—Research—Congresses.
2. Alcoholism—Research—Congresses. I. Millman, Robert B. II. Cushman, Paul. III. Lowinson, Joyce H. IV. Series. [DNLM: 1. Substance abuse—Congresses. W1 AN626YL v. 362]
Q11.N5 vol. 362 [HV5809] 500s 81-3973
[362.2'9'072] AACR2

PCP

Printed in the United States of America

ISBN-0-89766-117-6 (cloth)

ISBN-0-89766-118-4 (paper)

ANNALS OF THE NEW YORK ACADEMY OF SCIENCES

VOLUME 362

May 5, 1981

RESEARCH DEVELOPMENTS IN DRUG AND ALCOHOL USE *

Conference Chairman

ROBERT B. MILLMAN

Editors

ROBERT B. MILLMAN, PAUL CUSHMAN, JR., AND JOYCE H. LOWINSON

Conference Organizing Committee

ROBERT B. MILLMAN, Chairman; BENJAMIN KISSIN, JAY LARSEN, JOYCE H. LOWINSON, REV. JOHN H. MCVERNON, NORBERT J. ROBERTS, BARRY STIMMEL, AND NATHAN STRAUSS III

CONTENTS

* This series of papers is the result of a conference entitled Research Developments in Drug and Alcohol Use held 4–5 December, 1979 by the National Association on Drug Abuse Problems and the Committee on Public Health, New York Academy of Medicine.

Part IV. Issues in Opiate Dependence

Part V. Adverse Effects of Drugs of Abuse

Part VI. Alternative Perspectives on the Drugs of Abuse

Part VII. Acute and Protracted Aspects of the Abstinence Syndrome

Part VIII. Clinical Aspects of Detoxification from Opiates

Financial assistance was received from:

- BURROUGHS WELLCOME COMPANY
- DRY DOCK SAVINGS BANK
- ELI LILLY AND COMPANY
- ENDO LABORATORIES, INC.
- EXXON CORPORATION
- MERCK SHARP & DOHME, DIVISION OF MERCK & CO., INC.
- ROCHE LABORATORIES, DIVISION OF HOFFMANN-LA ROCHE, INC.
- SANDOZ CORPORATION
- G. D. SEARLE AND COMPANY
- SCHERING-PLOUGH CORPORATION
- SMITH KLINE & FRENCH LABORATORIES, DIVISION OF SMITHKLINE CORPORATION

INTRODUCTION

Robert B. Millman

Department of Public Health
The New York Hospital–Cornell Medical Center
New York, New York 10021

Paul Cushman, Jr.

Departments of Pharmacology, Medicine and Psychiatry
Medical College of Wisconsin and De Paul Rehabilitation Hospital
Milwaukee, Wisconsin 53193

Joyce H. Lowinson

Department of Psychiatry
Albert Einstein College of Medicine
Bronx, New York 10461

The use and abuse of psychoactive drugs and alcohol continues to be an important human behavior as well as a major societal problem. In response to this, there has been a remarkable burgeoning of the scientific base of this field in recent years, both in clinical and preclinical areas. These proceedings derive from a conference sponsored by the National Association on Drug Abuse Problems (NADAP) and the Committee on Public Health of The New York Academy of Medicine, "Research Developments in Drug and Alcohol Use" that was held in New York City in December, 1979. This conference was developed to provide a forum where scientists, treatment providers, and governmental representatives might consider some of these new developments and data with a view toward their more rapid application to the needs of patients as well as the stimulation of additional targeted, effective scientific investigations.

A previous conference also sponsored by NADAP, "Recent Developments in Chemotherapy of Narcotic Addiction," held in November 1977, in Washington, D.C. and published in 1978 as Volume 311 of the *Annals of The New York Academy of Sciences* established a fine precedent. We trust that the present meeting maintained a similar level of excellence with a significantly broader focus.

Psychoactive drug taking has been looked at according to unduly limited perspectives. This has been due to a multiplicity of factors. Workers in the field have often been isolated from the more traditional scientific disciplines. Psychiatry, neurology, and medicine are often loath to accept responsibility for these difficult patients and, consequently, to formulate research questions and develop answers. Basic scientists are often unaware of the pressing clinical issues in this field. Psychologists and sociologists are often unfamiliar with the biological aspects of drug-taking behaviors. Until recently, the field was not considered a legitimate or prestigious field of endeavor.

Whereas many of us have a parochial interest in some aspects of drug or alcohol use, the interests of our patients are often more eclectic. They take alcohol in addition to drugs of many classes, such that they confound our treatment efforts and research goals. It is clear that we have to know more about the various drug classes, their similarities and differences, and about their interactions. It makes little sense that alcohol treatment programs cannot handle patients dependent on other drugs or that methadone programs have insufficient resources to effectively treat their alcohol-dependent patients. To these ends, presentations on alcohol and a variety of other drugs were included in the program. The withdrawal syndromes from opiates and alcohol were considered with a view towards facilitating considerations of similarities, differences, and new areas to investigate.

The pharmacology and patterns of use of the various drugs of abuse are increasingly influencing knowledge of the psychobiology of the affective and cognitive psychiatric disorders. Agonistic and antagonistic actions of drugs as well as their withdrawal syndromes may, in fact, mimic or precipitate particular functional psychiatric syndromes. The pharmacological investigations of clonidine and buprenorphine may elucidate aspects of psychobiologic function while they are being evaluated for possible clinical efficacy. Presentations on opioid neurotransmitters, brain reward mechanisms, and neuropsychological determinants of opiate addiction are further indicative of this rapprochement between psychiatry and substance abuse. We are at a point now where we stand to learn a good deal from people working in heretofore removed areas.

Continuing evaluations of the characteristics, indications, and results of particular therapeutic modalities are also included in this volume. While new methods are being developed, it is essential that current procedures be critically and dispassionately considered. Presentations on methadone maintenance and detoxification, behavior modification techniques, and psychotherapeutic interventions are presented in this vein.

The program and the distinguished participants reflect the concerns and interests of the conference committee as well as a good many other people whose opinions we solicited. The papers were of high quality and provoked a good deal of lively and sophisticated discussion, a portion of which we have included in the proceedings. It is well recognized that much important work was omitted from the program. We are encouraged to develop similar meetings in the future that might include some of this work.

We would like to express our appreciation to the sponsors of this conference: NADAP and The New York Academy of Medicine, Committee on Public Health. The National Association on Drug Abuse Problems is a voluntary agency located in Manhattan and is devoted to the vocational rehabilitation of people with substance abuse problems. Representing a joint effort of management and labor, this active organization has focused on job development, vocational placement, as well as the training of substance abuse treatment teams. Beginning with the early methadone conferences, it has provided strong leadership and support in the planning, administration, and publication of major drug abuse-related conferences. The New York Academy of Medicine, founded in 1847, has long served as a forum to examine contemporary health problems and advances in the art and science of medicine. The Standing Committees on Public Health, Medical Education, and Medicine in Society have had significant impact on medical theory and practice through the years. We are also grateful to The New York Academy of Sciences for their expert and elegant publication of these proceedings.

We would like to particularly thank Dr. Norbert J. Roberts, Medical Director of the Exxon Corporation and Chairman of the Executive Committee of NADAP, and H. Daniel Carpenter, President of NADAP. As with the 1977 conference, they provided strong leadership and organizational skills throughout the planning process. Financial support for this meeting was provided by NADAP and members of private industry, whose names are listed following the table of contents of this volume.

Finally, we acknowledge with sincere gratitude the enthusiastic and knowledgeable work of the conference committee in developing the concept of this meeting and planning the individual sessions. We are proud of the conference and this publication and are encouraged to develop comparable conferences in the future.

PART I. EPIDEMIOLOGY AND CHARACTERISTICS OF DRUG AND ALCOHOL ABUSE

NATIONAL PATTERNS OF ALCOHOL USE AND ABUSE

Sheila Blume

New York State Division of Alcoholism and Alcohol Abuse
Albany, New York 12229

INTRODUCTION

When interviewed by members of the press, most of us in the field of alcoholism have had similar experiences. The first question asked is usually "just how many alcoholics *are* there in the United States?" The reporter wants to know whether there are five million, ten million, or, as estimated in a recent Journal of the American Medical Association editorial, 17 million.[7] In trying to answer what seems like a simple question, the alcohol specialist must confront some of the field's most difficult and perplexing problems. The first and most basic of these is the use of the term "alcoholism." At one extreme is the definition of alcoholism as a disease diagnosed according to the National Council on Alcoholism criteria,[18] which is expressed as a dichotomy: either a person is or is not an alcoholic. On the other extreme is the concept of problem drinking, defined by constructing scales based on the number and extent of various alcohol-related problems, such as public intoxication or drinking driver arrests, employment problems, and domestic violence, yielding a continuous distribution rather than a dichotomy. Yet another concept for defining alcoholism defines a level of "hazardous consumption" and counts the number of people whose average daily intake exceeds this consumption as "alcoholics." [9] The level of hazardous consumption for alcoholism is generally defined as a daily average of 15 centiliters of absolute alcohol: roughly 12½ ounces of 80 proof liquor or the equivalent. (The level of hazardous consumption putting one at risk for cirrhosis of the liver is considered somewhat lower, approximately ½ pint of 80 proof liquor per day.)

The second difficult problem touched by the seemingly simple question concerns the various sources of data upon which epidemiological estimates are made. For the alcohol studies field the principal sources are: 1) tax and population data, allowing the calculation of average per capita consumption, types of beverages consumed, and trends in consumption; 2) survey data, usually household surveys conducted by face to face or telephone interview, occasionally in schools by questionnaire; and 3) "catastrophe" counts, in which estimates of alcohol-related problems are made from reported death rates from cirrhosis of the liver, hospital admissions for alcohol psychoses or alcoholism, alcohol-related arrests, automobile crashes and other similar events.

Each of these sources yields both useful data and a series of methodological problems. Before reviewing these data, some of the theories advanced to explain them, and some of the problems in method, let us look at a "best guess" of the situation in the United States today. FIGURE 1[15,16] presents an estimated distribution of the drinking age population of the United States; men and women age 14 and older, for the year 1975. Of the 160 million Americans in this age range, 48 million are abstainers and 112 million drink alcohol. As many as 11.5 million may have serious alcohol problems, with approximately half that number, 5.75 million, probably identifiable as "alcoholic."

Epidemiology of Alcohol Use and Abuse

Tax and population data yield interesting views of trends in alcohol consumption over time. FIGURE 2 (Alcohol and Health, 1978) shows a general increase in total per capita consumption during the last 20 years with a particular increase in the consumption of beer and a slight recent decrease in the

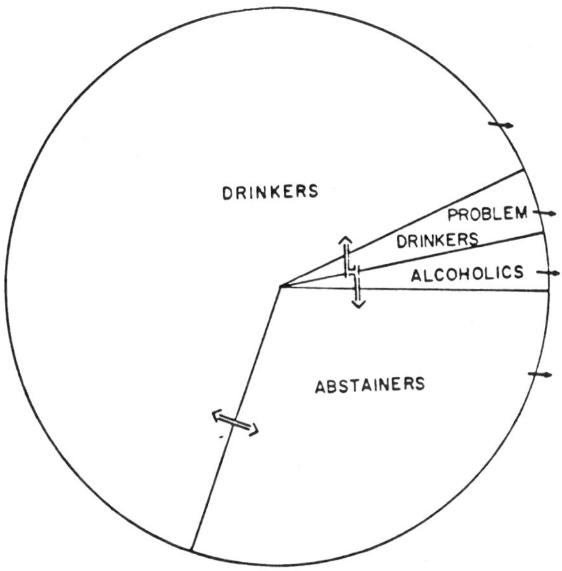

FIGURE 1. Estimated distribution of the drinking age population, U.S.A., 1975. Total, age 14 and older: 160 million = 100%. All drinkers (nonabstainers), 112 million = 70% (includes problem drinkers, 5.75 million = 5.2%; alcoholics, 5.75 million = 5.2%). (From Keller and Gurioli.[15] By permission of *Journal of Studies on Alcohol.*)

consumption of hard liquor. The problem with these figures is that, based as they are on tax records, they omit the consumption of illegal (bootleg, moonshine) alcoholic beverages. The use of such beverages is thought to have varied from as much as 15 percent of the legal beverage use 15 or 20 years ago to a relatively small percentage at the present time. If true, this would mean that the true increase in per capita consumption is considerably less than the apparent increase (Burk, 1976). This problem is magnified when efforts are made to compare per capita consumption between states, countries, and regions of the world. An unknown proportion of the alcohol purchased in any given state will be carried across a border and drunk elsewhere. Consumers may stock up when prices are lower. Tourists and other travelers residing in other

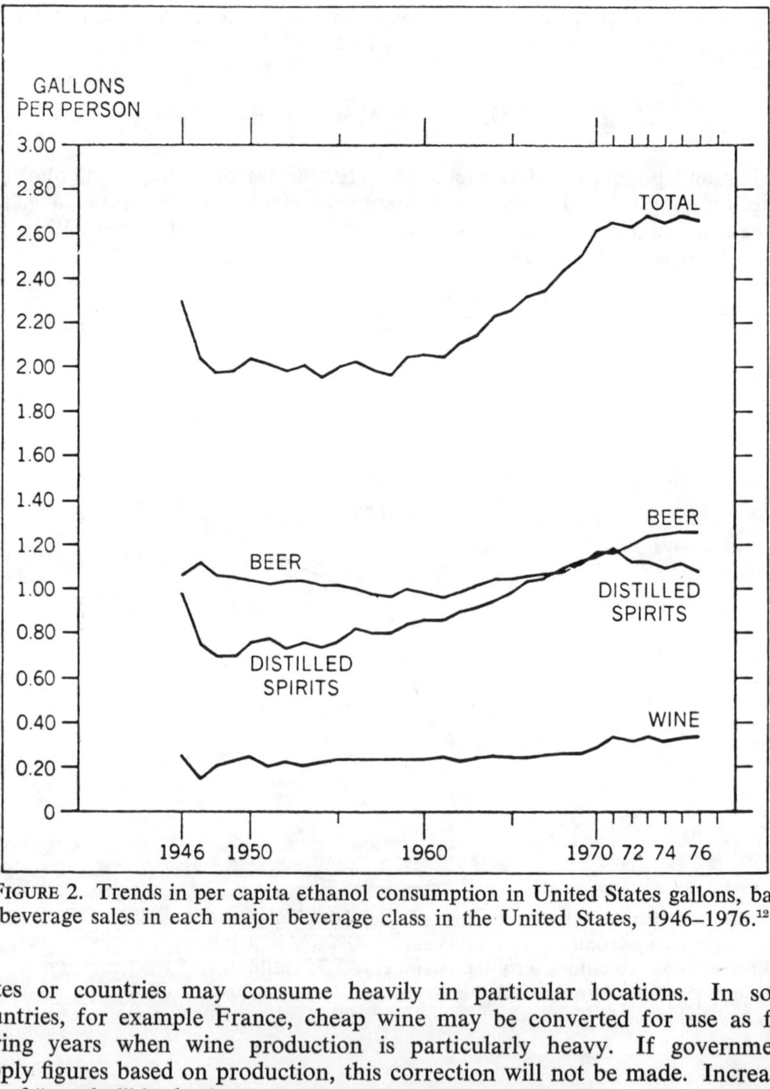

FIGURE 2. Trends in per capita ethanol consumption in United States gallons, based on beverage sales in each major beverage class in the United States, 1946–1976.[12]

states or countries may consume heavily in particular locations. In some countries, for example France, cheap wine may be converted for use as fuel during years when wine production is particularly heavy. If governments supply figures based on production, this correction will not be made. Increased use of "gasohol" in the future may compound this problem.

An interesting set of findings based on both tax-population and survey data is illustrated by FIGURE 3, a distribution of consumption curve.[8] Plotting the percentage of people who drink alcohol in a population along the *Y* axis and mean consumption, either annual or daily, on the *X* axis results in a log normal curve, sometimes referred to as a "Ledermann Curve" because of the work of Ledermann in the 1950s. Such a curve can be described by two quantities: the mean per capita consumption, and a measure of dispersion. Since the spread of the curve is thought to be a constant, the approximate curve may be plotted from a known mean. Those persons falling under the tail end of the curve are thought to be the "population at risk," the "problem drinkers," or the "alcoholics." It is argued, therefore, that any decrease in mean per capita consumption will move the curve to the left and greatly decrease the proportion of the population at the tail end of the curve. It has repeatedly been found that there is an inverse correlation between the real price of alcohol (the price divided by the average disposable income of the population) and mean per capita consumption. FIGURE 4 [8] illustrates that relationship for the province of Ontario, Canada. Furthermore, various measures of alcohol-related problems also correlate with mean per capita consumption and real price of alcohol. For example, FIGURE 5 plots the number of road accidents and the real price of rum in Trinidad and Tobago between 1956 and 1975.[3] Putting all these findings together, it has been recommended that governments adjust taxation to control the real price of alcoholic beverages, either to stabilize or to decrease the mean per capita consumption, as a method aimed at decreasing the incidence of alcoholism or alcohol-related problems in a particular population.[1] FIGURE 6 illustrates recent United States trends in the real price of distilled spirits, showing that the price has risen much less than the prices of other goods.[10] The above-summarized theory of primary prevention through taxation affecting per capita consumption has been hotly debated, but has not been seriously attempted anywhere in the world to date, to my knowledge.

Problems with the above theory are discussed by Room.[19] The accuracy of the measurement of mean per capita consumption presents a problem in itself as discussed above. By the nature of the distribution of consumption curve, small deviations in mean consumption lead to large changes in the population defined as hazardous drinkers or alcoholics. Definitions of alcoholism using single cut-off points of average consumption, as illustrated in FIGURE 7,[9] ignore important differences between individuals, particularly between men and women.

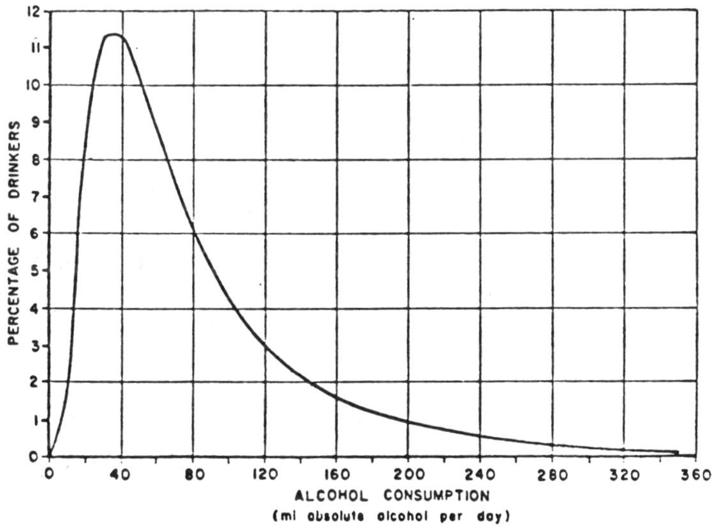

FIGURE 3. Distribution of drinkers according to average daily volume of consumption in a population with an annual consumption per drinker of 30 liters of absolute ethanol. (From DeLint and Schmidt.[8] By permission of Wiley-Interscience.)

Women weigh on an average 40 pounds less than men, and have an average per capita consumption of a bit more than half that of males in survey results. They differ in body content of fat relative to water content, and have higher peak blood alcohol readings following a standard dose of alcohol, as compared to men.[14] At the very least, male and female data should be plotted separately. Such cut-offs also ignore individual differences due to age, weight and physical health.

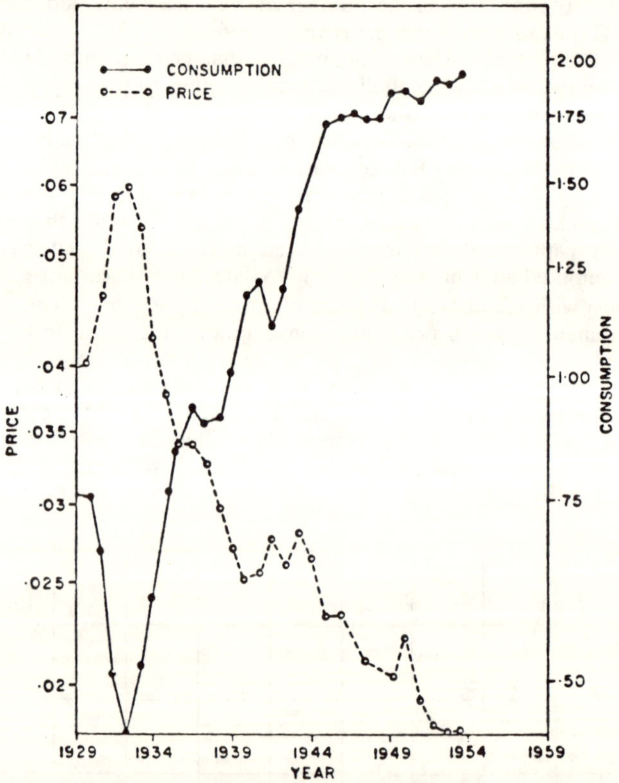

FIGURE 4. Alcohol price (P) and consumption (C). Ontario, 1929–1958. $P =$ the price of an average gallon of absolute alcohol expressed as a fraction of average disposable income; $C =$ consumption in gallons of absolute alcohol per person 20 years and older. (From DeLint and Schmidt.[8] By permission of Wiley-Interscience.)

Correlations between mean per capita consumption and alcohol problems do not necessarily indicate a cause and effect relationship. A small proportion of the population is responsible for a large proportion of the alcohol consumption. Room mentions that six percent of the population drinks 41 percent of the alcohol, and ten percent of the population drinks 60 percent of the alcohol. Thus average consumption figures are very sensitive to the drinking habits of a small proportion of the population. It has not been demonstrated that purposeful changes in price will effect this heavy drinking population. Room speculates

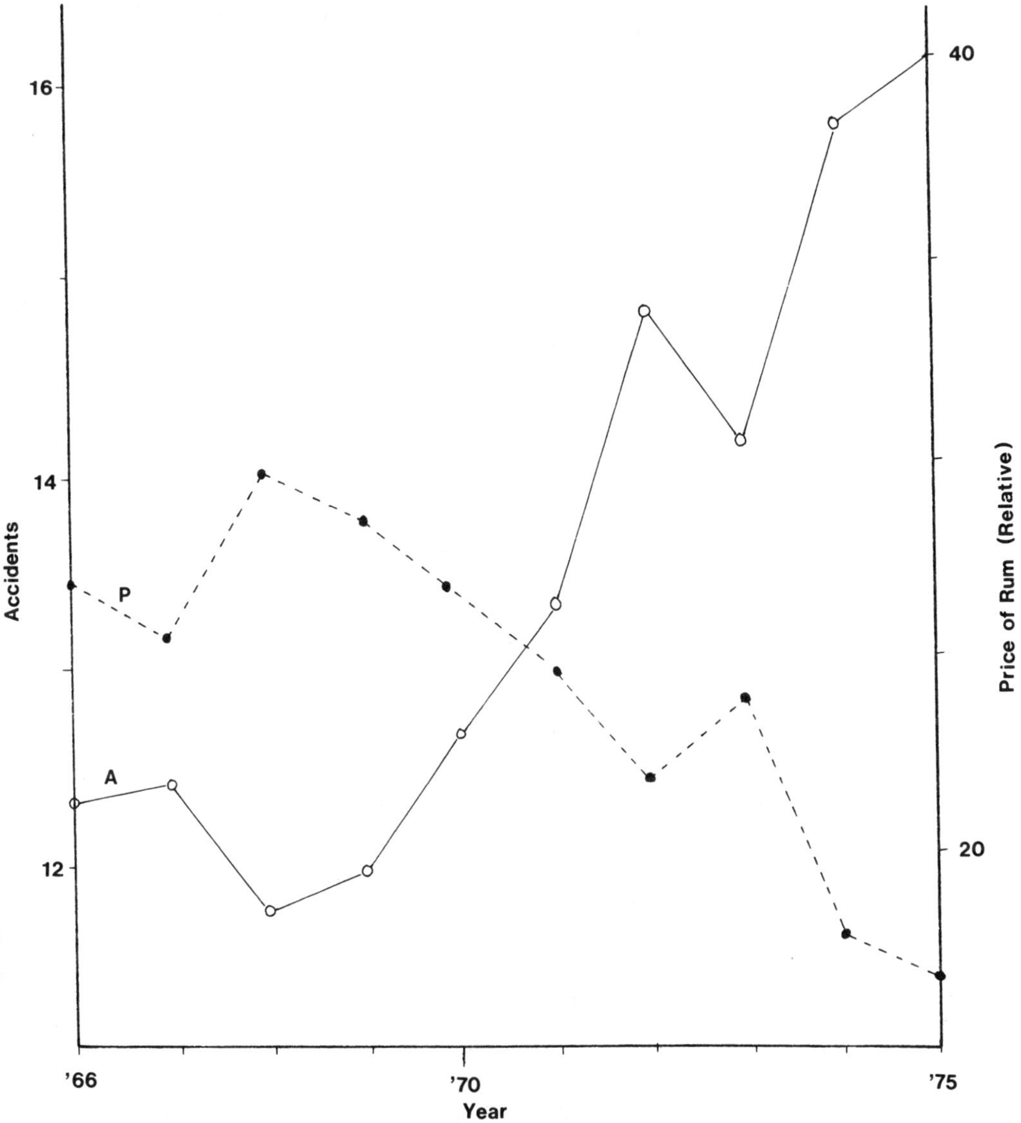

FIGURE 5. Road traffic accidents and the price of rum relative to income in Trinidad and Tobago, 1966–1975. —— Road accidents (no injury accidents); - - - - Price of rum (relative to per capita income). (From Beaubrun.[3])

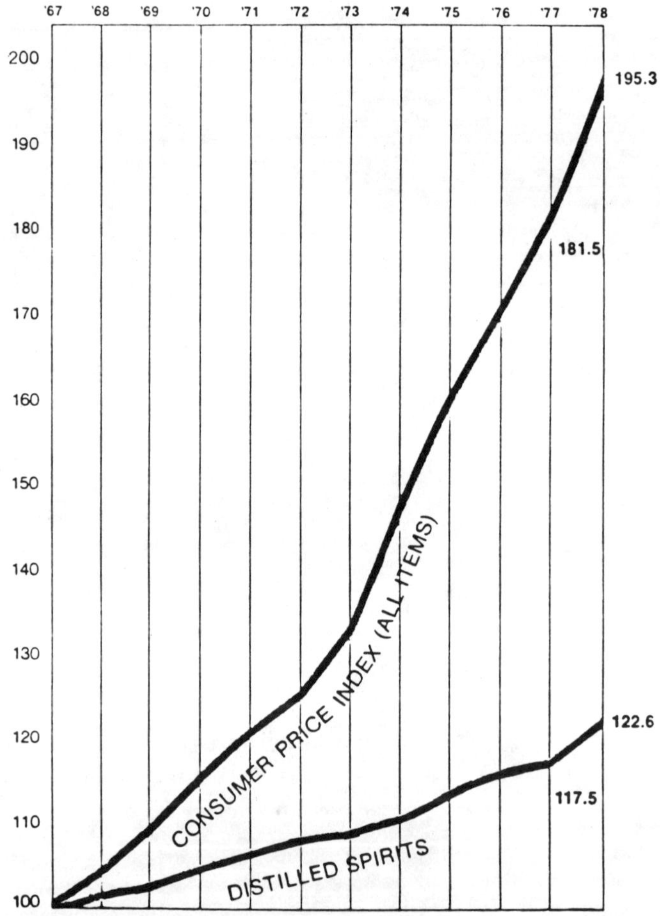

FIGURE 6. Retail liquor costs compared to the consumer price index.[10]

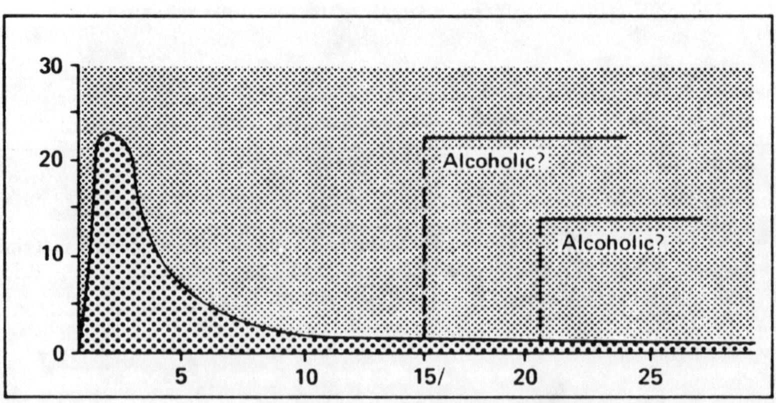

FIGURE 7. Frequency distribution of alcohol consumption ($\overline{c} = 151$).

that such changes are more likely to affect the poor than the rich. For example, during prohibition in the U.S., the average intake of the lower socioeconomic groups decreased greatly while the upper groups drank nearly as much as before.

Estimates of Alcoholism Based on Cirrhosis Mortality

E. M. Jellinek, in the early 1940s, developed a formula for calculating the number of people suffering from alcoholism in a population, based on rate of mortality from cirrhosis of the liver.[16] This so-called Jellinek formula was based on a number of assumptions. Both the percentage of alcoholics who developed cirrhosis and the death rate from cirrhosis were assumed to be constant. Although Jellinek later withdrew his formula, Keller used it subsequently to develop the probably conservative estimate of the number of alcoholic people in the United States shown in FIGURE 1. Problems with this formula include the fact that the death rate from cirrhosis will differ according to the availability and quality of medical care, which may vary over time and from place to place. The accuracy of the estimate will also be affected by the distribution of socioeconomic status in a population and by the death rate from other causes in the alcoholic sub-group of the population, which varies greatly from region to region.

Survey Results

The classical study in this field was reported by Cahalan *et al.*,[6] who conducted an extensive nation-wide survey of drinking practices and problems related to alcohol in the year 1964–5. FIGURE 8 is a summary of their findings on drinking patterns.[13] FIGURE 9 summarizes their findings on alcohol-related problems. It is clear from their data that one out of ten drinkers over the age of 21 reported a significant level of problems related to alcohol intake. This figure of 1/10 is the source for a number of public estimates of "alcoholism", but in my opinion defines the larger group which includes both problem drinkers and those suffering from the disease alcoholism. Later survey studies have yielded results similar to those of Cahalan *et. al.* Drinking practices surveys done on samples of young people, usually in the schools, have yielded high rates of alcohol-related problems. These problems, however, are usually defined quite differently from those in adults. The drinking of alcohol itself, or drinking to "drunkenness," usually undefined, is in itself considered a problem in teenagers. An important recent finding in youth survey research is that the traditional differences in drinking patterns between boys and girls have tended to diminish at the junior high and high school levels.[22]

Methodological difficulties in drinking surveys are discussed by Room,[19–21] Edwards,[11] and Armor *et al.*[2] When household surveys are done, the heaviest drinkers are not likely to be at home: homeless persons and those in institutions are not counted. Such an exclusion is relatively unimportant for behaviors that are widely distributed, but become more important in measuring behaviors with skewed distribution, such as alcohol intake. If calculations of total annual consumption of beer, wine and distilled spirits are made from data collected in household surveys, they do not account for all of the alcoholic beverages consumed, as reported in the tax-population data. Room calculated the quantities of alcoholic beverages accounted for by the American Drinking Practices

32% of the total adult population are abstainers. The remaining 68% drink at least once a year, with 12% of all adults classified as heavy drinkers.

77% of adult men and 60% of adult women drink at least once a year, with 21% of all men and 5% of all women classified as heavy drinkers.

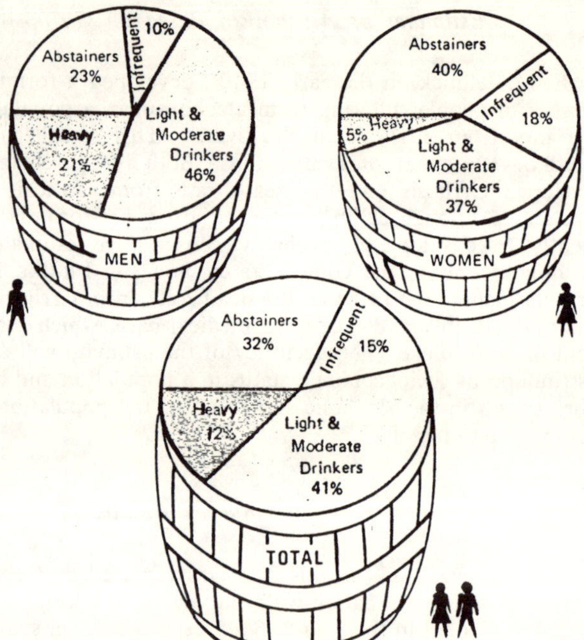

**Age 21+*

** Degree of drinking was classified according to a rather complex combination of the quantity of alcohol consumed per occasion and the frequency of drinking.*

- *Heavy drinking. Drink nearly every day with five or more per occasion at least once in a while, or about once weekly with usually five or more per occasion.*
- *Moderate drinking. Drink at least once a month, typically several times, but usually with no more than three or four drinks per occasion.*
- *Light Drinking. Drink at least once a month, but typically only one or two drinks on a single occasion.*
- *Infrequent Drinking. Drink at least once a year, but less than once a month.*
- *Abstainers. Drink less than once a year or not at all.*

FIGURE 8. Percent of abstainers and types of drinkers among adults, U.S.A. 1964–1965.[13]

Survey of Cahalan *et al.*[6] He found this survey accounted for only 60 percent of the sales of wine, 55 percent of the sales of beer, and 55 percent of the sales of distilled spirits. A similar calculation from the Harris poll data reported by Armor *et al.*,[2] showed that that survey accounted for 100 percent of the wine, 20 percent of the beer and 52 percent of the distilled spirits reported in tax population data.[20] A survey-derived calculation made in Finland in 1968 accounted for 42.5 percent of the total consumption derived from beverage tax data.[21]

The validity and reliability of self report survey data has been discussed at length by Room, and by Armor *et al.* They both conclude that there is probably considerable underestimation of quantity consumed, particularly by heavy drinkers and in regions of the country where "dry" sentiment prevails. Validity of problem-incidence data has seldom been investigated. In one study, only 30 to 65 percent of persons with a history of alcohol-related arrests checked "yes" to the appropriate question on a paper and pencil survey. In a test of reliability, between 10 and 50 percent of subjects who had reported an alcohol-related problem on an earlier survey, answered "never" in response to the same

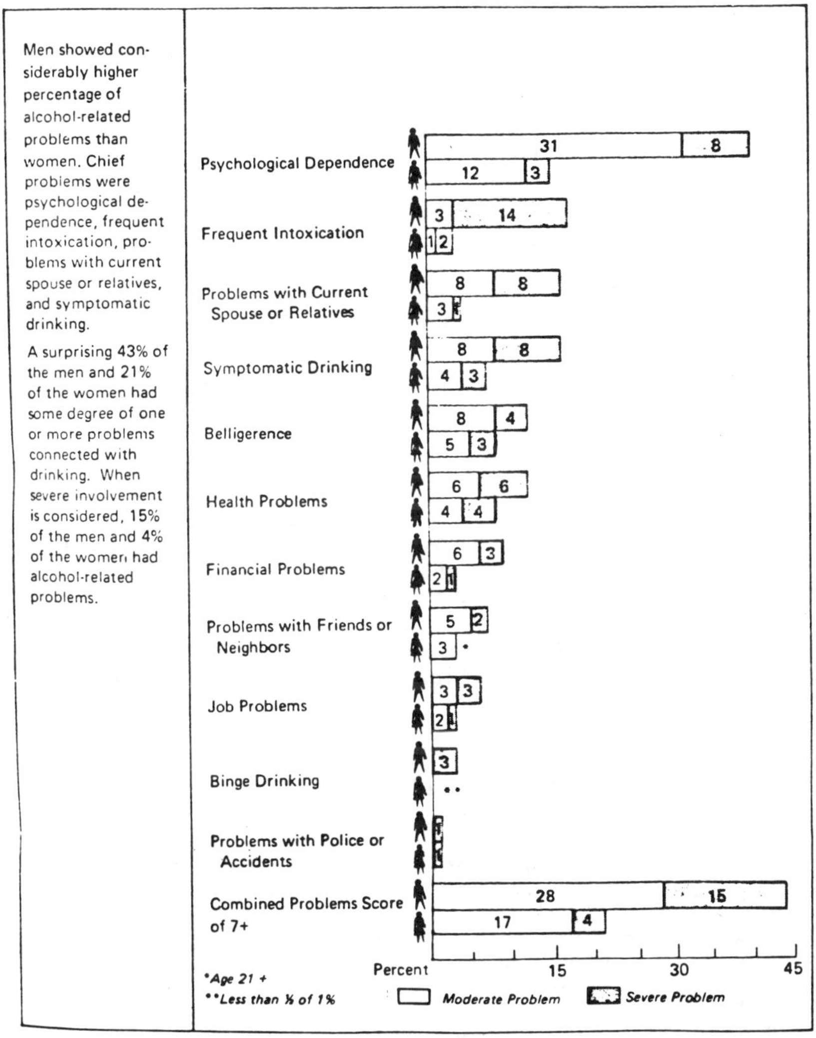

FIGURE 9. Prevalence of alcohol-related problems among adults, age 21 and over, in the United States during a 3-year period prior to 1967.[13]

question in a second test.[20] Interviewer characteristics are also thought to have an effect on the results obtained. The age, sex, and drinking habits of the interviewer correlate with survey results. Self interest, as perceived by the interviewee, will vary in direction. In a clinic population, the person interviewed may see it as being in his self interest to exaggerate upward the amount of alcohol consumed, while in a general population poll perceived self interest may dictate an underestimation.

Finally, in any look at alcohol-related problems, it must be remembered that these problems are of varied types. Some alcohol-related problems are physiological, related to the nature of alcohol as a drug. These include blackouts, shakes, delirium tremens, and other physical symptoms. Other problems are interpersonal in nature and therefore will be heavily influenced by cultural values and norms. A moderately drinking person may have severe marital problems with a spouse who is an abstainer on religious grounds. A very heavy drinker married to an alcoholic may have no such differences of opinion. Finally, some alcohol problems are defined by law and their incidence much influenced by enforcement policies. For example, males have a far higher rate of arrest and conviction for driving while intoxicated while women drivers stopped for similar reasons are less often arrested, charged and convicted of this offense.[4] If a state chooses to raise its legal minimum drinking age, by the stroke of a governor's pen, a large number of young drinkers will suddenly be in the "problem" category each time they obtain an alcoholic beverage. Thus simple counts of numbers of alcohol-related problems do not yield uniform results.

Conclusion

Although I have attempted to outline some of the difficulties involved in collecting and interpreting epidemiological data in the alcohol abuse field, I think it is fair to say that there is much helpful data now on hand and there is a reasonable expectation that methodology will improve over the years. The epidemiology of alcohol use is both an art and a science which seeks to understand a complex and overdetermined set of behaviors, with a set of imperfect tools, so that we can make difficult political decisions about impossible problems. I hope this overview has helped illuminate both our efforts and our imperfections.

References

1. Archibald, H. D. 1976. Alcohol and Public Policy. Proceedings of the Caribbean Institute on Alcoholism. St. Thomas, Virgin Islands.
2. Armor, D., J. Polich & H. Stambul. 1978. Alcoholism and Treatment. John Wiley and Sons. New York.
3. Beaubrun, M. H. November 29, 1977. Epidemiological Research in the Caribbean Context: Road Accidents and the Price of Rum in Trinidad and Tobago, 1966–1975. Addiction Research Foundation Seminar on International Collaboration. Toronto, Ontario.
4. Blumenthal, M. & H. Ross. February, 1973. Two Experimental Studies of Traffic Law, Volume 1. The Effect of Legal Sanctions on DWI Offenders. Department of Transportation. Washington, D.C., D.O.T., HS-800, 825.

5. BURK, C. G. October, 1976. Changing habits in American drinking. Fortune.
6. CAHALAN, D., I. CISIN & H. CROSSLEY. 1969. American Drinking Practices. Rutgers Center of Alcohol Studies. New Brunswick, N.J.
7. CASTELLI, W. P. 1979. How Many Drinks A Day? J. Am. Med. Assoc. **242:** 2000.
8. DELINT, J. & W. SCHMIDT. 1971. The Epidemiology of Alcoholism. *In* Biological Basis of Alcoholism. Y. Israel & J. Mardones, Eds. Wiley-Interscience, N.Y.
9. DELINT, J. & W. SCHMIDT. 1976. Alcohol and Mortality. *In* The Biology of Alcoholism. B. Kissin & H. Begleiter, Eds. Volume IV. Plenum. New York, N.Y.
10. DISCUS FACTS BOOK. 1978. 25th Edit. Distilled Spirits Council of the United States. Washington, D.C.
11. EDWARDS, G. 1973. Epidemiology Applied to Alcoholism. Q. J. Stud Alcohol **34:**28–56.
12. H.E.W. 1978. Alcohol and Health. Third Special Report to the U.S. Congress.
13. H.E.W. 1971. Alcohol and Health. First Special Report to the U.S. Congress.
14. JONES, B. M. & M. K. JONES. 1976. Women and alcohol: Intoxication, metabolism, and the menstrual cycle. Chap. 5. *In* Alcoholism Problems in Women and Children. M. Greenblatt & M. Schuckit, Eds. Grune and Stratton. New York, N.Y.
15. KELLER, M. & C. GURIOLI. 1976. Statistics on Consumption of Alcohol and Alcoholism. J. Stud. Alcohol. New Brunswick, N.Y.
16. KELLER, M. 1975. Problems of Epidemiology in Alcohol Problems. J. Stud. Alcohol **36:**1442–1451.
17. LEDERMANN, S. 1956. Alcool, Alcoolisme, Alcoolisation: Données Scientifiques de Caractère Physiologique, Economique et Social. Institut National d'Etudes Demographiques, Travaux et Documents, Cahier No. 29, Presses Universitaires de France, Paris.
18. NATIONAL COUNCIL ON ALCOHOLISM. 1972. Criteria for the diagnosis of alcoholism. Ann. Int. Med. **86:**764.
19. ROOM, R. 1978. Evaluating the effect of drinking laws on drinking. *In* Drinking. J. Ewing & B. A. Rcuse, Eds. Nelson Hall. Chicago.
20. ROOM, R. 1975. The accuracy of survey reports of drinking behavior. Unpublished paper.
21. ROOM, R. 1971. A comparison of survey and sales data in Finland. Drinking & Drug Practices Surveyor **3:**15–16.
22. WECHSLER, H. & M. MCFADDEN. 1976. Sex differences in adolescent alcohol and drug use: A disappearing phenomenon. J. Stud. Alcohol. 37.

INTERNATIONAL PATTERNS OF DRUG ABUSE AND CONTROL

Lee I. Dogoloff and Caroline M. Devine

White House Domestic Policy Staff
Washington, D.C. 20500

As the world becomes increasingly pluralistic and the interdependencies of nations become more numerous and more sensitive, we find that many of our most important problems are no longer clearly "domestic" or "foreign." Energy shortages, trade deficits, and agricultural prices, for example, are inextricably related to foreign considerations.

The domestic U.S. drug problem has always had international implications because many of the serious drugs of abuse originate in foreign countries. Effective curtailment of trafficking in illegal substances depends heavily on controls exerted as close as possible to the source. Once the illegal substances have reached our 96,000 mile borders, or have been distributed in the U.S., or in another nonsource country, control becomes a massive problem for law enforcement. Thus, the burden on the U.S. domestic law enforcement agencies can be significantly reduced to the extent that foreign governments are capable and willing to control drug production and trafficking within their own countries.

However, we cannot focus only on supply reduction. A demand out of control implies fearsome consequences to the social system of any country and makes the task of reducing supplies far more difficult. To the extent that the demand for illicit drugs can be reduced, so will the incentive to produce be diminished. Endorsing this interdependency in his August 2, 1977, Drug Abuse Message to the Congress, President Jimmy Carter stated:

> Drug addiction, which in recent years was viewed as a problem peculiar to America, now affects people throughout the world. We can no longer concern ourselves with merely keeping illicit drugs out of the United States, but we must join with other nations to deal with this global problem by combatting drug traffickers and sharing our knowledge and resources to help treat addiction whenever it occurs.

The prevention of drug abuse is a global effort and one which all nations must address. There was a time, perhaps, when it was possible for other countries to regard the illegal drug trade and its disastrous consequences as primarily a problem of concern to the United States. That time has passed. The illegal drug traffic has become massively international in its proportions, and it is no longer a uniquely or even primarily American problem.

In the past three years, due to both increased addiction rates and a willingness to openly face long-term problems, foreign governments, together with the United States, have officially recognized the widespread ramifications of drug cultivation, production, trafficking, and consumption. Drug abuse is no longer just a United States problem. Drug dependency by a citizenry in a foreign country can have the same weakening effects on that nation's society and economy as it can on ours. Furthermore, the drug traffic can and does produce vast sums of untaxed money which support the criminal community, corrupt officials, and even insurrections, which in all, further undermine the integrity and stability of a nation.

Given the inextricable links between the international drug traffic and United States drug abuse situation, a brief assessment of our drug abuse problem is indeed in order. In 1978, more than 280 million prescriptions were written for psychoactive drugs. On the illicit side of the drug spectrum, an estimated 450,000 Americans use heroin daily. Last year, 6.5 million individuals in the United States consumed 21 metric tons of pure cocaine equivalent; half these users were between 18 and 25 years old. At a minimum, the total marihuana consumption in the United States during 1978 was 5,200 metric tons.

The quantities of illicit drugs available to the U.S. are even more startling. The National Narcotics Intelligence Consumers Committee (NNICC) estimates that somewhere between 10,000 and 15,000 metric tons of marihuana; 19 and 25 metric tons of cocaine hydrochloride; and 3.7 and 4.5 metric tons of heroin were imported into the United States during 1978.

HEROIN

The amount of heroin available to the United States has fortunately decreased since 1977 when approximately 5.5 metric tons were smuggled into this country. The success of our efforts stems in large part from our cooperation with the Mexican Government, which has brought about a 20% decline in the amount of Mexican heroin available in the U.S.

But the heroin problem is regrettably endemic to the civilized world and must be continually monitored even when we see some glimmers of hope. Mexico still represents the source of 50% of the heroin in the United States and is followed by Southeast Asia which is responsible for 30% and the Middle East with 20%. Estimates by the U.S. Drug Enforcement Administration indicate that Western Europe had approximately 234,000 addicts in 1978, up from 200,000 the previous year. Last year, there were approximately 1,000 heroin-related deaths in Western Europe, and the number is expected to grow in 1979. The Federal Republic of Germany has alone witnessed one of the most dramatic increases in drug related deaths and injuries in all of Western Europe. In West Germany and Berlin, there were at least 447 drug related deaths in the first ten months of 1979. West German authorities estimate that there are between 60,000 and 80,000 hard drug users in the country.

While the reasons for these increases are not well defined, increased availability is surely a factor. There has been a distinct shift in the trafficking patterns such that the bulk of the European traffic has shifted from Southeast Asian to Middle Eastern sources. The Middle East's potential to produce heroin is serious. Under optimum conditions, that is assuming every kilogram of opium is converted into heroin, this region could produce 80 metric tons of heroin for worldwide consumption.

Both the increased availability and the shift in sources are visible in Western European seizure statistics provided by the Drug Enforcement Administration.

1. In 1978, 611 kilograms of heroin were seized in Europe, 429 kilograms from Southeast Asia, and 182 kilograms from the Middle East.

2. By June 1979, 262 kilograms of Middle Eastern heroin had already been seized, and by October 1979, only 245 kilograms of Southeast Asian heroin had been seized.

3. Moreover, the farmer's price for Mideast opium plummeted, from $200 a kilogram in 1978 to $50 in 1979, and at a time when Southeast Asian opium prices have increased by up to 500%.

Ironically, the United States may currently be the only country in the entire Western Hemisphere which is experiencing a decline in heroin availability and related deaths and yet, while the United States has not yet faced the full brunt of these shifting trafficking trends, our latest estimates indicate that 15–20% of the heroin consumed in the United States originates in Afghanistan, Pakistan, and Iran. This trend and its proven tendency for rapid acceleration are of immediate concern.

Cocaine

Cocaine continues to be widely abused and the long range trend forecasts increased abuse. Since 1974, cocaine-related injuries and deaths within the United States have tripled. The coca leaf is grown chiefly in Peru and Bolivia, although there have been recent reports of expanded cultivation in Colombia and possible incipient cultivation in Mexico. According to the latest available estimates, there are approximately 25,000 hectares under cultivation in Peru and 20,000 in Bolivia.

Although technically committed to eradication of the coca bush under the Single Convention, Peru and Bolivia are currently not able to fully implement its provisions because to do so would cause severe economic and social disruption. Furthermore, there have been recurring reports of newly cleared land being brought under coca cultivation in both countries. While some of this planting may represent replacement of meager or dead coca bushes, much of it is suspected to be new growth.

Many users believe that cocaine is relatively free from markedly undesirable effects and is generally safe. Cocaine's reputation for safety, however, is overstated since it is, in part, based on diluted doses of the drug taken relatively infrequently due to its high costs. Furthermore, its use and consequences are often difficult to detect by current reporting systems since it produces few "traditional" overdose deaths and emergency room episodes.

Despite the reported health consequences of cocaine use which range from increased heart rate and blood pressure to possible mental aberrations and destruction of the nasal lining, many still consider cocaine to be a "safe" drug. Unfortunately, a lack of adequate information is sometimes misinterpreted as indicating that a drug is "safe" when it would be more accurate to admit that our knowledge is simply insufficient to specify the full parameters of risk.

Marihuana

The principal countries from which marihuana is supplied to the U.S. are Colombia, Mexico, and Jamaica. Together they supply over 90% of the marihuana consumed in the United States. The amount of marihuana smuggled from these countries into the United States ranges from a minimum of 6,500 metric tons to a possible high of 15,000 tons.

Marihuana is a difficult crop to eradicate because it can be grown in areas of dense growth inaccessible by air. In addition, the plots are generally small and difficult to locate. Further complicating this eradication effort is the fact that today's marihuana trafficker is highly organized and financially independent, unlike the former small, dispersed and struggling marihuana smuggler of the past.

The marihuana traffic to the United States represents a multi-billion dollar industry. In 1978, marihuana was the top income producer, accounting for $15–23 billion or approximately 28–43% of the total income generated in the U.S. illicit market from imported drugs.

Since the mid-1970s, there has been a steady and rapid transformation in the international traffic of marihuana to the United States. As late as 1974, the U.S. marihuana market was supplied primarily by Mexico, with some shipments coming from Jamaica.

In 1975, the Federal Government estimated that annual marihuana imports totaled approximately 4,000 tons. By 1977, however, the user population within the U.S. had increased over 30 percent to an estimated 16 million regular users. During this time, Colombia supplanted Mexico as the principal marihuana source country. Of the estimated 10,000 to 15,000 tons of marihuana imported into the United States in 1977, intelligence indicated that nearly 60 percent came from Colombia. In 1978, the Colombian share was even greater—no less than 70 percent.

A number of factors have been responsible for the recent shift to Colombian marihuana in the United States:

1. A major one has been the success of the Mexican Government in eradicating marihuana cultivation and reducing supplies. The Office of the Attorney General of Mexico has been quoted as stating that eradication efforts have reduced the Mexican marihuana crop by 75 percent over the past two years. Information available today shows that Colombian marihuana is encountered almost exclusively throughout the northeast, mid-Atlantic, and Gulf Coast areas. It supplies most of the demand in the Great Lakes region and in many of the other midwestern States. It has emerged rapidly in the Pacific northwest, whose role as an import center for Colombian marihuana is evidenced by the seizures of several mother ships in this area since early 1978. Even in the southwestern United States, long the traditional stronghold of Mexican marihuana, Colombian marihuana is gaining in acceptance.

2. The major organizations dealing in Colombian marihuana have taken on corporate structure. Overnight, these organizations are capable of importing 5, 10, 20, or more tons of marihuana, breaking it down for distribution, putting it on the road for distant retail markets, and clearing profits of several million dollars. The Mexican marihuana trade, by contrast, is and has been more of a cottage-type industry. It is relied on by numerous small organizations and independent traffickers who deal in smaller loads and, for the most part, supply local markets. Their enterprise is lucrative, but compared to the Colombian operations, cannot as instantaneously produce the same massive profits.

Given increasing supplies available at the source and growing consumer preference, it can be expected that Colombian marihuana will continue to be preeminent in the United States under present interdiction capabilities. As of mid-1979, prices have not risen nor has there been any reported shortage in supply.

Federal Response

To deal with these problems, the Federal Government supports a three-part program to discourage drug abuse and to reduce the health and social consequences of such abuse. Essentially our three part program is comprised of the domestic drug law enforcement program; the domestic treatment, rehabilitation and prevention effort; and finally, the international activities. I would like to dwell on this last area for a moment for I consider our international activity to be the answer to many of our domestic drug abuse problems.

There are ten countries in the world which we view as priority targets for our foreign policy endeavors to encourage cooperation in effective programs to reduce the supply of illicit drugs entering the world market: Burma, Laos, Mexico, Thailand, Afghanistan, and Pakistan (countries in which significant amounts of opium are grown and traffickers manufacture heroin in illicit laboratories); Bolivia and Peru (the major coca producing countries); and Ecuador and Colombia (the major processing and transmitting areas for the cocaine traffic to the U.S.).

In most of these countries, the production and local consumption of opium and coca leaves are old traditions and integral parts of the culture and economy of the nation. The production of these drug crops provides an important source of income, and in some cases the only source to farmers in many of these countries. Any endeavors we pursue must take these factors into consideration.

Consequently, the United States supports a wide range of approaches involving partnerships with other countries and international organizations. Through existing foreign policy mechanisms, we have been able to elevate the attention given to international narcotics control cooperation. High-level United States political and diplomatic representation to foreign governments by both the Executive Branch and the Congress have been instrumental in increasing foreign commitments both financial and ideological to international narcotics control cooperation.

Crop eradication offers another opportunity to reduce the supplies of illicit drugs at their source. It has proven to be the most efficient and cost effective way to reduce the illegal cultivation in those countries which do not have an extensive history of poppy cultivation and opium use such as Mexico.

When drug cultivation is a traditional part of a country's culture and economics, and supports a large number of otherwise law abiding farmers, rural development and crop substitution are the first stages of a program to reduce supply at the source, and may be combined with an eradication program. The United States will continue to encourage and support, where possible, programs to replace illicit drug crops with other crops or activities that provide adequate and stable incomes for the people in the growing regions.

Integrated rural development is, however, a costly and long-term response well beyond the resources which have been appropriated specifically for the international narcotics control program. Consequently, we look to working with host country governments and the international organizations in joint efforts to solve mutual problems.

Together with the U.N. Fund for Drug Abuse Control, we have encouraged the multilateral institutions such as the U.N. Development Program and the International Financial Institutions to increase their participation in these efforts to reduce the supply of illicit drugs at their source. (The United States representatives to the loan committees of the Regional Development Banks and other financial institutions are now using their votes and influence to (1) encourage well-designed rural development and income substitution projects in countries which now produce dangerous drugs; and (2) ensure that assistance is not used to foster the growth of crops such as coca and opium.)

The United States concern with the drug abuse problem is one that will persist for many years. Experience indicates that solutions are not rapidly achieved and that social change does not readily come about in a free society. To the extent that drug abuse in the United States is the result of foreign grown materials, the cutting edge of our attack will be through foreign policy initiatives. Hence, one of the greatest challenges which we face in the coming years will rest with the success of our international effort.

WEST COAST AND EAST COAST DRUG ABUSE PATTERNS, 1979–80

David E. Smith

Department of Toxicology
Haight-Ashbury Free Medical Clinic
University of California
San Francisco, California 94102

Introduction

In December of 1979, I made a presentation at the New York Academy of Medicine Drug Abuse Symposium comparing West Coast against East Coast drug abuse patterns. At that time, I emphasized that we had seen the development of a new pattern of heroin addiction involving the smoking of Persian heroin; and an increase in the new users coming to our clinic addicted to heroin. This, in association with the readdiction of the traditional users who had a long history of intravenous use of heroin, produced a drug abuse indicator which, in the past, had heralded an increase in heroin use nationwide. At the time of the presentation, the audience of drug abuse workers from the New York area indicated that they had not yet observed the smoking of Persian heroin amongst the middleclass. Nor, had they seen any significant increase in patients addicted to heroin in seeking treatment. It was difficult to determine if our heroin indicators would remain valid, since our increase in Persian heroin had started about 1977 and was associated with the increase of Iranians coming from the Southwest Asian area prior to the revolution in Iran and bringing large quantities of Persian heroin with them. For a variety of complicated reasons however, many of which we do not yet understand, 1980 fulfilled our prediction and there was a large influx of Southwest Asian heroin coming from the Iran-Pakistan-Afghanistan area resulting in increased treatment admissions in the Northeast Corridor, including New York, New Jersey and Maryland. Dr. William Pollin, Director of the National Institute on Drug Abuse in 1980, appropriated additional funding for immediate assistance to these treatment programs expanding the capacity by an additional 350 treatment slots. Combined with matching state funds, these 350 extra treatment slots will be used for outpatient methadone maintenance and for heroin detoxification.

In the New York area, federally funded drug treatment programs increased 15%, whereas in the Baltimore area the increase was 36%; in the Newark area the increase was 54%. In addition, the National Institute on Drug Abuse indicated that there was an increase in heroin overdose deaths, which verified the predicted dramatic increase in the incidence and prevalence of heroin addiction in the Northeast Corridor. Study of prospective indicators then can predict increases in the incidence and prevalence of heroin addiction in different regions of the country. Other than increased availability of heroin, and new patterns of use, we are not sure of the cause and effect relationship, but it is important that increased study of these predictor phenomena be instituted, both for better planning and treatment and for the potential for increased prevention efforts.

California, in general, and the San Francisco Bay Area, specifically, has served as an indicator area for new drug abuse trends since the middle 60's. This paper will highlight new drug abuse trends which may have significance for the rest of the U.S. The basis for such an analysis comes from the review of clients seen at the Haight-Ashbury Free Medical Clinic coupled with the epidemiological analysis of our Clinic Research Director, Dr. John Newmeyer. In addition, through our Training and Consultation Program, we have interacted with other drug treatment facilities and made a systematic review of both street drug analysis reports and the drug abuse literature. This review is not intended to be all inclusive, but rather to highlight new drug abuse trends and it is organized by drug group.[1a]

Opiate Abuse

As shown in Figure 1, point-prevalent estimates for heroin addiction in San Francisco County 1973–1978 compiled by Dr. Newmeyer, heroin addiction in the Bay Area has followed a very cyclical course. Following the much heralded heroin epidemic of the late 60's and early 70's [1b] patterns of heroin addiction bottomed out in the 1973 area. About the time however, that public reports indicated that heroin addiction was on the wane, we saw an upturn which peaked in 1976 followed by a down cycle which plateaued in the 1977–1978 time period. At present, we are experiencing an increase in heroin addiction in the San Francisco Bay Area, and I predict that this increase will herald a nationwide increase in heroin addition.[2] As indicated by Newmeyer, we are seeing an increase in new clients who first became addicted to heroin in 1978 and 1979. In addition, there is evidence of new supplies of heroin to support this increased demand as demonstrated by the following statement:

> An increased flow of heroin from the Middle East and Southeast Asia has caused a sharp upsurge in heroin abuse in Western Europe and drug abuse experts are predicting that these sources of supply will raise the availability of the drug in the United States.[3]

In addition, we are seeing some new patterns of opiate abuse. For example, we have seen an increase in the smoking of Persian heroin, which is a very potent form of the drug that can produce physical dependence even when smoked rather than injected. We analyzed a sample of Persian heroin from one of our clients who had developed significant physical dependence by smoking the drug and found the sample to be 92% pure in contrast to our usual 3–5% street level heroin purity. It appears that this supply of heroin is coming from the Middle East including Iran. There is an increased growing of opium in Iran and other areas of the Middle East despite the current Iranian religious policy against narcotic drugs, as a result of the political and social disruption occurring in that area, as noted by the following statement: "Drug traffickers are taking advantage of political chaos to turn opium cultivation into a booming export industry." [3]

Relative to transport of Persian heroin in the U.S., it appears to be coming from a variety of sources as noted by a recent arrest in which an Iranian government employee was charged with smuggling an estimated $18,000 worth of opium into San Francisco. In general, the demand for heroin exceeds the supply and as a consequence these new sources of heroin plus a new generation of users will significantly increase the problem of heroin addiction. Policy

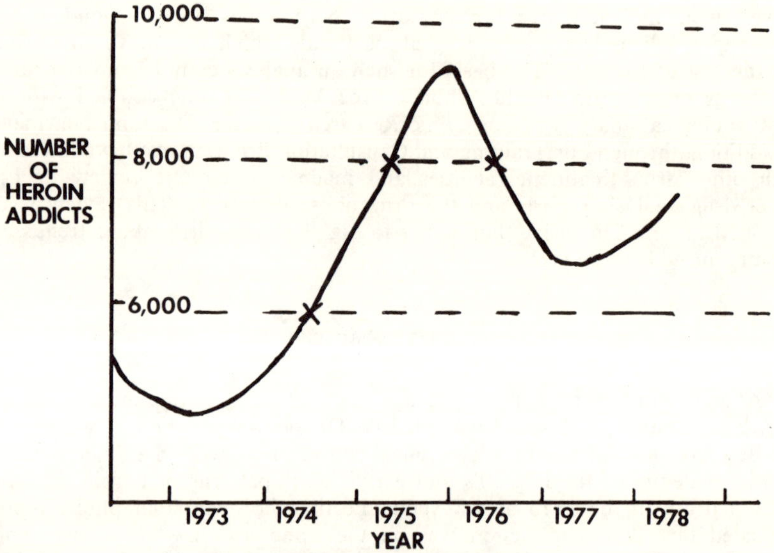

FIGURE 1. Point-prevalence estimates for heroin addiction, San Francisco County, 1973–1978.

makers must be warned that the problem of heroin addiction is far from resolved in the United States.

THE STIMULANTS

We have also seen an increase in stimulant abuse as well as polydrug abuse in the Bay Area. For the purposes of analysis, we have broken down the polydrug abuser into the streetwise vs. nonstreetwise polydrug abuser (see TABLE 1). The streetwise polydrug abuser is primarily involved with the street drug culture, whereas the nonstreetwise polydrug abusers obtain their drugs primarily through physicians and are involved with prescription drug abuse. Using this analysis, we have found that diversion of pharmaceutically manufactured amphetamines into the drug culture is down substantially,[4] but diversion of other central nervous stimulants such as methylphenidate (Ritalin®) is up.[5] In addition, there is an increase in the combined use of heroin and Ritalin called "speedballing" and we have seen an increase in the intravenous abuse of cocaine. Relative to new patterns of stimulant abuse, the most significant is the smoking of cocaine freebase. The closest parallel to this new pattern of stimulant abuse was described by Jeri *et al.*,[6] where he reported the Peruvian experience with coca paste, a crude extract of coca leaves containing cocaine sulphate, ecgonine, other coca alkaloids, benzoic acid and kerosene residue which was placed on tobacco or marijuana cigarettes and smoked.

A substantial pattern of high-dose cocaine toxicity, including the cocaine psychosis was reported with this pattern. In the Bay Area we have seen a substantial increase in the use of "freebase kits" to convert cocaine hydrochloride to cocaine freebase.[7] As a result, the cocaine freebase is very volatile, with a melting point of 98 degrees centigrade and it vaporizes easily. Users smoke freebase in pipes which support the freebase on one or more mesh screens, although the cocaine freebase is also volatilized by putting the material on aluminum foil and heating it from below while snorting the vapor through a tube. This pattern is called "chasing the dragon." A substantial amount of cocaine can be delivered into the bloodstream via this method of volatilization and one obtains an intense rush which more parallels the injection of cocaine hydrochloride, rather than the snorting of cocaine hydrochloride.[10, 11] This initial euphoria is quickly followed by irritability and during this phase users report feeling compelled to do some more freebase. Due to its local anesthetic properties on the bronchial mucosa, bronchial irritation is not noted initially by

TABLE 1

STREETWISE VS. NONSTREETWISE CRITERIA *

Parameter	Streetwise	Nonstreetwise
Primary means of support	(+2) Dealing drugs Prostitution Stealing Friends Spouse Welfare None	(−2) Legitimate employment Welfare Student Spouse None
Dress	(+1) Unconventional	(−1) Conventional
Personal appearance and grooming	(+1) Unconventional	(−1) Conventional
Knowledge of street jargon	(+1) Yes	(−1) No
Means of funding drug habit	(+2) Stealing Prostitution Dealing Drugs Welfare	(−2) Legitimate employment Welfare
Ability to purchase drugs from "street" drug dealers if drugs are not available through channels	(+2) Yes	(−2) No
Living in a geographical area known as a youth drug sub-culture	(+1) Yes	(−1) No

* The distinction between streetwise and nonstreetwise is made by summing the values of parameters one through seven. A zero score indicates an uncertain state which we indicate as "unable to classify." In using this schemata, if an individual falls into a category which appears on both the streetwise and nonstreetwise cells (such as welfare for parameter one), a zero is assigned for the value of that parameter.

the users, but many report bronchial irritation after smoking cocaine freebase, which may last for several days. Bronchitis can be severe and users report coughing up blood and stained sputum for weeks, following sustained use. Cocaine freebase is prepared from a water solution of cocaine hydrochloride by precipitating the freebase with ammonia, sodium hydroxide or other strong alkali. Ethyl or petroleum ether is then added to the water solution to extract the cocaine freebase. The ethyl ether is then placed in a dish and allowed to evaporate, using one of a variety of commercial kits to basify the cocaine. In addition, as previously described, new forms of heroin can also be smoked in a similar fashion and we have seen individuals who had avoided injection of the drug initially becoming involved in the smoking of cocaine freebase, and, as a result of the intense stimulation and resultant side effects, smoke heroin as a downer and come into our clinic deeply involved in the "upper and downer" cycle with physical dependence on heroin.[9]

As a consequence, we feel that the expanded and evolving pattern of cocaine freebase, particularly viewed in association with heroin freebase, either in an upper downer cycle or combined in a "speedball" [10] represents a new and potentially very serious drug abuse pattern. The major limitations at the present time are the high cost of both drugs, but smoking of cocaine freebase can lead to high-dose drug-induced psychosis, cocaine overdose or pulmonary complications. In addition, the preparation of the freebase can produce ether fires because of the high degree of inflammability of the material.

We continue to see varying forms of prescription drug abuse in nonstreetwise polydrug abusers, including both nonnarcotic and narcotic drug abuse patterns such as Talwin® addiction in physicians. However, we have not seen in the San Francisco Bay Area the increased use of "Ps" and "blues" (Talwin and pyrobenzamine) which has been reported in the Midwest area, particularly Chicago and St. Louis.

Sedative-Hypnotic Abuse

The San Francisco Bay Area continues to have a substantial problem with alcohol combined with sedative-hypnotic abuse in both nonstreetwise and streetwise polydrug abusers. Additional work needs to be done in defining the toxicity of various patterns of prescription sedative-hypnotic abuse such as long-term low-dose diazepam use.[15] I have particular concern, however, relative to the increase in methaqualone abuse. This drug, when first introduced as a prescription sedative-hypnotic was widely abused.[12] But, as a result of increasing controls of the manufacture of the drug, we saw a decrease of abuse. However, recently there has been technological breakthroughs in clandestine laboratories and as a result, there has been an increasing black market synthesis of methaqualone. The consumer in the drug culture believes the methaqualone is from pharmaceutical sources and still continues to pay a relatively high price for the drug. A recent street drug analysis report of one of these black market samples indicated that it not only contains methaqualone, but two other chemicals apparently used in the synthesis, namely, toludine and acetylonthronilic acid. Gleason, *et al.*[13] gives these two contaminants a toxicity rating of 4 with the ability to potentially damage liver, kidneys and bone marrow. The consumer in the drug culture purchases methaqualone believing that it is pharmaceutically pure, but the contaminants in this new black market synthesis may produce new patterns of toxicity in addition to the high abuse potential of methaqualone itself. The expansion of clandestine lab technology will, I believe, add new toxicological consequences as such patterns of drug abuse increase.

Psychedelic Drugs

We have seen an increase in the use of LSD in the San Francisco Bay area, but, we have seen a relatively small increase in the incidence of panic reaction or bad trips. It appears that the expanded consumption of LSD is occurring in a consumer population which has had previous experience with the drug and is not abusing it chronically or in a group of adolescents who have adequately prepared themselves in order to minimize the adverse effects associated with LSD. LSD use then occurs within a cultural context that tends to minimize abuse.

In contrast, other drugs that are viewed as psychedelic by nature by the consumer have moved toward more chronic abuse patterns with higher toxicity.[14] Although, there is a good deal of experimentation in one time use of PCP that can lead to acute toxic consequences,[15] there is a trend towards chronic abuse on a more regular basis, which can have substantial additional neuropsychological toxicity. PCP has been in the Bay Area for a long time and was first defined as a street drug in the Haight-Ashbury District in San Francisco.[16] Its explosive increase occurred in the 70's as part of the result of black market synthesis with relative high availability and low cost. However, as described by Newmeyer, a number of factors have changed, including increased law enforcement efforts that have made the drug somewhat less available and more expensive, plus a growing awareness of the consumer population of its toxicity which, as predicted by Newmeyer, "may make 1979 the high water mark in the popularity of PCP."

Unfortunately, we have seen the appearance of other disassociative anesthetics such as Ketamine on the street and those who study new drug abuse patterns must be aware that in excess of 30 PCP analogues exist, which make new drug abuse patterns with new toxic consequences from this drug group inevitable. We have also seen an increase in drug combinations that previously appeared unlikely. For example, a subject of the chronic PCP abuse population moves back and forth between heroin and PCP. PCP is smoked or injected on a chronic basis until toxic consequences appear and then the individual uses heroin to calm those side effects. When dependence and cost become major deterrents to continue the use of heroin, they revert back to the use of PCP. This drug switching between different drug groups poses particular challenges to drug-specific programs which are oriented only to the treatment of opiate addiction such as methadone maintenance programs.

In summary, the only constant about the drug scene is that it will change. And workers in the drug abuse field must keep a constant awareness of new drug abuse patterns in order to make the treatment procedures and prevention techniques effective.

References

1a. Harvey, William. 1980. Mississippi Enterprise. St. Louis, Mo.

1b. Smith, D. E., *et al.* 1972. It's So Good, Don't Even Try It Once: Heroin In Perspective. Prentice-Hall.

2. INABA, D., G. JOHNSON & D. E. SMITH. 1980. Persian heroin in the San Francisco Bay area 1977–1980. The new wave? Newsletter. California Society for the Treatment of Alcoholism and Other Drug Dependencies: **7**(2).
3. BOLIN, J. K. 1979. U.S. faces another heroin challenge. U.S. J. Drug Alcohol Dep.
4. MORGAN, J. P. *et al.* 1978. Street amphetamine quality and the controlled substances act of 1970. J. Psychedelic Drugs **10**(4).
5. NEWMEYER, JOHN A. 1978. The epidemiology of the use of amphetamine and related substances. J. Psychedelic Drugs **10**(4).
6. JERI, F. R., *et al.* 1978. The syndrome of coca paste. J. Psychedelic Drugs **10**(4).
7. WESSON, DONALD R. 1979. Smoking cocaine freebase. Newsletter. California Society for the Treatment of Alcoholism and Other Drug Dependencies **6**(4).
8. MEYERS, F. H., A. J. ROSE & D. E. SMITH. 1968. Incidents involving the Haight-Ashbury population and some uncommonly used drugs. J. Psychedelic Drugs **1**(2).
9. SMITH, D. E., *et al.* 1973. Uppers and Downers. Prentice-Hall.
10. WESSON, DONALD R. 1979. Smoking cocaine freebase. Newsletter. California Society for the Treatment of Alcoholism and Other Drug Dependencies **6**(4).
11. SMITH, D. E. 1979. Importance of gradual dosage reduction following low-dose Benzodiazepine therapy. Newsletter. California Society for the Treatment of Alcoholism and Other Drug Dependencies **6**(2).
12. SMITH, D. E., *et al.* 1973. Uppers and Downers. Prentice-Hall.
13. GLEASON, M. N., R. E. GOSSELIN & H. C. HODGE. 1963. Clinical Toxicology of Commercial Products: 119. Williams & Wilkins.
14. NEWMEYER, JOHN A. 1979. The epidemiology of PCP use in the late 1970s. To be published in Proceedings of the National PCP Conference.
15. SMITH, D. E., *et al.* 1978. The diagnosis and treatment of the PCP abuse syndrome. NIDA Research Monograph Series 21. *In* PCP Phencyclidine Abuse: An Appraisal. R. Petersen and K. Stillman, Eds.
16. MEYERS, F. H., A. J. ROSE & D. E. SMITH. 1968. Incidents involving the Haight-Ashbury population and some uncommonly used drugs. J. Psychedelic Drugs **1**(2).

DRUG ABUSE PATTERNS ON THE EAST COAST

Reverend John Hamilton McVernon

National Association on Drug Abuse Problems, Inc.
New York, New York 10017

It is more than a little surprising that the conference committee chose as a person to sketch current trends in drug use a man who is neither a researcher, nor a scientist nor a physician but one trained in philosophy and in, an even more obscure field of study, theology.

There may be some logic to the choice: Edmund Carpenter—the person whose ideas were popularized by Marshall McLuhan—quotes John Cullen as saying "I don't know who discovered water, but I am certain it wasn't a fish." [1] When you are in the midst of something, you tend to take its nature and its currents for granted. Perhaps my distance will help.

What really changes in this field are the styles of drug use, the substances used and the populations involved. What changes, too, are society's reaction to drug users and the level of concern about drug problems. Heroin use and heroin addiction are nothing new in New York City. When the numbers of heroin addicts inched up to 100,000 [2] a journal linked the high rate of heroin use to two factors in the city's life: the hectic pace and the crowding.

That was the situation before 1920. And the problem was then one of what we would call today "prescription drug misuse," which ought to give pause to some of those who clamor for tighter controls on the problem medications today.

For many, involvement with heroin is a source of identity and an economic enterprise that gives meaning to their day in a society which seems to have shut off most other avenues of accomplishment. One wonders if the proliferation of street corner vendors hawking everything from digital time pieces to Rush is a sign of a new underground economy that will serve as an alternative to the life style of the dope dealing hustler.

Inflationary pressure has made itself felt in the economy of drug traffic. Higher prices seem to contribute to the swing to pentazocine and peribenzamine in New Orleans and Chicago, and pentazocine and methylphenidate in Philadelphia, and phenmetrazine and pentazocine in Washington, D.C. These are unusual replacements for heroin since the drugs fit the role only as psychological substitutes rather than physiological ones. All are mixtures reminiscent of the old Bombita.

During the summer months, one New York medical center experienced a tenfold increase in intake for heroin detoxification and city-wide we experienced doubling of applications for that service. The same phenomenon was observed in New Haven. In other areas there appeared to be a move from heroin to prescription drugs, notably methaqualone, a change made more readily possible by the pipeline which brings from West Germany legitimately produced bulk, which is capsuled in Colombia and introduced to the U.S. through Florida.

Observers of the popular music scene are alerting the disc jockeys to expect a long-term resurgence of rock. When we were in the midst of what *The Wall*

Street Journal described as a "go-go economy" that mood played into disco, which is bright and optimistic. The stylish drug was cocaine, the drug of the flapper era. The rock-and-roll renaissance they trace to the energy crisis and growing fears about the economy. Rock has always been more aggressive, an outlet for frustration and tension at a time when people are scared.

If graffiti are any index of trends, one New York subway wall bears the legend: "Disco is dead, Rock is head."

Acid rock was the overture of the heroin fad of the early '70s and the return of hard times might signal the return of hard drugs. If heroin use does increase, one consolation is that we might not see heroin deaths increase. A study of the experience of The Emergency Medical Service in New York City shows that an overdose victim who is alive when the ambulance arrives has the best prospect for survival as compared to other categories of critical patients. So, using groups ought to be encouraged to avail themselves of that help since so many deaths may be utterly unnecessary.

A remarkable aside, at the time of the Pope's visit to Manhattan, street drugs apart from heroin, phencyclidine, marijuana and methaqualone, were unavailable. Street workers suggest that the drought was not the result of spiritual awakening but law enforcement saturation at the most prominent points of sale.

Among the exotica, phencyclidine continues to be much discussed as a dangerous drug. We are cautioned that here is one case that justifies the scare tactics that were, admittedly, counterproductive when talking about marijuana. Given the passage of a few months time the PCP panic will give way to a subsequent cause for alarm. When the drug was first misused in the Midwest in the middle '60s there were not the bizarre effects and panic reactions since the users hadn't been psyched up to expect that kind of a trip. Even with all the hype, the security folks from the New York Board of Education haven't one case of bad reaction to PCP on school property or during school time among their many thousands of students. If PCP is as widely used as the media observes and has as high a potential for harm as some claim, we ought to be picking our way over the victims as we stroll along Central Park South.

In October, 1979 Metromedia aired a documentary on the subject, calmly entitled "Angel Death," with stories about fried babies—real balanced stuff. The PCP user is today's version of the coked up hop-head of the '20s or the junkie of the '50s.

It reminds me of the events that took place a hundred years ago or so in England when one of the first gorillas to be brought to that country for exhibition escaped into the countryside and was apprehended—in fact was arrested and put on trial—and upon questioning because its answers were unintelligible, an assumption was made that the gorilla was French and it was executed as a spy.

We have believed some ridiculous things about people who use drugs, too, and we haven't yet broken the habit.

Maybe the next panic potion will be isobutyl nitrite. I thought that could never happen in America. How could anything that makes sex better be bad.

I was mistaken. I forgot the power of the myth of the child. Kids are taking it. What are the ill effects? They get high. (Appealing to our fear that somewhere someone is having more fun than we are). And even worse, when queried, these little people (whom we like to call children) know that it is used in homosexual circles. Presto, you have the makings of a real problem by combining fear of drugs and fear of sex so we can initiate a new anti-kid pogrom.

Our gullibility is currently being exploited by a number of anti-drug coalitions, relatively strong in Michigan and New York. They take the data on drug use and drug traffic and drug problems and having summarily dismissed the thesis that drug dependence is often the result of a series of unhappy decisions an individual makes in a painful life situation, attribute the dope problem to the British, big business, the Hong Kong connection, and the Zionists (read Jews).

The supposititious arguments are in a volume titled "Dope Inc." and because the topic of drugs has such mythical power some people believe this fable.

In the industrial setting, employee assistance coordinators are picking up increasing numbers of workers with drug problems. The drug involvement they see is typically not the classic addict profile, nor do the employees with drug problems manifest the same kind of personal and job deterioration the alcohol-dependent worker does.

The employed problem drug user is more often disoriented rather than dysfunctional. Many are young females who stumble into heavy drug use by taking medications to counteract the undesired effects of the contraceptive formulations. Some are recreational smokers who start letting work time be fun time. A few are weekend heroin users who catch a "jones." And others are men and women under stress who, on their own or through inappropriate professional care, get into prescription drugs above their heads.

Two goals have to be accomplished. The first is to see that employers don't overreact to drug use and make a developing difficulty a full blown problem.

The second is to see that the initial intervention—because the magic word "drugs" has been mentioned—doesn't leap to referrals to long-term care either in the therapeutic community, the chemotherapeutic program or even care on the model of alcohol treatment.

As a rule this pattern of inappropriate drug taking responds to good information, practical counseling, with, of course, an adequate regimen of detoxification where appropriate.

Alcohol problems continue to predominate, though that may be a function of the fact that most employee assistance coordinators are "friends of Bill Wilson," people who themselves came out of a background of alcoholism. One finds what one looks for.

The epidemic of adolescent alcoholism has apparently been licked. Media monsters are made for slaying anyway. Dickens observed the same sad situation among young people and alcohol in his time. Unfortunately, he wasn't well enough equipped to label what he observed in medical terminology. If anyone persists in the misguided notion that young people and drink were never as well acquainted in the past as they are today, please study the writings of Jacob Riis:

"1901, the growler looms up in the New York street boy's life, baffling the most persistent efforts to reclaim him. There is no escape from it; no hope for the boy, once its blighting grip is upon him. Thenceforward the logic of the slums, that the world which gave him poverty and ignorance for his portion owes him a living, is his creed, and the career of the 'tough' lies open before him, a beaten track to be blindly followed to a bad end in the wake of the growler." [3]

Now that we are somewhat calmer about that epidemic, I hear there are professional voices raised in doubt about the fetal alcohol syndrome, too. It would seem that if this characteristic physiognomy were a common result of the heavy use of alcohol, folk-wisdom would have picked it up and incorporated it in what once were called "old wives tales."

Some months ago a conversation about marijuana took place in this city, an exchange on the topic among men and women active in prevention and treatment programs which showed that a new working definition of the substance was being developed that excluded pot from the category: drug. So when the question is asked of applicants to programs "What drugs do you use?" the typical respondent doesn't bother to mention "smoke." It isn't classed as a drug.

Some of the drug-free therapeutic communities have had marathons to thrash out the problem of pot smoking staff and answer the questions: Is use of marijuana cause for a graduate to fall from good standing? Is it to be considered drug use?

One large program admits that pot would be allowed except for the bad vibrations that would be touched off in the community and the pressure which would be exerted by the police.

Some workers in prevention and chemotherapeutic programs see marijuana use as potentially positive for their clients. In the former it delays dealing with multiple life crises and in the latter medicates the discomfort of heroin withdrawal.

Concerning the realm of prevention there is increasing dissatisfaction with the "warm-fuzzie/cold-pricklie" approach to the topic. Once the accepted wisdom was that when a person could identify what was causing them pain and express that hurt they were okay.

Time has shown that ventilation isn't always therapeutic. Prevention programs now are mixing feeling and fact; others provide alternate environments; some are really intervention efforts with young people who have initiated use.

A very interesting project comes out of the American Health Foundation where mental health and the avoidance of addictive behavior are integrated in a person-centered approach. The thesis is that my well-being is determined not solely by nature or nurture but by what I do with what I have. Staying healthy is my job. And as I can be the source of my well-being by eating right and resting well, by exercise and keeping tabs on the signs of good health and illness in my own system, so less and less do I expect outside influences to do the job for me. I depend less on the professional, less on placebos and more on myself. I take responsibility.

It is not tautological to observe that the person who takes many drugs is likely to take more drugs. And the person who has little inclination to medicate physical problems is even less inclined to be involved with chemicals as solutions for emotional problems.

In the drug-free therapeutic community, which generally receives support from without, significant internal questioning has been heard from a group of French social workers.

In their setting, social service has historically been linked to the Church and the therapeutic community seems to continue the role of the helping agency as a transmitter of the traditional ethic.

Even here in secular America, a treatment center is more like the seminary I attended than contemporary seminaries are. The staff are the clergy of the therapeutic ritual, answers to all questions are written in stone, the inner life of the resident is laid bare through a confession of faults and the client fluctuates emotionally between exhilaration and humiliation.

The fact that the process "works" for some clients does not necessarily mean it is therapeutic. The validity of the criticism that the treatment center does not allow for the development of new sorts of guiding values will be tested by the willingness of programs to hear this kind of comment and react productively to it.

The entire future of drug use and drug problems will be affected by changing patterns of populations. As our citizens age increasing numbers of older persons will be persons who have had experience with psychotropics. As the opportunity for greater leisure increases the appeal of taking trips without leaving the farm increases.

At the same time it is possible, since human history is characterized by cycles, that our young will react conservatively to the games we play with our minds. Will Durant, now in his high old age, got a glimpse of 42nd Street and feels we've gone too far and that the coming decades will see a swing from personal freedom to social responsibility.

The revolutionary children of China see the opium habit as a remnant of the oppressive past, and heroin, LSD and grass may, by the year 2,000, be very much part of a bygone era.

Of course people will still be getting high on power, or religion, or electronic implants. The task is not to keep from playing with the mind but to keep the cost of the game low and have the players come out winners.

References

1. Carpenter, Edmund. 1970. They Became What They Beheld. Ballantine. New York, N.Y.
2. Musto, David, M. 1973. The American Disease: 108. Yale University Press. New Haven, Conn.
3. Riis, Jacob, A. 1971. How the Other Half Lives: 165. Dover. New York, N.Y.

Article really does not focus on subject of East Coast Drug Abuse. There is an implied "soft line" acceptance of drug use instead of a concentration on drug abuse.

GENERAL DISCUSSION

Robert B. Millman, *Session Chair*

Department of Public Health
The New York Hospital-Cornell Medical Center
New York, New York 10021

RICHARD RESNICK: Carl Verebey, here in New York, has recently shown that opiates like morphine can protect against the development of PCP stereotopy in animals. It brought to mind that we don't see PCP problems in methadone-maintained patients. I wonder whether others have had similar experiences.

DAVID SMITH: The observation that methadone might reverse some of the toxicity of PCP is very interesting. It doesn't appear that the opiates have a major protective effect against PCP intoxication in man. For example, methadone-maintenance patients who use high doses of PCP do develop agitation and toxic psychosis.

CHAIRMAN MILLMAN: This PCP-methadone interaction relates to the question of possible tolerance to the antipsychotic effects of the opiates. Certainly the opiates have antipsychotic properties, so it's not surprising that acutely administered methadone would be an effective treatment of PCP toxicity. Whether chronic methadone will affect psychotic signs, which ones, at what dose, etc., are very interesting issues.

SIDNEY COHEN: Dr. David Smith, why are people changing cocaine hydrochloride to coca paste or free coca base? I would think that free base would produce less "bang." How do you understand this phenomenon?

JAMES COOPER: We are presently attempting to include the 8–11-year age group in National Drug Abuse surveys.

DAVID SMITH: I don't see many persons who report exchanging parenteral cocaine for smoking free base. What I do see, are former cocaine snorters who now smoke free base. The maximum effect is still intravenous. I am concerned that individuals who wouldn't be likely to get into high-dose patterns may, by smoking free base, develop cocaine toxicity.

JAMES HALIKAS (*Medical College of Wisconsin*): Are there any data on stable recreational or social use of these drugs on a chronic basis? Rev. John McVernon suggested some people might be having fun through moderate use of some of these drugs. We know that people can drink alcohol socially for a long time safely and without increasing the dose. It appears to be true for some regular marijuana users. What about some of these other drugs?

JAMES COOPER: In our study of the effects of drugs on sexual functioning, different populations reported quite different results. For example, regarding PCP and sexual dysfunction, the group admitted to our drug-treatment program was very dysfunctional. Thus one might conclude that PCP produces all sorts of sexual dysfunction. Yet another PCP-using population, not assembled because of problems of abuse, reported using the drug successfully without sexual dysfunction. This points out one of the difficulties in epidemiological and clinical studies. The patient population which enters treatment may leave you with a biased view and not reflect others not entering treatment.

DAVID SMITH: Heroin chipping also falls into that category. Lee Robins has some data implying that if someone had tried it more than six times they were likely to become addicted. Yet we've always heard anecdotally of large numbers of recreational heroin users who've never become addicted.

CHAIRMAN MILLMAN: Norman Zinberg in Boston has reported on a small number of apparently controlled heroin users who use intermittently for long periods of time and do not become dependent. In New York we're also hearing about, and occasionally seeing, large numbers of people, mostly affluent, who use heroin intermittently and do not get into trouble. There is little question that people are able to use all the other drugs in the same way, at least for periods of time. We need to follow these people—no easy task.

SHEILA BLUME: I think that the more we learn about the natural history of alcohol abusers, the more we realize that the category labeled problem drinkers in the circular pie chart is very diverse. About a third of the drinkers in a two-year cycle go in and out of that category. The total number remains the same, but the individuals within that problem drinking category change all the time. We have a lot to learn about the natural history of alcohol problems.

BARRY STIMMEL: Since tranquilizers are so easily available, they probably produce the largest number of persons with chronic adverse psychic consequences. Yet we don't often see these consequences in the emergency rooms because people can control their use much better than heroin and PCP.

SHELDON ZIMBERG: In view of the data which indicate an increasing prevalence of the use of marijuana and greater strengths of the substance that's being smoked, are we seeing more frequent episodes of adverse reactions and more severe reactions to the use of marijuana?

DAVID SMITH: Our evidence is that the incidence of severe reaction is decreasing and that's characteristic of all the psychedelics over the past 10 or 15 years. As people learn to handle them, the incidence of side effects decreases. The acute adverse reactions we commonly see are due to the combination of alcohol and marijuana.

HERBERT D. KLEBER: As far as I can see, the paraquat scare drove out the use of Mexican marijuana, which has 1% THC and markedly increased the use of Colombian, California, etc., with THC rates of anywhere from 2% to 7%. The cost rose from $20 an ounce up to $40 to $200 or more. Also, petty crimes in schools increased. Whether it will also lead to more medical complications, we'll have to wait and see.

METABOLIC INTERACTIONS BETWEEN OPIATES AND ALCOHOL *

Mary Jeanne Kreek

The Rockefeller University
New York, New York 10021

Coexistence of narcotic and ethanol abuse, contrary to medical school teaching of a decade ago, is common. Combined narcotic and alcoholic addictive disease is also common, and alcohol abuse or alcoholism often persists during and also following chronic pharmacological treatment for heroin addiction. Both alcohol- and narcotic-related problems require clinical management.

Speculations concerning some type of common bond between the two addictive diseases of alcoholism and narcotic addiction are tempting, yet our current knowledge does not permit us to claim any definite relationship at this time. The state of the art in both areas of research is advancing rapidly and in many directions. The discovery of specific opiate receptors, their endogenous ligands including the various endorphins and enkephalins, and more recently, the suggestion that many different such receptor-ligand systems may exist both for opioid compounds, as well as for other types of exogenous and presumably endogenous compounds, has been one of several very exciting new advances. New analytical techniques have been developed which now allow more precise and specific measurement of a variety of endogenous and exogenous substances. Nevertheless, despite many recent advances in our understanding of opioid and alcohol disposition and effects, at this time no commonality between narcotic addiction and alcoholism has been clearly documented.

Both alcoholism and narcotic addiction, individually and together, may have profound effects on the physiological, medical, behavioral and social status of an individual with these disorders. Relationships may exist between the two clinical problems, which may or may not have any relationship to the yet undefined etiology or mechanisms underlying each separate addictive disease entity, or to the production and maintenance of the tolerant and dependent states. There are several theoretical possibilities of types of narcotic-ethanol interactions. Dispositional interactions could occur in which the absorption, distribution, metabolism or excretion of one agent might be affected by the other. Pharmacodynamic interactions of several types might occur. These could be general interactions at diverse sites resulting in altered pharmacological effects of one or both agents, or interactions localized at some specific site of action, such as at a single type of receptor system. Other various types of interactions could occur altering drug action, such as possible specific metabolic interactions. Additive, synergistic or opposing effects of ethanol and

* Supported by grants from the National Institute on Drug Abuse (DA-01138); the National Institutes of Health, General Clinical Research Center Grant (RR-00102); and the New York State Division of Substance Abuse Services (C-147605). The opinions expressed within are not necessarily those of this office. This investigation was supported in part by a Research Scientist Development Award (DA-00049) from the ADAMHA awarding institute, the National Institute on Drug Abuse.

narcotics could alter the physiological or pathological effects of either of these agents.

The observations by Ross and colleagues that both chronic morphine and chronic ethanol treatment in animal models result in selective depletion of calcium in the brain, and that in each case this depletion can be prevented by naloxone, have suggested the existence of possible common central nervous system metabolic mechanisms relating ethanol and narcotics.[1] Similarly, both chemical and biological observations of Cohen, Davis, Walsh, Blum, Myers, Melchior and others have suggested that acetaldehyde or other aldehydes from endogenous sources or exogenous ethanol may react under physiological conditions with endogenous neurotransmitter amines to form tetrahydroisoquinoline alkaloids which share some properties with narcotics.[2–6] These findings have further stimulated speculations concerning a commonality between opiate and ethanol addictions. It has also been suggested that ethanol releases endorphins, thus resulting in opiate-like effects.[7, 8] At this time, there are unresolved conflicting reports of the effects of narcotics, usually morphine, and the narcotic antagonist, naloxone, on ethanol drinking behaviors in rodents, suggesting that each of these agents may decrease, have no effect on, or increase ethanol consumption.[5, 9–13] Also, there have been several observations that ethanol may act by a specific or nonspecific mechanism to ameliorate or prevent signs of naloxone-precipitated abstinence syndrome in animals receiving chronic narcotic treatment.[6, 14–19] For instance, ethanol significantly reduces diarrhea occurring in the setting of naloxone-precipitated narcotic withdrawal following morphine treatment in the rat.[18] Recently, observations and studies have suggested that naloxone both does and does not lessen the symptoms of acute ethanol intoxification in man.[20, 21]

A demonstration of the existence of dispositional interactions between ethanol and narcotics would not in any way necessarily link the etiology or mechanisms underlying alcoholism or narcotic addiction, yet could explain some of the observations made when the two coexist. Significant dispositional interactions between ethanol and narcotics could alter the development and maintenance of the tolerant and dependent state by effecting atypical and possibly intermittent availability of each agent to critical sites of action. Drug-seeking behavior for each agent could thus also be altered.

This report will focus on the clinical problems of coexistence of narcotic dependency and ethanol abuse, on one observed apparent metabolic interaction between ethanol and a narcotic in humans, and then on studies of dispositional interactions between narcotics and ethanol in both *in vitro* and *in vivo* animal models and in man.

Although alcohol abuse with its many complications is probably the major medical problem in the United States at this time, with the annual number of deaths due to cirrhosis increasing markedly in recent years, it is nevertheless difficult to estimate the relative prevalence of alcohol abuse and alcoholism in certain population subgroups; for instance, in heroin addicts and former addicts now in chronic methadone maintenance treatment. Limited available information suggests that the prevalence of alcohol use may be very high in appropriately matched nonopiate using subgroup populations of similar demographic characteristics to the opiate-using group. Although there is no documented evidence of an increased prevalence of alcohol-related problems in narcotic-dependent groups, the two problems do coexist in large numbers of both heroin addicts and patients during and following chronic chemotherapy for addiction.[22–25]

Alcohol abuse was documented as a concomitant problem with heroin addiction in the initial prospective study of all patients entering methadone maintenance treatment between 1964 and 1966.[22, 23] Of the first 214 patients, 92 remained in chronic high-dose methadone treatment for three or more years. Of this long-term treatment group, approximately 20% were identified as heavy users of alcohol at time of admission to treatment for heroin addiction, drinking more than 4 oz equivalent of whiskey per day; after three or more years of methadone treatment, a total of 25% of all patients remaining in treatment were using these large amounts of alcohol on a chronic basis. Alcohol-related liver disease, with or without coexisting post-viral chronic liver disease, as well as other clinical problems related to alcohol abuse, were common in this group. Alcohol-related problems were the cause for discharge in many of the patients who left treatment in less than three years, and accounted for death of one patient in the prospective study group.

Alcohol abuse is also prevalent in young former narcotic addicts.[26, 27] In a study carried out in a special methadone maintenance and detoxification clinic for youthful drug abusers, 16–23 years old with documented chronic heroin addiction, 15 of 46 patients available for special evaluation, of the total 90 patients in the clinic, were found to be chronic heavy users of alcohol, consuming a mean of 17 oz equivalent of whiskey daily. The alcohol abusers were similar to nonabusers with regard to age (a mean of 19.5 and 20 years, respectively) and duration of methadone maintenance treatment (34.3 and 36.5 months, respectively). The mean levels of two tests of liver function, SGOT and SGPT, however, were significantly higher in the alcohol abuser group than in the nonalcohol abusers (mean SGOT levels: 76 ± 19 SEM versus 40 ± 4 SEM; and mean SGPT levels: 99 ± 21 SEM versus 53 ± 7 SEM, respectively).

A prospective clinical follow-up study recently has been carried out in one adult methadone maintenance clinic to determine the prevalence of alcohol abuse and to evaluate the progression of liver disease in patients continuing to use large amounts of alcohol. Of 218 patients in treatment in the clinic at time of initiation of the study, 31% were identified by staff as chronic alcohol abusers, consuming more than 4 oz equivalent of whiskey daily on a chronic basis, with or without objective criteria for a diagnosis of alcoholism.[28, 29] After two years of follow-up, 59% of those patients identified as chronic alcohol abusers had been discharged, voluntarily or involuntarily, from methadone treatment, in many cases for reasons related to chronic alcohol abuse. For most of these patients, there was failure to treat both alcohol-related problems and opiate addiction. However, 41% of patients identified initially as chronic alcohol abusers remained in methadone treatment for two years of follow-up. Although in most cases attempts at intervention in alcohol abuse had failed, narcotic addiction remained under satisfactory management, and patients remained in continuing medical follow-up care.

Ninety percent of the patients initially identified as chronic abusers of alcohol had abnormal liver function tests at the beginning of the study period, as contrasted to around 60% usually observed in general populations of patients in chronic methadone treatment. Preliminary analysis of data from this study shows that of the 28 patients remaining in treatment during the two years of study, only 25% (7 cases) showed laboratory evidence of deterioration of liver function during the prospective study period. These findings of lack of rapid progression of liver disease in most patients are probably what would be expected in a group of alcohol abusers not in methadone maintenance treatment. There was no evidence of any synergistic effects of methadone and ethanol when used together with respect to progression of liver disease, which has been suggested by many clinical observers working in methadone treatment programs. It is certainly possible, however, that exceptionally severe or rapidly progressive liver disease might occur in some patients, which could be due to the superimposition of the hepatotoxic effects of ethanol on a liver already damaged by viral hepatitis and one of its chronic sequellae. Over two-thirds of all patients in methadone treatment have evidence of chronic liver disease, most commonly due to one of the chronic sequellae of viral hepatitis. Also, the possibility that interactions between methadone and ethanol may occur which are especially deleterious to the liver has certainly not been fully excluded by these clinical studies.

An unexpected finding was made in the initial prospective studies of patients entering and during methadone treatment. In a population with generally poor nutrition, a variety of chronic infectious diseases, and a high prevalence of chronic liver disease, either of post-viral or alcohol-induced types, serum albumin levels were elevated in 17% of patients at time of admission to chronic methadone treatment, and after three or more years of treatment levels were elevated in 32%.[22, 23] Subsequently, similar findings were made in a retrospective study of adult patients, and in a prospective study of adolescent patients.[26, 27] In collaboration with Dr. Marcus Rothschild and Dr. Murray Oratz, studies of the possible effects of methadone on albumin metabolism have been carried out in rabbits treated on a chronic basis with methadone.[30] The changes observed during methadone treatment included increased total amounts of intra- and extravascular albumin, coupled with increased, not decreased, rates of albumin degradation. In other studies, Rothschild and colleagues have shown that ethanol reduces synthesis of albumin in the rabbit model *in vivo* and *in vitro*.[31, 32] Also, low levels of serum albumin are commonly observed in chronic alcohol abusers. Thus, it is of especial interest that in the recent study of methadone maintenance patients who are also chronic heavy users of alcohol, it was found that 13% of patients had elevated levels of serum albumin after 27 to 75 months of methadone treatment.[28, 29]

Significant dispositional interactions between ethanol and a few other drugs in both animal models and in man have been described by Lieber and Rubin, Kalant and Khanna, and others.[33–40] It has been observed that ethanol may have two distinctly different effects on drug metabolism. Administration of large amounts of ethanol may inhibit drug metabolism, possibly by direct inhibition of hepatic microsomal function. However, after chronic administration of ethanol followed by sufficient time to allow clearance of ethanol from the body, accelerated metabolism of some drugs has been observed, possibly due to the documented effect of chronic ethanol treatment, resulting in enhancement of hepatic microsomal drug-metabolizing enzyme activities.

We have carried out several studies to determine whether or not there are any significant dispositional interactions between ethanol and narcotics following acute and chronic administration in animal models and in man. In previous studies of the hepatic extraction of long- and short-acting narcotics using ar isolated perfused rabbit liver preparation carried out in collaboration with Drs. Rothschild and Oratz, it was shown that the long-acting narcotic, methadone, was avidly extracted (86%) from portal venous blood in a single pass through the liver and that the extent of extraction was independent of rate of hepatic blood flow, but was decreased by increasing the total amounts of methadone injected beyond 7.5 mg per bolus (see TABLE 1).[41] It was also shown that unchanged methadone was slowly released from the liver into hepatic effluent blood, suggesting that the liver may serve not only as a site of biotransformation of methadone, but also as a reservoir for storage and subsequent release of unchanged compound (see TABLE 2). Hepatic extractions of the short-acting narcotics, morphine, heroin and meperidine were all significantly lower (27%, 59% and 66%, respectively) than that of methadone in a single pass (see TABLE 3). Subcellular distributions of methadone and morphine also were significantly different, with methadone and its metabolites found primarily in fractions containing nuclei, mitochondria, microsomes and other membranes, whereas morphine was primarily found in the supernatant cytosol (see TABLE 4).

Recently, studies have been carried out with Drs. Rothschild and Oratz to determine the effects of ethanol preperfusion on acute hepatic distribution and metabolism of narcotics in the isolated perfused rabbit liver.[42] In these studies, it was shown that preperfusion with ethanol (200 mg/dl of ethanol for 75 minutes) did not significantly alter the acute hepatic extraction of either of the long-acting narcotics, methadone or LAAM, or of the short-acting narcotics, morphine or meperidine. Also, preperfusion with ethanol did not alter either the subcellular localization of narcotics or the proportions of unchanged

TABLE 1 *

HEPATIC EXTRACTION OF METHADONE

A. Hepatic Extraction of Methadone and Its Separate Enantiomers †

Compound	Amount injected ‡ (mg free base)	Number of perfusion studies	Hepatic extraction § (% of total amount injected)
dl-methadone	1.5	6	86.1 (±0.81 SEM)
d-methadone	0.75	2	83.6 (±2.46 SEM)
l-methadone	0.75	2	84.5 (±3.86 SEM)

B. Hepatic Extraction of Methadone: Effect of Varying Amounts Injected

Compound	Amount injected ‡ (mg free base)	Number of perfusion studies	Hepatic extraction § (% of total amount injected)
dl-methadone	1.5	6	86.1 (±0.81 SEM)
dl-methadone	7.5	2	88.8 (±2.56 SEM)
dl-methadone	15.0	3	75.2 (±2.52 SEM) ¶
dl-methadone	75.0	3	55.7 (±3.57 SEM) ‖

* (From M. J. Kreek, M. Oratz and M. A. Rothschild.[41] By permission of *Gastroenterology*.)

† Hepatic extraction as measured, after two minutes of open perfusion following a single bolus of drug, is slightly underestimated.

‡ Total mass of methadone injected into portal vein cannula as a single bolus.

§ Percentage of total radioactivity from methadone in liver after two-minute open perfusion.

¶ Significantly different from hepatic extraction of 1.5 mg dl-methadone, $p < 0.05$.

‖ Significantly different from hepatic extraction of 1.5 mg dl-methadone, $p < 0.01$.

TABLE 2 *

CONCENTRATION OF UNCHANGED DL-METHADONE IN HEPATIC EFFLUENT PLASMA †

Time after injection of radioactivity (seconds)	Concentration of unchanged dl-methadone (μg/ml)	Total amount of unchanged dl-methadone in 15 second sample (μg)
0–15	0–.43	0.40–1.57
15–30	.64–.48	2.36–1.76
30–45	.47–.26	1.51–0.98
45–60	.26–.17	1.04–0.64
60–75	.13–.17	0.43–0.59
75–90	.17–.17	0.57–0.55
90–105	.17–.17	0.57–0.70
105–120	.19–.17	0.67–0.62

* (From M. J. Kreek, M. Oratz and M. A. Rothschild.[41] By permission of *Gastroenterology.*)

† Concentration of unchanged dl-methadone in hepatic effluent plasma, determined by gas liquid chromatography following bolus injection of methadone (1.5 mg free base) into portal vein of isolated perfused rabbit liver (single study).

TABLE 3 *

HEPATIC EXTRACTION OF MORPHINE, DIACETYLMORPHINE (HEROIN), MEPERIDINE, 1-α-ACETYLMETHADOL AND NALOXONE †

Compound	Amount injected ‡ (mg free base)	Number of perfusion studies	Hepatic extraction § (% of total amount injected)
morphine	1.5 mg	6	27.4 (±2.30 SEM) ¶
diacetylmorphine (heroin)	1.5 mg	3	59.2 (±2.11 SEM) ¶
meperidine	1.5 mg	4	65.8 (±2.32 SEM) ¶
1-α-acetylmethadol (LAAM)	1.5 mg	2	90.8 (±3.30 SEM)
naloxone	1.6 mg	4	40.4 (±5.31 SEM) ¶

* (From M. J. Kreek, M. Oratz and M. A. Rothschild.[41] By permission of *Gastroenterology.*)

† Hepatic extraction as measured after two minutes of open perfusion following a single bolus of drug is slightly underestimated.

‡ Total mass of drug injected into portal vein cannula as a single bolus.

§ Percentage of total radioactivity from methadone in liver after two-minute open perfusion.

¶ Significantly different from hepatic extraction of 1.5 mg dl-methadone, $p < 0.01$.

methadone or the major *N*-demethylated metabolites in each of the hepatic subcellular fractions.

Although these findings suggest that acute exposure to ethanol by preperfusion does not cause significant alterations in the acute hepatic extraction and subcellular distribution of either long- or short-acting narcotics in the isolated perfused rabbit liver, and does not impair the immediate hepatic biotransformation of methadone within the short two-minute open perfusion period, Whitehouse and coworkers have reported that acute ethanol administration to the

TABLE 4 *

DISTRIBUTION OF RADIOACTIVITY FROM METHADONE AND MORPHINE IN SUBCELLULAR FRACTIONS OF RABBIT LIVER

	Methadone	*Morphine*
Fraction 1 Whole liver homogenate	Mean 85.0% † ±SEM 1.13 N 4	Mean 28.4% † ±SEM 2.87 N 4
Fraction 2–3 Supernatant (12,000g × 10 minutes)	Mean 46.9% ‡ ±SEM 3.65 N 4	Mean 82.8% ‡ ±SEM 2.54 N 4
Fraction 4 Sediment (12,000g × 10 minutes) (RBC's, nuclei, mitochondria, bound polysomes, membranes)	Mean 49.8% ‡ ±SEM 1.99 N 4	Mean 12.3% ‡ ±SEM 3.64 N 4
Fraction 5 Supernatant (165,000g × 90 minutes) (cytosol)	Mean 36.1% ‡ ±SEM 2.75 N 4	Mean 80.3% ‡ ±SEM 2.17 N 4
Fraction 6 Sediment (165,000g × 60 minutes) (microsomes)	Mean 8.5% ‡ ±SEM 1.37 N 4	Mean 0.7% ‡ ±SEM 0.34 N 4

†—% of total radioactivity injected $\left(\frac{\text{radioactivity in liver}}{\text{total radioactivity injected}}\right)$

‡—% of radioactivity in each fraction based on total radioactivity in whole liver homogenate $\left(\frac{\text{radioactivity in fraction}}{\text{total radioactivity in whole liver homogenate}}\right)$

N—Number of separate perfused rabbit liver studies performed.

* (From M. J. Kreek, M. Oratz and M. A. Rothschild.[41] By permission of *Gastroenterology*.)

rat *in vivo* may alter the hepatic uptake and biliary excretion of methadone.[43] However, as in this study using rabbit liver, no alterations in net metabolism of radiolabeled methadone were demonstrated in their studies using the whole rat model.[43]

Chronic studies have been carried out in my laboratory using the rat as an experimental animal to determine whether there are any significant interactions between ethanol and methadone in that setting.[44] In several other studies, we have determined plasma levels of methadone in the rat, using specific and sensitive gas liquid chromatographic techniques. The plasma levels achieved after chronic treatment with 5 mg/kg per day by the subcutaneous route are greater than those following chronic treatment with 30 mg/kg per day by the oral route, and during the first two hours after drug administration, both are in the range of plasma levels observed in humans during methadone maintenance treatment. The plasma disappearance rates are similar with a $t_{1/2}$ of 70 and 90 minutes, respectively.[45, 46] The oral route of administration following subcutaneous and oral administration in the rat has been used in the ethanol interaction studies, since alcohol is ingested in humans.

Sprague-Dawley rats were treated with methadone (25 mg/kg per day), or a water placebo, daily by gavage for two weeks and then treated concomitantly with methadone, or water, plus ethanol (2 g/kg per day p.o.), or isocaloric sucrose for two weeks. On the day following the last dose of ethanol, rats were sacrificed at sequential time points following a last oral dose of methadone. Plasma levels of methadone were determined by gas liquid chromatography. Plasma levels of methadone were significantly lower at one hour after the oral dose in animals treated on a chronic basis with both methadone and ethanol than those treated with methadone alone and were also lower in ethanol-treated animals at two hours following the methadone dose. Thus, chronic treatment with ethanol along with methadone effected a lowering of plasma levels of methadone when ethanol itself was not present in the body. This effect is probably due to enhancement of hepatic microsomal mixed function oxidase drug-metabolizing enzyme activities by chronic ethanol exposure. Similarly, Borowsky and Lieber recently have shown that following chronic treatment of rats with ethanol alone, decreased levels of unmetabolized methadone are present in liver and brain following a single radiolabeled tracer dose of methadone as compared with the levels in control animals not receiving ethanol.[47] They also showed that chronic ethanol administration to rats increases the rate of *in vitro N*-demethylation of methadone.[47]

In these studies, as well as in other preliminary studies in our laboratory, it had been shown that chronic treatment with ethanol alters methadone disposition in the rat. However, the effects of chronic methadone treatment on ethanol disposition in the rat have not been studied previously. Clinical anecdotes have suggested that the response to alcohol may be reduced in maintenance patients. There are conflicting reports on the effects of narcotics on hepatic microsomal enzyme function in rodents or in man showing enhancement, inhibition or no effects. It has been well established by numerous investigators that chronic treatment with ethanol alone effects an acceleration in ethanol elimination rates, the so-called "adaptive increase," although there is still controversy as to the precise mechanisms involved in this effect.[48–55]

Recently, we have carried out studies to determine the effects of chronic treatment with methadone alone and methadone along with ethanol on ethanol elimination in the rat.[56] Animals were first stabilized on chronic treatment with methadone or were sham-treated with water. Then each group was subdivided, methadone or water continued and ethanol or isocaloric sucrose administered by liquid diet for three weeks. Animals were pair-fed for both liquid and solid diet throughout the study. Voluntary consumption of ethanol exceeded 20 g/kg per day. At the end of the study, weights were similar in all groups. On the final day, ethanol (2 g/kg) was administered intravenously, blood ethanol levels determined by head-space gas liquid chromatography and blood ethanol disappearance rates were calculated. Chronic treatment with methadone alone effects an acceleration in ethanol disappearance rates and the resultant more rapid rates are significantly greater than those following chronic treatment with ethanol alone. Combined chronic treatment with ethanol and methadone resulted in an even greater acceleration of ethanol elimination rates, with the resultant rates significantly greater than those following chronic treatment with either ethanol or methadone alone. Therefore, in the rat during chronic treatment, significant interactions between ethanol and the long-acting narcotic, methadone, have been observed.

The question has been raised frequently of whether or not it is medically and pharmacologically safe for a patient maintained on methadone to use alcohol intermittently on a "social" basis, although there are no clinical reports suggesting that such usage may result in any unexpected or unusual undesirable effects. A study was carried out with Drs. Paul Cushman and Enoch Gordis to determine whether acute "social" use of ethanol alters methadone metabolism as reflected by plasma levels of methadone and whether methadone alters ethanol metabolism as reflected by blood disappearance rates.[57]

Five well-stabilized patients in chronic maintenance treatment, maintained on 30 to 100 mg/day of methadone, without evidence of liver disease and without a history of alcohol abuse, were studied first while receiving methadone alone, with measurements of plasma levels of methadone. Then each patient was restudied following administration of 90 ml of a 50% solution of ethanol (around 3¾ oz equivalent of whiskey) given one hour after the usual daily oral dose of methadone, with measurement of plasma levels of methadone and blood levels of ethanol, and finally studied a third time with the same amount of ethanol given 20 to 38 hours after the last oral dose of methadone, with measurements of blood levels of ethanol. Plasma levels of methadone were similar, both when methadone was administered alone, as in usual daily treatment, and when methadone treatment was followed in one hour by ethanol (see FIGURE 1). The mean blood ethanol disappearance rates were similar when the ethanol was given one hour, or 20 to 38 hours after the last dose of methadone, 2.1 and 2.3 mg per liter per minute, respectively. These blood disappearance rates observed in these methadone-maintained patients were similar to the disappearance rates reported in healthy control subjects, which range from 1.5 to 4.0 mg per liter per minute.[58]

Since disulfiram (or Antabuse®) is the only pharmacological agent which has been shown to be effective as an adjunctive tool in the management of chronic alcohol abuse, we have recently carried out clinical studies in collaboration with Drs. Ted Tong and Neal Benowitz of the University of California at San Francisco to determine if there are any significant dispositional interactions between methadone and disulfiram.[59, 60] Patient volunteers, well-stabilized on steady doses of methadone, with no evidence of polydrug or alcohol abuse, were studied first while receiving methadone alone, then at the end of a one-week period of concomitant administration of disulfiram (500 mg/day p.o.), and finally after disulfiram was discontinued. Although the mean trough plasma methadone concentrations were lowest and apparent terminal half-lives of methadone shortest during disulfiram treatment, these differences were not statistically significant. However, there was an increase in the relative amounts of the major *N*-demethylated pyrrolidine metabolite excreted in urine during disulfiram treatment. Thus although disulfiram may alter methadone disposition, in this study using short-term administration of disulfiram in doses used in the management of alcoholism, no significant dispositional or clinical interactions were observed.

In summary, alcohol abuse is common in heroin addicts, former addicts on methadone maintenance treatment, and also possibly especially common in former addicts and methadone-maintained patients during narcotic withdrawal and afterwards while in the drug-free state. There is no clear evidence, however, that the overall prevalence of alcohol abuse in these narcotic addicts and former addicts is greater than in appropriately matched control groups. Also, although many exciting and provocative experimental and clinical observations

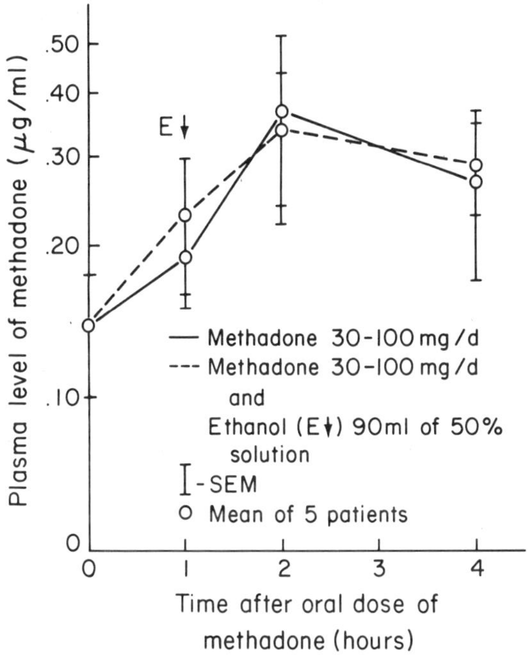

FIGURE 1. Methadone plasma disappearance curves on methadone and ethanol or methadone alone; plasma levels of methadone in five stabilized maintenance patients (not alcohol abusers) after oral dose (30 to 100 mg) alone and after oral dose followed in one hour by 90 ml of a 50 percent solution of ethanol; determination by gas liquid chromatography. (From Kreek.[44] By permission of Raven Press.)

have been made, there is no definite evidence of any link between the addictive diseases of narcotic addiction and alcoholism. However, clinical observations have been made which suggest that interactions may occur between narcotics and ethanol, affecting the available levels of each, and thus possibly the "drug hunger" for each, and also possibly altering the steady state maintenance treatment with methadone when alcohol is used in large amounts on a regular and chronic basis. Several studies have been carried out by our laboratory and by others documenting some specific dispositional interactions between narcotics and ethanol. Clinical studies of possible interactions between methadone and ethanol in methadone-maintained patients who are also chronic abusers of and dependent upon alcohol are now in progress.

Summary

1. Acute preperfusion with ethanol does not alter significantly the initial hepatic extraction or subcellular distribution of narcotics, or the immediate biotransformation of the long-acting narcotic, methadone, using the isolated perfused rabbit liver. However, the acute administration of ethanol may alter distribution and/or impair hepatic drug metabolism in perfusion studies of longer duration, or *in vivo*, as has been suggested by others in studies of several drugs.

2. Following chronic treatment with both ethanol and methadone in the rat, plasma levels of unmetabolized methadone, determined by gas liquid chromatography, are significantly lowered.

3. Following chronic treatment with methadone alone, blood elimination rates of ethanol are accelerated to a greater extent than following chronic treatment with ethanol alone in the rat; following chronic treatment with both methadone and ethanol, rates of ethanol elimination are accelerated to a significantly more rapid rate than following treatment with either agent alone.

4. To date, clinical studies in patients on chronic steady-dose methadone maintenance treatment, without liver disease, polydrug abuse, or heavy use of ethanol, show no significant acute dispositional interactions between methadone and ethanol.

5. Clinical studies in patients on chronic steady-dose methadone maintenance treatment, without liver disease, polydrug abuse, or heavy use of ethanol, show no significant dispositional interactions between methadone and disulfiram (Antabuse®) when the latter was given for one week for study purposes only.

6. Clinical studies of possible dispositional interactions between methadone and ethanol in methadone-maintained patients, who are also chronic abusers of alcohol, are now in progress.

References

1. Ross, D. H., M. A. Medina & H. L. Cardenas. 1974. Morphine and ethanol: selective depletion of regional brain calcium. Science **186:**63–65.
2. Cohen, G. & M. Collins. 1970. Alkaloids from catecholamines in adrenal tissue: possible role in alcoholism. Science **167:**1749–1751.
3. Davis, V. E. & M. J. Walsh. 1970. Alcohol, amines and alkaloids: a possible basis for alcohol addiction. Science **167:**1005–1007.
4. Cohen, G. 1976. Alkaloid products in the metabolism of alcohol and biogenic amines. Biochem. Pharmacol. **25:**1123–1128.
5. Myers, R. D. & C. L. Melchior. 1977. Alcohol drinking: abnormal intake caused by tetrahydropapaveroline in brain. Science **196:**554–556.
6. Blum, K., M. G. Hamilton, M. Hirst & J. E. Wallace. 1978. Putative role of isoquinoline alkaloids in alcoholism: a link to opiates. Alcoholism **2:**113–120.
7. Ho, A. K. S. & C. C. Ho. 1979. Toxic interactions of ethanol with other central depressants: antagonism by naloxone to narcosis and lethality. Pharm. Biochem. Behav. **11:**111–114.
8. Verebey, K. & K. Blum. 1979. Alcohol euphoria: possible mediation via endorphinergic mechanisms. J. Psychedelic Drugs **11:**305–311.

9. SINCLAIR, J. D., J. ATKINS & S. WALKER. 1973. Morphine-induced suppression of voluntary alcohol drinking in rats. Nature **246:**425–427.
10. BLUM, K., J. E. WALLACE, J. D. EUBANKS & H. A. SCHWERTNER. 1975. Effects of naloxone on ethanol withdrawal, preference and narcosis. Pharmacologist **17:**197.
11. ROSS, D. H., I. GELLER & R. J. HARTMANN. 1976. Ethanol preference in the hamster: effects of morphine sulfate and naloxone, a long acting morphine antagonist. Proc. Western Pharmacol. Soc. **19:**326–330.
12. HO, A. K. S. & R. C. A. CHEN. 1976. Interactions of narcotics, narcotic antagonists, and ethanol during acute, chronic, and withdrawal states. Ann. N.Y. Acad. Sci. **281:**297–310.
13. HO, A. K. S., R. C. A. CHEN & M. J. MORRISON. 1977. Opiate-ethanol interaction studies. *In* Alcohol and Opiates: Neurochemical and Behavioral Mechanisms. K. Blum, Ed.:189–202. Academic Press. New York.
14. BLUM, K., S. FUTTERMAN, J. E. WALLACE & H. A. SCHWERTNER. 1977. Naloxone-induced inhibition of ethanol dependence in mice. Nature **265:**49–51.
15. JONES, M. A. & G. R. SPRATTO. 1977. Ethanol suppression of naloxone-induced withdrawal in morphine-dependent rats. Life Sci. **20:**1549–1556.
16. BASS, M. B., H. J. FRIEDMAN & D. LESTER. 1978. Antagonism of naloxone hyperalgesia by ethanol. Life Sci. **22:**1939–1946.
17. HO, A. K. S., R. C. A. CHEN & C. C. HO. 1978. Interaction toxicity between ethanol and narcotics in mice with reference to alpha-1-acetylmethadol (LAAM). Pharm. Biochem. Behav. **9:**195–200.
18. HO, A. K. S., R. C. A. CHEN & M. J. KREEK. 1979. Morphine withdrawal in the rat: an assessment by quantitation of diarrhea and modification by ethanol. Pharmacology **18:**9–17.
19. KHANNA, J. M., A. D. LE, H. KALANT & A. E. LEBLANC. 1979. Cross-tolerance between ethanol and morphine with respect to their hypothermic effects. Eur. J. Pharmacol. **59:**145–149.
20. SORENSEN, S. C. & K. MATTISSON. 1978. Naloxone as antagonist in severe alcohol intoxication. Lancet **2:**688–689.
21. MACKENZIE, A. I. 1979. Naloxone in alcohol intoxication. Lancet **1:**733–734.
22. KREEK, M. J. 1973. Medical safety and side effects of methadone in tolerant individuals. J. Am. Med. Assoc. **223:**665–668.
23. KREEK, M. J., L. DODES, S. KANE, J. KNOBLER & R. MARTIN. 1972. Long-term methadone maintenance therapy: effects on liver function. Ann. Intern. Med. **77:**598–602.
24. STIMMEL, B., M. COHEN & R. HANBURY. 1978. Alcoholism and polydrug abuse in persons on methadone maintenance. Ann. N.Y. Acad. Sci. **311:**99–109.
25. OTTENBERG, D. J. *et al.* 1978. The problem-drinking drug addict. National Institute on Drug Abuse Services Research Administrative Report (U.S.G.P.O.) 281–265–1224.
26. KREEK, M. J. 1978. Medical complications in methadone patients. Ann. N.Y. Acad. Sci. **311:**110–134.
27. ROSS, A., M. J. KREEK & E. KHURI. Alcohol abuse in adolescent former heroin addicts in methadone treatment. In preparation.
28. BEVERLEY, C. L., M. J. KREEK, A. O. WELLS & J. L. CURTIS. 1980. Effects of alcohol abuse on progression of liver disease in methadone-maintained patients. *In* Proceedings of the 41st Annual Scientific Meeting of the Committee on Problems of Drug Dependence, Inc. L. S. Harris, Ed. National Institute on Drug Abuse Research Monograph Series: 399–401. Rockville, Md.
29. BEVERLEY, C. L., M. J. KREEK, A. O. WELLS, J. L. CURTIS & J. G. RUCKEL. Effects on progression of liver disease of chronic alcohol abuse in methadone-maintained patients. In preparation.
30. ROTHSCHILD, M. A., M. J. KREEK, M. ORATZ, S. S. SCHREIBER & J. G. MONGELLI. 1976. The stimulation of albumin synthesis by methadone. Gastroenterology **71:**214–220.

31. ROTHSCHILD, M. A., M. ORATZ & S. S. SCHREIBER. 1974. Alcohol, amino acids and albumin synthesis. Gastroenterology **67:**1200–1213.
32. ORATZ, M., M. A. ROTHSCHILD & S. S. SCHREIBER. 1976. Alcohol, amino acids and albumin synthesis. II. Alcohol inhibition of albumin synthesis reversed by arginine and spermine. Gastroenterology **71:**123–127.
33. RUBIN, E. & C. S. LIEBER. 1968. Hepatic microsomal enzymes in man and rat: induction and inhibition by ethanol. Science **162:**690–691.
34. RUBIN, E., H. GANG, P. S. MISRA & C. S. LIEBER. 1970. Inhibition of drug metabolism by acute ethanol intoxication. Amer. J. Med. **49:**801–806.
35. KHANNA, J. M. & H. KALANT. 1970. Effect of inhibitors and inducers of drug metabolism on ethanol metabolism *in vivo*. Biochem. Pharmacol. **19:**2033–2041.
36. RUBIN, E. & C. S. LIEBER. 1971. Alcoholism, alcohol, and drugs. Science **172:** 1097–1102.
37. KHANNA, J. M., H. KALANT & G. LIN. 1972. Significance *in vivo* of the increase in microsomal ethanol-oxidizing system after chronic administration of ethanol, phenobarbital and chlorcyclizine. Biochem. Pharmacol. **21:**2215–2226.
38. KHANNA, J. M., H. KALANT, Y. YEE, S. CHUNG & A. J. SIEMENS. 1976. Effect of chronic ethanol treatment on metabolism of drugs *in vitro* and *in vivo*. Biochem. Pharmacol. **25:**329–335.
39. KALANT, H., J. M. KHANNA, G. Y. LIN & S. CHUNG. 1976. Ethanol–a direct inducer of drug metabolism. Biochem. Pharmacol. **25:**237–342.
40. MEZEY, E. 1979. Ethanol: metabolism and adverse effects. Viewpoints on Digestive Diseases **II(2):**1–4.
41. KREEK, M. J., M. ORATZ & M. ROTHSCHILD. 1978. Hepatic extraction of long- and short-acting narcotics in the isolated perfused rabbit liver. Gastroenterology **75:**88–94.
42. KREEK, M. J., M. A. ROTHSCHILD, M. ORATZ, J. MONGELLI & A. C. HANDLEY. 1979. Effects of ethanol on hepatic distribution and metabolism of narcotics in the isolated perfused rabbit liver. Alcoholism **3:**183. Abstract.
43. WHITEHOUSE, L .W., D. TEMPLETON & C. J. PAUL. 1979. Ethanol inhibition of hepatic uptake of dl-(2-^{14}C)methadone in the rat and its consequence. J. Stud. Alcohol **40:**7–18.
44. KREEK, M. J. 1978. Effects of drugs and alcohol on opiate disposition and actions. *In* Factors Affecting the Action of Narcotics. M. W. Adler, L. Manara and R. Samanin, Eds.: 717–740. Raven Press. New York, N.Y.
45. KREEK, M. J., C. L. GUTJAHR, J. W. GARFIELD, D. V. BOWEN & F. H. FIELD. 1976. Drug interactions with methadone. Ann. N.Y. Acad. Sci. **281:**350–370.
46. KREEK, M. J. 1979. Methadone disposition during the perinatal period in humans. Pharmac. Biochem. Behav. **11**, Suppl.: 7–13.
47. BOROWSKY, S. A. & C. S. LIEBER. 1978. Interaction of methadone and ethanol metabolism. J. Pharmacol. Exp. Ther. **207:**123–129.
48. LIEBER, C. S. & L. M. DECARLI. 1972. The role of the hepatic microsomal ethanol oxidizing system (MEOS) for ethanol metabolism *in vivo*. J. Pharmacol. Exp. Ther. **181:**279–287.
49. THURMAN, R. G., H. G. LEY & R. SCHOLTZ. 1972. Hepatic microsomal ethanol oxidation: hydrogen peroxide formation and the role of catalase. Eur. J. Biochem. **25:**420–430.
50. LIEBER, C. S., L. M. DECARLI, S. MATUZAKI, K. OHNISHI & R. TESCHKE. 1978. The microsomal ethanol oxidizing system (MEOS). Methods Enzymol. **52:** 355–367.
51. FIENMAN, L., E. BARAONA, S. MATSUZAKI, M. KORSTEN & C. S. LIEBER. 1978. Concentration dependence of ethanol metabolism *in vivo* in rats and man. Alcoholism **2:**381–385.
52. WENDELL, G. D. & R. G. THURMAN. 1979. Effect of ethanol concentration on rates of ethanol elimination in normal and alcohol-treated rats *in vivo*. Biochem. Pharmacol. **28:**273–279.

53. Bleyman, M. A. & R. G. Thurman. 1979. Comparison of acute and chronic ethanol administration on rates of ethanol elimination in the rat *in vivo.* Biochem. Pharmacol. **28:**2027–2030.

54. Thurman, R. G., T. Yuki, M. A. Bleyman & G. Wendell. 1979. The adaptive increase in ethanol metabolism due to pretreatment with ethanol: a rapid phenomenon. Drug Alcohol Depend. **4:**119–129.

55. Lieber, C. S. 1979. Moderator's comments. Drug Alcohol Depend. **4:**151–152.

56. Wendell, G. D. & M. J. Kreek. 1979. Effects of chronic methadone treatment on rate of ethanol elimination in the rat *in vivo.* Alcoholism **3:**200. Abstract.

57. Cushman, P., M. J. Kreek & E. Gordis. 1978. Ethanol and methadone in man: a possible drug interaction. Drug Alcohol Depend. **3:**35–42.

58. Casella, G. A., G. A. Deneau & S. J. Mulé. 1978. The effect of ethanol on the metabolism of chronically-administered 1-α-acetylmethadol (LAAM) in the rhesus monkey. Res. Commun. Chem. Pathol. Pharmacol. **21:**351–354.

59. Liebson, I., G. Bigelow & R. Flamer. 1973. Alcoholism among methadone patients: a specific treatment method. Am. J. Psychiatry **130:**599–601.

60. Tong, T. G., N. L. Benowitz & M. J. Kreek. 1980. Methadone-disulfiram interaction during methadone maintenance. J. Clin. Pharmacol. **20:**506–513.

OPIATE ADDICTION AND ALCOHOLISM: THE FEASIBILITY OF COMBINED TREATMENT APPROACHES *

Barry Stimmel, David Korts, Murry Cohen, George Jackson, Victor Sturiano, and Raymond Hanbury

Departments of Medicine, Biostatistics, Community Medicine, and Psychiatry
Mount Sinai School of Medicine of The City University of New York
New York, New York 10029

This discussion will focus on two aspects of the interaction between narcotic addiction and alcoholism: 1) the effectiveness of a single center to treat both alcoholics and narcotic addicts and 2) the importance of study design in trying to develop a therapeutic approach for management of the alcoholic-narcotic addict.

Both of these subjects have generated a great deal of controversy and are particularly relevant. The money allocated for treatment programs on both federal and state levels is declining. There is a real need to consolidate resources to provide the most effective therapy. Epidemiologically, the profile of the heroin addict is also changing. There is a greater prevalence of polydrug use amongst heroin addicts, with alcohol being one of the more prominent drugs of abuse. A brief review of each area is therefore timely.

Combined Treatment of Alcoholics and Narcotic Addicts

The concept of treating alcoholics and narcotic addicts within the same facility is usually met with a great deal of resistance on the part of both clients and staff. The narcotic addict is viewed as being a sociopathic, manipulative, aggressive individual, whereas the alcoholic is considered to be far more passive and, in general, of a different social class with considerably less deviant criminal behavior. Treating both types of individuals within a single clinical setting is generally conceived as being at best ineffective with respect to narcotic addicts and at worst detrimental to the alcoholic, whose passivity is viewed as a cause for his becoming a potential victim of the more aggressive addict.

Unfortunately, although opinions can be easily elicited concerning the ineffectiveness of combined treatment, when one turns to the literature to review the evidence, a marked paucity of data exists. This perhaps led the Division of Special Treatment and Rehabilitation of NIAAA and the Division of Resources Development of NIDA in 1974 to enter into a joint effort to develop demonstration projects which could help provide answers concerning the feasibility of treating alcoholics and polydrug abusers within the same facility. As a result of this effort, projects were approved and funded under the consortium titled The National Drug/Alcohol Collaborative Project (NDACP).

Although the final report of this consortium has not yet appeared, there have been two studies that have been published which provide evidence of the effectiveness of a combined treatment approach. Ottenberg and Rosen, in a

* This paper in part deals with a Demonstration Project funded by the National Institute of Drug Abuse.

review of 1½ years of combined therapy of 484 alcoholics and 201 narcotic addicts found that the initial divisiveness that appeared between these two groups eventually gave way to successful therapeutic efforts.[1] The retention rate of alcoholics in joint treatment was 59%, as compared to 56% in the preceding years when this group was treated separately.

A multicenter study in the Veterans Administration system, carried out by Baker *et al.*[2] compared patient performance six months after the start of therapy in alcoholic clients and in narcotic-dependent clients treated in both conventional and combined treatment settings. Both the conventional and the combined facilities produced sizeable patient improvement. The difference in outcome for alcoholics treated in the conventional setting as compared to those treated in the combined milieu, although statistically better, was quite small and not clinically relevant. Unfortunately, this study was hampered by an inability to randomly assign clients to the different treatment modalities.

The findings of these two studies, suggesting that narcotic-dependent persons and alcoholics can be managed effectively in a single facility, unfortunately has done little to alter the longstanding consensus that therapeutic effectiveness must be synonymous with directing a treatment effort at a homogeneous population. The fallacy of this statement lies in the belief that either alcoholics or narcotic addicts comprise two distinct populations. As emphasized by Diesenhaus,[3] an enormous heterogeneity exists within both groups, emphasizing a need for varied treatment settings and therapeutic modalities.

Classification of clients entering the Colorado Alcohol and Drug Abuse Treatment Facility,[3] one of the participants in the NDACP, revealed a five class typology of substance abusers (TABLE 1). Persons who consumed excessive quantities of alcohol could be found in four of the five types, the exception being the heroin abuser group. Those who abused heroin were found in three of the five typologies. A considerable overlap therefore existed between alcoholics and heroin users, suggesting the ability of combined treatment facilities to be effective in treating narcotic addicts and alcoholics who have basically similar personality structures.

A second study providing a rationale for combined therapy is that of Dudley *et al.*[4] who quantitatively measured psychosocial variables in both heroin addicts and alcoholics. These investigators found that both groups exhibited a high rate of life change. The direction of change was found to vary between groups with alcoholics constantly underperceiving the significance of life change and disease and heroin addicts overperceiving these differences. Theoretically, in a combined treatment approach, those heroin addicts who are manipulative and viewed as antisocial would be counterbalanced by the alcohol group who would be able to supply the necessary peer behavior control. Alcoholic clients might be able to benefit from contact with heroin addicts who could aid in increasing their understanding and perception.

Another factor perpetuating the belief of ineffectiveness of combined treatment is the frequently encountered bias of staff working in such facilities. The importance of views of the staff participating in the treatment process has been emphasized by Cole and Cole,[5] who interviewed staff at 15 different treatment agencies. These investigators noted that the staff with the most positive attitudes were those working in agencies that had started as combined treatment facilities. Staff in agencies that originated as alcohol treatment centers, later adding facilities for combined treatment, were far less likely to have favorable expectations concerning success in working with both populations, as were staff who were found in facilities treating a single group of patients. On the basis of the interviews, these investigators concluded that given a receptive treatment staff, combined treatment probably has the potential and flexibility to provide treatment to both alcohol abusers and narcotic addicts. It was felt that such treatment would probably be equal to or even more efficient with respect to effective utilization of resources than separate treatment.

Unfortunately, traditional treatment agencies, which represent the majority of existing clinical programs, tend to view substance abusers as consisting of three mutually exclusive populations: the alcoholic, the polydrug abuser, and the narcotic addict. Available evidence to date suggests that with the exception of age differences the opposite actually prevails.[1, 3, 4, 6, 7] A great deal of heterogeneity exists within each group, and only by taking advantage of this heterogeneity, with the establishment of programs specifically dealing with existing personality problems, regardless of substance abuse, can the most efficacious form of therapy be provided.

Alcoholism and Methadone Maintenance

Most surveys concerning prevalence and complication of alcoholism in persons on methadone maintenance are retrospective in nature. Although a causal relationship between methadone maintenance and alcoholism has never been demonstrated, it is still commonly believed to exist. Those studies that have been published, in general, report that individuals defined as alcoholic while on maintenance have a poorer retention rate, experience more complications, and are considered to be more psychologically disturbed than their nonalcoholic peers.[8–10] Unfortunately, retrospective, nonblinded studies contain many confounding variables which make interpretations of any conclusions somewhat hazardous. Even with respect to defining the prevalence of alcoholism in methadone maintenance, retrospectively identifying alcoholics on the basis of their visibility in the clinic does not allow for an accurate assessment of either incidence or prevalence of this condition. Since only those alcoholics whose alcoholism becomes visible can be identified, it is more than likely that a considerable number of alcoholics may exist who, in fact, progress satisfactorily through methadone maintenance. By only focusing on the former group, conclusions drawn from such studies will be quite misleading. It is therefore quite important to prospectively categorize entrants into a study with the

TABLE 1

TYPOLOGY OF SUBSTANCE ABUSERS

	Percent of Population Studied
Low Need—Marginal Use and Problem Abuser	38
Heroin Abuser	4
Downer Abuser	25
Downer-Upper Mixer	19
High Need—Multiple Substance Abuser	14

categorization preferably being carried out by individuals who will not be involved in the actual therapy.

The effectiveness of therapy for the alcoholic also cannot be adequately assessed if one preselects only those alcoholics who are having difficulty in adjusting for the therapeutic effort. A number of alcoholics may be functioning well. Another undetermined number who are presently having trouble may, without any intervention, resolve their "visible" problems. It is therefore important to have a control group of clients who, although receiving standard clinic services, are not specifically selected for therapy directed toward their alcoholism. In order to guard against selector bias and a bias inherent in self-selection in the client, such assignment should be randomized. It should be emphasized that since all clients are being provided with counselling, no one is being denied services. The difference is that a service of unproven efficacy can now be compared with the standard services offered in the specific clinic.

Any study dealing with alcoholism in methadone maintenance must be conducted in a scientific manner consistent with prospective, randomized investigations if valid conclusions are to be reached.

As a working model, a program recently funded by the National Institute of Drug Abuse as a demonstration project will be described. In July of 1977, the Mount Sinai School of Medicine initiated a prospective, randomized control study to determine: (1) the prevalence of alcoholism in persons on methadone maintenance; (2) the basic differences between the alcoholic methadone-maintained client and the nonalcoholic client; (3) the effect that alcoholism would have on the therapeutic effort; and (4) the most effective means of managing alcoholism in patients on methadone maintenance.

Participants in this study were recruited from all patients entering the Methadone Maintenance and Aftercare Treatment Program (MMATP) as well as those enrolled at the time. It is anticipated that more than 61% of all possible participants will ultimately enroll in the study with the number of participants exceeding 600. All persons entering the study are classified prospectively within the first several weeks of entry into the study on the basis of multiple sources of input. The criteria used in classifying an individual as alcoholic are based on those suggested by the National Council of Alcoholism (TABLE 2 and TABLE 3).

Treatment staff are blinded in that they are not able to separate participants and nonparticipants or identify the category into which a client is categorized.

Once separation of alcoholic clients has occurred, these individuals are randomly assigned to three treatment groups. One group undergoes the classical abstinence therapy; the second group is exposed to a behavioral modification-controlled drinking approach; and the third group represents a control population. This latter group receives all of the general clinical services as well as individual counselling but does not enter a specific group process directed toward control of their alcoholism. All other participants in the study who have been categorized as being nonalcoholic are treated as controls and therefore consequently receive no specific alcohol related treatment.

As soon as treatment and control groups have been established, task focused orientation groups are formed for those clients randomized into actual treatment groups. This phase of treatment concentrates on the antecedents, consequences, and control of drinking as well as emphasizing the importance of participating in the assigned treatment modality. After this brief orientation session, the specific treatment groups commence.

TABLE 2

MAJOR CRITERIA OF ALCOHOLISM

Withdrawal Symptoms or Blackouts
Daily Consumption of One-Fifth of Whiskey or Equivalent
Presence of Confirmed Alcohol-Associated Illnesses with History of Current Drinking
Repetitive Drinking with Loss of Control over Previous Month
Blood Alcohol Greater Than 150 mg% without Intoxication

It should be emphasized that in spite of the existence of a randomized trial, in the establishment and maintenance of the various treatment groups consistent criteria are observed. Individuals may be excluded from the actual study for many reasons, including: the appearance of overt psychotic behavior, inability to form a relationship with any staff member, the appearance of any serious complications associated with alcoholism necessitating a specific therapeutic intervention, or inability to articulate or benefit from the group setting.

At quarterly intervals all participants in this study, both alcoholic and nonalcoholic, are reviewed to determine if a reclassification is appropriate. A client not originally identified as an overt alcoholic can be considered for reassignment to the "overt" group on the basis of annual health review results, a blood alcohol level of greater than 300mg%, or documentation by a staff member of various symptoms and signs of alcoholism. Progress in treatment and outcome are being followed prospectively, utilizing a wide range of parameters.

Although final data analysis has not been performed, approximately 20% of all persons entering the study can be classified as alcoholic. Preliminary analysis of baseline demographic characteristics, psychological indices or indices of social productivity reveals little difference between the alcoholic and nonalcoholic groups. The prevalence of alcoholism in nonparticipants does not differ from that of participants, suggesting that preselection is not of paramount importance among participants.

Of most interest is that the initial one-year retention rate in methadone maintenance does not reveal any differences with respect to alcoholic and nonalcoholic clients. Over a one-year period, 78% of all alcoholics were retained in maintenance as compared to 82% of nonalcoholics. This finding differs not only from that previously reported in the literature but also from the impression of those therapists participating in the study.

The reasons for these initial findings have been alluded to above. Unawareness of initial categorization of clients into alcoholic or nonalcoholic eliminated therapist bias with respect to evaluation of a client's functioning prior to

TABLE 3

MINOR CRITERIA OF ALCOHOLISM *

Consistent Odor of Alcohol Breath
Blood Alcohol in Morning Specimen
Blood Alcohol Level of Greater Than 300 mg% at Any Time
Presence of Known Major Alcohol-Associated Illnesses

* Any two criteria needed for diagnosis.

entering methadone maintenance. A number of persons who were indeed alcoholic but able to function satisfactorily were targeted in this study through the prospective categorization process who otherwise might have been included in the nonalcoholic pool. These clients, who denied the existence of any alcohol problem, in fact represented almost 50% of the alcohol group.

Similar retention rates reported for alcoholics and nonalcoholics in this study as compared to lower retention of alcoholics reported in most programs is not surprising when one considers the "philosophical" environment surrounding methadone maintenance. A frequently expressed opinion of treatment staff is that an alcoholic on methadone maintenance should be detoxified from methadone since it is less harmful to be on illicit heroin than drink while on methadone. Although existing evidence suggests that illicit heroin causes a much greater risk than drinking and that individuals who inject heroin still continue to drink, this belief leads to a self-fulfilling prophecy concerning retention of alcoholics in methadone maintenance. The lack of adequate follow-up subsequent to detoxification in most programs does not permit any further information to be generated concerning outcome of alcoholics and mistaken beliefs are perpetuated.

Conclusions

In summary, in order to adequately assess the feasibility of a combined treatment approach in alcoholism and in narcotic dependency, as well as to address the most efficacious manner of treating alcoholism in the narcotic-dependent person, the subject must be pursued in a scientific and scholarly manner. Existing evidence suggests that individuals who are alcoholic and those who use narcotics comprise an extremely heterogeneous population. If one is aware of the similarities as well as the differences, a treatment plan may be able to be formulated that concentrates on the person rather than the disease.

If these therapies are accompanied by an adequate evaluation process utilizing well-established scientific design, considerable advances in knowledge may be able to be obtained concerning the treatment of alcohol and narcotic dependency. Until such randomized, prospective, controlled studies are supported, evidence of the relative superiority of either combined or separate treatment for alcoholism and narcotic dependency remains subjective and, consistent with the process of scientific inquiry, must be viewed as such.

References

1. Ottenberg, D. J. & A. Rosen. 1971. Merging the treatment of drug addicts into an existing program for alcoholism. Q. J. Stud. Alcohol **32:**94–103.
2. Baker, S. L., T. Lorei, H. A. McKnight & J. L. Duvall. 1977. The Veterans Administration's comparison study: alcoholism and drug abuse—combined and conventional treatment settings. Alcoholism: Clin. Exp. Res. **1:**285–291.
3. Diesenhaus, H. 1979. Combined treatment—where are we at? The U.S. Journal August:7.
4. Dudley, D. L., D. K. Roszell, J. E. Mules & W. H. Hague. 1974. Heroin vs. alcohol addiction—quantifiable psychosocial similarities and differences. J. Psychosom. Res. **18:**327–335.

5. Cole, S. G. & E. A. Cole. 1979. Alcohol and drug abuse treatment: perceived effectiveness of inpatient combined treatment programs. Am. J. Drug Alc. Abuse **6:**109–123.

6. Kissen, B. 1973. Which addicts and alcoholics should be treated together and which separately? Proc. 6th Annu. Eagleville Conf.: 44–49.

7. Ciotola, P. V. & J. F. Peterson. 1976. Personality characteristics of alcoholics and drug addicts in a combined treatment program. J. Stud. Alcohol **37:** 1229–1235.

8. Bihari, B. 1974. Alcoholism and methadone maintenance. Am. J. Drug Alc. Abuse **1:**79–89.

9. Maddux, J. F. & B. Elliott. 1975. Problem drinkers on methadone. Am. J. Drug Alc. Abuse **2:**245–254.

10. Shut, J., K. File & T. Wohlmuth. 1973. Alcohol use by narcotic addicts in methadone maintenance treatment. Q. J. Stud. Alcohol **34:**1356–1359.

GENERAL DISCUSSION

Enoch Gordis, *Session Chair*

Mount Sinai Medical Center
New York, New York 10029

CHAIRMAN ENOCH GORDIS: Interactions of opiates and ethanol are important because alcoholism is probably the leading cause of failure in drug treatment programs. It's important to point out that we do not know whether alcoholism is more common among people in methadone programs than it is in the matched population of non-narcotic users in the same area.

There are two interesting clinical observations that merit research attention. One, alcohol and the opiates do not seem to relieve each other's withdrawal symptoms. Thus in treating the withdrawal from one, you have to use drugs specific for that addiction.

Second, there seems to be something intractable about alcoholism in people who have a history of heroin use. At least in conventional alcoholism programs, the usual management of alcoholism in people who formerly used heroin leads to results that are much worse than in the alcoholic population who have not used heroin. We need to learn how to handle mixed alcohol and opioid abuse. So, here we have some evidence of some relation between the two addictions and some evidence of their independence. Heroin users who drink are in double jeopardy for severe hepatic consequences of the addiction. That is still another reason why this topic is of such great importance.

Not included in this session is the suggestion that the isoquinoline-opiate-like compounds may be involved in alcoholism one way or another. Also, there are some old experiments in animals which suggest that perhaps liver damage itself may increase the appetite for alcohol.

CATHERINE TRESE (*North Charles Foundation of the Cambridge Hospital, Cambridge, Mass.*): Dr. Stimmel, what is your operational definition for alcoholism?

BARRY STIMMEL: We basically used the NCA criteria. A person had to have one of the major criteria, which are the presence of withdrawal symptoms or blackouts, daily consumption of a fifth of whiskey or its equivalent or more, confirmed presence of an alcohol-associated illness with history of current drinking, repetitive drinking with loss of control during the previous month, blood-alcohol level greater than 150 mg.% without intoxication, etc. The patient had to have two minor criteria; for example, consistent odor of alcohol on the breath, blood alcohol in a morning specimen, blood-alcohol level greater than 300 mg.% at any time, and the presence of a known alcohol-associated illness.

TOVE ROSEN (*New York State Psychiatric Institute and Columbia University*): I would like to draw your attention to the different roles of central nervous system tissue. The nervous tissue does not react pathologically or pharmacologically as a homogeneous tissue, unlike many other body tissues. Its different anatomical regions react differently, a fact which may bear on both behavior and treatment. Finally, I would also like to mention that there is a different vulnerability between the prenatal nervous system, the immediate postnatal, juvenile, adult, and senile nervous systems.

SHELDON ZIMBERG: I wonder why Antabuse® was not considered as a treatment modality. One study used Antabuse as a contingency for the continued use of methadone with some interesting results.

I wonder what problems you had in the use of Antabuse that made you discontinue it, because it's a widely used, standard drug in the treatment of alcoholics.

BARRY STIMMEL: We started using Antabuse, really, in 1970. We never made it contingent on taking methadone because of certain ethical issues.

Many in our socioeconomic group of patients had organic syndromes or neurologic disturbances. We found that our people kept on taking it and drank alcohol, nevertheless. They kept building up high levels of acetaldehyde despite vomiting or other alcohol-Antabuse reactions. Dr. Stanley Gitlow, who also has a lot of experience with Antabuse, reported that most people he treats with Antabuse never drink because they are afraid of producing the alcohol-Antabuse reaction. However, in the socioeconomic group of our clinic populations, many challenged Antabuse with alcohol consistently. For some of them the drive for alcohol was so great they kept on drinking, nevertheless.

SHELDON ZIMBERG: Well, I'm not sure that it is solely a socioeconomic problem. We deal with a similar population at the Hospital for Joint Diseases in Harlem and do not find problems with the methadone-treated alcoholics taking Antabuse. I wonder whether it was their psychopathology or whether it was the staff's feeling about Antabuse. Coercive models, some using Antabuse as a requirement, are widely used in the treatment of alcoholics in industry. You get into treatment or you lose your job. Methadone patients could also be coerced if they realized that they could not get their methadone unless they got their Antabuse. I'm sorry that you didn't try this approach.

BARRY STIMMEL: We felt the coercive use of Antabuse would have a high dropout rate. Our staff wanted to use it, and would still like to use it, but we can't get too many patients to take it.

CHARLES RIORDAN (*Yale University*): As I recall from your former studies, your average of intake is about age 25, is it not?

BARRY STIMMEL: Yes, it's older now.

CHARLES RIORDAN: It's still important to emphasize that 20% of people at that age defined as alcoholics by your criteria represent a very serious problem.

TOM MCCLELLAN (*Philadelphia*): Dr. Stimmel, I was impressed by the stringent criteria that you used in defining the alcoholic. I don't quite understand how these patients would not be recognizable to the entire staff as alcoholics.

BARRY STIMMEL: That's not too difficult to understand. The initial categorization was made when people were coming into the program. It was a while before the staff knew the patients well. There is no way the staff would really know that the person had a history of drinking with withdrawal symptoms or blackouts.

TOM MCCLELLAN: Oh, so it wouldn't necessarily have to be current alcoholism?

BARRY STIMMEL: Oh, it would be current. There would be a history of drinking within the last three months, a history of withdrawal symptoms or blackouts. Unless a staff member specifically elicited that information, he or she would not necessarily know at the outset of treatment. Although physicians would know of alcohol-associated illness, the staff members would not likely know because they did not elicit that as part of their history.

PAUL CUSHMAN, JR. (*Milwaukee*): Dr. Kreek, I'm puzzled about possible species differences and the difficulty in extrapolating from the rodent data to man. The rabbit had no change in the tissue distribution of methadone in the ethanol-treated animal versus controls. That seems to be consistent with the studies in man, where methadone plasma levels were the same after a modest amount of alcohol compared with the same person when not fed alcohol. Now, does the rabbit handle methadone the same way as man does or does the rabbit handle methadone the same way as the rat does?

MARY JEANNE KREEK: In humans, you and Dr. Gordis and I jointly showed that single large social doses of alcohol did not affect the plasma levels of methadone. Because of many questions about these findings, we decided to go back into our most basic animal model, the isolated rabbit preparation, where, as in man, we did not find any acute alcohol effects. Now, neither the rabbit nor the rat metabolizes methadone identically with man. However, the routes of metabolism are quite similar in that both proceed primarily by successive *N*-demethylation. The rodents hydroxylate the *N*-demethylative products; man does not to any extent. The important bottom line is that in rodents and in man all metabolites (with one exception—a very, very minor metabolite) are pharmacologically inactive. The parent compound, methadone, is itself the only active component. I think that's a critical issue as far as drawing this analogy. I would like to stress that pharmacokinetic differences in rodents, cats and dogs, and even primate models can be very different from man. Therefore, if one is dosing once or twice a day with methadone in a rodent model, one cannot expect the same sustained steady state as we have in a human receiving methadone or another long-acting narcotic given once daily by the oral route. We have reason to believe that methadone in the rabbit is stored in the liver and released unchanged; this sharply contrasts with the short-acting narcotics like morphine or heroin, which are taken up, metabolized, and released or excreted. Possibly, the liver in man may also serve as a storage bin for an unchanged compound, which allows steady-state treatment.

Part III. Neurobiological Correlates of Behavior

DRUGS OF ABUSE AND THE ENDOGENOUS REINFORCEMENT SYSTEM: THE RESISTANCE OF INTRACRANIAL SELF-STIMULATION BEHAVIOR TO THE INEBRIATING EFFECTS OF ETHANOL

Aryeh Routtenberg

Departments of Psychology and Biological Sciences
Cresap Neuroscience Laboratory
Northwestern University
Evanston, Illinois 60201

The central theme of this review is that drugs of abuse by depressing or inhibiting a variety of neural mechanisms, while leaving the endogenous reinforcement system (ERS) still functional, permit thereby the ascendency of this specific brain mechanism in mediating addiction. If the ERS is crucial to the survival of the organism there may, indeed, be significant reasons why it is resistant to, for example, the depressing influence of ethanol.

The ERS is anatomically specifiable. It is formed by those pathways which both support intracranial self-stimulation (ICSS) and participate in the memory formation process.[1]

The ERS can be detected using a simple test. Animals with electrodes implanted into specific brain locations will press a pedal in a Skinner box to activate the brain tissue at the tip of the electrode. This intracranial self-stimulation demonstration was first made by Olds and Milner [2] in 1954 with electrode placements in the septal area. It was subsequently shown by Olds and Olds [3] that the highest rates of pedal pressing for the lowest current levels were found with electrodes in the posterolateral hypothalamus, where ascending and descending fiber pathways, including the medial forebrain bundle, are located. I shall return to a brief discussion of these pathways shortly.

Of special interest to the view that the ERS can exert powerful control over behavior is our demonstration [4] that animals will forego food essential to their survival in order to obtain rewarding hypothalamic stimulation. If such self-destructive behavior can be mediated by activation of the ERS, is it possible that the abuse of drugs and the self-destructive sequelae of addiction are also mediated by the activity of the ERS? The data to be reviewed do not discourage this hypothesis.

Early ICSS Mapping Studies

The evidence which I will now review strongly recommends the view that dopamine-containing fiber systems originating in the ventral midbrain, coursing through the diencephalic sites in postero-lateral hypothalamus and terminating in particular cortical (e.g., frontal, entorhinal) and subcortical (e.g., neostriatum, nucleus accumbens) telencephalic sites, are key pathways in the ERS.

Although we had not appreciated it at the time, our mapping studies aimed at determining sites of self-stimulation within the rat cerebrum demonstrated certain interesting parallel locations with subsequently described catecholamine systems.[5] We had quite innocently set out to provide an overview of sites within brain that most consistently supported ICSS. Our early work on the midbrain, pons and medulla [6] demonstrated that the highest rates of self-stimulation were found in the ventral tegmental area, both in Tsai's area and in the substantia nigra. Subsequent mapping with finer electrodes [7] demonstrated that self-stimulation from the substantia nigra was in the compact zone. Thus, in our study of over 100 points within the brainstem the highest ICSS rates were found in the ventral tegmental area.

These brain locations have been shown to contain dopaminergic cell bodies.[5] The axons of these cell bodies ascend in the lateral portions of the medial forebrain bundle to, for example, prefrontal cortex. It is likely that lateral hypothalamic, or medial forebrain bundle ICSS, which Olds [8] viewed as the focus of the ERS, is, in fact, activating the ascending dopaminergic axons. It is likely that axons other than these dopaminergic ones are activated: for example, descending nondopaminergic ones from frontal cortex.

In another mapping experiment, we studied the points within frontal cortex which supported ICSS. We found that the major sites of self-stimulation were in the medial prefrontal and sulcal prefrontal cortex.[9, 10] These studies were carried out prior to the work of Tassin *et al.*,[11] who demonstrated that the sites in frontal cortex where we observed the most intense self-stimulation were, in fact, the sites where the highest concentrations of dopamine were discerned. It has also been shown with retrograde tracing methods [12] that cell bodies within the ventral tegmentum project forward to the sulcal prefrontal cortex, as well as the medial prefrontal cortex.

In sum, self-stimulation has been demonstrated at various locations along this dopaminergic neural element: the cell body, the axon and the terminals (for detailed reviews of the role in the frontal cortex in self-stimulation, see Routtenberg and Santos-Anderson,[13] Mora [14] and Routtenberg [15]).

Lesion Studies

While the evidence indicating a role for the dopamine systems in ICSS is highly suggestive,[16] it is necessary to demonstrate that destruction of this system degrades ICSS in order to *prove* the involvement of dopamine in ICSS.

A particularly clear example of the role of this approach demonstrating the role of dopamine in self-stimulation is the work of Clavier and Gerfen.[17] With horseradish peroxidase (HRP) tracing techniques, they have demonstrated that the location of the particular cells that project to the sulcal prefrontal cortex is slightly anterior to the ventral tegmental area of Tsai at the mesodiencephalic junction. They have further shown that 6-hydroxydopamine (6-OHDA) injections into this cell body region significantly reduces self-stimulation in the sulcal prefrontal cortex. Thus, by knowing precisely the cell bodies of origin of the dopaminergic innervation of the sulcal prefrontal cortex and by selective neurotoxic destruction of these cell bodies, there is now excellent evidence for the crucial participation of this dopaminergic link in the ICSS behavior mediated by frontal cortex.

Other Dopamine Systems

There is evidence reviewed elsewhere [18] of the role of other dopaminergic systems in ICSS, in particular, the nigroneostriatal system and the entorhinal cortex. Rather than detail the evidence with respect to these systems, it would be better to emphasize the fact that there exist several different dopaminergic pathways in brain which can be related to ICSS. Indeed, even though it is likely that noncatecholamine systems also participate in the ICSS effect, the evidence to date most strongly implicates these dopamine systems as forming a key link in the endogenous reinforcement system.

The Effects of Alcohol on the Endogenous Reinforcement Substrate

Although there has not yet emerged a clear picture of the influence of ethanol on ICSS, certain main points concerning its influence can be described. St. Laurent and Olds [19, 20] described the effect of ethanol on self-stimulation and found that it had different effects, depending on the location of stimulation. It appeared that ICSS in the subcortical telencephalic sites, such as the septal area, could be increased while ICSS in hypothalamus could be decreased by ethanol. These results were by no means universal. Indeed, the most apparent conclusion, on the basis of their presented data, is that ICSS remains surprisingly unaffected by ethanol administration. St. Laurent and Olds [19] note that "Alcohol . . . had practically no effect when electrodes were implanted in posterior, focal areas of the self-stimulation system, and this was true even when doses were raised to the point where an almost comatose state was produced." (p. 97)

We have confirmed this observation in the following manner (Routtenberg and Miller, unpublished observations). Male albino rats were implanted with electrodes either in the posterolateral hypothalamus or the dentate gyrus of the hippocampus. Self-stimulation in saline-injected rats was 700–900 in 15 min for the former placements and 25–100 in 15 min for the latter (10–20 μA, 60 Hz. sine wave current). A dose of 2.1 gm/kg ethanol produced a near comatose state in our animals 5 min after the intraperitoneal injection of a 25% ethanol solution. These animals would lie prostrate, not moving, both in their home cage or in the Skinner box where self-stimulation behavior had previously been tested.

While these animals did not *initiate* brain stimulation administration, if the experimenter applied a few 0.5 sec trains of stimulation the animal would crawl to the pedal and commence pressing at rates not dissimilar from the undrugged state. This was true for both hypothalamic and hippocampal placements. When the stimulation was turned off, the animals retreated to their stupor. Thus, it would be more accurate to state that the lack of effect of ethanol can be demonstrated *after* experimenter-applied stimulation is given. Precisely what mechanism gives rise to this reversal of stupor is not known, but the parallel (suggested by Dr. E. Gordis) with pressure effects on lipid membranes and reversal of anesthesia is intriguing.[21]

It would appear, therefore, that despite the obvious debilitating effects of ethanol, the neural mechanisms which support intracranial self-stimulation are still capable of maintaining this behavior.

I would like to argue from these results, then, that the ERS is not significantly depressed by ethanol. Moreover, given the concomitant widespread depression of other neural systems, the ERS is capable of exerting a powerful control over behavior. Thus, I would predict that under the influence of ethanol, animals would still forego food essential to their survival in order to obtain brain stimulation reward. Interestingly, chlorpromazine, at dosages (1–2 mg/kg) with little motoric or obvious behavioral effects, will eliminate this nonadaptive self-destructive behavior.[22]

In sum, our results and those of St. Laurent and Olds[19, 20] support the view that alcohol is remarkable in its *inability* to depress ICSS in the medial forebrain bundle. We have also found that self-stimulation in the hippocampal formation appears to be unaffected by similar doses of ethanol. St. Laurent and Olds[19, 20] suggested that telencephalic self-stimulation may be influenced by ethanol while hypothalamic self-stimulation may not. This intriguing view will require a careful dose-response and current threshold ICSS study at different anatomical locations.

With respect to the *resistance* of the endogenous reinforcement system to the depressant effects of alcohol, one might be especially interested to know what properties the ERS has, so that it can resist the powerful pharmacological actions of ethanol. From an evolutionary perspective it might be that because the reward system is crucial for the maintenance of moment-to-moment behavior, protection of the ERS from external agents has certain survival properties. In some fashion the lack of effect of alcohol may illustrate this capacity of the ERS to tolerate wide excursions from the norm.

Dopamine and Alcohol

There is evidence that ethanol may, in fact, facilitate the action of dopamine. Such evidence supports the notion that ethanol does not dampen the influence on the endogenous reward system (ERS). Indeed, it may be the case that under certain conditions the influence of ethanol is to make the endogenous reward system more responsive to emotionally-laden (social, aggressive, sexual, hunger) stimuli.

With respect to the effects of ethanol on dopamine, the review by Tabakoff *et al.*[23] should be consulted. Acute administration of ethanol has been shown to lead to an increased release of dopamine[24] as well as causing increase in synthesis.[25] It has been shown that release is increased by ethanol using neostriatal synaptosomes[26, 27] and that following dopamine withdrawal there is a decrease in dopamine-stimulated adenylate cyclase using a subcortical forebrain tissue. Wajda *et al.*[28] have shown that acute administration of alcohol at 4 gms/Kg, which produces a loss of the righting reflex, caused a significant increase in dopamine levels. No influence of ethanol on tyrosine hydroxylase or choline acetyl transferase activities was noted. It is apparent that ethanol has facilitatory effects on dopamine at a time when self-stimulation behavior is unaffected and motoric capacity is significantly altered.

Brain Self-Stimulation and Memory

Several lines of evidence have indicated that the brain pathways of reward play a key role in memory consolidation processes (e.g., Routtenberg[38]). Briefly, brain areas that support self-stimulation when stimulated during or after learning, have specific effects on the animal's capacity to recall the task (see Clavier and Routtenberg[18]). Thus, there exists the cross-association between ICSS sites and the memory consolidation system. It is, therefore, reasonable to refer to these pathways as part of the ERS.

If alcohol has little effect on brain stimulation, one might expect it to have little effect on memory. Although there is considerable evidence that ethanol does influence memory (e.g., Miller *et al.*[29]; Gerrein and Chechile[30]), these losses may be related to state-dependent effects, rather than a specific loss of memory.[31]

Particularly impressive is the study of Prado de Carvello *et al.*,[32] who showed that high doses of ethanol (3 gms/Kg) had no effect on retention in either active or passive avoidance conditioning. Thus, ethanol is ineffective both in altering the memory formation mechanism and in depressing ICSS. Losses of memory in ethanol abuse may be related to the long-term deteriorating influence of ethanol.[33]

It may be the case, then, that the special property of the ERS which resists the effect of ethanol may be precisely the memory function, for without memory the animal cannot survive.

Potential Avenues for Future Research and Some Speculations

An intriguing report by Lorens and Sainati[34] has suggested the possibility that self-stimulation is potentiated by alcohol and that this effect may be mediated by the opioid system. Although this finding is not firmly established (Lorens, personal communication; Bloom, personal communication), it is to be emphasized that there is an important lack of effect of ethanol on ICSS coordinated with a major loss of motoric capacity.

Given the suggested intact functioning of the ERS in the presence of ethanol, is it possible that the brain mechanisms which mediate abuse, are, in fact, the neural substrate of the ERS? Thus, for example, tolerance to morphine can be reversed by disruptive electrical stimulation of the frontal cortex.[35] This suggests the possibility that memory-like components of the drug abuse syndrome[36] may be mediated by the ERS. The long-term alterations in certain dopamine systems[37] following chronic ethanol administration encourage the further exploration of the ERS-dopamine-ethanol association both with regard to intracranial self-stimulation reward and the memory formation of drug tolerance and abuse.

References

1. Routtenberg, A. 1978. The reward system of the brain. Scientific American **26:**122–131.
2. Olds, J. & P. Milner. 1954. Positive reinforcement produced by electrical stimulation of septal area and other regions of rat brain. J. Comp. Physiol. Psychol. **47:**419–427.
3. Olds, M. E. & J. Olds. 1963. Approach-avoidance analysis of rat diencephalon. J. Comp. Neurol. **120:**259–295.
4. Routtenberg, A. & J. Lindy. 1965. Effects of the availability of rewarding septal and hypothalamic stimulation on bar-pressing for food under conditions of deprivation. J. Comp. Physiol. Psychol. **60:**158–161.
5. Routtenberg, A. 1975. Intracranial self-stimulation: Catecholamine brain pathways and memory consolidation. *In* Nebraska Symposium on Motivation. J. K. Cole and T. B. Sonderegger, Eds.:161–182. University of Nebraska Press. Lincoln, Neb.

6. ROUTTENBERG, A. & C. MALSBURY. 1969. Brainstem pathways of reward. J. Comp. Physiol. Psychol. **68:**22–30.
7. HUANG, Y. H. & A. ROUTTENBERG. 1971. Lateral hypothalamic self-stimulation pathways in *Rattus norvegicus*. Physiol. Behav. **6:**589–596.
8. OLDS, J. 1962. Hypothalamic substrates of reward. Physiol. Rev. **42:**544–604.
9. ROUTTENBERG. A. 1971. Forebrain pathways of reward in *Rattus norvegicus*. J. Comp. Physiol. Psychol. **75:**269–276.
10. ROUTTENBERG, A. & M. SLOAN. 1972. Self-stimulation in the frontal cortex of *Rattus norvegicus*. Behav. Biol. **7:**567–572.
11. TASSIN, J. P., J. BOCKAERT, G. BLANC, L. STINUS, A. M. THIERRY, S. LAVIELLE, J. PRÉMONT & J. GLOWINSKI. 1978. Topographical distribution of dopaminergic innervation and dopaminergic receptors of the anterior cerebral cortex of the rat. Brain Res. **154:**241–252.
12. DIVAC, I., A. KOSMAL, A. BJÖRKLUND & O. LINDVALL. 1978. Subcortical projections to the prefrontal cortex in the rat as revealed by the horseradish peroxidase technique. Neuroscience. **3:**785–796.
13. ROUTTENBERG, A. & R. SANTOS-ANDERSON. 1977. The central role of prefrontal cortex in intracranial self-stimulation: A case history of anatomical localization of motivational substrates. *In* Handbook of Psychopharmacology. L. L. Iversen, S. D. Iversen & S. H. Snyder, Eds.:**8:**1–21. Drugs, Neurotransmitters and Behavior. Plenum Press. New York, N.Y.
14. MORA, F. 1977. The neurochemical substrates of prefrontal cortex self-stimulation: A review and an interpretation of some recent data. Life Sci. **22:**919–930.
15. ROUTTENBERG, A. 1979. Anatomical localization of phosphoprotein and glycoprotein substrates of memory. Prog. Neurobiol. **12:**85–113.
16. WISE, R. A. 1978. Catecholamine theories of reward: A critical review. Brain Res. **152:**215–248.
17. CLAVIER, R. M. & C. R. GERFEN. 1979. Neural inputs to the self-stimulation region in the sulcal prefrontal cortex of the rat: Horseradish peroxidase study. Brain Res. Bull. **4:**347–353.
18. CLAVIER, R. M. & A. ROUTTENBERG. 1980. In search of reinforcement pathways: A neuroanatomical odyssey. *In* Biology of Reinforcement: Facets of Brain Stimulation Reward. A. Routtenberg, Ed.: 81–105. Academic Press. New York, N.Y.
19. ST. LAURENT, J. & J. OLDS. 1967. Alcohol and brain centers of positive reinforcement. *In* Alcoholism—Behavioral Research, Therapeutic Approaches. Ruth Fox, Ed.: 80–101. Springer Publishing Company. New York, N.Y.
20. ST. LAURENT, J. 1972. Brain centers of reinforcement and the effects of alcohol. *In* Biology of Alcoholism. B. Kissin & H. Begleiter, Eds.: **2:**85–106. Plenum Press. New York, N.Y.
21. TRUDELL, J. R., W. L. HUBBELL, E. N. COHEN & J. J. KENDIG. 1973. The extent of small-molecule exclusion from spin-labeled phospholipid model membranes. Anesthesiology **38:**207–211.
22. ROUTTENBERG, A. & G. C. BULLOCH. 1971. Self-starvation and rewarding brain stimulation: Effects of chlorpromazine and pentobarbitol. Learn. Motiv. **2:** 83–94.
23. TABAKOFF, B., C. MELCHIOR, S. URWYLER & P. L. HOFFMAN. 1979. Alterations in neurotransmitter function during the development of ethanol tolerance and dependence. Second Magnus Huss Symposium. Stockholm, Sweden.
24. CARLSSON, A., T. MAGNUSSON & T. H. SVENSSON. 1973. Effect of ethanol on the metabolism of brain catecholamines. Psychopharm. **30:**27–36.
25. CARLSSON, A. & M. LINDQUIST. 1973. Effect of ethanol on the hydroxylation of tyrosine and tryptophan in rat brain *in vivo*. J. Pharm. Pharmacol. **45:**457–470.
26. SEEMAN, P. & T. LEE. 1974. The dopamine-relasing actions of neuroleptics and ethanol. J. Pharmacol. Exper. Therap. **190:**131–140.

27. HOFFMAN, P. L. & B. TABAKOFF. 1977. Alterations in dopamine receptor sensitivity by chronic ethanol treatment. Nature. **268:**551–553.
28. WAJDA, I. J., I. MANIGAULT & J. P. HUDICK. 1977. Dopamine levels in the striatum and the effect of alcohol and reserpine. Biochem. Pharmacol. **26:** 653–655.
29. MILLER, M. E., V. J. ADESSO, J. P. FLEMING, A. GINO & R. LAUERMAN. 1978. Effects of alcohol on the storage and retrieval processes of heavy social drinkers. J. Exp. Psychol. (Human Learn.). **4:**246–255.
30. GEREIN, J. R. & R. A. CHECHILE. 1977. Storage and retrieval processes of alcohol-induced amnesia. J. Abnorm. Psychol. **86:**285–294.
31. PETERSEN, R. C. 1977. Retrieval failures in alcohol state-dependent learning. Psychopharmacol. **55:**141–146.
32. PRADO, C. DE, D. A. VENDITE & I. IZQUIERDO. 1978. A near-lethal dose of ethanol, given intraperitoneally, does not affect memory consolidation of two different avoidance tasks. Psychopharmacol. (Berlin) **59:**71–74.
33. RILEY, J. N. & D. W. WALKER. 1978. Morphological alterations in hippocampus after long-term alcohol consumption in mice. Science **201:**646–648.
34. LORENS, S. A. & S. M. SAINATI. 1978. Naloxone blocks the excitatory effect of ethanol and chlordiazepoxide on lateral hypothalamic self-stimulation behavior. Life Sci. **25:**1359–1364.
35. KESNER, R. P., D. J. PRIANO & J. R. DEWITT. 1976. Time-dependent disruption of morphine tolerance by electroconvulsive shock and frontal cortical stimulation. Science **194:**1079–1081.
36. TABAKOFF, B. & R. F. RITZMANN. 1977. The effects of 6-hydroxy-dopamine on tolerance to and dependence on ethanol. J. Pharm. Exper. Therap. **203:**319–331.
37. TABAKOFF, B. & P. L. HOFFMAN. 1979. Development of functional dependence on ethanol in dopaminergic systems. J. Pharm. Exper. Therap. **208:**216–222.
38. ROUTTENBERG, A. 1979. The participation of brain stimulation reward substrates in memory: Anatomical and biochemical evidence. Fed. Proc. **38:**2446–2453.

OPIATES, OPIOID PEPTIDES AND PSYCHIATRY

Glenn C. Davis

Psychiatric Clinical Research Unit
University of Tennessee Center for the Health Sciences
Memphis, Tennessee 38163

Monte S. Buchsbaum and William E. Bunney, Jr.

Biological Psychiatry Branch
National Institute of Mental Health
Bethesda, Maryland 20205

Introduction

In this decade there has been an explosion of basic information in the neurosciences. The discovery of the opiate receptor [1–3] followed by discovery of endogenous ligands for this receptor [4, 5] spearheaded a revolution in peptide neurochemistry. As with most exciting discoveries, there have been early attempts to relate disease states to alterations in the synthesis, metabolism or action of these new opioid peptides. In fact these attempts have preceded an undersanding of the normal functions of the opioid peptides. In this paper we will augment existing reviews [6–8] in hopes of characterizing the boundaries of the research in opiate and opioid pharmacology in psychiatric patients.

Clinical interest in endorphins has been generated for a number of reasons. Psychotomimetic reactions to many opiates have been reversed by the narcotic antagonist naloxone. Cyclazocine, a mixed agonist-antagonist, has been reported to have antidepressant efficacy. A recent intriguing report [9] found an antihallucinatory effect of naloxone; this has stimulated a number of pilot studies. In fact, the broad behavioral actions of opiates on mood, cognition, endocrine function, and pain sensitivity made the discovery of endogenous opiate-like compounds particularly intriguing—could there be an excess or deficiency of these compounds in schizophrenia, depression or mania.

Experimental evidence that opiate-like peptides (endorphins) play a role in symptoms of some psychiatric illnesses comes from several sources: direct pharmacological testing of narcotic antagonists and endorphins in psychiatrically ill populations, measurement of endorphin levels in human cerebrospinal fluid (CSF) and plasma and studies of endorphin mediation of physiological functions, such as endorphin influences on pain regulation, pituitary function and temperature regulation.

Schizophrenia

Narcotic Antagonists

The simplest endorphin hypothesis of schizophrenia suggests that some symptoms in this illness directly result from an excess of these opiate-like peptides and thus implies that opiate (and hence endorphin) antagonists could be used as a test of the hypothesis and also provide effective treatment. Gunne *et al.*,[9] in an open study, were the first to suggest that naloxone might be useful in schizophrenia. These authors reported that 0.4 mg of naloxone administered intravenously reversed or attenuated auditory hallucinations for from 5 to 90 minutes in four schizophrenics. Subsequently, Emrich and coworkers [10] gave either 1.2 or 4 mg of naloxone intravenously to 20 patients and found that delusional symptoms and hallucinations decreased at 2, 4, and 6 hours after injection. Thus, Emrich *et al.*[10] replicated the findings of Gunne and associates in a double-blind, placebo-controlled study using a higher dose of naloxone, although they observed the therapeutic effects at different time points. Watson *et al.*[11] gave 10 mg of naloxone to 11 schizophrenics (screened from 1000 patients for frequent auditory hallucinations) and reported significant attenuation of hallucinations for 24 to 48 hours. We reported [12] that one target symptom (unusual thought content) improved after naloxone administration in 14 schizophrenic patients when compared with placebo, but we failed to demonstrate improvement in hallucinations or global psychoses ratings. Lehmann *et al.*[13] reported that five patients studied in a double blind and placebo controlled study improved in total BPRS rated psychopathology, as well as thought disturbance and hallucinatory behavior six hours after injection of 10 mg of naloxone. Thus, a number of published studies have reported at least some symptomatic improvement although a variety of doses were used and different time courses for improvement found.

On the other hand, a number of studies [14–21] have failed to demonstrate clinical improvement in the symptoms of schizophrenia either acutely after naloxone, or during chronic treatment with naltrexone.

Interestingly, Lipinski *et al.*[21] reported significant improvement on the continuous performance task after naloxone. The continuous performance task is a measure of vigilance and attention that has been suggested to be a core psychophysiological abnormality in schizophrenia (for a possible relationship between the attention dysfunction of schizophrenia and opioid peptides see Davis *et al.*[22]).

We have suggested that there is a therapeutic interaction of narcotic antagonists with neuroleptics. In support of this suggestion, note that the patients of Gunne *et al.*[9] were treated with various neuroleptics at the time of naloxone testing, as were half of the patients of Watson *et al.*[11] When our two study populations are combined (total $N = 24$), thought disorder improved in the group of patients stabilized on neuroleptics ($p < .05$ paired t-test) and not among medication-free patients. Thus, if there is a therapeutic effect of narcotic antagonists, it may be secondary to an interaction with neuroleptics.

It should be noted that a series of small sample size studies, each failing to reach statistical significance, increase the danger of prematurely rejecting the hypothesis that endorphins are implicated in the symptoms of psychiatric disorders. Such a premature rejection is further exacerbated by the likelihood that multiplicity of biological factors may be responsible for the group of schizophrenias.

Beta-Endorphin

In a preliminary uncontrolled study, Kline *et al.*[23] reports improvement in symptoms of schizophrenia after the administration of beta-endorphin. The symptom improvement was found two weeks after a single beta-endorphin injection. Acutely, these patients seemed to be a little worsened by beta-endorphin injection. Several other research groups have administered beta-endorphin to schizophrenics; however, to our knowledge, no reports have yet appeared in the literature.

Des-Tyrosine-Gamma-Endorphin

Verhoeven *et al.*[24] report transient improvement in both an open and a double-blind crossover study of the compound des-tyrosine-gamma-endorphin (DTγE). In their double-blind study, slight but significant improvement occurred with the first day of treatment as well as major improvements with subsequent treatments; by day four psychotic symptoms had almost disappeared. This compound is particularly interesting since it does not possess opiate-like activity (because of the removal of the *N*-terminal amino-acid residue, tyrosine). Based on the similarity of the activity of DTγE and halperidol in animal tests, DeWied[25] concluded that DTγE might be produced normally as a metabolic product of a larger endorphin peptide and function as an endogenous "neuroleptic." Furthermore, he suggests that schizophrenia may be caused by a reduced availability of DTγE or a closely related neuropeptide. Thus, the "second" endorphin hypothesis suggests that disturbances in neuropeptide metabolism could be involved in the pathogenesis of schizophrenia. No other reports of therapeutic effects of DTγE have appeared in the literature, although a number of research groups are studying this compound.

FK 33–824

Jorgensen, Fog and Veilis[26] treated eight schizophrenic patients with FK 33-824, a methionine-enkephalin analogue, in an open pilot study for three days. Three schizophrenic patients had dramatic symptomatic improvement.

Blood and CSF Endorphin Levels

There have been two approaches to the measurement of endorphins in human blood and cerebrospinal fluid (CSF) : the measurement of endorphin peptides by specific radioimmunoassay and the measurement of opiate receptor-active substances by radio-receptor assays. Terenius and his colleagues have pioneered the use of chromatographic fractionization of human CSF, with its endorphin activity tested by radio-receptor assay. These investigators report that CSF contains opiate receptor-active substances in two major chromatographic fractions. In an early study of endorphin levels in psychotic patients,[27] four cases with chronic schizophrenia were studied before and after treatment with neuroleptics. Endorphin fraction 2 levels were found elevated in all four patients on at least one sampling period. Two patients who benefited from clozapine treatment showed a clear-cut drop in their fraction 2 levels, whereas two patients maintained increased endorphin levels and did not improve on this drug. These investigators could not distinguish, on the basis of clinical symptomatology, between schizophrenics with high and those with normal endorphin fractions. A summary of this work may be found in Terenius, Wahlstrom and Johansson.[28]

Domschke, Dickschas and Mitznegg [29] measured beta-endorphin by radioimmunoassay in paranoid schizophrenics with auditory hallucinations in the acute stage of their disease and in seven chronic schizophrenics with at least ten years of illness. All patients were concurrently receiving neuroleptic drugs. These authors reported that acute schizophrenics had beta-endorphin concentrations ten times higher than controls, whereas the beta-endorphin levels in the CSF of the chronic schizophrenics were half of normal.

Emrich *et al.*[30] reported a tendency for higher levels of immunoreactive beta-endorphin-like material in the CSF and plasma of schizophrenic patients, although they could not replicate this trend in a second series of experiments. They also noted that electroconvulsive therapy increased the plasma beta-endorphin-like immunoreactivity. In summary, studies of plasma and CSF levels of endorphin in schizophrenia are compatible with an abnormality in endorphin function.

Depression

Narcotic Antagonists

There are fewer reports linking narcotics or opioid peptides to affective illness. Fink *et al.*[31] were the first to report that narcotic antagonists might be beneficial in depressive illness; cyclazocine brought about clinical improvement in their open study of depressed outpatients. Terenius, Wahlstrom and Agren [32] administered naloxone, 0.4–0.8 mg t.i.d., for 6–12 days in depressed patients without any positive effects on mood levels. However, an abrupt worsening of symptoms was noted in two of the six cases when naloxone was discontinued. Furthermore, CSF endorphin fraction 1 decreased as a function of treatment. We did not see improvement in mood after naloxone administration in a pilot study of four depressed patients, one treated for three days.[33]

Beta-Endorphin

Kline and his colleagues [23, 34] administered beta-endorphin to a number of depressed patients in an open study and reported transient improvement in the mood of some subjects. Angst *et al.*[35] administered beta-endorphin to six depressed patients, precipitating mania or hypomania in four.

CSF Endorphin Levels

Terenius *et al.*[27] have also reported elevations in CSF fraction 1 and 2 in patients with manic-depressive illness; both manic and depressive phases. Additional evidence that endorphins might play a role in the depressive process may be found in the work of Almay *et al.*,[36] who found CSF endorphins in pain patients correlated with patient self-ratings of depression. Interestingly, we [37] have reported that almost 20% of endogenously depressed patients are significantly more insensitive to experimental pain than normals.

Mania

There are behavioral and preliminary clinical findings to suggest that mania, an illness characterized by hyperactivity, arousal, grandiosity, pressure of thoughts and speech, euphoria and loss of judgment might be associated with an elevation of endogenous opiates. Three groups have reported the results of acute clinical trials of naloxone in manic patients. Janowsky and associates[38, 39] studied 10 patients and reported generalized and often dramatic antimanic effects of 20 mg of naloxone, while Emrich and his associates[40] were unable to demonstrate naloxone-induced changes in two patients using 4 and 24 mg of naloxone. Davis *et al.*[33] reported a dose-dependent reduction of manic speech production and pressure of thought in one of four manic patients, but a subsequent study by Davis *et al.*[49] including an additional 10 patients with a wide range of manic symptomatology administered 20 mg of naloxone, did not demonstrate beneficial effects on behavioral ratings.

Catatonia

Bloom *et al.*[41] proposed that the catatonic-like action of opiates and of beta-endorphin in rats suggest that the human symptom of catatonia (such as found in catatonic schizophrenia) might be an appropriate target symptom for a therapeutic trial of naloxone. Davis *et al.*[33] report clinical improvement in psychomotor retardation at 1 hour post-injection in a catatonic patient. On the other hand, "mannerisms and posturing," a psychomotor analogue of "catatonia," did not improve in 14 schizophrenic patients. Schenk and his colleagues (reported at the World Congress on Biological Psychiatry, Barcelona, 1978) administered naloxone continuously for 3–21 days to 22 psychotic patients with catatonic stupor (17 of whom were schizophrenic) and reported immediate improvement in many. Improvement was accompanied by deepening of respiration and an arousal reaction in EEG. Abrams *et al.*[42] did not observe improvement in catatonia in one patient administered 1.2 mg of naloxone intravenously.

Discussion

Evidence that narcotic antagonists improve the psychotic symptoms of schizophrenia or affective illness is weak at present, nevertheless, failure to demonstrate improvement with naloxone does not rule out a role for endorphins in such disorders. The behavioral effects of such an excess may be the consequences of subsequent actions of endorphins and not easily modified in the acute experiment. Possible therapeutic effects might require changes, homeostatic compensations or even drug effects which require time to develop.[8] Most of the therapeutic agents used in psychiatry (tricyclic antidepressants, lithium, neuroleptics) require more than a single dose and more than one day for their target effects. Thus, the failure of an acute antipsychotic efficacy is a weak test of a compound's therapeutic value. Only few studies have used the orally administered narcotic antagonist naltrexone which provides continuous receptor blockade with single day dosing.[18–20] All three studies were single blind and appropriate to the small sample size, no statistical analysis was reported. Larger trials of naltrexone in addition to acute studies will be necessary to better address endorphin hypotheses of psychiatric disorders.

Naloxone's potency as an antagonist varies in physiological preparations [42, 46] and three receptor sites were postulated for narcotic studies in chronic spinal dog.[44–45] Thus, *in vitro* and *in vivo* pharmacological studies suggest the presence of more than one opioid receptor. Thus, naloxone may be more potent in blocking some endorphin effects than others.

Biological and psychophysiological indicators of endorphin hyperactivity may be potent markers for screening patients with psychiatric illnesses for "endorphin-related" subgroups. Possible candidates for such an approach include individual measures of pain insensitivity, altered respiratory rates, diminished pupillary diameter, evoked potential measures of somatosensory function, and more specific plasma and CSF endorphin levels, as such assays become available.

We have been particularly interested in using measures of pain insensitivity as a marker for identification of endorphin subgroups. Both schizophrenic patients and affectively ill patients exhibit pain insensitivity to acute somatosensory stimulation [37, 47] and pain reports have been associated with changes in CSF opiate-like activity.[48] If pain insensitivity is a marker for "hyper-endorphinism," as we suggest, then psychiatric patients with insensitivity may be screened from the larger population and admitted to treatment protocols with narcotic antagonists for careful attention to psychiatric symptom attenuation.

Thus a role for endorphins in the symptoms of psychiatric illnesses has not been identified. While the initial hope that a simple excess or deficiency of endorphins might be responsible for schizophrenic hallucinosis or mania has not been substantiated, new clinical strategies for targeting patient subgroups and new developments in peptide neurochemistry especially in endorphins still suggest the importance of these compounds to normal and abnormal behavior.

References

1. Pert, C. B. & S. H. Snyder. 1973. Properties of opiate-receptor binding in rat brain. Proc. Natl. Acad. Sci. U.S.A. **70:**2243–2247.
2. Simon, E. J., J. M. Hiller & I. Edelman. 1973. Stereospecific binding of the potent narcotic analgesic (^{3}H) entorphine to rat brain homogenate. Proc. Natl. Acad. Sci. U.S.A. **70:**1947–1949.
3. Terenius, L. 1973. Characterization of the "receptor" for narcotic analgesics in synaptic plasma membrane fraction from rat brain. Acta Pharmacol. Toxicol. **33:**377–384.
4. Hughes, J., T. W. Smith, W. H. Kosterlitz, L. A. Fothergill, B. A. Morgan & H. R. Morris. Identification of two related pentapeptides from the brain with potent opiate agonist activity. Nature **258:**577–580.
5. Cox, B. M., K. E. Opheim, H. Teschemacher & A. Goldstein. 1975. A peptide-like substance from pituitary that acts like morphine 2. purification and properties. Life Science **16:**1777–1782.
6. Verebly, K., J. Volavka & D. Clouet. 1978. Endorphins in psychiatry. An overview and a hypothesis. Arch. Gen. Psychiatry **35:**877–888.
7. Watson, S. J., H. Akil, P. A. Berger & J. D. Barchas. 1979. Some observations on the opiate peptides and schizophrenia. Arch. Gen. Psychiatry **36:** 35–41.

8. DAVIS, G. C., M. S. BUCHSBAUM & W. E. BUNNEY, JR. 1979. Research in endorphins and schizophrenia. Schizophr. Bull. **5:**244–250.
9. GUNNE, L. M., L. LINDSTROM & L. TERENIUS. 1977. Naloxone-induced reversal of schizophrenic hallucinations. J. Neural Trans. **40:**13–19.
10. EMRICH, H. M., C. CORDING, S. PIERRE, A. KOLLING, D. V. ZERSSEN & A. HERZ. 1977. Identification of an antipsychotic action of the opiate antagonist naloxone. Pharmakopsychiatr **10:**265–270.
11. WATSON, S. J., P. A. BERGER, H. AKIL, M. J. MILLS & J. D. BARCHAS. 1978. Effects of naloxone on schizophrenia. Reduction in hallucinations in a subpopulation of subjects. Science **201:**73–76.
12. DAVIS, G. C., W. E. BUNNEY, JR., E. G. DEFRAITES, J. E. KLEINMAN, D. P. VAN KAMMEN, R. M. POST & R. J. WYATT. 1977. Intravenous naloxone administration in schizophrenia and affective illness. Science **197:**74–77.
13. LEHMANN, H. V. NAIR & N. S. KLINE. 1979. β-Endorphin and naloxone in psychiatric patients: Clinical and biological effects. Am. J. Psychiatry **136:** (6)762–766.
14. VOLAVKA, J., A. MALLYA, S. BAIG & J. PEREZ-CRUET. 1977. Naloxone in chronic schizophrenia. Science **196:**1227–1228.
15. JANOWSKY, D. S., D. S. SEGAL, F. BLOOM, A. ABRAMS & R. GUILLEMIN. 1977. Lack of effect of naloxone on schizophrenic symptoms. Am. J. Psychiatry **134:**926–927.
16. GUNNE, L. M., L. LINDSTROM & E. WIDERLOV. 1979. Possible role of endorphins in schizophrenia and other psychiatric disorders. *In* Endorphins in Mental Health Research. E. Usdin, W. E. Bunney, Jr. & N. S. Kline, Eds.:547–552. Macmillan Press, Ltd. New York, N.Y.
17. KURLAND, A. A., O. L. MCCABE, T. E. HANLON & D. SULLIVAN. 1977. The treatment of perceptual disturbance in schizophrenia with naloxone hydrochloride. Am. J. Psychiatry **134:**1408–1410.
18. SIMPSON, G. M., M. H. BRANCHLEY & J. H. LEE. 1977. A trial of naltrexone in chronic schizophrenics. Curr. Ther. Res. **22:**909–913.
19. GITLIN, M. & J. E. ROSENBLATT. 1978. Possible withdrawal from endogenous opiates in schizophrenics. Am. J. Psychiatry **135:**377–378.
20. MIELKE, D. H. & D. M. GALLANT. 1977. An opiate antagonist in chronic schizophrenia; a pilot study. Am. J. Psychiatry **134:**1430–1431.
21. LIPINSKI, J., R. MEYER, C. KORNETSKY & B. M. COHEN. 1979. Naloxone in schizophrenia: negative results. Lancet **I:**1292–1293.
22. DAVIS, G. C., M. S. BUCHSBAUM & W. E. BUNNEY, JR. 1980. Alterations of evoked potentials link research in attention dysfunction to peptide responsive symptoms of schizophrenia. *In* Neural Peptides and Neuronal Communications. M. Trabucchi & E. Costa, Eds. :473–487. Raven Press. New York, N.Y.
23. KLINE, N. S., C. H. LI, H. E. LEHMANN, A. LAJTHA, E. LASKI & T. B. COOPER. 1977. β-endorphin-induced changes in schizophrenic and depressed patients. Arch. Gen. Psychiatry **34:**1111–1113.
24. VERHOEVEN, W. M. A., H. M. VAN REE & D. DEWIED. 1979. Improvement of schizophrenic patients treated with (DES-Tyr^1)-γ-endorphin (DTγE). Arch. Gen. Psychiatry **36:**294–298.
25. DEWIED, D. 1978. *In* Characteristics and Function of Opioids. J. M. Van Ree & L. Terenius, Eds.: 113–131. Elsevier, North Holland.
26. JORGENSEN, A., R. FOG & B. VEILIS. 1979. Synthetic enkephalin analogue in treatment of schizophrenia. Lancet **I:**935.
27. TERENIUS, L., A. WAHLSTROM, L. LINDSTROM & E. WIDERLOV. 1976. Increased CSF levels of endorphins in chronic psychosis. Neurosci. Letters **3:**157–162.
28. TERENIUS, L., A. WAHLSTROM & L. JOHANSSON. 1979. Endorphins in human cerebrospinal fluid and their measurement. *In* Endorphins in Mental Health Research. E. Usdin, W. E. Bunney, Jr. & N. S. Kline, Eds.:553–560. Macmillan Press, New York, N.Y.

29. DOMSCHKE, W., A. DICKSCHAS & P. MITZNEGG. 1974. CSF β-endorphin in schizophrenia. Lancet **I:**1024.
30. EMRICH, H. M., V. HOLLT, W. KISSLING, M. FISCHLER, H. LASPE, H. HEINEMANN, D. V. ZERSSEN & A. HERZ. 1979. β-Endorphin-like immunoreactivity in cerebrospinal fluid and plasma of patients with schizophrenia and other neuropsychiatric disorders. Pharmakopsychiatr. **12:**269–276.
31. FINK, M., J. SIMEON, T. M. ITIL & A. M. FREEDMAN. 1970. Clinical antidepressant activity of cyclazocine—a narcotic antagonist. Clin. Pharmacol. Ther. **11:**41–48.
32. TERENIUS, L., A. WAHLSTROM & H. AGREN. 1977. Naloxone (Narcan) treatment in depression: clinical observations and effects on CSF endorphins and monoamine metabolites. Psychopharmacology **54:**31–33.
33. DAVIS, G. C., W. E. BUNNEY, JR., M. S. BUCHSBAUM, E. G. DE FRAITES, W. DUNCAN, J. C. GILLIN, D. P. VAN KAMMEN, J. KLEINMAN, D. L. MURPHY, R. M. POST, V. REUS & R. J. WYATT. 1979. Use of narcotic antagonists to study the role of endorphins in normal and psychiatric patients. *In* Endorphins in Mental Health Research. E. Usdin, W. E. Bunney, Jr. & N. S. Kline, Eds. :393–406. Macmillan Press. New York, N.Y.
34. KLINE, N. S. & H. E. LEHMANN. 1979. β-Endorphin Therapy in Psychiatric Patients. *In* Endorphins in Mental Health Research. E. Usdin, W. E. Bunney, Jr. & N. S. Kline, Ed.:500–517. Macmillan Press, Ltd. New York, N.Y.
35. ANGST, J., V. AUTENRIETH, F. BREM, M. KOVKKOV, H. MEYER, H. H. STASSEN & U. STORCK. 1979. Preliminary results of treatment with β-endorphin in depression. *In* Endorphins in Mental Health Research. E. Usdin, W. E. Bunney, Jr. & N. S. Kline, Eds.:518–528. Macmillan Press, Ltd. New York, N.Y.
36. ALMAY, B. G. L., R. JOHANNSON, L. VON KNORRING, L. TERENIUS & A. WALHSTROM. 1978. Endorphins in chronic pain. I. Differences in CSF endorphin levels between organic and psychogenic pain syndromes. Pain **5:**153–162.
37. DAVIS, G. C., M. S. BUCHSBAUM & W. E. BUNNEY, JR. 1979. Analgesia to painful stimuli in affective illness. Am. J. Psychiatry **136:**(9)1148–1151.
38. JANOWSKY, D., L. JUDD, L. HUEY, N. ROITMAN, D. PARKER & D. SEGAL. 1978. Naloxone effects on manic symptoms and growth hormone levels. Lancet **II:** 320.
39. JANOWSKY, D. S., L. L. JUDD, L. HUEY & D. SEGAL. 1979. Effects of naloxone in normal, manic and schizophrenic patients: evidence for an alleviation of manic symptoms. *In* Endorphins in Mental Health Research. E. Usdin, W. E. Bunney, Jr. & N. S. Kline, Eds.:435–447. Macmillan Press, Ltd. New York, N.Y.
40. EMRICH, H. M., C. CORDING, S. PIERR, A. KOLLING, H. S. MOLLER, D. VON ZERSSEN & A. HERZ. 1979. Actions of naloxone in different types of psychoses. *In* Endorphins in Mental Health Research. E. Usdin, W. E. Bunney, Jr. & N. S. Kline, Eds.: 452–460. Macmillan Press, Ltd. New York, N.Y.
41. BLOOM, F., D. SEGAL, N. LING & R. GUILLEMIN. 1976. Endorphins: profound behavioral effects in rats suggest new etiological factors in mental illness. Science **194:**630–632.
42. ABRAMS, A., D. BRAFF, D. JANOWSKY, S. HALL & D. SEGAL. 1978. Unresponsiveness of catatonic symptoms to naloxone. Pharmakopsychiatr. **11:**177–179.
43. LORD, J. A. H., A. A. WATERFIELD, J. HUGHES & H. KOSTERLITZ. 1977. Endogenous opioid peptides: multiple agonists and receptors. Nature **267:** 495–499.
44. GILBERT, P. E. & W. R. MARTIN. 1976. The effects of morphine and nalorphine-like drugs in the nondependent, morphine-dependent and cyclazocine-dependent chronic spinal dog. J. Pharm. Exp. Ther. **198:**66–82.
45. MARTIN, W. R., C. G. EADES, J. A. THOMPSON, R. E. HUPPLER & P. E. GILBERT. 1976. The effects of morphine and nalorphine-like drugs in the independent and morphine-dependent chronic spinal dog. J. Pharm. Exp. Ther. **197:**517–532.

46. Snyder, S. H., S. R. Childers & G. W. Pasternak. 1978. Opiate receptors: A) functional heterogeneity demonstrated with apparently irreversible naloxone derivative; B) regulation by guanine nucleotides. *In* Advances in Pharmacology and Therapeutics. J. Jacob, Ed. Vol. 1. Receptors. 39–46. Pergamon Press. New York, N.Y.
47. Davis, G. C., M. S. Buchsbaum, D. P. Van Kammen & W. E. Bunney, Jr. 1979. Analgesia to pain stimuli in schizophrenics reversed by naltrexone. Psychiatr. Res. **1:**61–69.
48. Von Knorring, L., B. G. L. Almay, F. Johannson & L. Terenius. 1978. Pain perception and endorphin levels in cerebrospinal fluid. Pain **5:**359–365.
49. Davis, G. C., I. Extein, V. I. Reus, W. Hamilton, R. M. Post, F. K. Goodwin & W. E. Bunney Jr. 1980. Failure of naloxone to reduce manic symptoms. Am. J. Psychiatry **137:**1583–1585.

GENERAL DISCUSSION

Herbert Kleber, *Session Chair*

Department of Psychiatry
Yale-New Haven Medical Center
New Haven, Connecticut 06519

Y. F. JACQUET (*New York City*): Dr. Davis reported on naloxone doses at least 25–50 times more than is required to reverse opiate overdose. Now in view of the known multiple actions of naloxone, do you think it's possible that you're affecting some system other than the endorphin? For example, the Gamma Amino Butyric Acid system?

GLENN DAVIS: Let me address that in several ways. If you look at a lot of the doses used in animals to produce endocrine effects, for instance, prolactin effects, these doses of naloxone are not out of proportion to the doses that are used in animals to produce such opiate agonist effects. I didn't claim that we were studying only endorphin effects. We could be studying many things. We currently don't know. That's why we're using high doses.

Let me answer it in another way which may be more satisfactory to you. In our evoked potential paradigm, various doses of naloxone produce effects in opposite directions to the ones we get with morphine. Now, that doesn't mean that the behaviors that we're talking about are specific effects, but they are what we see in terms of evoked potential.

Y. F. JACQUET: I'm not talking about nonspecific effects. Naloxone has been known to antagonize GABA and even nitrous oxide. Many naloxone actions are beginning to emerge, which may or may not involve opiate receptor mechanisms.

GLENN DAVIS: I agree. Whether those are indirect actions via opiates is still not effectively ruled out, either.

HERBERT KLEBER: One problem with the earlier studies is that the doses were so low that you often didn't see any effect. I agree that it is better to at least show there is an effect and then go back and try to figure out what that effect was.

ENOCH GORDIS (*Mt. Sinai Medical Center, New York City*): Dr. Routtenberg, the striking awakening effect of your electrode experiment was very evident from that movie. In alcoholism, one thing that's clear is that in many of the alcohol experimental setups, high atmospheric pressures are able to awaken drunken animals. Then they'll promptly slip back into torpor again once the high atmospheric pressure is released. I'm wondering whether you could comment on any possible commonality. Except for that one experiment with pressure, I don't know anything else which rapidly awakens ethanolized animals after which they can immediately fall back asleep again. You implied that this endogenous reinforcement system might somehow explain the persistent use of ethanol. Somehow the ethanol is replacing the electric shock? Is that correct?

ARYEH ROUTTENBERG: Perhaps a wild hypothesis at this point comes from evidence that this system has a very potent effect on memory formation and retrieval processes. Indeed, there is one study that showed that stimulation of the frontal cortex attenuated tolerance to morphine. These agents may persistently engage a memory mechanism, in part residing within this dopamine system and perhaps the opioid system, as well.

JAMES KETCHAM (*Los Angeles*): Dr. Davis, does the apparent elevation of beta endorphin in acute schizophrenia and decline in chronic schizophrenia suggest that this system might be playing some positive role? It's interesting that Bliss, Pinkus and Hoglan etc., back in the early 1950s, made similar observations that corticosteroids were elevated in acute schizophrenia and lower in chronic schizophrenia. Since endorphins and ACTH are concomitantly released, might we not be just seeing another aspect of a stress response?

GLENN DAVIS: Yes, I didn't mean to give you the impression that my belief was that these were involved causally in any of these illnesses. First we must examine if there is an association. Then we must address whether this is homeostatic or it's compensatory homeostatic or whether it's some other functional alteration.

N. G. BACOPOULOS (*Dartmouth Medical School*): I have a question and comment for Dr. Routtenberg, which takes us back to the wonderful world of rats and ethanol. At the University of Iowa, we gave ethanol to rats in the same dose and the same manner as you're doing, measuring dopamine metabolism in the brain. We found a drastic reduction of dopamine turnover in the substantia nigra, which fits rather interestingly with some of your data. We also found a reduction in some terminal regions, such as the caudate nucleus, although not in others, suggesting a sort of anesthetic effect throughout the dopamine neuron neuraxis. With apomorphine, a dopamine agonist, we could reverse some of the behavioral effects, mostly motor incoordination, that accompanied this biochemical change. These data fit very nicely with yours. There is one theoretical point I'd like to take up, i.e., that ethanol does not interfere with the dopaminergic system or with the endogenous reinforcement system. I'd like to submit that it's conceivable that ethanol exerts a pre-synaptic blockade of dopaminergic function which can be surmounted by your electrical stimulation. If you administer chlorpromazine and block dopamine receptors, you would not expect to surmount it as easily with electrical stimulation as you have reported because the dopamine released would not affect the blocked receptors. So, I think that ethanol, dopamine, and the reinforcement system are definitely integrated in a very complex way.

ARYEH ROUTTENBERG: I second your views on the complexity. Boris Haverkoff, who has done quite a bit of work on the dopamine system, reports ethanol to have a variety of very interesting effects on the dopaminergic system. Some of them are selective anatomically, i.e., on the mesolimbic system rather than the nigra neostriatal system.

In terms of long-lasting effects, Haverkoff believes that ethanol uncouples the connection between the pre-synaptic and post-synaptic system. But I'm glad you raised that point because I wouldn't want to leave the impression that it has no effect on the dopaminergic system. It clearly does have such an effect, but it doesn't seem to mitigate against this brain stimulation reward effect.

N. G. BACOPOULOS: I think both what you've said and what I've said point to the fact that there are ways in which the acute behavioral effects of ethanol can be disrupted or reversed, and those ways both appear to stimulate dopaminergic pathways.

ROSS FISHMAN: The cell stimulation demonstration in your studies used food-seeking behavior. Would a rat continue to operate the intracranial stimulation if, for example, to do so meant that it would have to tolerate getting foot shock?

ARYEH ROUTTENBERG: Yes.

ROSS FISHMAN: Then is there any evidence that the intracranial stimulation itself may be reducing the pain or at least making it more tolerable?

ARYEH ROUTTENBERG: Yes.

ROSS FISHMAN: Behind these questions is my interest in the amotivational syndrome manifested under the influence of several drugs which influence both food-seeking and escape-avoidance behaviors. Might some drugs of abuse have their effect not only by reducing overall activity levels, but also by producing some sustained activity of the endogenous reinforcement system?

ARYEH ROUTTENBERG: I believe that explains the phenomena. There are several reports that brain stimulation does have analgesic properties. The anatomic sites do not overlap entirely with the analgesic system, but there are several areas in common.

GABRIEL NAHAS (*Columbia University*): I would like to ask Dr. Routtenberg about the drugs which animals will readily self-administer, i.e., opiates, cocaine, amphetamines, etc. Is there any correlation between these self-administered drugs in animal models and their point of impact on the brain work system? Aren't there several points of impact described by Gary Stein, for the self-inducing drugs, the drug-inducing drugs, and the drug-reducing ones?

ARYEH ROUTTENBERG: Yes, there is a very definite link between self-administration, for example, of amphetamine and the dopaminergic reward system.

NEUROPSYCHOLOGICAL IMPAIRMENT IN OPIATE ADDICTS: RISK FACTORS *

Bruce J. Rounsaville, Robert A. Novelly and Herbert D. Kleber

Department of Psychiatry
School of Medicine
Yale University
New Haven, Connecticut 06519

Cecilia Jones

Austin Riggs Center
Stockbridge, Massachusetts 01262

The relationship between neuropsychological impairment and opiate addiction has been infrequently studied and the results have been contradictory. In a multi-center collaborative study of polydrug abuse, Grant *et al.* found that 37% of poly-drug users, many of whom used opiates, showed neuropsychological deficits based on clinician's ratings of test results using the Halstead-Reitan Neuropsychological Battery.[1] Risk factors for impairment included heavy use of CNS depressants and opiates, increased age, poorer academic achievement, and a history of CNS related medical events and developmental difficulties such as general anesthesia, or learning disabilities. These findings support earlier pilot investigations,[2, 3] which also reported a high incidence of neuropsychological impairment (45% to 64%) in multiple drug abusers following their entry into treatment. Another recent study found opiate addicts to have marked perceptual disturbances on the Bender Gestalt Test.[4]

In contrast, four studies [5–8] have failed to detect any differences in neuropsychological status between polydrug users or opiate addicts and normal controls. The most recent of these investigations [5, 6] are well-designed studies which employ either the extensive and widely used Halstead-Reitan Battery [5] or selected tests from that battery.[6]

The present study is designed to extend previous work in this area by evaluating neuropsychological functioning of opiate addicts with an abbreviated, economical battery of tests that could be used more routinely for detecting neuropsychological impairment in clinical programs. In earlier studies, neuropsychological tests revealed deficits which were not found by medical history interviews or gross neurological exams, since evidence of a neurological disorder was an exclusion criterion for these investigations.[1, 3] If, as some studies suggest, a substantial number of addicts do manifest signs of neuropsychological impairment, then detection of these deficits may be important for treatment planning. Grant, *et al.* have suggested that "persons with such deficit might respond better to highly structured, problem-oriented interventions in which communications are simple and straightforward than to therapies producing high emotional arousal."[1] (p. 183) Rehabilitative efforts also may need to address limitations in an individual's ability to learn and change that may be uncovered through the use of a neuropsychological test battery.

* This work was supported by N.I.D.A. Contract No. 271–77–3410, Herbert D. Kleber, principal investigator.

In the current paper, we will present data regarding, 1) the prevalence of neuropsychological impairment in a sample of opiate addicts evaluated early in treatment, 2) antecedents of neuropsychological impairment in this group, and 3) concomitant clinical and behavioral characteristics associated with neuropsychological impairment in addicts.

METHODS

Setting and Sample

Opiate Addicts

Seventy-two opiate addicts were evaluated at the Screening and Evaluation Unit of a Drug Dependence Treatment Center one to three weeks after applying for treatment. The three major modalities of treatment offered opiate addicts in this setting are Methadone Maintenance, Outpatient Narcotic Antagonist Treatment, and a Residential Drug-Free Therapeutic Community. At the time of evaluation, clients were either in the process of evaluation and still using illicit opiates ($N = 15$), recently maintained on methadone ($N = 37$), or recently detoxified and participating in treatment ($N = 20$). To monitor the interference of drug state on test results, urine specimens were obtained on 65 of the subjects and analyzed to detect recent drug use. Clients were also rated clinically on a Drug Interference Scale [1] and testing was deferred if they showed any behavioral signs of drug toxicity or abstinence effects.

Neuropsychological evaluation was a voluntary part of lengthy psychological and diagnostic testing of clients seen at screening. The voluntary nature and the length of the battery prohibited the evaluation of a consecutive or randomized sample. However, a comparison of the current group with a set of 25 consecutive clients evaluated at this screening unit immediately after the completion of this phase of the study revealed no significant differences in age, sex, race, social class, educational level and I.Q. Thus, the sample was felt to be representative of clients seen early in treatment in this setting.

Epileptic Comparison Group

The epilepsy group was matched, using a group match procedure, for age, sex, handedness, and education and consisted of individuals meeting the following criteria: 1) a neurological diagnosis of either a partial or partial-complex or absence seizure disorder, with epileptic or epileptiform discharges on serial EEG examinations and without evidence of hysterical components, 2) no evidence of either focal or diffuse abnormalities on CT scan as reported by the neuroradiologist, and 3) no history of psychiatric hospitalization, drug or alcohol abuse. A total of 60 epilepsy patients were included, 20 of whom had a diagnosis of primary generalized (absence) epilepsy, and 40 of whom were diagnosed as having either partial or portial-complex (psychomotor) epilepsy. Of the latter group, 20 had the maximal EEG abnormality over the left hemisphere while 20 had a maximal right hemisphere EEG abnormality. All patients were noninstitutionalized, and were being treated at a hospital clinic.

Neuropsychological Battery

Measures were selected to provide maximal diagnostic power with considerations of portability, brevity of administration, relative freedom from cultural bias, and coverage of a range of cerebral functions. Tests included the following: A. Motor measures-grip strength, Finger tapping,[9] Pegboard; B. Perceptual/Visual measures—Trails A and B,[10] Visual search; [11] C. Speech/Language measures—color naming, H-words; [12] D. New associative learning-digit symbol substitution test,[13] and E. Intellectual Functioning-Vocabulary, similarities, block design, and picture arrangement tests from Wechsler Adult Intelligence Scale.[14]

For all subtests, impairment was defined as a score of greater than one standard deviation from the standard mean in the direction of impairment. A summed overall impairment rating was derived from subtest scores by summing the number of tests on which impaired ratings were made. Thus, the rating of overall impairment was based on objective test scores and not on a global clinical judgment. This battery was administered and scored by either a Master's or a Doctoral level psychologist.

Other Measures of Clinical Status

To evaluate clinical features associated with neuropsychological functioning, the following tests were also administered: a) the Maudsley Personality Inventory, measuring two factors, neuroticism and extroversion; [15] b) the Beck Depression Inventory, a self-reported depressive symptom scale; [16] c) the SCL 90 based on the Hopkins Symptom Checklist,[17] a checklist assessing nine areas of psychiatric symptoms commonly seen in outpatients; d) the Social Adjustment Self Report, a measure of social functioning over the preceding two weeks,[18] and e) the Schedule for Affective Disorders and Schizophrenia (SADS) which is a semi-structured interview for assessing psychiatric history and symptoms.[19]

Results

Sociodemographic and Clinical Characteristics of the Sample

There were no significant differences between the opiate addicts and epileptics on age (addicts mean = 27.9; epileptics mean = 29.2), sex (addicts 72% male; epileptics 67% male), educational level (addicts mean = 11.5; epileptics mean = 11.8) or handedness (addicts 91% right; epileptics 87% right). In addition, addicts were predominantly white (58%), unemployed (56%), and in lower socioeconomic groups (84% in Holingshead's classes IV and V).

In the addict sample the mean number of years of opiate use was 8.2. Poly-drug use was common as measured by the number of drugs used heavily for at least three months. Twenty-eight percent of the sample abused opiates alone, 43% abused opiates and 1–3 additional classes of drugs, and 29% abused opiates and 4–6 additional classes of drugs.

Neuropsychological Impairment in Opiate Addicts

Overall impairment was moderate to severe in 53% of opiate addicts, mild in 26% and absent in 21%. As shown in TABLE 1, the epileptic group had a distribution of overall impairment levels that was not significantly different from the addict group.

To evaluate the areas of greatest impairment and to further differentiate the two groups, the addicts and epileptics were compared according to the number with impaired performance on the individual tests as shown in TABLE 2. Epileptics were significantly more impaired than addicts in the two most specific measures of rapid verbal fluency, color naming and H words. Impairment in opiate addicts was most common on pegboard, visual search, digit symbol, and intellectual functioning tasks.

Despite findings that a substantial number of addicts had impaired ratings on most measures, the range of IQ scores on the group was normal, with a mean verbal IQ of 97, performance IQ of 97, and full scale IQ of 104. Impairment in intellectual functioning displayed in TABLE 2 is a compound measure of both low IQ (14% less than 85) and verbal performance discrepancy (28%).

To sum up, the sample of opiate addicts showed evidence of general cerebral dysfunction and was generally comparable to a sample of ambulatory patients with a diagnosed neurological disorder.

Risk Factors Associated with Neuropsychological Impairment in Opiate Addicts

In this section aspects of the subjects' histories and current functioning will be compared across three subgroups: 1) unimpaired addicts, 2) mildly impaired addicts, and 3) moderately-severely impaired addicts. These subgroups will be compared on categorical data (e.g., presence or absence of childhood hyperactivity) using the χ^2 statistic and on ordinal or continuous data (e.g., number of years of opiate use) using one way analysis of variance.

The association between a factor and neuropsychological impairment is presented as significant if $p < .05$.

Childhood Dysfunctional Behavior and Neuropsychological Impairment

Evidence from childhood of behavioral disturbance was compared in opiate addicts with absent, mild and moderate/severe neuropsychological impairment. As displayed in TABLE 3, poor educational record, earlier school dropout, and

TABLE 1

OVERALL NEUROPSYCHOLOGICAL IMPAIRMENT IN OPIATE ADDICTS AND EPILEPTICS

	Subject Group				
Degree of Impairment	Epileptics		Opiate Addicts		χ^2
	N	%	N	%	
None	8	14	15	21	
Mild	20	33	19	26	N.S.
Moderate-severe	32	53	38	53	

TABLE 2

COMPARISON OF OPIATE ADDICTS AND EPILEPTICS IN COMPONENTS OF NEUROPSYCHOLOGICAL IMPAIRMENT

Area Tested	Subject Groups: Epileptics (n = 60) % impaired	Subject Groups: Opiate Addicts (n = 72) % impaired	Significance of Difference (χ^2)
Motor			
Grip Strength	32	28	n.s.
Finger Tapping	50	42	n.s.
Pegboard	77	76	n.s.
Perceptual/Visual			
Trails A	28	17	n.s.
Trails B	42	37	n.s.
Visual Search	42	49	n.s.
Speech/Language			
Color Naming	57	22	*
H Words	57	24	*
New Associative Learning			
Digit Symbol	37	50	n.s.
Intellectual Functioning			
WAIS Full Scale <85 or Verbal Performance Disparity	37	42	n.s.

* = $p < .001$.

childhood hyperactivity were significantly related to greater neuropsychological impairment in the addict sample.

Drug State at Interview

Urine screening for drugs was performed on 65 subjects at the time of neuropsychological testing. Of those subjects, 20 had no opiates in the urine. Five subjects who had positive tests for opiates also had other substances in the urine, such as cocaine or tranquilizers, but this group was not evaluated

TABLE 3

RELATIONSHIP BETWEEN CHILDHOOD DYSFUNCTIONAL BEHAVIOR AND NEUROPSYCHOLOGICAL IMPAIRMENT IN OPIATE ADDICTS

Childhood History Items Significantly Correlated with Greater Impairment	Childhood History Items Not Correlated with Greater Impairment
Quality of Educational Record (good, fair, poor)	Firesetting (absent, present)
	Cruelty to Animals (absent, present)
Highest Grade Level (< High School, High School, > High School)	Bedwetting after age 5 (absent, present)
	Stuttering (absent, present)
Childhood Hyperactivity (absent, mild, severe)	Age of First Arrest for Delinquency (15, 16–20, 21 up)

separately. No significant relationship was noted between neuropsychological impairment and current drug status measured by urine opiates. Of those with positive tests, 58% were moderately/severely impaired, 29% mildly impaired, and 13%, unimpaired while 50% were moderately/severely impaired, 30% mildly impaired, and 20% unimpaired in the group with negative urines.

Drug History

Drug history was measured in three ways: a) years of use more than once each week, b) greatest frequency of use (ranging from occasionally to several times daily) for 3 months or more, and c) a composite rating defined on the SADS which evaluates amount of drug use, evidence of addiction, and interference with functioning. Unimpaired, mildly impaired and moderately/severely impaired opiate addicts differed in their history of drug use in only two areas: cocaine and alcohol use. More impaired addicts had a history of using alcohol more intensively for at least a 3 month period and they were rated on the SADS scale as having more severe history of cocaine use.

CNS Related Medical History

A history of CNS related medical events was not differentially distributed in opiate addicts with absent, mild or moderate/severe neuropsychological impairment as displayed in TABLE 4.

Psychiatric Symptoms, Personality, and Social Functioning

Current symptom status, as measured by the Beck Depression Inventory, and the SCL 90, was not significantly related to neuropsychological functioning, as shown in TABLE 5. Similarly, no difference in recent social functioning as measured in the SAS-SR or in the personality traits of neuroticism or extroversion measured on the Maudsley Personality Inventory.

Criminal History

Assuming that neuropsychological impairment seen in this sample is not a short term phenomenon, it might be expected to be associated with criminal behavior particularly of a violent sort, as the work of Lewis, *et al.*[20] has shown. However, the arrest record for different types of crimes and the total number of incarcerations did not differ in those with and without neuropsychological impairment among the opiate group, as shown in TABLE 5.

DISCUSSION

Prevalence of Neuropsychological Impairment in Opiate Addicts

Detecting general neuropsychological impairment in one-half of our sample, our findings corroborate those of Grant *et al.*,[1–3] and contrast with earlier studies.[5–8] Moreover, it is noteworthy that only around one-fifth of our sample had completely normal profiles.

This finding is supported by the comparability of the addict and epileptic groups in distribution of general impairment and on most individual measures of neuropsychological functioning. The epileptic group, while representing a population with a recognized neurological disorder, when compared with normals is not likely to be grossly neurologically impaired.[21] When compared with opiate addicts, the epileptic group was more impaired only on measures of verbal fluency. This is consistent with the fact that two-thirds of the epileptics had psychomotor epilepsy with a focus in either the right or left temporal-frontal region.

TABLE 4

RELATIONSHIP BETWEEN DRUG AND MEDICAL HISTORY AND NEUROPSYCHOLOGICAL IMPAIRMENT IN OPIATE ADDICTS

Area Significantly Correlated with Greater Impairment	Area Not Significantly Correlated with Greater Impairment
Greatest Frequency of Use	Greatest Frequency of Use
Alcohol	Opiates
	Barbiturates
	Other Sedatives
	Amphetamines
	Cocaine
	Marijuana
	Hallucinogens
	Inhalants
Severity of Use (SADS Rating n = 55) *	Severity of Use (SADS Rating n = 55) *
Cocaine	Opiates
	Sedatives/hypnotics/tranquilizers
	Amphetamines
	Marijuana
	Hallucinogens
	Inhalants
	Number of Years of Use
	Opiates
	Barbiturates
	Other Sedatives
	Amphetamines
	Cocaine
	Marijuana
	Hallucinogens
	Inhalants
	Alcohol
	Medical History
	Abnormal Gross Neurological Exam
	Syphillis History
	Seizure History
	Head Injury History
	Drug Overdose History
	General Anesthesia History
	Syncope History

* Missing data on 17 subjects.

Evaluating the measures in which addicts perform most poorly, it appears that those tasks which call for greatest integration of different cortical areas are most affected, while measures of focal cortical regions are comparatively unimpaired in this group. For instance, there was a linear relationship between the number of subjects impaired on motor tasks (grip, finger tapping, and pegboard) and the increasing need for integration of different cortical areas. Similarly, although verbal and performance IQ measures were not impaired in the group as a whole, verbal performance discrepancies were commonly noted. In the addict group as a whole, neuropsychological impairment appears to be diffuse and not localized. Thus, this sort of dysfunction is likely to be missed in clinical evaluations which do not rely on psychological testing, and may be an important factor in some addicts' impaired ability to sustain integrated efforts at work or to learn new vocational tasks.

The failure of Fields and Fullerton,[5] and Bruhn and Maage[6] to detect evidence of general cerebral impairment in opiate addicts, may be related to differences in the way that neuropsychological deficit was inferred. These studies made judgments of impairment solely on the basis of statistical differences between their sample and control groups on the individual tests employed. However, in addition to examining scores on a test-by-test basis, the present investigators (like those of Grant and Associates)[1–3] assigned individual impairment ratings by taking each subject's total test scores and their patterning into consideration. This procedure, which allows deviations on several measures to be summed as accruing evidence of neuropsychological deficit is, thus, a more sensitive method of detecting impairment in individual subjects and represents the type of evaluative approach most often used clinically.

TABLE 5

RELATIONSHIP BETWEEN PSYCHIATRIC SYMPTOMS PERSONALITY, SOCIAL FUNCTIONING, AND CRIMINAL BEHAVIOR AND NEUROPSYCHOLOGICAL IMPAIRMENT IN OPIATE ADDICTS

Areas Not Significantly Correlated With Great Impairment
Depressive Symptoms (Beck Depression Inventory)
General Symptoms (SCL 90)
Personality (Maudsley Personality Inventory Neuroticism and Extroversion)
Social Functioning (Social Adjustment Scale)
Criminal History
Number of Arrests
Violent Crimes
Property Crimes
Drug Related Crimes
Other Crimes
Number of Incarcerations

Antecedents of Neuropsychological Impairment

Given a high prevalence of neuropsychological impairment in opiate addicts, this impairment may precede use of opiates and predispose those effected to drug use, or it may result from drug use or the hazardous lifestyle associated with involvement in a drug culture. The significant relationship between poor school performance and childhood hyperactivity and neuropsychological impairment supports the proposition that this dysfunctioning preceded drug use for some. Conversely, the lack of a significant relationship between severity of most nonalcoholic drug use and neuropsychological impairment fails to support the proposition that the amount of nonalcoholic drug use is a cause of this impairment. It is noteworthy that the greatest frequency of alcohol use was significantly related to neuropsychological impairment, extending previous findings [3] and underscoring the need to address alcohol abuse in the treatment of opiate addicts. The correlation of neuropsychological impairment and cocaine use may be related to either preferential use of cocaine among those with neuropsychological impairment or impaired neuropsychological functioning resulting from excessive cocaine use. Given the association between childhood hyperactivity and neuropsychological impairment and the lack of previous evidence of neuropsychological impairment caused by cocaine use, the correlation is possibly explained by the use of cocaine as treatment for their deficit by those with neuropsychological impairment.

Limitations of Current Study

Several features of the current study may limit the generalizability of our findings. Although our sample was not random, it was not detectably different from a consecutive sample of opiate addicts applying for our treatment. The sample was heterogenous for current use of opiates, but the detoxified group did not differ from those on methadone or illicit opiate in neuropsychological impairment. The fact that no association was found between positive urines and neuropsychological status strongly suggests that the test results were not significantly altered by recent drug ingestion by our subjects. Our findings are on the basis of a less extensive battery than that performed by Grant *et al.*,[1–3] or Fields and Fullerton,[5] but the abbreviated testing was purposefully designed in an effort to pilot the use of a battery of instruments that would be more efficient and economical for more general clinical use than the full Reitan Battery. It is unlikely that poor motivation due to psychological symptoms or personality pathology were responsible for these findings because measures of these factors were not significantly correlated with neuropsychological impairment in our sample. Moreover, the normal range of IQ scores provides evidence for adequate motivation to perform on these tasks.

Most importantly, we do not have data from a demographically matched normal control group using this particular neuropsychological battery. Our determination of degree of impairment is based on published norms for each individual instrument. However, these norms are frequently not available from subjects with low educational achievement or with subjects in lower socioeconomic groups. Finlayson *et al.*[22] has shown a linear relationship between neuropsychological impairment and educational level and Amante *et al.*[23] has shown that intellectual and perceptual motor deficits are more common in subjects at lower socioeconomic levels. Both the addict and the epileptic samples in this study had on the average, less than a high school education. This may be a determinant of the poor performance in these samples. Such a view is supported by the correlation within the addict group between lower educational achievement and neuropsychological impairment and by the findings of Grant *et al.*[1] suggesting a similar relationship between educational level and impairment.

Finally, the stability of neuropsychological impairment in our sample may be questioned as it was detected on entrance to treatment when the addicts most typically are in a psychological, social or pharmacological crisis, which might lead to impaired performance. Grant *et al*[1] have reported substantial improvement in a significant minority of impaired drug abusers when three month reevaluations were performed. Follow-up data is needed on our sample to determine whether the impaired scores indicate relatively stable characteristics and to evaluate the prognostic significance of neuropsychological impairment in opiate addicts. A follow-up study and an evaluation of a demographically matched normal control group are in progress. Given the contradictory nature of published reports on neuropsychological functioning of drug abusers and opiate addicts, replication studies are needed to more definitively establish the extent and the nature of the relationship between drug abuse and neuropsychological impairment.

Summary

Neuropsychological functioning in opiate addicts has been infrequently studied and results have been contradictory. More recent studies by Grant *et al.* detected global neuropsychological impairment in from 37% to 64% of polydrug abusers, many of whom used opiates, while four previous studies failed to demonstrate that opiate addicts were more impaired than nondrug using comparison groups.

In the current study, a sample of 72 opiate addicts applying for treatment at an out-patient drug program were tested using a one-hour battery of neuropsychological measures designed to assess briefly and economically the area covered by the lengthy Reitan Battery. The majority of the addict group were polydrug users and had used opiates for an average of 8.2 years. Results of testing in this group were compared with results obtained on a sample matched for age, education, sex and handedness of 60 epileptics with no evidence of structural CNS lesions. Individual test measures and an overall impairment rating were made.

Results indicated 53% of the addicts had moderate/severe neuropsychological impairment, 26% had mild impairment, and 21% were unimpaired. This distribution was not significantly different from that found in the epileptic comparison group, in which 53% had moderate/severe impairment, 33% mild impairment, and 14% no impairment. Comparison of individual test scores in the two groups revealed that the epileptic group was more impaired than the opiate group only in measures of verbal fluency.

A search for antecedents of neuropsychological impairment in opiate addicts revealed that those with more impairment were more likely to have a history of childhood hyperactivity, earlier school dropout, poor educational achievement, and a greater severity of alcohol and cocaine use. Neuropsychological impairment was found to be not significantly correlated with measures of CNS related medical history (such as head injuries), duration of severity of illicit drug use in any category other than cocaine, criminal history, psychiatric symptoms, social functioning, or personality pathology.

Our findings support previous studies revealing neuropsychological impairment in a substantial proportion of opiate addicts and suggest the value of evaluating this aspect of their functioning as a guide to rehabilitative efforts. Limitations of this study and the need for further research are discussed.

References

1. Grant, I., K. M. Adams, A. S. Carlin, P. M. Rennick, L. L. Judd, K. Schooff & R. Reed. 1978. Organic impairment in polydrug users: risk factors. Am. J. Psychiatry **135:**2.
2. Grant, I., I. Mohns & M. Miller. 1976. A neuropsychological study of polydrug users. Arch. Gen. Psychiatry **33:**973–978.
3. Grant, I. & L. Judd. 1976. Neuropsychological and EEG disturbances in polydrug users. Am. J. Psychiatry **133:**1039–1042.
4. Korin, H. 1974. Comparison of psychometric measures in psychiatric patients using heroin and other drugs. J. Abnorm. Psychol. **83:**(2)208–212.
5. Fields, S. & J. Fullerton. 1975. Influence of heroin addiction on neuropsychological functioning. J. Consult. Clin. Psychol. **43:**(1)114.
6. Bruhn, P. & N. Maage. 1975. Intellectual and neuropsychological functions in young men with heavy and long-term patterns of drug abuse. Am. J. Psychiatry **132:**4.
7. Brown, R. R. & J. E. Partington. 1942. A psychometric comparison of narcotic addicts with hospital attendants. J. Gen. Psychol. **27:**71–79.
8. Pfeffer, A. Z. & D. C. Ruble. 1948. Chronic psychosis and addiction to morphine. Arch. Neurol. Psychiatry **56:**665–672.
9. Russell, E. W., C. Neuringer & G. Goldstein. 1970. Assessment of Brain Damage: A Neuropsychological Key Approach. John Wiley. New York, N.Y.
10. Reitan, R. M. 1958. Validity of the trail making test as an indicator of organic brain damage. Percept. Mot Skills **8:**271–276.
11. Goldstein, G., R. B. Welch, P. M. Rennick & C. H. Shelby. 1973. The validity of a visual searching task as an indicator of brain damage. J. Clin. Consulting Psychol. **41:**(3)434–437.
12. Rennick, P. M. Norms for the Lafayette Clinic Neuropsychological Assessment Battery. P. M. Rennick Neuropsychological Fund. Lafayette Clinic. Detroit, Mich.
13. Kaufman, A. 1965. The substitution test: a survey of studies on organic mental impairment and the role of learning and motor factors in test performance. Cortex **9:**47–63.
14. Duke, R. B. 1967. Intellectual evaluation of brain-damaged patients with a WAIS short form. Psychol. Rep. **20:**858.
15. Eysenck, H. J. 1959. The Manual of the Maudsley Personality Inventory. Univ. of London Press. London, England.
16. Beck, A. T., C. H. Ward, M. Mendelson, *et al.* 1961. An inventory for measuring depression. Arch. Gen. Psychiat. **4:**461–471.
17. Derogatis, L., R. Lipman, K. Rickels, *et al.* 1974. The Hopkins symptom checklist (HSCL): a self-report symptom inventory. Behav. Sci. **19:**1–16.
18. Weissman, M. M. & S. Bothwell. 1976. The assessment of social adjustment by patient self-report. Arch. Gen. Psychiatr. **33:**1111–1115.
19. Endicott, J. & R. L. Spitzer. 1978. A diagnostic interview: The Schedule for Affective Disorders and Schizophrenia. Arch. Gen. Psychiat. **37:**837–844.
20. Lewis, D. O., S. S. Shanok, J. H. Pincus & G. H. Glaser. 1979. Violent juvenile delinquents: psychiatric, neurological, psychological, and abuse factors. J. Am. Acad. Child Psychiatry:307–319.
21. Klove, H. & C. G. Matthews. 1974. Neuropsychological studies of patients with epilepsy. *In* Clinical Neuropsychology: Current Status and Applications. R. Reitan & L. Davison, Eds. John Wiley.

22. Finlayson, M. A. J., K. A. Johnson & R. M. Reitan. 1977. Relationship of level of education to neuropsychological measures in brain-damaged and nonbrain-damaged adults. J. Consul. Clin. Psychology **45:**536–542.
23. Amante, D., V. W. VanHouten, J. H. Grieve, C. A. Bader & P. H. Margules. 1977. Neuropsychological deficit, ethnicity, and socioeconomic status. J. Consul. Clin. Psychology **45:**524–535.

PSYCHOTHERAPY FOR OPIATE ADDICTION: SOME PRELIMINARY RESULTS

George E. Woody, Charles P. O'Brien,
A. Thomas McLellan, and Jim Mintz

University of Pennsylvania Medical Center
Philadelphia, Pennsylvania 19104

While numerous surveys and clinical reports have reported multiple psychiatric problems among opiate addicts,[1–3] most authorities doubt the efficacy of psychotherapy for this condition. Until now, no systematic study of psychotherapy in addicts has been conducted. Many of the psychiatric problems seen in addicts, particularly anxiety states and depression, have traditionally been felt to respond to psychotherapy in nondrug abusers. Some recent clinical reports indicate that a variety of psychiatric problems may accentuate drug use in addicts,[4] thus any treatment that reduces the severity of these problems may add something to the commonly used rehabilitation techniques. During 1976-1978, a series of conferences on these issues were sponsored by NIDA. The conferees agreed that widespread psychopathology existed in drug addicts and that controlled studies of psychotherapy were needed. Earlier studies had been thwarted by extremely high drop-out rates but the conferees felt that this problem would be lessened by methadone treatment. It became clear that any examination of the efficacy of psychotherapy with addicts should be done in combination with methadone treatment. We report preliminary results from one such controlled study.

METHOD

Subjects

The subjects are opiate addicts who are starting a new treatment episode with methadone maintenance. Patients eligible for this study must be between 18 and 55 years of age, cannot be psychotic, must not have subnormal intelligence, or a persistent organic brain syndrome. They must also have some interest in psychotherapy and give informed consent to participate. After initial screening for eligibility, patients complete an intake evaluation and are randomly assigned to one of three treatment conditions: drug counseling alone (DC), counseling plus supportive-expressive therapy (SE) and counseling plus cognitive-behavioral therapy (CB). An outline of the design is seen in FIGURE 1. All sessions are taped and 15 minute segments of each tape are rated by independent observers. These ratings classify therapy type and evaluate speech content and pattern of both therapist and patient.

Treatments

Drug Counseling

Drug counseling is a treatment that focuses on identifying specific needs and delivering concrete services. Its major focus is on providing external services rather than dealing with intrapsychic processes. Counselors monitor progress by reviewing urinalysis reports and vocational situations. They provide liaison services with physicians, courts and social agencies. A typical counseling situation might begin when a counselor meets with his patient, reviews the clinic chart and observes that the urine tests show opiates. He questions the patient regarding what has been happening and how he is feeling. The patient says his methadone dose is not yet high enough, that he is having withdrawal symptoms beginning about 16 hours after he takes his methadone and that he has been using heroin. The counselor then arranges for the patient to meet with the program physician to be evaluated for an increase in his methadone dose. At the same time, the patient mentions that he has a court appearance in two weeks and requests a note for the judge saying that he is participating in a treatment program. The counselor has the patient sign a release of information statement, prepares a note and then gives it to the patient to take to his lawyer. Counselors sometimes also intervene directly in emergencies such as loss of a

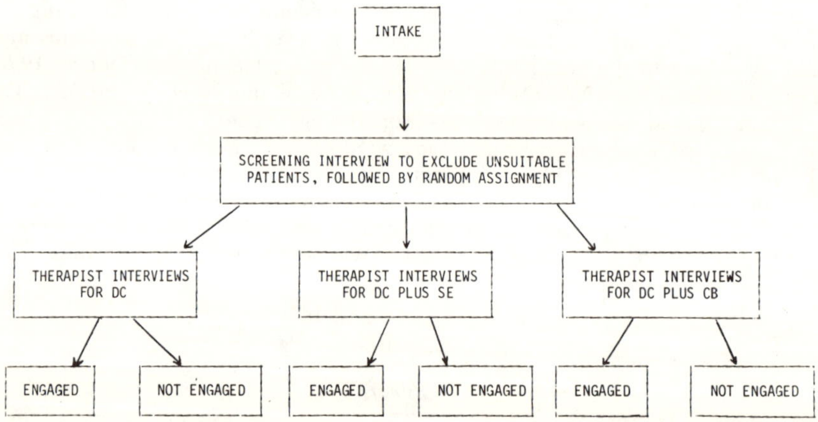

FIGURE 1. An outline of the overall treatment design.

place to live, family crises, or discharge of intense affects, such as anxiety or anger. In these situations they meet with the patient, form an opinion regarding the cause of the problem and often arrange for a meeting with a program physician who then works toward a solution with the counselor and the patient. Drug counseling is similar to the treatment described by Wolberg,[5] and it is described in a treatment manual.[6]

Supportive-Expressive Therapy

Supportive-expressive therapy is an analytically-oriented, focal psychotherapy modeled after that described by Sifneos[7] and Malan.[8] It aims to help the patient identify and work through problematic relationship themes. The therapist identifies these themes via the relationship with the patient (transference), or according to what the patient says about other important relationships such as those with his wife or other family members. Special attention is paid to the meanings that the patient attaches to the drug dependence. For example, a therapist might have a patient who denies having any problems. He keeps appointments out of "curiosity" or because he thinks he "ought to" but he maintains that things are going well in spite of being unemployed and having an unstable living situation. When he has a problem with his girlfriend, he refuses to discuss it, misses several sessions and uses drugs, then asks his counselor to have his methadone dose increased. In this case, the therapist quickly identifies the patient's denial as it appears in the transference, in the relationship with his girlfriend and in his drug use. The therapist works with the patient, aiming to diminish the denial. If the therapist is successful, treatment should help the patient to address his problems more directly, and thus increase the likelihood of finding better solutions to life problems than using drugs.

Cognitive-Behavioral Therapy

Cognitive-behavioral therapy is a treatment that aims to identify and change false beliefs, unhealthy moods and problematic behavior. It is a treatment that has been developed by Dr. Aaron T. Beck and has been shown to be effective for treating certain types of depression. Dr. Beck and his colleagues have found that depressed patients often have false beliefs such as being helpless or worthless and that these negative cognitions have profound influences on mood. Beck and his colleagues have found that reversing these false beliefs can significantly improve the patient's mood. For example, a person is withdrawn, depressed and feels that he is worthless and cannot succeed at anything. A CB therapist, having identified these false beliefs, attacks them actively and directly, aiming to show the patient how and why they are untrue. If the therapist succeeds in reversing them, the patient's mood usually brightens and the associated social withdrawal decreases markedly. During CB therapy, the patient may be required to do "homework" such as recording daily activities and thoughts or deliberately altering certain behaviors. Some false beliefs commonly seen in narcotic addicts are, "I'm a junkie, I'll never get better" or "I can't possibly feel good without drugs." The CB therapist identifies these beliefs and works actively with the addict in the same way that he would with a depressive.

Both CB and SE therapies are described in treatment manuals,[9, 10] as is DC. The manuals were used from the very start in the training and continuing supervision of all therapists and counselors. Dr. Beck is supervising the CB therapists and Dr. Lester Luborsky is training and supervising the SE therapists. The DC therapists are supervised by the clinic physicians, nurses and social workers.

Initiating Treatment

After being randomly assigned to one of these three treatment conditions, the patient is given a brief explanation of the kind of treatment he will receive in the manner described by Orne.[11] The importance of keeping regular appointments is also emphasized at this time. All patients are then required to have at least three meetings with their counselor and their therapist (if they are assigned a therapist) within the first four weeks. These mandatory sessions are required to make sure that all patients have an opportunity to gain some familiarity with the treatment conditions. After these three sessions are completed, patients are encouraged but not required to keep appointments. Patients who do not complete these initial sessions are not counted as part of the study, though data is collected on their progress. Those patients who are assigned a therapist have an opportunity to continue with that person for six months. Evaluation is done at one month post-intake, seven months post-intake and 12 months post-intake. A variety of test studies over these periods of time are done and they are summarized in FIGURE 2.

RESULTS AND DISCUSSION

A summary of all clinic intakes and patient study assignments is presented in FIGURE 3. As seen, about two-thirds (n = 75) of all patients who met the

	INTAKE	1 MONTH	7 MONTH	12 MONTH
CONSENT FORM	✓			
MAUDSLEY PERSONALITY INVENTORY	✓	✓	✓	✓
BECK DEPRESSION INVENTORY	✓	✓	✓	✓
SOCIAL ADJUSTMENT SCALE (WEISSMAN)	✓	✓	✓	✓
SCL 90	✓	✓	✓	✓
SHIPLEY	✓			
RELATIONSHIP INVENTORY - COUNSELOR		✓		
RELATIONSHIP INVENTORY - THERAPIST		✓		
HELPING RELATIONSHIP - COUNSELOR		✓		
HELPING RELATIONSHIP - THERAPIST		✓		
PATIENT TERMINATION FORM			✓	
SCHEDULE FOR AFFECTIVE DISORDERS & SCHIZOPHRENIA - LIFE TIME VERSION	✓			
RESEARCH DIAGNOSTIC CRITERIA	✓			
DSM III	✓			
PREVIOUS TREATMENT FORM	✓			
SCHEDULE FOR AFFECTIVE DISORDERS - CHANGE VERSION	✓	✓	✓	✓
ADDICTION SEVERITY INDEX	✓	✓	✓	✓
BACKGROUND DATA INTERVIEW (BLAINE)	✓			
SOCIAL INFORMATION FORM (LUBORSKY)	✓			
FOLLOW-UP FORM				✓
THERAPIST FACILITATIVE BEHAVIOR		✓		
GOALS OF THERAPY - THERAPIST		✓		
TERMINATION FORM - THERAPIST			✓	
COUNSELOR FACILITATIVE BEHAVIOR		✓		
TERMINATION FORM - COUNSELOR			✓	

FIGURE 2. Psychotherapy study schedule of testing.

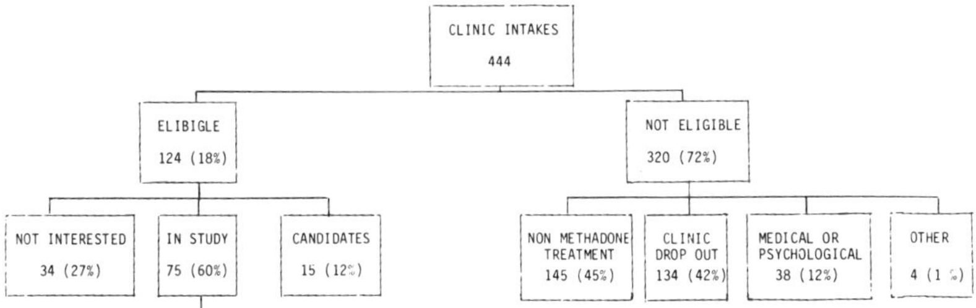

	CB	SE	DC	TOTAL
ACTIVE	7	4	7	18
COMPLETED	15	13	16	44
EARLY DROP OUT	3	5	2	10
ADMIN. DROP OUT	0	2	1	3
TOTAL	25	24	26	75

FIGURE 3. Screening log summary, March 1978–October 1979.

criteria for inclusion had entered the study as of October 30, 1979. Thirteen were early drop-outs. Three of these were administrative drop-outs—one patient was found to be schizophrenic and two patients were discovered to be nonveterans and thus ineligible for treatment. As seen, about half of those not eligible for the project were in this category because they were assigned to non-methadone treatment.

The background status of the first 53 patients who started the project is seen in TABLE 1. The only significance between group differences found was a slightly lower income for the SE group.

TABLE 2 summarizes the frequency of appointments for the first 44 patients to complete six months of therapy. The frequency of appointments with both counselors and therapists for the psychotherapy groups is listed separately (all patients had counselors; two out of every three patients also had psychotherapists). In interpreting this data, it is important to know that the therapists were available an average of 10 hours per week, while counselors were available 35 hours per week. Thus the higher frequency of appointments with counselors could very likely reflect availability rather than acceptability. As seen, a little less than half of the patients in the psychotherapy groups are moderately to heavily engaged with their therapists. It must be emphasized here and throughout the remainder of the paper that this data is preliminary, thus all numbers are small and final conclusions cannot be made. For example, it will be interesting to see if the differences in frequency of appointments seen between the SE and CB groups holds up when more data is available.

FIGURES 4, 5, 6 and 7 show outcome data on the first 35 patients to complete their one-year follow-ups. As seen in FIGURE 4, all groups are showing improvement on the Beck Depression Inventory and the SCL-90, but the psychotherapy groups appear to improve more than the counseling alone group on the Beck. FIGURE 5 shows the percentage of patients in each group who received psychotropic medications each week. Flurazepam hydrochloride (Dalmane)®, chloral hydrate, doxepin (Sinequan)®, and oxazepam (Serax)®

TABLE 1

BACKGROUND AND STATUS AT START OF TREATMENT

	I SE	II CB	III DC	TOTAL
N	15	18	20	53
Age	26 ± 4	28 ± 4	27 ± 4	27 ± 4
Race ($p < .10$)				
% Black	40	33	55	43
% White	60	67	45	57
Yrs. Educ.	12.0	11.8	12.0	12.0
Marital Status				
% Never Married	46	39	40	42
% Div./Sep.	8	28	30	24
% Married/Cohabit.	46	33	30	34
Soc.-Econ.-Stat.				
% Above Average	18	11	20	17
% Average	39	33	40	40
% Below Average	43	56	40	43
Income Prev. Mo.*	$1035	$1244	$1138	$1154

* = $p < .05$ (Groups underlined are *not* significantly different).

prescriptions account for the great majority of these medications. As seen, the psychotherapy groups received fewer prescriptions than the drug counseling group. It is important to note that no medications are prescribed by any therapist. Similarly, the methadone doses during the first six months were lower in the psychotherapy groups (FIGURE 6) and the urine tests showed less abuseable drugs for the psychotherapy groups as compared to the drug counseling group (FIGURE 7). We find these data very interesting and definitely suggestive that the psychotherapy is providing an additional positive effect. Some of these results may not be clinically meaningful (such as the difference between 45 and 35 mg of methadone), but others (BDI 6 vs. 10; 16% vs. 10% positive urines) probably are. We think it is significant that all the positive results favor the psychotherapy groups.

TABLE 2

PATIENT ENGAGEMENT IN COUNSELING AND THERAPY
COMPLETED PATIENTS, OCT. 1979 (N = 44)

Number of Sessions	Engagement	DC only	CB DC	CB CB	SE DC	SE SE
3	Intro Sessions	0	0	1(7%)	0	0
4–9	Lightly Engaged	1(6%)	5(35%)	8(53%)	4(31%)	5(38%)
10–18	Moderately Engaged	3(50%)	5(33%)	4(27%)	5(38%)	7(54%)
19+	Heavily Engaged	7(44%)	5(33%)	2(13%)	4(31%)	1(8%)
	Total No. Patients Per Group	16	15		13	
Average No. Sessions	Average No. Sessions	18	14	10	14	12

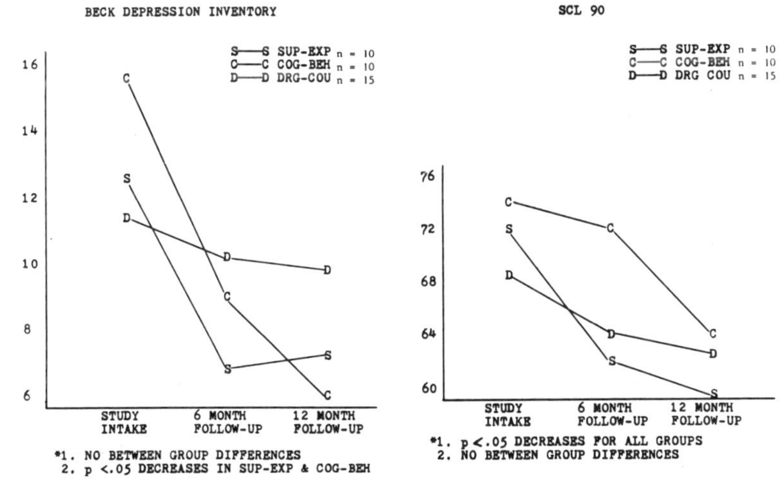

FIGURE 4. All groups show improvement on the Beck Depression Inventory and the SCL-90.

Similar findings are seen in TABLE 3 where Addiction Severity Index (ASI) ratings of patients at intake and at six months are shown. The ASI is a clinical/research interview, designed to assess problem severity in six areas of functioning: medical, employment/support, substance abuse, legal, family/social, and psychological. In each problem area, objective data on the number and extent of problem symptoms is collected along with patients' subjective reports on the duration, severity, and importance of the treatment problem. The interviewer assimilates the two types of information to produce a rating (0–9) of the subjects' problem severity, operationally defined as "need for treatment." These

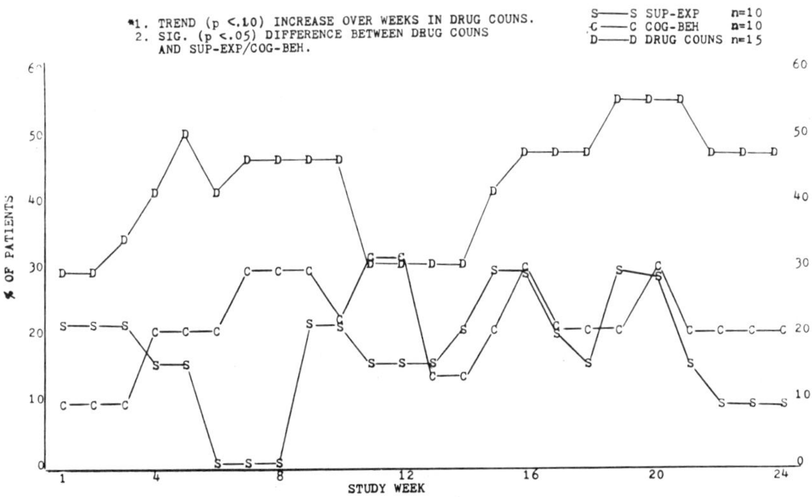

FIGURE 5. Patients receiving ancillary medication by group.

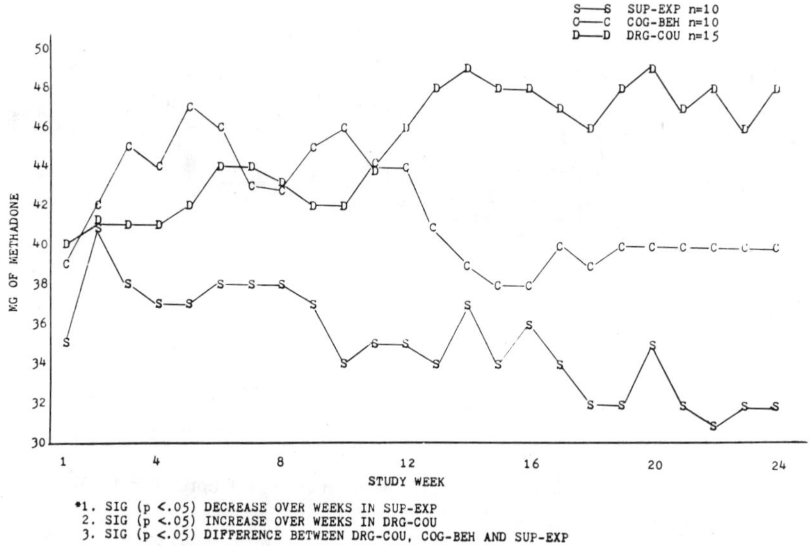

FIGURE 6. Mean methadone dosage by group.

severity ratings have been shown to be reliable and valid general estimates of patient status in each area.[12]

Similar to previous results, all groups are getting better but the psychotherapy patients are showing more improvement than patients receiving counseling alone.

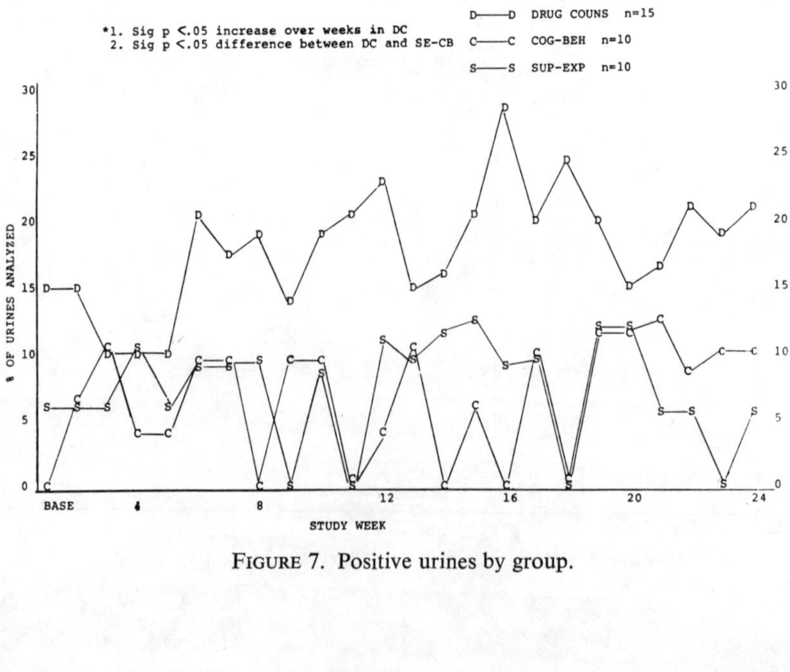

FIGURE 7. Positive urines by group.

TABLE 3

ASI GROUP STATUS COMPARISONS PRE-AND POST STUDY

N	SE 10			CB 10			DC 15			Between Groups Significance	
	Start		6-Mo.	Start		6-Mo.	Start		6-Mo.	Start	6-Mo.
Medical Severity	1.4		2.0	2.0		2.3	2.3		2.8		
Days bothered by med. probs.	2		5	4		6	5		8		
Employment Severity	4.0		3.0	4.0	†	2.8	3.4		4.0		†
Days Worked	8	†	14	7		12	11		13	†	
Money Earned	$354	†	$486	$430	*	$690	$504	†	$576	†	†
Drug Abuse Severity	4.0	*	1.6	4.3	†	2.3	4.1	†	2.9		†
Days used drugs	12	†	4	13	†	6	12		7		
Money spend on drugs (wk.)	$69	*	$8	$81	*	$31	$92	*	$35		†
Legal Severity	2.5	†	1.0	4.0	†	1.8	2.7		2.2		†
Days of criminal activity	4		3	7	†	3	4		4		
Illegal income	$144	*	$39	$272	*	$58	$178	*	$87	†	†
Psychological Severity	2.9	†	1.9	2.6	†	1.5	2.7		2.8		†
Days bothered by psych. probs.	6		4	5		4	5		6		
Family/Social Severity	2.4	†	1.5	2.6		1.8	2.6		2.3		†
Days bothered by F/S probs.	9		6	9		6	10		9		†
Days in Controlled Environment	1		2	0.5		1.5	1		1		

† = $p < .05$.
* = $p < .01$.

Summary

In summary, this preliminary analysis suggests two important points. First, that narcotic addicts enrolled in a methadone treatment program are receptive to psychotherapy. Secondly, that psychotherapy may add something to routine counseling services. As seen, the psychotherapy patients, in this very preliminary analysis, are using fewer drugs (including prescription drugs, methadone and illicit drugs) and they report fewer psychiatric symptoms than those receiving drug counseling alone. We do not think that the design of this project rules out the possibility that these results are nonspecific effects (seeing a "doctor," having an opportunity to see two helpers rather than one), however, we also see nothing here to support the idea that narcotic addicts cannot benefit from the services of professionally trained psychotherapists.

These early analyses represent only a very small portion of the entire range of data collected. We will be especially interested in identifying reasons for improvement in those patients who respond. Preliminary analysis of segments of tapes by the independent raters shows that the raters correctly identified 80% of the therapy tapes. Comparing these independent taped ratings with outcome measures may be a valuable way to assess possible relationships between amount and kind of therapy and treatment outcome. Finally, patient ratings of therapists including the patient's views of the helping relationship may supply additional important information regarding why improvement occurs.

References

1. Weissman, M. W., F. Slobetz, B. Prusoff, M. Mesritz & P. Howard. 1976. Clinical depression among narcotic addicts maintained on methadone in the community. Am. J. Psych. **133:**1434–1438.
2. Woody, G. E., C. P. O'Brien & K. Richels. 1975. Depression and anxiety in heroin addicts: A placebo-controlled study of doxepin in combination with methadone. Am. J. Psych. **132:**447–450.
3. Wurmser, L. 1972. Drug abuse: Nemesis of psychiatry. Am. Scholar 393–407.
4. Khantzian, E. J., J. E. Mack & A. F. Schatzberg. 1974. Heroin use as an attempt to cope: Clinical observations. Am. J. Psych. **131**(2):160–164.
5. Wolberg, L. R. 1967. The Technique of Psychotherapy. 2nd Edit. Grune & Stratton. New York, N.Y.
6. Stockdale, D., F. Hargrove & G. E. Woody. 1977. Individual Treatment Manual for Drug Counseling.
7. Sifneos, P. 1972. Short-Term Psychotherapy and Emotional Crises. Harvard Univ. Press. Cambridge, Mass.
8. Malan, D. 1963. A Study of Brief Psychotherapy. J. B. Lippincott. Philadelphia, Pa.
9. Beck, A. T. & G. D. Emery. 1977. Individual Treatment Manual for Cognitive Behavioral Psychotherapy of Drug Abuse. Copyright by A. T. Beck.
10. Luborsky, L. 1977. Individual Treatment Manual for Supportive-Expressive Psychoanalytically Oriented Psychotherapy: Special Adaptation for Treatment of Drug Dependence. Copyright by Lester Luborsky.
11. Orne, M. & P. Wender. 1968. Anticipatory socialization for psychotherapy: Method and rationale. Am. J. Psych. **124:**88–98.
12. McLellan, A. T., L. Luborsky, G. E. Woody & C. P. O'Brien. 1980. An improved diagnostic evaluation instrument for substance abuse patients: The Addiction Severity Index. J. Nerv. Ment. Dis. **168:**26–33.

CLINICAL STATUS OF METHADYL ACETATE (LAAM)

J. D. Blaine and P. R. Renault

Clinical Behavioral Branch, Division of Research
National Institute on Drug Abuse
Rockville, Maryland 20857

D. B. Thomas

Biometric Research Institute
Washington, D.C. 20007

J. A. Whysner

Medical Research Applications
McLean, Virginia 22101

Introduction

Over thirty years ago, Chen[1] and Isbell[2] first reported on the chemistry, analgesic activity and addiction liability of the methadone-derivative methadyl acetate, LAAM. The early clinical studies of LAAM focused on its morphine-like analgesic properties[3,4] and its opiate-like clinical pharmacological profiles.[5,6] Fraser, Isbell and coworkers demonstrated that a single oral dose of LAAM could relieve and prevent the occurrence of opiate abstinence for up to 72 hours, after the abrupt discontinuation of morphine in morphine-dependent subjects. In the early 1960s, LAAM's usefulness as an analgesic was studied. However, its onset of action, when given parenterally, was delayed and erratic; this problem, as well as its prolonged time course of activity, limited its usefulness for analgesia.

About ten years ago, Jaffe and coworkers first utilized d,1-methadyl acetate (both stereoisomers were included in this preparation) in a narcotic addiction treatment program.[7,8] They found that d,1-methadyl acetate administered orally on Monday, Wednesday, and Friday could be safely and effectively substituted for daily methadone maintenance. Further small-scale controlled clinical trials by this group[9–11] and others[12–15] provided early evidence that LAAM and methadone had comparable safety and effectiveness as maintenance treatments for chronic heroin addiction. Results accumulated on over 750 patients treated with LAAM substantiated early findings that clinically significant toxicity or adverse reactions were absent among LAAM patients and the methadone control group. Also, it was apparent that there had been adequate pharmacological substitution for intravenous heroin since opiate abstinence symptoms did not occur, and there was reduction in intravenous heroin use among the study patients.[15]

The encouraging results from these early clinical trials, coupled with evidence of long-term safety from concurrent animal toxicity studies,[16] gave support for further pharmaceutical development of LAAM. Between 1973 and 1976, two larger scale controlled cooperative Phase II clinical trials were performed to demonstrate the safety and effectiveness of LAAM.[17,18] Finally, an extensive, carefully monitored, cooperative Phase III clinical trial was carried out from 1976 to 1979 to confirm LAAM's safety and effectiveness in a large patient sample, whose background characteristics approximated the population who might receive the drug when it becomes available for general clinical use. Information was obtained to evaluate alternative dosage schedules, incidence of side effects and adverse reactions, potential medical contraindications, and cross-drug interactions.[19]

The major clinical studies of LAAM in males have been completed. The data have been extensively analyzed, and a New Drug Application (NDA) is now under review by the Food and Drug Administration (FDA). The purpose of this paper is to provide an overview of the major safety and efficacy findings from these later, larger-scale cooperative clinical studies. Also, some clinical issues and questions emerging from these studies will be discussed.

Phase II and III Studies

The purpose of the three large-scale multi-site cooperative trials was to establish the safety and efficacy of LAAM, relative to methadone, in a large number of patients followed under a common protocol (Table 1). The first of these, the Veterans Administration Cooperative Study, was a double-blind, fixed-dose study with patients randomized to either LAAM (80 mg. TIW) or one of two doses of methadone: a high (100 mg.) or a low (50 mg.) daily dose. LAAM patients received placebo on their nondrug scheduled days. The protocol specified forty weeks of treatment. Study patients were eligible for the trial if they met the existing criteria (1973) for admission to methadone maintenance programs, as defined by the FDA, and were males between the ages of 18 and 60. Patients were excluded for incapacitating or life-threatening conditions, disease requiring regular repeated medication, frankly psychotic states, epilepsy, current severe alcoholism, and pending criminal charges. Upon signing an informed consent, eligible patients were given a physical examination with psychiatric evaluation, chest X-ray, electrocardiogram, urinalysis, and blood studies.

In the 12 participating clinics, 430 men were inducted; 142 received LAAM and 142 and 146 patients received methadone at 100 mg. and 50 mg. daily, respectively. The first dose in all three groups was 30 mg., which was incremented by 10 mg. on each succeeding Monday until the patient achieved his target dose.

Safety

In order to evaluate safety problems or possible drug toxicity, laboratory data (hematology, blood chemistry, and urinalysis), vital signs and weight were obtained before treatment, at every four-week intervals during treatment, and upon a patient's termination. To evaluate patient complaints, a symptom-sign list of difficulties commonly reported by maintenance patients was elicited weekly for the first eight weeks and then every four weeks thereafter. The complete physical examination was repeated at the twelfth week and at the end of the study. Clinic physicians were obliged to report any adverse reactions to the medical monitor of the study coordinating committee and to follow the patients' course when possible. For all early patient terminations, clinics were

TABLE 1

PHASE II AND III LAAM/METHADONE COMPARATIVE STUDIES—STUDY DESIGN

	VA	SAODAP	Phase III
Sample Size	430 (Males)	772 (Males)	3649 (Males to-date)
Population	Street (Heroin) Addicts	Crossover (Methadone) Patients	Crossover and Street Patients (See Protocols below)
Design	Double-blinded/Fixed dose	Open/Randomized to drug/ Variable dose	Open for drug/Randomization and blind for dosage regimen (Varies with Protocols)
No. of Clinics	12	16	89
Protocols	No. One—Randomized to: Methadone 50mg: 7 days a week (N = 146) Methadone 100mg: 7 days a week (N = 142) LAAM 80mg: 3 days a week (N = 142)	No. One and No. Two—Randomized to: Methadone: 7 days a week (N = 308) LAAM: 3 days a week (N = 328) No. Three—Randomized to: Methadone: 7 days a week (N = 71) LAAM: Methadone Monday through Thursday, LAAM Friday (N = 65) No. (VANGARD) Patients from initial study continued beyond 40 weeks on LAAM (N = 145) or Methadone (N = 129)	No. One Crossover and Street Patients Placed on LAAM 3 days a week (N = 2308) No. Two Crossover and Street Patients Randomized (open) to: LAAM: 3 days a week (N = 816) or Methadone: 7 days a week (N = 525) Supplemental Induction Regimens: No. Three Crossover Patients Randomized to: 3 open dosage regimens of LAAM (N = 178) No. Four Crossover and Street Patients Placed on LAAM and blinded to one of 3 dosage regimens (N = 445) No. Five Crossover and Street Patients Placed on LAAM and blinded to one of 3 dosage regimens (N = 120) Control Group open on Methadone (N = 78) No. Six Patients from initial 40 week study (Protocols 1–5) continued on in an open study on: LAAM (N = 1011); or Methadone (N = 234)

required to determine a primary reason from a pre-established list and also to provide a supporting narrative, detailing the circumstances of the termination. Over the course of this study (and the preceding studies described below), various analyses were carried out to evaluate safety parameters. Statistically, comparisons of changes from baseline and between groups were carried out to detect subtle effects that might have been clinically important. Various algorithms to isolate individuals with outlying values were employed to identify cases for review by the medical monitor. Finally, instances of possible adverse reactions and terminations for reasons that might have been related to the study medication were reviewed by the medical monitor and the study's medical advisory panel.

Efficacy

This study was not designed to establish absolute efficacy, since no placebo or nontreatment group was included. However, previous work had established the ability of both methadone and LAAM to suppress opiate withdrawal and maintain individuals without the supplemental use of illicit narcotics. Thus, it was judged reasonable to assume that both drugs were effective (and also that the three dosing regimens used in this particular study were adequate substitutes for morphine). Although none of the available indices of efficacy are entirely unambiguous, they do provide, in aggregate, a fairly comprehensive picture of patient functioning over the course of the study. The reduction of the use of illicit opiates was considered a primary measure of efficacy and was monitored by a weekly urine screen. The particular test of each patient's urine screen was scheduled according to a random sequence supplied centrally. Specimens were sent to the clinical laboratory at the Sepulveda VA Hospital, where they were tested for morphine, barbiturates, amphetamines, and a variety of other substances. Patient reports and staff assessments of illicit drug use were also recorded at four-week intervals and upon termination of treatment. Retention of patients in maintenance treatment over the trial (40 weeks) was another measure indicative of efficacy. Also, checked reasons for early termination were categorized according to whether they were related to treatment with the drug or for some other reasons.

Secondary to these immediate goals were a variety of indicators of a patient's psychosocial functioning. A global evaluation rating based upon staff consensus was evolved when a patient terminated from the study: several parameters were assessed by this instrument. Finally, a variety of other kinds of information was gathered, either by patient report or staff assessment, regarding contingent effects such as encounters with the law, employment, and patient mood.

The SAODAP Cooperative Study of LAAM compared with methadone differed from the VA protocol in that all patients entered into the study had already been stabilized on methadone for at least three months. Also, the study utilized an open rather than double-blind controlled design. Patients who were randomly assigned to LAAM were abruptly switched (crossed-over) to LAAM on their first study day at a dose which was the same dose as that of methadone (1.0 crossover ratio). Clinicians were allowed to vary dosage in response to changing states of physical dependence or individual requirements. In this study, 636 patients were randomized to either LAAM (N = 328) or methadone (N = 308).

Of the two Phase II studies, the VA trial constituted the primary clinical investigation; the SAODAP Study evaluated the feasibility of crossing patients from methadone to LAAM and also provided adjunct safety and efficacy data. The relative strengths and weaknesses of these two study designs have been discussed previously.[17–19] It is clear that the open design of the SAODAP study increased the level of complaints by patients who were aware that they were assigned to LAAM, an experimental drug. Also, clinicians were more likely to terminate patients with difficulties if they know they were receiving LAAM. Finally, a LAAM patient who tired of the burden of completing forms, being interviewed, and giving urine and blood samples could drop from the study and return to methadone (a drug upon which he had been previously stabilized); no such option was available to the methadone patients. Thus, the interpretations of efficacy data generated in this study must be viewed with caution, although it does provide LAAM safety data on more than twice the number of patients as had been exposed to the drug in the VA study.

The Phase III trial was intended to provide LAAM to a large number of maintenance patients who would be representative of the future intended clinical population and to provide nationwide experience with LAAM. The focus of the study was on producing a large amount of safety-related data on low-incidence phenomena sufficient to provide the FDA with information to approve an NDA for LAAM. Toward this end, most patients in the study were inducted into an uncontrolled trial (Protocol I). For previous methadone patients, crossover ratios of 1.2–1.3 were utilized. Here, data collection involved a complete physical examination, with laboratory studies done and vital signs taken before an initial dose of study medication was given and also upon a patient's termination. Efficacy data included a weekly urine screen for illicit drugs and a termination global evaluation by the clinic staff.

In order to make a comparison with methadone, a second protocol (II) provided for a 60:40 randomization of patients to either LAAM or methadone on an open basis. In this study 816 patients were assigned to LAAM and 525 to methadone. In this protocol the symptom-sign checklist and the Profile of Moods Scale (POMS) were also collected at specified intervals. Finally, several other protocols (III, IV, V) were developed to evaluate the effects of various schedules of induction and crossing-over. These protocols employed various regimens of supplementation with LAAM or methadone and/or gradual increases in LAAM dosage with paralleled decreases in methadone dosages: they have been described in detail elsewhere.[20]

Patient induction in the Phase III trial was closed in April 1979, and data collection ceased on September 15, 1979. A total of 3,649 patients in 89 clinics were inducted into the 40-week trial (3,124 on LAAM and 525 on methadone). Of these, about 20% were street inductees and 80% were crossed over from prior methadone maintenance. A total of 1,133 LAAM patients and 287 methadone patients completed the 40-week phase of the trial. In addition, a continuation phase produced data on 540 patients who had a minimum of 80 weeks experience and 134 patients who were in the trial at least 120 weeks.

In total, over the three studies, a total of 4,715 patients were followed; 3,594 of these were given LAAM and 1,121 were assigned to methadone.

Safety Results

There were no deaths among LAAM patients in the VA study, 4 in the SAODAP study, and 17 in the Phase III trial. Nine of these deaths involved mixed-drug overdose reactions, but in none did LAAM appear to be the primary cause of death in those instances in which the clinic involved had followed the protocol. However, alcohol and other sedative-hypnotics (especially Valium®) were always involved, and drug interactions cannot be ruled out. This topic has recently been discussed at greater length.[21]

During the VA trial, 11 patients terminated primarily for side effects. Of those, only three were not explainable as withdrawal symptoms that manifested early in this fixed-dose study. One methadone-100 patient was terminated because of a pruritic maculopapular rash that developed on study-day two while the patient was still receiving only 30 mg. of the drug. Another patient was terminated for possible bone marrow suppression. The third was a LAAM patient who terminated for fatigue and pains in the chest and both arms; the physician determined that his condition was not related to the study medication. There were no adverse reactions reported in the SAODAP study.[18]

In the larger Phase III trial, three LAAM patients suffered allergic reactions, characterized by combinations of the following: chills, nausea or vomiting, pruritus, myalgia, skin rash, and high or low temperature. One patient terminated for memory loss and rash. Another LAAM patient terminated with vomiting, photophobia, and weakness following a single dose; another manifested diplopia in response to the initial dose. This last reaction was confirmed by a challenge test. Over all the trials, the frequency of the most common of these reactions, except skin rashes, is well under one per thousand patients. Skin rashes, as an isolated finding, occurred somewhat more frequently in both LAAM and methadone patients.

Detailed statistical analyses were carried out on all of the quantitative safety data and involved cross-sectional tests among drug treatment groups, trend analysis of changes from the prestudy scores, and a variety of other models. Due to the large number of variables upon which data were collected and the extensiveness of the analysis plan, a large number of test of significance were calculated, and several of these showed sporadic significant differences between drug treatment groups. There was a persistent, but small, mean drop in red blood cell count, hematocrit and hemoglobin levels in LAAM patients in most protocols across the trials. This change was not clinically meaningful ($\Delta \approx -2\%$) and no individuals were noted as having difficulties in this area. Likewise, in all trials there was a persistent slight mean elevation ($\Delta \approx +1\%$) in blood pressure, both systolic and diastolic, in the methadone groups. Again, no individuals manifested clinically significant changes, nor were there any terminations for this reason.

The symptom-sign record showed the usual complaints associated with patients taking opiates. Complains of constipation, delayed ejaculation, and impotence were particularly common across all trials; of these, constipation was most likely to cause chronic problems for individuals. In the open trials, there was a tendency for a greater number of complaints by LAAM patients although, in the double-blind VA trial, these differences among treatment groups were greatly reduced. LAAM patients reported more difficulties associated with the underdosing syndrome during the initial eight weeks of the trials. These problems were transient: there were fewer complaints later in the studies and also few differences between the LAAM and methadone groups. However, in the VA study, the methadone-50 group experienced mild underdosing symptoms that did persist later into the trial.

Efficacy Results

The primary measure of efficacy, illicit opiate use as detected by weekly urine screens, is most readily interpretable in the double-blind VA trial. FIGURE 1 displays the proportion of urines dirty for opiates across the 40 weeks of this study. The frequency of dirty urines is significantly higher ($p < .05$) in the methadone-50 group from the sixth week on, while LAAM patients have significantly lower frequencies of dirty urines than either methadone group after the thirty-second week.

This relationship was further explored by an analysis of the cohorts of patients who completed at least 24 weeks and 40 weeks in the study (FIGURE 2).

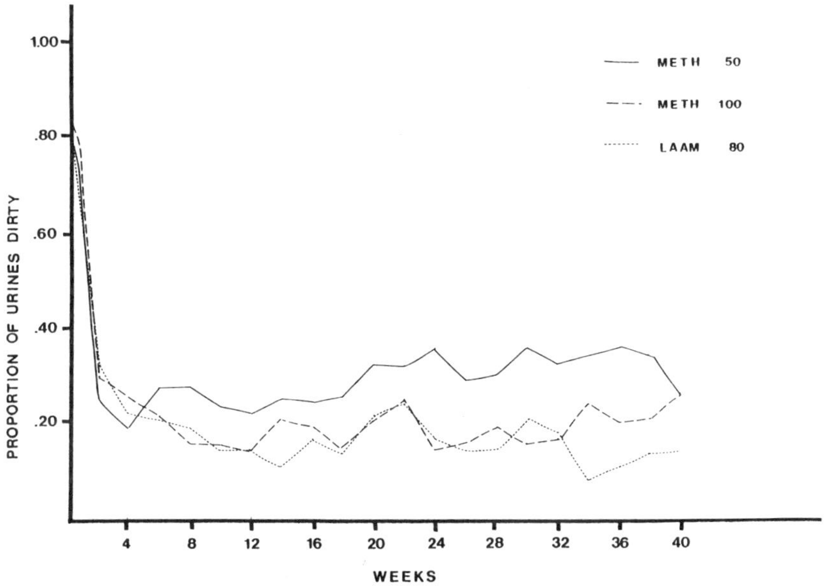

FIGURE 1. Veterans Administration Study: Proportion of urines "dirty" for morphine by study week.

These groups were compared for frequencies of dirty urines during the initial 8 weeks and thereafter. Examination of these proportions indicates that none of the groups in either cohort differed significantly during the first 8 weeks. However, later in the study, methadone-50 patients increased their use of illicit opiates, while the LAAM-80 group showed a pronounced drop in the use of these agents. The cohort analysis shows that this finding reflects a true decrease in illicit opiate use over time, rather than an apparent decrease due to possible differential termination of persistently illicit-opiate-using LAAM subjects. All of the group differences reach statistical significance ($p < .05$) during the later period. While the differences among study medication groups are not as pronounced in the other open trials, the tendency for LAAM patients to have a lower frequency of dirty urines generally persists.

The retention of subjects by study medication group across the 40 weeks of the VA study is shown in FIGURE 3. Here, it is evident that the high-dose methadone group has the highest retention: 54% of the patients finished the trial. The methadone-50 and LAAM-80 groups were somewhat lower, with 43% and 32%, respectively, remaining in the study to 40 weeks. All group differences reach statistical significance ($p \leq .01$). Inspection of the case records of premature terminators showed that a number of LAAM-80 patients, and somewhat fewer methadone-50 patients, terminated during the initial 8 weeks with complaints of underdosing. A second survival curve (FIGURE 4) was generated which "censors out" those individuals. Examination of these

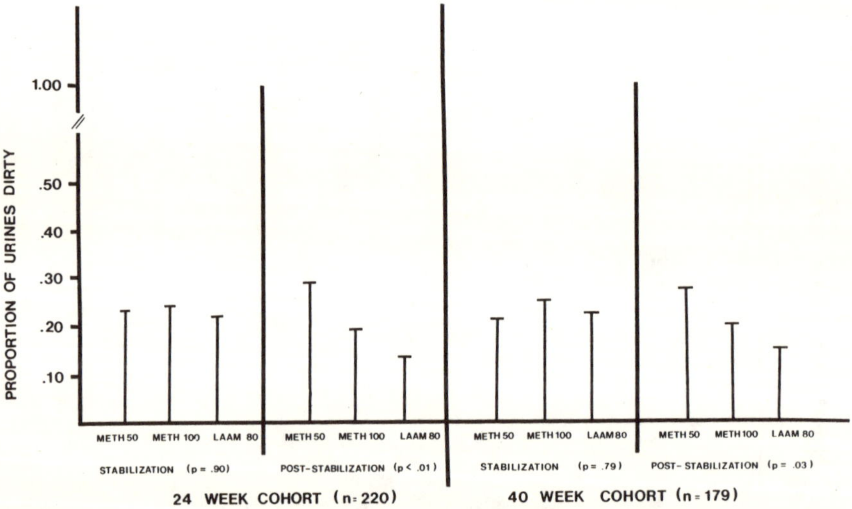

FIGURE 2. Veterans Administration Study: Proportion of urines "dirty" for morphine for the 24 and 40 week cohorts during and after stabilization.

distributions indicates that the group differences are roughly halved, and no group differences reach statistical significance.

Analysis of the patient retention patterns in the SAODAP and Phase III trials shows similar patterns of subject terminations. The effect of removing the earliest terminators who complained of underdosing symptoms has an even more pronounced effect on the proportion of LAAM patients retained. Reviewing the records of LAAM patients who continue in the studies show that the underdosing complaints generally do not persist after stabilization. The distributions of premature terminations within clinics show that in many of them there was no difference, in the rates of early terminations, between LAAM and methadone. Generally, this was true of clinics with the highest overall retention. These relationships would suggest that something other than simple pharmacological effects are involved in the differential drop out rates.

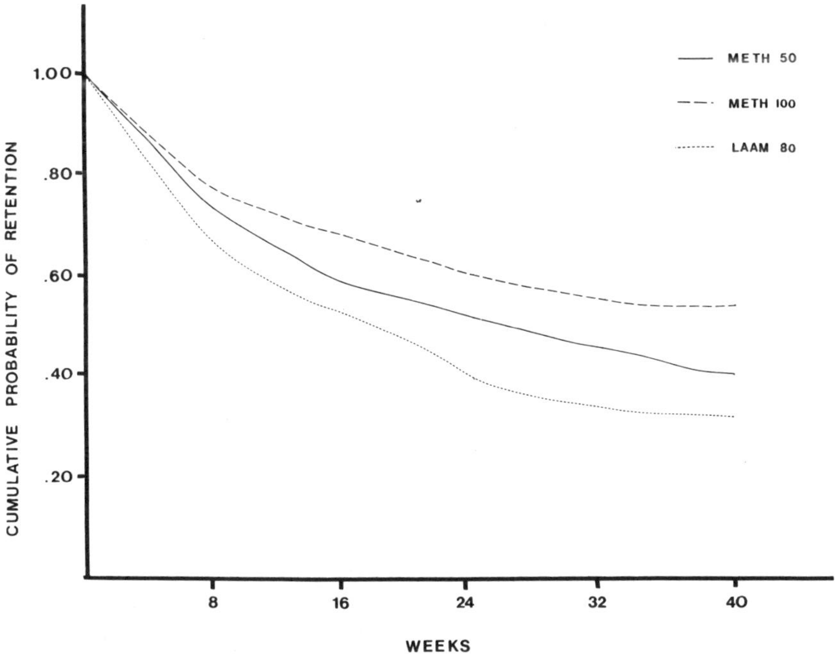

FIGURE 3. Veterans Administration Study: Cumulative probability of retention.

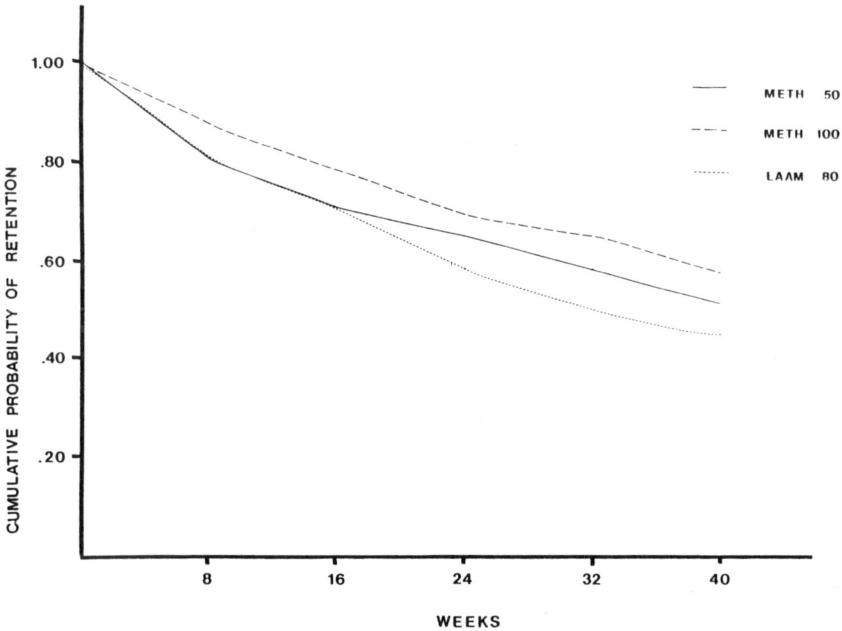

FIGURE 4. Veterans Administration Study: Cumulative probability of retention censoring subjects terminating for underdosing symptoms during stabilization.

Discussion of Results, Conclusions and Implications

Safety Toxicity

Based on the extensive clinical experience with over 3,500 LAAM patients and 1,150 methadone patients in these three large cooperative clinical trials, the evidence unquestionably indicates that LAAM and methadone are comparably safe medications over extended periods (up to 120 weeks). There was no evidence of systematic, progressive, or clinically meaningful changes in any laboratory parameter indicating toxicity. Also, serious adverse reactions were exceedingly rare for both LAAM and methadone. The rate of occurrence was comparable, about two per thousand overall for both drugs. The various manifestations were idiosyncratic and did not reflect any specific organ system involvement.

The only patient-reported complaints were the usual ones associated with opiate dependence: undermedication, overmedication, or nonspecific somatic symptoms (especially impotence, constipation and delayed ejaculation). These opiate effects were generally minimal to mild in severity, transient, occurring more frequently during stabilization (induction or crossover period), and decreasing in frequency thereafter. No medical contraindications or therapeutic cross-drug interactions were found.

The only probable clinical precaution for either of these opiate maintenance agents involves the potentially hazardous interaction with other psychoactive drugs that have depressant actions, especially alcohol, benzodiazapines, sedative-hypnotics and other opiate analgesics. Thus, patients (especially those with uncontrolled polydrug abuse) should be cautioned that the use of these other drugs during maintenance on LAAM or methadone can produce a lethal mixed overdose. Patients are most vulnerable during the stabilization period when tolerance to the depressant effects of the maintenance drugs is not well established and underdosing symptoms are more frequently present.

At first glance, LAAM patients appear more vulnerable to this mixed overdose than methadone patients. However, this conclusion cannot be made with any certainty, due to the absence of an adequate control groups to reliably estimate the incidence of mixed-overdose deaths during methadone induction.

Clinical reports indicate a notable psychotropic difference between LAAM and methadone that is prominent during dosage stabilization. Some LAAM patients feel less sedated or narcotized than methadone patients at comparable dosage levels. These LAAM patients may experience a decreased ability to accurately assess and adjust their psychophysiologic states due to the differing psychoactive properties of LAAM and methadone. Due to the lack of previous experience with LAAM, they may believe that the drug is not working, which may lead to attempts to self-medicate with illicit drugs to correct this assessment of their physiological state. Alternatively, some LAAM patients may simply perceive that they are experiencing less drug-induced euphoria than they are accustomed to feel with methadone and take illicit drugs to alter their state of consciousness.

Efficacy

The evidence indicates that, in general, LAAM and methadone are both efficacious maintenance medications. Both produced dramatic decreases in heroin use by street heroin addicts; these decreases persisted throughout maintenance. The data across all studies indicate that LAAM is somewhat more effective in reducing heroin use. In the double-blind fixed-dose VA study, the data indicated that the LAAM group had statistically and clinically significantly lower levels of involvement with illicit opiates than both methadone groups. The methadone-50 group had persistent multiple complaints related to undermedication after induction than either the LAAM-80 or methadone-100 groups. These findings suggest that the LAAM-80 and methadone-100 regimens were equally efficacious in suppressing the opiate abstinence syndrome, whereas, patients treated with the methadone-50 regimen occasionally relied on illicit opiates to suppress withdrawal. These results are supported by a further study by Ling.[22] These LAAM-methadone differences were less apparent in the SAODAP and Phase III studies, which were compared primarily of patients previously stabilized on methadone at a mean maintenance dose of 50–60 mg. and whose protocols permitted individualized dosage adjustments when necessary. Illicit opiate use was lower among LAAM patients in these studies.

In the VA study, support for the efficacy of both LAAM and methadone is found in the improvement noted in patients in the staff's global assessment of rehabilitation: especially in the two categories, decreased illicit drug use, and criminal justice problems. In the open studies, the results generally favor LAAM, although the specific parameters of marked improvement varied. The major clinical parameter in which methadone is consistently superior to LAAM is termination for symptoms of undermedication—"drug not holding"—during the drug stabilization period. When the retention curves are censored for these terminations, LAAM and methadone retentions are comparable. Again, it should be emphasized that the majority of all premature terminations are for nondrug-related reasons.

Several different phenomena that are artifacts of the study designs appear to contribute to this consistent finding of lower LAAM patient retention.[20] In the open SAODAP and Phase III studies, methadone patients had already been stabilized on this drug. Thus, there was no period of pharmacologic instability for them. Also, knowledge of assignment to either the "experimental drug," LAAM, or the familiar control drug, methadone, introduces the possibility of bias for both patients and staff. The methadone patients and staff knew methadone's effects and no alternative maintenance medication was available for methadone patients if they were dissatisfied with its effects; detoxification being the only other option. In the LAAM group, similar complaints of dissatisfaction with the drug effects were dealt with by terminating the patient from the study and switching him back to methadone. Examination of the dosage records indicates that physicians, inexperienced with and uncertain about LAAM, were often hesitant in responding to undermedication complaints among LAAM patients by increasing a patient's dosage. The fixed-dose protocol of the VA study did not permit individualized dose adjustment to alleviate undermedication. Patients in both the LAAM and the two methadone groups appear to have attempted to compensate for undermedication during induction by self-medicating with heroin. However, the LAAM patients terminated more frequently during induction. This appears to be related to the longer time required for pharmacokinetic stabilization on LAAM (8 weeks) as opposed to that required for low-dose methadone (3 weeks).

The different pharmacokinetic parameters among individuals taking LAAM, as reported by Finkle,[23] may account for the observed discrepancy between two findings: lower illicit heroin use after stabilization, but higher proportions of terminators for undermedication before stabilization. The mean elimination (Beta) half-lives for LAAM and its active metabolites are as follows: [24]

LAAM:	92 ± 7%
n-LAAM:	71 ± 3%
dn-LAAM:	143 ± 6%

For comparison, the elimination half-life of methadone is about 22 ± 7 hours (range, 14–40 hours).[25, 26] When the dose of a drug is given on the half-life or at a shorter interval, approximately 5 half-lives are necessary before steady-state stabilization is achieved. Thus, the average individual reaches stabilized blood LAAM levels in 460 hours (20 days) for LAAM, 355 hours (15 days) for n-LAAM, and 715 hours (30 days) for dn-LAAM, as contrasted with 5 days for methadone. Some proportion of LAAM patients who terminated early due to undermedication may have been slow metabolic converters of LAAM, resulting in undermedication during the early weeks of the trial. Those with a faster metabolic conversion of LAAM may have achieved blood and tissue levels of active drug more rapidly, comparable to the rates in the higher-dose methadone group.

However, given the extremely long half-lives of LAAM and its metabolites and the average dosing interval of 56 hours, substantial amounts of the drug will accumulate in the blood and tissues. This is not the case with methadone, which is dosed on the half-life. Available data indicate that steady state levels of LAAM, nor-LAAM, and di-nor-LAAM are approximately 2.5 to 4.0 times higher than the first-dose levels at the point of crossover from methadone to LAAM. When a 1.0 mg./kgl. dose of LAAM was taken three times a week for a total of ten doses (21 days), the average plasma concentrations 48 hours after the tenth dose were 79 nanograms/ml. for LAAM, 184 nanograms/ml. for nor-LAAM, and 102 nanograms/ml. for di-nor-LAAM (total concentration, 365 nanograms/ml.) [24] In contrast, the average methadone concentration 24 hours after a daily 1.0 mg./kg. dose was 265 nanograms/ml.[26] Thus, although considerably more time is required for LAAM patients to reach stabilized blood levels than for methadone patients, the levels of LAAM and its metabolites actually achieved are considerably higher than the levels of methadone. Furthermore, these levels remain relatively constant through the 48 to 72 hour interdose interval, whereas the methadone level declines by an average of 45%.

Considerable effort was exerted in the Phase III studies to try a variety of dosage schedules to decrease the rate of early LAAM patient terminations. However, none of these alternate induction or crossover regimes produced either statistically or clinically significant improvement in retention or underdosing complaints, compared with the standard three-times-weekly dosage schedule. Although not fully tested in a controlled study, the slightly more rapid schedule for induction of street patients used in the Phase III study, in which a 10 mg. dose increase was given at every third dose, appears to represent some improvement over the VA street induction schedule in which a 10 mg. increase in dosage was made at every fourth dose.

A consistent finding in all these studies was that the inter-clinic differences in early termination rates were greater than the methadone vs. LAAM group differences. For example, in the VA study, the percentage of early terminations was 30% or less in two clinics but 75% or higher in seven clinics. One clinic had about 70% termination the first 88 weeks. At the same time, incidence or underdosing complaints is rather uniformly distributed among clinics. Also, individuals who terminated early did not appear to have significantly more severe complaints than those who did not. Thus, whether a LAAM patient terminates for mild to moderate undermedication symptoms may be more influenced by the practices of clinical staffs, rather than by pharmacological factors. Factors that appear to be associated with retention in maintenance treatment are (1) confidence in the medication, (2) experience, and (3) an available supportive-emphatic therapeutic staff.

Areas for Future Research

Several areas emerge from this review as promising for future research. In terms of the pharmaceutical development of LAAM, a large body of data on comparative detoxification from LAAM and methadone maintenance remains unanalyzed. Given the pharmacokinetic differences between the drugs, LAAM could diminish the severity of abstinence symptoms in the final phase of detoxification and post-detoxification. Clinical reports lend support to this possibility. Second, the analysis of the long-term safety and efficacy data generated in the Phase III trail should be completed. Also, studies comparing the clinical psychopharmacology, safety and efficacy of LAAM and methadone in women should be performed. The possibility of interactions between LAAM and other psychoactive drugs should be explored, although animal studies do not reveal any differences between LAAM and methadone.[27]

A research area deserving high-priority is the elucidation of the particular patient characteristics that determine differential success with LAAM or methadone. Clinical experience has revealed that some patients do well on one drug while others do not. Some patients appear to benefit more than others from the psychopharmacological effect of LAAM, an effect referred to by patients as "feeling normal." Others appear to prefer the different feeling state of methadone. Pharmacokinetic and metabolic differences among patients should be investigated further, as should the relationship between the psychotropic differences between LAAM and methadone and personal expectations about the subjective state of maintenance.

A scientifically interesting area deserving high-priority clinical research is the elucidation of the particular patient characteristics that determine differential success with LAAM or methadone. Clinical experience has revealed that some patients do well on one drug but not the other. Clinicians have reported that dramatic turnabouts in some patients' rehabilitation have occurred when switched to LAAM from methadone, and these individuals are vehement in their desire to remain on this drug. Some patients appear to benefit more than others from the psychopharmacological effect of LAAM, an effect referred to by patients as "feeling normal." Others appear to prefer the different feeling state of methadone. Pharmacokinetic and metabolic differences among patients should be investigated further, as should the relationship between the psychotropic differences between LAAM and methadone and personal expectations about the subjective state of maintenance.

Finally, strategies of treatment program management should be sought, to optimize treatment outcomes with both of these safe and effective medications.

ACKNOWLEDGMENT

The authors would like to thank Gail Levine for her critical comments on the manuscript and drawing the various figures.

REFERENCES

1. CHEN, K. K. 1948. Pharmacology of methadone and related compounds. Ann. N. Y. Acad. Sci. **51:**83–97.
2. ISBELL, H., A. WICKLER, A. J. EISENMAN, M. DAINGERFIELD & E. FRANK. 1948. Liability of addiction to 6-dimethlamino-4-4-diphenyl-3-hepatone in man. Arch. Intern. Med. **82:**362–392.
3. KEATS, A. S. & H. K. BEECHER. 1952. Analgesic activity and toxic effects of acetylmethadol isomers in man. J. Pharmacol. Exp. Ther. **105:**210–215.
4. DAVID, N. A., H. J. SEMLER & P. R. BURGNER. 1956. Control of chronic pain by DL-alpha-acetylmethadol. J. Am. Med. Assoc. **161:**599–603.
5. FRASER, H. F. & H. ISBELL. 1952. Actions and addiction liabilities of alpha-acetylmethadols in man. J. Pharmacol. Exp. Ther. **105**(4):458–465.
6. FRASER, H. F., T. L. NASH, G. D. VANHORN & H. ISBELL. 1954. Use of miotic effect in evaluating analgesic drugs in man. Arch. Inter. Pharmacodyn. Ther. **98:**443–451.
7. JAFFE, J. H., C. R. SCHUSTER, B. B. SMITH & P. H. BLACHLY. 1969. Comparison of DL-alpha-acetylmethadol and methadone in the treatment of narcotics addicts. Pharmacologist **11:**256.
9. JAFFE, J. H. & E. C. SENAY. 1971. Methadone and 1-methadylacetate. Use in management of narcotics addicts. J. Am. Med. Assoc. **216:**1303–1305.
10. JAFFE, J. H., E. C. SENAY, C. R. SCHUSTER, P. F. RENAULT, B. B. SMITH & S. DIMENZA. 1972. Methadyl acetate vs. methadone. A double-blind study in heroin users. J. Am. Med. Assoc. **222:**437–442.
11. SENAY, E. C., P. F. RENAULT, S. DIMENZA, W. E. COLLIER, S. J. DANIELS & W. DORUS. 1975. Three times a week LAAM equals seven times a week methadone: A preliminary report of a control study. Probl. Drug Dep. 543–550.
12. ZAKS, A., M. FINK & A. M. FREEDMAN. 1972. 1-alpha-acetylmethadol in maintenance treatment of opiate dependence. Proceedings of Fourth National Conference on Methadone Treatment: 207–210. San Francisco, Calif.
13. SAVAGE, C., E. KARP, S. CURRAN, T. E. HAWLON & O. L. MCCABE. 1976. A methadone/alpha-acetylmethadol (LAAM) Maintenance: A Comparative Study. Compr. Psychiatry **17:**6415–6424.
14. GOLDSTEIN, A. & B. JUDSON. 1974. Three critical issues in the management of methadone programs: Critical Issue 3: Can the community be protected against the hazards of take-home methadone? Addiction. Peter G. Bourne, Ed.: 140–148. Academic Press. New York, N.Y.
15. BLAINE, J. D. 1978. Early clinical studies of levo-alpha-acetylmethadol (LAAM): An opiate agonist for use in the medical treatment of chronic heroin dependence.. *In* The International Challenge of Drug Abuse. R. C. Peterson, Ed., **19:**249–259. NIDA Research Monograph Series. DHEW. Rockville, Md.
16. WOLVEN, A. & S. ARCHER. 1976. Toxicology of LAAM. *In* Rx 3x/week LAAM: Alternative to Methadone. J. D. Blaine and P. F. Renault, Eds., **8:**29–38. NIDA Research Monograph Series. DHEW. Rockville, Md.
17. LING, W., C. J. KLETT & R. GILLIS. 1978. A Cooperative Clinical Study of Methadyl Acetate. Arch. Gen. Psychiatry **35:**345–353.
18. LING, W., V. C. CHARUVASTRA, S. C. KAIM & C. J. KLETT. 1976. Methadyl Acetate and Methadone as maintenance treatments for heroin addicts. Arch. Gen. Psychiatry **33:**709–720.

19. Blaine, J. D., P. F. Renault, G. L. Levine & J. A. Whysner. 1978. Clinical use of LAAM. Ann. N. Y. Acad. Sci. **311**:214–231.
20. Klett, C. J. 1978. The SAODAP Cooperative Studies of LAAM: Unblinded Comparison with Methadone. *In* The International Challenge of Drug Abuse. R. C. Petersen, Ed. NIDA Research Monograph Series. DHEW. Rockville, Md. **19**:271–276.
21 Thomas, D. B., J. A. Whysner & M. C. Newmann. 1980. The Phase III Clinical Evaluation of LAAM: I. Comparative Epidemiology of LAAM and Methadone. NIDA Research Monograph Series. In press.
22. Ling, W., M. Blakis, E. D. Holmes, C. J. Klett, W. E. Carter. 1980. Re-stabilization on methadone after methadyl acetate (LAAM) maintenance. Arch. Gen. Psychiatry **37**:194–196.
23. Finkle, B. S., T. A. Jennison, D. M. Chinn, W. Ling & E. D. Holmes. The plasma and urine disposition of 1-d-acetyl-methadol and its principal metabolites in man. Clin. Pharmacol. Ther.
24. Barnett, G. 1979. Personal Communication based on pharmacokinetic analysis of data obtained in NIDA Contract No. 271–76–3233 entitled "Metabolism, Pharmacokinetics and quantification of LAAM and metabolites in biological specimens." B. Finkle, Principal Investigator.
25. Inturrisi, C. E. & K. Verebely. 1972. The Levels of Methadone in the plasma in methadone maintenance. Clin. Pharmacol. Ther. **135**:633–637.
26. Verebely, K., J. Volarka, S. J. Mulé & R. Resnick. 1975. Methadone in Man: pharmacokinetic and excretion studies in acute and chronic treatment. Clin. Pharmacol. Ther. **18**:180–190.
27. Braude, M. D. 1978. Personal communication regarding finding of contract with Parke, Davis & Company. Detroit, Mich.

GENERAL DISCUSSION

William A. Frosch, Session Chair

The New York Hospital–Cornell Medical Center
New York, New York 10021

BARRY STIMMEL (*Mount Sinai School of Medicine, New York City*): I'd like to address my comments to Dr. Woody. I would like to compliment him and his colleagues on excellently designed studies. However, based on the data you presented, I find that I cannot agree with any of your interpretations. In the data presented, of the 440 people in your universe, only about 75, or less than 20%, ultimately were eligible and agreed to enter the study. In your data for the first-year follow-up, there were only 10 people in each cohort, and only between 30% and 50% of these were actively committed to therapy. So I have great difficulty in attributing any significance to the changes that you've shown. It's very hard to assign relevance when you say that the dose of methadone dropped about 10 mg. when half of those people in those groups may not have been participants in the study. Do you think that with time you will be able to generate enough people in each group to get a relevant study?

GEORGE WOODY: For a drug addict, private psychotherapy once a week for three months, or every other week for six months, may have a different meaning than for a college student with a neurosis who is going to a psychiatric clinic in a large hospital.

The numbers are small, but there were some significant differences, e.g., the Beck depression scores were higher at intake for the CB group. For the other groups there were no statistically significant differences in the Beck or the methadone dosages or the other measures at intake to the study.

ARNOLD WASHTON (*New York Medical College*): We in New York Medical College are also looking at the effects of psychotherapy on the outcome of addiction treatment. In our case, we studied patients on naltrexone as opposed to your patients on methadone.

In connection with what Dr. Stimmel just said, we assumed from the outset that psychotherapy is not a treatment generally applicable to the addicted population as a whole. We, too, have settled for the point of view that we will work with whatever number of patients remain in the study for a sufficiently long period of time to get some information about its efficacy. Related to the practical problems of getting sufficiently large numbers in studies of this type, why did your patients refuse the treatment?

For example, some patients who are randomly assigned to therapy might refuse participation in the study because of what they've heard about psychotherapy, which they do not want. Others who are slated by random assignment to get no therapy may have dropped out because they, in fact, wanted psychotherapy. So, I'd like to know, in your experience, what the reasons have been for refusing the treatment.

GEORGE WOODY: It's always hard to tell. There could be a lot of reasons. Sometimes it's a purely practical reason. Other times we have patients who become involved in treatment and then they seem to back away from it. In our estimation, part of the resistance to therapy in some people was fear of the process. The patient who seems to have a lot of very strong dependency needs, meets with his therapist three or four times and then starts developing feelings of anger, disappointment, and tension. That seems to us to be related to the therapeutic process. During the early part of the study, some patients refused treatment because they wanted psychotherapy and were not slated to get it.

JAMES MADDUX (*San Antonio*): I have a question for Dr. Woody on his important study. Heroin users are not well known for their capacity to engage in any kind of ongoing psychotherapy. Of those who you said were willing to start, how many of them had dropped out by the end of three months' treatment? And of those who did stay, what did the therapists do to hold them in therapy?

GEORGE WOODY: A lot of the patients at least said they wanted therapy, though about 20% dropped out early in treatment. The therapists' main maneuver is to try to avoid the resistance to keeping regular appointments that comes up in the course of therapy with many of these patients.

JAMES MADDUX: They were able to continue on methadone if they did drop out?

GEORGE WOODY: Yes, that's right.

PETER GESSNER (*Buffalo, New York*): Dr. Mendelson, you mentioned that the people had to respond continuously for three hours to obtain the drug or the money. Could you be a little more explicit; what rate of pressing did they require?

JACK MENDELSON: Simply, the subject had to respond every second in order for the response to count. Responses made more frequently than one second would not count. So that over a period of one hour, a subject would have to emit 3,600 responses in order to get an hour's worth of points. Multiply that by three and you've got one dose of heroin.

BARRY STIMMEL: And a sore thumb.

JACK MENDELSON: That is a lot of behavior. I'm sure some of you are concerned with the conceptualization of craving, a very difficult concept to get a handle on. Someone craves something. How do you know it? They use it, that's why they crave it. It's circular. This is not to demean an individual's subjective feeling states and verbal reports of craving. What we've tried to do is operationalize through behavior an output that an individual can give to us through time which essentially says, "I want the drug," or "I want the money," and each button-press over an hour, two hours, or nine hours, tells us exactly what the subject desires at that particular moment.

MARY JEANNE KREEK: Dr. Mendelson, I wonder if in your very elegant studies with buprenorphine you have seen any subjective or objective differences in response to heroin as the trial went on. Wording it a different way, did you ever try to use heroin placebo in the self-administration design and were these subjective or objective findings in each patient assessed?

JACK MENDELSON: We did not use in any of our designs a heroin placebo, but we did very carefully assess the reaction to heroin following self-administration. Succinctly, the blockade that was achieved with buprenorphine was equivalent to what one would see with the pretreatment of 50 to 100 mg. of naltrexone. The subjects did not perceive that they were getting a heroin effect.

Does tolerance develop through time to the antagonist effects? I don't know. In our studies, we couldn't answer that because once subjects were on buprenorphine, they could make the discrimination that they were on it after a blocked self-administration of heroin. Thus, it was more prudent for them to work for money than for heroin. So we didn't have any heroin probes. But tolerance very definitely develops to buprenorphine agonist effects.

MARY JEANNE KREEK: The liking for buprenorphine on a milligram weight basis was almost similar to, or slightly greater than, the liking for morphine, according to yours and the earlier studies. Did that liking for buprenorphine itself decrease with time?

JACK MENDELSON: No, the liking persisted. There was something rather curious about what buprenorphine did in terms of subjective feeling states. It seemed to produce a sense of well-being without producing the "high," the "rush," the "coasting," or the "soap-boxing."

Y. F. JACQUET: I wanted to ask whether the behavioral effects that you observed during buprenorphine maintenance were due to an antagonist action, that is, blockade of the opiate receptor, or to some agonist action, or would you say it was a mixed action?

JACK MENDELSON: I would say mixed. The question is an important one. Is the blockade effect due to the induction of cross-tolerance? For lack of better terminology, it may resemble cross-tolerance following stabilization of methadone. Or it may be due to an antagonistic effect. I suspect that it's a mixture of both. The antagonistic action is very pronounced and very real.

I would just amplify on that a bit. In the clinical studies that have been done to determine the efficacy of buprenorphine for the treatment of pain, the potency, as I have pointed out, is 25 or more times greater than that of morphine. However, the duration of action is about equivalent.

In other words, the duration of action of pain relief for a dose of buprenorphine, equivalent to 10 mg. of morphine, is about 4 to 6 hours. However, other agonistic actions do appear to remain for very long periods of time. For example, meiosis persists for a duration of over 24 hours, so that agonist action certainly is dissociated from the analgesic action.

PART V. ADVERSE EFFECTS OF DRUGS OF ABUSE

ADVERSE EFFECTS OF MARIJUANA: SELECTED ISSUES

Sidney Cohen

Department of Psychiatry
Neuropsychiatric Institute
University of California at Los Angeles
Los Angeles, California 90024

Our consciousness about the impact of environmental factors upon human physical and psychological health has been raised in recent years. Of particular interest is the presence of those suspect molecular configurations that penetrate one orifice or other. The smoke of certain plant materials has been under study, and more recently, the pyrolytic products of the dried leaves and tops of *Cannabis sativa* have come under scrutiny.

In considering the custom of the deliberate inhalation of marijuana smoke, three elements are worth examining for any adverse consequences that might accrue from long term exposure.

Chronicity of Use

Although untoward effects from the acute use of marijuana are known, they are infrequent and usually of lesser import. It is the consistent indulgence in substantial amounts that increases the element of risk. For this reason the continuing trend toward increasing frequency of use is perturbing. The daily user was once infrequently counted, now daily and multiple daily use seems to be the mode. As with alcohol and other psychotropic drugs, the total dose over time is decisive in the emergence of many pathological changes.

One other direction that the unfolding marijuana scene is taking is, therefore, disquieting. It is the tendency for younger age groups to become increasingly involved in the habit. This gives the chronic user a longer time period to acquire cannabis-related adverse effects.

The Mode of Incorporation

The predominant technique for achieving the intoxicated state is by inhaling the gaseous and particulate products of cannabis combustion. This method is not the most fortunate from a public health standpoint. When combusted plant materials (specifically tobacco and cannabis) are regularly inhaled, the bronchial mucosa is exposed to polyaromatic hydrocarbons (PAHs) and other noxious compounds. The question of chronic inflammatory and neoplastic reactions arises. These will be discussed later.

The Repetitive Intoxicated State

No matter how achieved, intoxication poses certain risks, particularly in a complex, high technology society. These dangers are well known; there is no need to dwell upon them. Of greater concern are the protracted, sometimes daylong intoxications over years. Being stoned during much of one's waking hours is particularly undesirable during the formative years when critical coping techniques should be mastered. When preadolescents and adolescents employ marijuana, but not only marijuana, to distance themselves from the problems and frustrations of their existence, they do themselves a substantial disservice. They deprive themselves of learning time and, may never learn the strategies for living this admittedly difficult life.

It is these three elements: high density use over time, the inhalation of smoke products, and the practice of frequent intermittent intoxications that I find most disquieting in the developing marijuana story. I would like to select two areas, the pulmonary and the residual psychological effects for somewhat more detailed consideration although other systems such as the endocrine, the immunologic and the synthesis of cellular proteins have also been brought into question.

Chronic Pulmonary Issues

Carcinogenesis

In 1912 Adler [1] wrote a monograph on lung cancer. The disease was such a rarity at that time that the author actually questioned the importance of his article by asking at the onset: "Is it worthwhile to write a monograph on primary malignant tumors of the lung?" By the 1930s the answer was clear. A sharp increase in bronchogenic carcinoma took place that has continued to the present, and the evidence that the etiologic factor is cigarettes is most persuasive. The question arises: Are we in the prodromal phases of another wave of lung cancer morbidity, this time due to cannabis?

Let us look at some data. Hoffman *et al.*[2] analyzed the gaseous and particulate phases of marijuana and tobacco smoke for carcinogens, cocarcinogens and cilia toxic agents. On the basis of their results, presented in TABLES 1 and 2, they concluded that "with the exception of the cannabinoids and nicotine, both inhalants are qualitatively similar." Actually, marijuana smoke contains 50% more of carcinogenic PAHs including benzo(a)pyrene. Novotny [3, 4] disagrees with the notion of qualitative similarity of marijuana and tobacco smoke. He found a number of higher molecular weight PAHs that were not detectable in tobacco smoke. The tobacco cigarette used in Hoffman's analysis was Kentucky Burley, equivalent to a standard high tar cigarette. The comparison would have been weighed in favor of tobacco if a low tar cigarette had been analyzed.

Only a small percentage of tobacco smokers develop lung cancer. Those who do apparently develop high levels of aryl hydrocarbon hydroxylase (AHH) induction after smoking. Marijuana smoke likewise induces AHH, and it is that enzyme that converts the PAHs into their ultimate carcinogenic form.

A standard assay for the carcinogenicity of tobacco tar is the application of smoke condensates to mouse skin. Cottrell *et al.*[5] applied marijuana smoke condensate to mouse skin for five days and observed metaplasia of the sebaceous glands, a finding that correlates well with carcinogenic activity. Hoffman *et al.*[2] applied tobacco or marijuana condensates to the shaved backs of mice for 74 weeks. They observed tumors in both groups with more tumors and fewer

TABLE 1

GAS PHASE ANALYSIS *

	Marijuana Cigarette	Tobacco Cigarette
Carbon Monoxide (Vol.%)	3.99	4.58
(mg.)	17.6	20.2
Carbon Dioxide (Vol.%)	8.27	9.38
(mg.)	57.3	65.0
Ammonia (μg)	228	178
HCN (μg)	532	498
Isoprene (μg)	83	310
Acetaldehyde (μg)	1,200	980
Acetone (μg)	443	578
Acrolein (μg)	92	85
Acetonitrile (μg)	132	123
Benzene (μg)	76	67
Toluene (μg)	112	108
Dimethylnitrosamine (ng)	75	84
Methylethylnitrosame (ng)	27	30

* (From Hoffman *et al.*[2])

survivors in the tobacco group. Acetone extracts of the leaves were not mutagenic. It is the tars, not the cannabinoids that are the causative factor in tumor formation.

Human and animal lung explant investigations examining the changes produced by tobacco and marijuana smoke have been conducted over the past several years.[6] Inhibition of DNA synthesis and atypical cell proliferation progressing to malignant transformation occurred in three to six months as compared to the controls which required 12–24 months. When the malignant

TABLE 2

PARTICULATE MATTER ANALYSIS *

	Marijuana Cigarette	Tobacco Cigarette
Phenol (μg)	76.8	138.5
o-Cresol (μg)	17.9	24
m-,p-cresol (μg)	54.4	65
2,4 and 2,5 dimethylphenol (μg)	6.8	14.4
Cannabidiol (μg)	190	—
Δ^9 THC (μg)	820	—
Nicotine (μg)	—	2,850
Napthalene (ng)	3,000	1,200
1-methyl Napthalene (ng)	6,100	3,650
2-methyl Napthalene (ng)	3,600	1,400
Benzo(a)anthracene (ng)	75	43
Benzo(a)pyrene (ng)	31	22.1

* (From Hoffman *et al.*[2])

cells were injected into mice, fibrosarcomas developed. The marijuana smoke was said to be more effective in producing the malignant cells than tobacco smoke, but it should be emphasized that the smoke of both drugs acted as carcinoma accelerators, not initiators, since the control group eventually developed sarcomas.

Inflammatory and Obstructive Lung Disease

In some animal studies[7-9] equivalent amounts of marijuana and tobacco produced changes consisting of bronchiolitis suggestive of early emphysema. Clinical studies of American soldiers consuming large amounts of hashish in the European theatre reported bronchitis, asthma and rhinopharyngitis.[10] Biopsies of the bronchial mucosa revealed atypical cells, basal cell hyperplasia and squamous cell metaplasia more consistently for the marijuana and tobacco groups than of those who smoked either drug alone. Overseas studies in Costa Rica, Jamaica and Greece of chronic cannabis users did not confirm the decrement in pulmonary dysfunction mentioned above.

In this country experimental investigations have generally shown evidence of early constrictive pulmonary disease in marijuana and marijuana-tobacco users.[11] In at least one study the narrowing of the airway was much greater for marijuana than for tobacco.[12]

Pulmonary alveolar macrophage activity is impaired with both tobacco and marijuana smoke when tested against staphyloccocus albus.[13] Aspergillosis is a rare cause of pulmonary disease in marijuana users and is reported only in those who bury their marijuana in the earth for aging, and who also happen to be immunosensitive to that fungus.

Assuming that the coal tars in tobacco and cannabis are approximately equivalent, then it may seem obvious that cigarette smokers are at greater risk simply because they smoke more. While the gap is closing, the average smoker of tobacco consumes 10 to 20 times more by weight than the average cannabis smoker. The different techniques of usage may equalize some of the disparity in dose since the cannabis smoker tends to inhale deeply and keep the smoke in the lungs as long as possible. It is interesting that neither of the active ingredients, nicotine nor delta-9-tetrahydrocannabinol contribute much to either the chronic respiratory disease nor to formation of lung neoplasms. Their impact is observed on other organ systems.

Of considerable clinical significance are the additive effects of marijuana and tobacco smoking. Their combined use is frequent, and in a recent publication,[14] 23 of 23 heavy cannabis and tobacco users had one or more histopathologic abnormalities on bronchial biopsy. Two of seven cannabis only smokers and one of three tobacco only smokers showed such pathology with none of three nonsmokers having any histopathologic lesions.

Residual Mental Effects

To me another significant question about cannabis, is whether long term, substantial use leads to psychological impairment during the interval when drugs are not used. Although some information is available that contributes to an answer to this question, the level of confidence for any sort of position on this point is not high.

In this matter the chronic, heavy juvenile consumer is again at particular risk. First, he will have a longer life span to develop adverse mental symptoms, and secondly, the developing brain may be more sensitive to cannabis than the adult brain. Our research efforts into this matter are deficient. We do not know the numbers of consistent users in the 8 to 12 year-old-age group. We have not studied a sample of young people intensively over time to arrive at an impression of the impact, if any, upon their mental functioning while not intoxicated. We have not even tested young animals thoroughly for their unintoxicated performance and behavior after long term exposure. I must emphasize that I am not speaking about the occasional use of marijuana, rather of what could be called chronic cannabism extending over years or decades.

The issue revolves around the condition clinically called the amotivational syndrome. Mental dulling, emotional blunting and loss of drive and goal directedness are the personality changes described. No doubt some of these people are amotivated for reasons other than drugs, and marijuana simply reinforces their withdrawal. Others seem to be obtunded by the drug and have no choice but to function in a more passive, less goal directed manner. Not infrequently, a veneer of pseudoequanimity and pseudoenlightenment overlays the mild confusion and memorial difficulties.

That some people become ambitionless and sluggish under the influence of a considerable amount of cannabis should not be surprising. THC is a central nervous system depressant and chronic daytime intoxication with any sedative will demotivate people. The fact that it takes weeks to years for the process to reverse itself is more difficult to explain, and the long retention time of THC in lipids like brain tissue does not directly resolve the issue. It is necessary to postulate organic brain impairment, and Heath's [15] depth electrode work may or may not be the neuroelectrical expression of the clinically manifest impairment.

The youngsters call the amotivational syndrome, "burnout." They identify their friends as burnt out, less frequently themselves, or they recognize their own impairment in retrospect only after stopping marihuana use for a few months. Not everyone seems to recover their mental agility, alertness and motivation even after months.

We are well aware of the neurotoxicity of chronic alcoholism. What about cannabism? Does it also produce a chronic brain syndrome? It is possible to selectively cite the literature either way; little is gained in a review of this confusing literature now.

Summary

I have selected two areas of concern about cannabis that have emerged because new patterns of usage are perceptible over the past few years. In the case of pulmonary pathology there is good reason to suspect that long term use can result in inflammatory or neoplastic changes, particularly when the lung has a double burden of dealing with both tobacco and cannabis smoke. With reference to chronic, substantial cannabis use and its impact on brain function, the definitive studies are yet to be done. If clinical impressions are meaningful, some people, especially young people, can sustain temporary and perhaps permanent impairment of nonintoxicated mental performance.

References

1. Adler, I. 1912. Primary malignant growths of the lungs and bronchi. Longmans, Green & Company. New York, N.Y.
2. Hoffman, D. L., K. D. Brunemann, G. B. Gori & E. L. Wynder. 1975. On the carcinogenicity of marijuana smoke. Recent Adv. Phytochemistry **9**:63–81.
3. Novotny, M., M. L. Lee & K. D. Bartle. 1975. A possible basis for the higher mutagenicity of marijuana smoke as compared to tobacco smoke. Experientia **32**(3):280–282.
4. Novotny, M., M. L. Lee & K. D. Bartle. 1976. Gas chromatography mass spectrographic and nuclear magnetic resonance spectrometric studies of carcinogenic polynuclear aromatic hydrocarbons in tobacco and marijuana smoke condensates. Anal. Chem. **28**(2):405–411.
5. Cottrell, J. C., S. S. Sohn & W. H. Vogel. 1973. Toxic effects of marijuana tar on mouse skin. Arch. Environ. Health. **26**:277–278.
6. Leuchtenberger, C. & R. Leuchtenberger. 1976. Cytological and cytochemical studies of the effects of fresh marijuana cigarette smoke on the growth and DNA metabolism of animal and human lung cultures. *In* Pharmacology of Marijuana. M. C. Braude & S. Szara, Eds. **2**:595–612. Raven Press. New York, N.Y.
7. Fleishman, R. W., J. R. Baker & H. Rosenkrantz. 1979. Pulmonary pathologic changes in rats exposed to marijuana smoke for one year. Toxicol. Appl. Pharmacol. **47**:557–566.
8. Roy, P. E., F. Magnan-Lapointe & N. D. Huy. 1976. Chronic inhalation of marijuana and tobacco smoke in dogs. Pulmonary pathology. Res. Commun. Chem. Pathol. Pharmacol. **14**(2):305–317.
9. Sullivan, M. F. & D. H. Willard. 1978. The beagle dog as an animal model for smoking studies. Toxicol. Appl. Pharmacol. **45**:445–462.
10. Tennant, F. S., M. Preble & T. J. Pendergast. 1971. Medical manifestations associated with hashish. J. Am. Med. Assoc. **216**:1965–1968.
11. Tashkin, D. P., B. J. Shapiro & Y. E. Lee. 1976. Subacute effects of heavy marijuana smoking on pulmonary function in healthy men. N. Engl. J. Med. **294**:125–129.
12. Tashkin, D. P., B. M. Calvarese, M. S. Simmons & B. J. Shapiro. 1978. Presented at the annual meeting of the American Thoracic Society. Boston, Mass.
13. Huber, G. L., G. A. Simmons, C. R. McCarthy, M. B. Cutting & R. Laguarda. 1975. Depressant effects of marijuana smoke on antibactericidal activity of pulmonary alveolar macraphages. Chest. **6**:769–773.
14. Tennant, F. S., R. L. Guerry & R. L. Henderson. 1980. Histopathologic and clinical abnormalities of the respiratory system in chronic hashish smokers. Substance Abuse & Alcohol. In press.
15. Heath, R. G. 1976. Marijuana and delta-9-tetrahydrocannabinol: Acute and chronic effects on brain function of monkeys. *In* Pharmacology of Marijuana. M. C. Braude & S. Szara, Eds. **2**:345–356. Raven Press. New York, N.Y.

ADVERSE EFFECTS OF COCAINE: SELECTED ISSUES

Lester Grinspoon and James B. Bakalar

Department of Psychiatry
Harvard Medical School
Boston, Massachusetts 02115

Until recently scientific knowledge about cocaine use and abuse was very limited, and most of it was based on studies more than fifty years old. There were no controlled experiments on human beings; even the clinical literature was sparse and affected by the limitations and prejudices of an earlier era. Recently cocaine has been gaining popularity on the street faster than any other drug, and, partly as a result, more significant work has been done on it in the last five years than in the preceding forty. This research is of several kinds: controlled experiments on human beings and animals, animal studies aimed at discovering theoretical models of psychosis, studies on medical uses, clinical reports on adverse effects and treatment, surveys and sociological reports on illicit use, chemical detection and identification studies. There have been no surprising discoveries, but we have put our knowledge on a sounder basis and filled gaps in it. And since illicit use has become so widespread, it is easier to judge the effects and dangers of cocaine as it is ordinarily used, avoiding the bias and sensationalism that often accompany insufficient information. Our emphasis will be on work done in the last five years even when the results are a confirmation or summary of knowledge familiar from earlier work.

Acute Effects

The central stimulant and sympathomimetic effects of cocaine are familiar: euphoria, energy, increased heart rate and blood pressure, confidence, dilated pupils, constriction of peripheral blood vessels, rise in body temperature and metabolic rate. A recent study [1] examines the cardiovascular and subjective effects of intravenous cocaine in nine subjects. Cocaine, dextroamphetamine, and placebo were administered in a controlled, double-blind experiment. The effects of cocaine on heart rate, blood pressure, respiratory rate, and mood increased as the dose was raised from 4 to 32 mg. Major effects were experienced only at doses of 16 mg. and above; subjects rated doses of 24 and 32 mg. as among the highest they had ever taken. Dextroamphetamine (10 mg.) was equivalent to 8–16 mg. of cocaine, and subjects usually had trouble distinguishing between the two drugs, although the effects of dextroamphetamine were sometimes perceived as lasting longer. The authors conclude that the stimulant action of cocaine resembles that of amphetamine. In another controlled study intranasal (snorting) and intravenous routes were compared. Nineteen illicit cocaine users took doses of 10 mg. and 25 mg. intranasally and intravenously, and 100 mg. intranasally. The 10 mg. intranasal dose had no observable subjective or physiological effect; at 25 mg. there was a rise in systolic blood pressure (no other physiological effects) and some euphoria (the most commonly reported feeling was relaxation). One hundred mg. affected mood strongly and also raised heart rate and diastolic blood pressure, but not respiratory rate or body temperature. Intravenous cocaine had marked physiological and mood effects even at the 10 mg. dose. In its effect on blood pressure, 25 mg. of intravenous cocaine was equivalent to 20 mg. of oral dextroamphetamine in another study. Twenty to thirty minutes after the 25 mg. intravenous dose and 45–60 minutes after the 100 mg. intranasal dose, a few subjects suffered a mild letdown during which they experienced lethargy, irritability, and a desire for more cocaine.[2] The average street dose of cocaine, it is worth noting, is 20 to 50 mg. intranasally.

A report on the effects of intravenous cocaine in rhesus monkeys at doses of .05 to 5 mg. per kg. indicates increases in respiratory rate, body temperature, and heart rate only at the largest dose, while increases in pupil size and changes in motor activity and other behavior begin at 0.2 mg. per kg. Changes in behavior were more clearly correlated with dose than physiological changes, and they occurred at much lower doses; for example, monkeys would press levers for a dose as low as 0.05 mg. per kg.[3]

Cocaine has been administered to depressed patients orally and intravenously.[4, 5] Oral cocaine produced no consistent changes in mood and behavior up to a dose of 200 mg., although it reduced sleep time. Intravenous cocaine at doses of 2.5 to 25 mg. produced marked physiological and mood effects: heart and respiratory rates and blood pressure rose, and patients experienced a tearful emotional catharsis.

In another study cocaine was administered to normal subjects in 10% solution intranasally at doses of 0.19 to 1.5 mg. per kg. There was no consistent cardiovascular effect, and the peak blood concentration came about 60 minutes after application, much later than the high point of euphoria reported in street use of cocaine.[6]

The last five years have put us in a better position than before to estimate the kinds and magnitude of adverse reactions. Studies of recreational users suggest that for the great majority, undesired effects are rare and not serious.[7–9] But some authorities familiar with the street scene insist that both laboratory experiments and surveys tend to underestimate their number and severity.[10] The most common undesirable effect is a feeling of irritability and lassitude after the effects subside, with a desire for more of the drug. Physicians in attendance at rock music concerts and elsewhere have reported an acute anxiety reaction with symptoms including high blood pressure, racing heart, anxiety, and paranoia.[11] More severe effects like tactile and other hallucinations and delusions are uncommon but do occur. Hospitals rarely see cases of cocaine psychosis, but a few have been reported, mainly in habitual cocaine abusers;[10] it is qualitatively similar to amphetamine psychosis but lasts a shorter time, and for that reason, among others, rarely comes to the attention of physicians.

In high doses cocaine can cause depression of the medullary centers and death from cardiac or, more often, respiratory arrest. But in practice severe physical poisoning and death from the toxic effects are rare. There are no well-documented anaphylactic (allergic) reactions.[12] Six cases of death from cocaine poisoning in 1970–1973 are recorded in a 1974 paper:[13] in every case the cocaine was apparently either injected intravenously or eaten in large quantities. Another study of cocaine-related death[14] finds five documented cases and adds nine more, three of which involved cocaine alone, always taken intravenously; in the other cases alcohol, morphine, or other drugs were also involved. In a three-year survey of Dallas County, Texas, the authors of this study found only two of a total of at least 228 deaths caused by drugs in which cocaine was present at all. Another recent study uses data from coroners' and medical examiners' offices over an area with a population of 63,000,000.[15] In the period 1971–1976, 111 fatalities were found in which cocaine was somehow involved. Twenty-five of the 111 were not toxic overdoses but deaths by murder, suicide, or accident related to drug use. Only twenty-six of the 111 cases involved cocaine alone, without other drugs. The increase from 2 deaths associated with cocaine in 1971 to 29 in the first six months of 1976 suggests both more cocaine use and more awareness of cocaine on the part of coroners and medical examiners. Of the twenty-six deaths associated with cocaine alone, four (15.4%) were from oral cocaine, either suicides or smuggling incidents; two (7.7%) were from intranasal use; the rest were from intravenous injection or the method of administration was unknown. Six of the 26 were suicides. Most of the deaths were from respiratory arrest preceded by seizures. Deaths from opiates and cocaine in combination were more common than deaths from cocaine alone. A still more recent study of 68 deaths associated with the recreational use of cocaine from the Medical Examiner's Office of Dade County in Florida found that over a 10-year period, 24 persons died directly of the toxic effects of cocaine. The drug was taken intravenously in 11 instances, orally in 7, and nasally in 5 (the method of administration was undetermined in one case). All but one of the oral cocaine fatalities were due to overdoses which arose from attempts to use the gastrointestinal tract as a place to hide the drug from authorities.[16] From May 1975 to April 1976 medical examiners reported to the Federal Drug Abuse Warning Network (DAWN) 57 cocaine-related deaths, including 6 (out of 4,668 drug-related deaths) that involved cocaine alone.[17]

For acute cocaine overdose, the recommended treatment is administration of oxygen (under pressure if necessary) with the patient's head down in the Trendelenburg position, muscle relaxants if required to accomplish this, and, if there are convulsions, intravenous short-acting barbiturates (e.g., 25–50 mg. sodium pentothal).[18] For the anxiety reaction with hypertension and tachycardia, 10 to 30 mg. of intravenous or intramuscular diazepam has been recommended. An alternative that seems to be a specific antagonist of cocaine's sympathomimetic effects is propranolol (Inderal®), a blocker of peripheral adrenergic receptors. Fifty cases have been successfully treated with one mg. of propranolol injected intravenously every minute for up to eight minutes.* [11,19]

Because cocaine increases energy and confidence and can produce irritability and paranoia, it has often been said to cause physical aggression and crime. Although it clearly can do so in some circumstances[20] there is no evidence of any consistent association. The effects on aggressive behavior have been studied in mice, monkeys, and pigeons.[21, 22] Like caffeine and nicotine, cocaine in-

* A warning should be added. In a letter to the *New England Journal of Medicine* (December 1, 1977), John D. Catravas and several colleagues at the University of Mississippi describe a controlled experiment in which they gave dogs intravenous propranolol (6 to 10 mg. per kg.) and an hour later a fatal dose of cocaine. The propranolol did not prevent or retard death, although pretreatment with chlorpromazine did. The authors warn that propranolol is effective at best only against moderate overdose and should not be regarded as a protection against lethal dangers.

creases nonattack behavior produced by a noxious stimulus more than it increases attack behavior; in contrast, dextroamphetamine causes a relative increase in attack responses. What little evidence there is suggests that cocaine is not as conducive to aggression as other drugs like alcohol, barbiturates, and amphetamines.

Chronic Effects

These have recently been summarized with detailed references.[20] It is important not to attribute to ordinary recreational use the kinds of pathological effects observed in high-dose intravenous injection by laboratory animals. If it is used no more than two or three times a week, cocaine creates no serious problems.[7, 9] Taken daily in fairly large amounts, it can disrupt eating and sleeping habits, produce minor psychological disturbances including irritability and difficulty in concentration, and create a serious psychological dependence.[7, 8] Although there is no physical dependence, sometimes mild withdrawal with anxiety and depression arise. Perceptual disturbance (especially pseudohallucinations), paranoid thinking, and rarely, psychoses also occur in chronic users.[7, 10] Runny or clogged noses are common; often they are treated with nasal decongestant sprays. Less often, noses may become inflamed, swollen, or ulcerated; in the older literature there are reports of perforated septa, but it is hard to find them today. All the undesirable effects (except, of course, nasal problems) are much more commonly produced by intravenous injection.

In experiments where unlimited access to intravenous cocaine is provided, animals will kill themselves by voluntary injections. In one recent experiment, for example, monkeys to whom intravenous cocaine was available 23 hours a day (infusion of 0.2 mg. per kg.) developed hyperactivity, tactile hallucinations, ataxia, severe weight loss, tremors, and convulsions as they continued to inject the drug; they died within five days. Methamphetamine and dextroamphetamine had similar effects.[23]

Although human beings do not use cocaine in this way, craving can become a serious problem for those who have constant access to it. Users sometimes find it necessary to deny themselves access to cocaine for a few days or weeks;[8] some have been known to try to lock up their bank accounts so that they will not spend all their money on it.[24] Because of this potential for psychological dependence and the accompanying problems, people familiar with cocaine are aware of a need for caution in using it.

Dependence potential varies with route of administration. For example, animal experiments continue to show that intravenous cocaine is one of the most powerful, possibly the most powerful of drug reinforcers.[25–27]

Recently some people have taken to smoking cocaine in the form of cocaine base, which is less subject to decomposition on heating than cocaine hydrochloride, the form in which it is usually taken intranasally. In a group of 99 cocaine users recently studied by Ronald Siegel, 8 were regular smokers of cocaine base. The pattern of use is similar to that of intravenous injection and may present similar dangers of dependency and overdose.[9] Monkeys smoking cocaine-base cigarettes containing 0.58% cocaine titrate their doses to about 160 mg. of cocaine a day and show no serious adverse effects; the result is similar when they chew cocaine hydrochloride chewing gum. But smokers in Peru use a concentrated paste containing 40% to 85% cocaine sulfate; this may resemble intravenous cocaine in its effects.[28] It is not yet clear how common cocaine smoking is likely to become or how dangerous it will prove to be.

Other issues explored in recent research are tolerance and sensitization. Recent experience has confirmed that at the usual recreational doses tolerance to the euphoric effect does not arise. One study on monkeys found progressive tolerance to the convulsive effect of daily high intravenous doses (starting at 3.1 mg. per kg.), which disappeared after 40 days when the drug was discontinued. Tolerance also developed for cardiac and respiratory stimulant effects in this experiment.[29] But other studies have found that chronic treatment lowers rather than raises the convulsive threshold in rats.[30] More undisputed are the phenomena of reverse tolerance or sensitization observed in animal experiments. Rats show increasing hyperactivity and stereotyped movements for an hour or two after each of a series of daily injections of the same dose.[31-33] This increased sensitivity endures for as much as seven weeks after the drug is discontinued.[34] Several theories have been developed to account for the sensitization effect,[30] which is also produced by amphetamines. It may partly account for the fact that stimulant psychoses occur mainly in chronic abusers who take a higher dose than usual for a short time.

At present chronic cocaine abuse does not commonly appear as a medical problem, and there is little literature on treatment. For chronic cocaine abusers who appear at clinics in a state of anxiety, diazepam or chloral hydrate has been recommended. For long-term treatment the only recommendations are very general—counselling or psychotherapy.[18]

Animal experiments and some human cases show that cocaine has a real potential for abuse, but at the present level of use it does not present many serious social or medical problems. For example, according to the records of DAWN, in May 1975–April 1976 cocaine alone or in combination with other drugs was involved in only 3.6% of cases at drug crisis intervention centers and less than one percent of drug cases in hospital emergency rooms.[17] The Client Oriented Data Acquisition Process (CODAP) reports that 1.2% of clients appearing at federally funded drug treatment facilities in 1975–1976 (about 650 clients in all) gave cocaine as their primary drug of abuse; another 4% reported cocaine as a secondary drug problem.[35] It is hard to say what the reality behind the statistics is, since they say nothing about the nature or real causes of the problems faced by cocaine users. Some authorities contend that there is much hidden cocaine abuse, especially in combination with depressants like barbiturates, heroin, and alcohol,[10] some of which has serious consequences that do not come to the attention of any treatment system. In general, cocaine seems to present some of the same dangers as the amphetamines, but in a less severe form. Most cocaine users have learned ways of taking the drug that prevent adverse effects. Whether the present high price and limited accessibility are also crucial in forestalling abuse remains to be seen.

References

1. Fischman, M. W., C. R. Schuster, L. Resnekov, J. F. E. Schick, N. A. Krasnegor, W. Fennell & D. X. Freedman. 1976. Cardiovascular and subjective effects of intravenous cocaine in rats. Arch. Gen. Psychiatry **33**:983–989.
2. Resnick, R. B., R. S. Kestenbaum & L. K. Schwartz. 1977. Acute systematic effects of cocaine in man: A controlled study by intranasal and intravenous

routes of administration. *In* Cocaine and Other Stimulants. E. H. Ellinwood, Jr. and M. M. Kilbey, Eds. Plenum. New York, N.Y.

3. Wilson, M. C., J. A. Bedford, J. Buelke & A. H. Kibbe. 1976. Acute pharmacological activity of intravenous cocaine in the rhesus monkey. Psychopharmacol. Communications **2:**251–261.
4. Post, R. M., J. Kotin & F. M. Goodwin. 1974. The effects of cocaine on depressed patients. Am. J. Psychiatry. **131:**511–517.
5. Post, R. M., J. C. Gillin, R. J. Wyatt & F. K. Goodwin. 1974. The effect of orally administered cocaine on sleep of depressed patients. Psychopharmacologia **37:**59–66.
6. Byck, R., P. Jatlow, P. Barash & C. Van Dyke. 1977. Cocaine: Blood concentration and physiological effect after intranasal application in man. *In* Cocaine and Other Stimulants. E. H. Ellinwood, Jr. and M. M. Kilbey, Eds. Plenum. New York, N.Y.
7. Siegel, R. K. 1977. Cocaine: Recreational use and intoxication. *In* Cocaine 1977. R. C. Petersen and R. C. Stillman, Eds. U.S. Government Printing Office. Washington, D.C.
8. Waldorf, D., S. Murphy, C. Reinarman & B. Joyce. 1977. Doing coke: An ethnography of cocaine users and sellers. Drug Abuse Council. Washington, D.C.
9. Siegel, R. K. 1979. Long-term effects of recreational cocaine use: A four year study. Presented at the International Seminar about the Medico-Sociological Aspects of Coca and Cocaine. Lima, Peru.
10. Wesson, D. R. & D. E. Smith. 1977. Cocaine: Its use for central nervous system stimulation including recreational and medical uses. *In* Cocaine 1977. R. C. Petersen & R. C. Stillman, Eds. Government Printing Office. Washington, D.C.
11. Rappolt, R. T., G. R. Gay & D. S. Inaba. 1976. Propranolol in the treatment of cardiopressor effects of cocaine. N. Engl. J. Med. **295:**448.
12. Van Dyke, C. & R. Byck. 1977. Cocaine: 1884–1974. *In* Cocaine and Other Stimulants. E. H. Ellinwood, Jr. & M. M. Kilbey, Eds. Plenum Press. New York, N.Y.
13. Price, K. R. 1974. Fatal cocaine poisoning. J. Forensic Sci. Soc. **14:**329–333.
14. Lundberg, G. D., J. C. Garriott, P. C. Reynolds, R. H. Cravey & R. F. Shaw. 1977. Cocaine-related death. J. Forensic Sci. **22:**402–408.
15. Finkle, B S. & K. L. McCloskey. 1977. The forensic toxicology of cocaine. *In* Cocaine 1977. R. C. Petersen & R. C. Stillman, Eds. U.S. Government Printing Office. Washington, D.C.
16. Wetli, C. V. & R. K. Wright. 1979. Death caused by recreational cocaine use. J. Am. Med. Assoc. **241:**2519–2522.
17. Petersen, R. C. 1977. Cocaine: An overview. *In* Cocaine 1977. R. C. Petersen & R. C. Stillman, Eds. U.S. Government Printing Office. Washington, D.C.
18. Gay, G. R. & D. S. Inaba. 1976. Acute and chronic toxicology of cocaine abuse: Current sociology, treatment, and rehabilitation. *In* Cocaine: Chemical, Biological, Clinical, Social and Treatment Aspects. S. J. Mulé, Ed. CRC Press. Cleveland, Ohio.
19. Rappolt, R. T., G. R. Gay & D. S. Inaba. 1977. Propranolol: A specific antagonist to cocaine. Clin. Toxicol. **10:**265–271.
20. Grinspoon, L. & J. B. Bakalar. 1976. Cocaine: A Drug and Its Social Evolution. Basic Books. New York, N.Y.
21. Hutchinson, R. R., G. S. Emley & N. A. Krasnegor. 1976. The effects of cocaine on aggressive behavior. *In* Cocaine: Chemical, Biological, Clinical, Social and Treatment Aspects. S. J. Mulé, Ed. CRC Press. Cleveland, Ohio.
22. Hutchinson, R. R., G. S. Emley & N. A. Krasnegor. 1977. The effects of cocaine on the aggressive behavior of mice, pigeons, and squirrel monkeys. *In* Cocaine and Other Stimulants. E. H. Ellinwood, Jr. & M. M. Kilbey, Eds. Plenum Press. New York, N.Y.

23. Johanson, C. E., R. L. Balister & K. Bonese. 1976. Self-administration of psychoactive drugs: The effects of unlimited access. Pharmacol. Biochem. Behav. **4:**45–51.
24. Resnick, R. B. & E. Schuyten-Resnick. 1976. Clinical aspects of cocaine: Assessment of cocaine abuse behavior in man. *In* Cocaine: Chemical, Biological, Clinical, and Social Treatment Aspects. S. J. Mulé, Ed. CRC Press. Cleveland, Ohio.
25. Woods, J. 1977. Behavioral effects of cocaine in animals. *In* Cocaine 1977. R. C. Petersen & R. C. Stillman, Eds. U.S. Government Printing Office. Washington, D.C.
26. Goldberg, S. R. & R. T. Kelleher. 1977. Reinforcement of behavior by cocaine injections. *In* Cocaine and Other Stimulants. E. H. Ellinwood, Jr. & M. M. Kilbey, Eds. Plenum Press. New York, N.Y.
27. Johanson, C. E. & C. R. Schuster. 1975. A choice procedure for drug reinforcers: Cocaine and methylphenidate in the rhesus monkey. J. Pharm. Exper. Therap. **193:**676–688.
28. Siegel, R. K. & M. E. Jarvik. 1979. Self-regulation of coca-chewing and cocaine-smoking by monkeys. Presented at the InterAmerican Seminar about the Medico-Sociological Aspects of Coca and Cocaine. Lima, Peru.
29. Matsuzaki, M. 1976. Effects of cocaine on the electrical activity of the brain and cardiorespiratory functions and the development of tolerance in the central nervous system. *In* Cocaine: Chemical, Biological, Clinical, Social, and Treatment Aspects. S. J. Mulé, Ed. CRC Press. Cleveland, Ohio.
30. Stripling, J. S. & E. H. Ellinwood, Jr. 1977. Sensitization to cocaine following administration in the rat. *In* Cocaine and Other Stimulants. E. H. Ellinwood, Jr. & M. M. Kilbey, Eds. Plenum Press. New York, N.Y.
31. Post, R. M. & H. Rose. 1976. Increasing effects of repetitive cocaine administration in the rat. Nature. **260:**731–732.
32. Stripling, J. S. & E. H. Ellinwood, Jr. 1976. Cocaine: Physiological and behavioral effects of acute and chronic administration. *In* Cocaine: Chemical, Biological, Clinical, Social, and Treatment Aspects. S. J. Mulé, Ed. CRC Press. Cleveland, Ohio.
33. Kilbey, M. M. & E. H. Ellinwood, Jr. 1977a. Reverse tolerance to stimulant induced abnormal behavior. Life Sci. **20:**1063–1076.
34. Kilbey, M. M. & E. H. Ellinwood, Jr. 1977b. Chronic administration of stimulant drugs: Response modification. *In* Cocaine and Other Stimulants. E. H. Ellinwood, Jr. & M. M. Kilbey, Eds. Plenum Press. New York, N.Y.
35. Siguel, E. 1977. Characteristics of clients admitted to treatment for cocaine abuse. *In* Cocaine 1977. R. C. Petersen & R. C. Stillman, Eds. U.S. Government Printing Office. Washington, D.C.

ALCOHOLISM: MEDICAL COMPLICATIONS

Charles S. Lieber

Alcohol Research and Treatment Center
Section and Laboratory of Liver Disease and Nutrition
Bronx Veterans Administration Medical Center and
the Mount Sinai School of Medicine (CUNY)
New York, New York 10029

Alcoholism is now generally recognized to be a major, if not the major, social problem confronting our society today. Of particular concern has been its steady growth. Indeed, over the last three to four decades there has been a significant increase in alcoholism, with present statistics estimating 10 million alcoholics in the United States alone. In large American hospital systems, such as that of the Veterans Administration, the incidence of alcoholism and its medical complications is considered second only to cardiovascular disease.

In particular, the prevalence of cirrhosis of the liver has now reached such a magnitude that this complication of alcoholism represents, in and by itself, a major public health problem. We now recognize that 75% of all deaths attributable to alcoholism are due to cirrhosis of the liver. In the United States, cirrhosis has overtaken diabetes as the fifth cause of mortality; in large urban areas, it has become the third cause of all deaths in the active age group of 25 to 65 years. Although not all cirrhotic subjects are alcoholics, it is generally recognized that a majority of patients with cirrhosis do admit to excessive alcohol consumption.

For some years, my associates and I have been studying the physiologic effects of alcohol on the body, especially on the liver. These findings have had significant implications for the management of acute and chronic alcoholism. Until 20 years ago it was generally believed that alcohol intake was not directly, but only indirectly, responsible for the liver disease of the alcoholic. It was considered that liver disorders were not due to alcohol itself but merely to the nutritional deficiencies so commonly associated with alcoholism and that, given an adequate diet, alcohol was not more toxic to the liver than other caloric rich substances such as fats or carbohydrates. This concept had direct impact on the management of the alcoholic. When reluctant to stop drinking, the alcoholic was advised by his physician that he could preserve normal liver function provided that he maintained a normal diet. This approach, however, was not very satisfactory. A number of individuals appeared to develop alcoholic liver disease despite an apparently adequate diet. Subsequently, our findings, along with those of other investigators, clearly established that even in the absence of dietary deficiencies ethanol can produce both acute and chronic changes, both structural and functional, directly in the liver [1] and indirectly in other organs and organ systems.[2] Some of these changes are irreversible, and, contrary to prior medical dogma, most of these changes are not caused simply by malnutrition in the chronic alcoholic; rather, they are the direct toxic effects of alcohol or its breakdown products. In addition, we have worked out in considerable detail many of the biochemical mechanisms by which alcohol produces its pathologic effects.

The effects of hepatic cellular metabolism and structure were found to depend mainly on the dose and duration of intake. The metabolism of ethanol, even at moderate concentrations, results in alteration of a number of hepatic functions because of the change in the hepatic redox state (NAD/NADH ratio) associated with the oxidation of ethanol via the alcohol dehydrogenase pathway.[3] This results, for instance, in decreased lipid oxidation,[4, 5] hyperlactacidemia and hyperuricemia.[6] The most striking and injurious effects occur after the chronic consumption of relatively large amounts of ethanol.

Prior to the development of this phase of injury, however, one can distinguish an initial stage of "adaptation." Indeed, chronic ethanol consumption, at least in its early stages, produces adaptive proliferation and metabolic changes in the endoplasmic reticulum (also called microsomal fraction), which results primarily in increased metabolism of ethanol,[7] other drugs,[8] and accelerated lipoprotein production [9] (with hyperlipemia). Side effects of the increased microsomal activity include activation of the hepatotoxicity of various compounds (through their conversion to toxic metabolites in the endoplasmic reticulum) [10] conversion of procarcinogens to carcinogens,[11] acceleration of testosterone catabolism [12] and energy wastage. Deleterious effects of chronic alcohol consumption may also result from an interference with protein secretion and the retention of protein with the associated swelling or ballooning of the hepatocyte.[13] Extended periods of excessive ethanol intake then result in damage to mitochondria, possibly as a consequence of the toxic effects of acetaldehyde,[14] the first product of ethanol metabolism that interacts readily with various proteins. Mitochondrial damage, in turn, results in decreased acetaldehyde metabolism, responsible, at least in part, for an unusually elevated acetaldehyde level in the alcoholic.[15]

The reproduction, in the baboon,[16] of the entire spectrum of alcohol-induced liver injury despite the concurrent ingestion of an adequate diet ingestion confirmed not only the direct toxic effects of alcohol but also led to the discovery that pericentral sclerosis is a precursor lesion which portends evolution towards cirrhosis.[17] The baboon studies also revealed characteristic amino acid changes, which, when applied to man, provided a biochemical index of heavy drinking based on the elevation of alpha-amino-n-butyric acid and glutamyl transpeptidase.[18] This biochemical change may allow for the detection of relapses of heavy drinking at a relative early stage of alcoholism,[19] whereas the pericentral sclerosis, perhaps with associated characteristic increases in the blood of mitochondrial enzymes (such as glutamic dehydrogenase),[20] may help screen those individuals who are in the process of developing cirrhosis.

The concept of the direct toxicity of ethanol upon the liver was also expanded to the gut,[21] the heart,[22] the testicles,[23] and the hematological system.[24] Hematological abnormalities, however, are not only due to the direct toxic effects of ethanol, but seem to be a major consequence of associated nutritional deficiencies, primarily folate deficiency. Abnormalities of the central nervous system also appear to be primarily due to vitamin deficiency, although the direct toxic effects of ethanol on the peripheral and central nervous system have not been ruled out. Similarly, it is not clear to what extent the abnormalities in the metabolism of bone,[25] calcium and other minerals, now more distinctly recognized in the alcoholic, are due to nutritional factors and to what extent direct effects of ethanol are involved. In any event, although malnutrition can occur in the alcoholic and, when present, should be corrected, it is now evident that we must give up the hope of fully preventing alcohol-related complications by merely controlling the diet; it is essential to control alcohol intake.

References

1. LIEBER, C. S., D. P. JONES & L. M. DECARLI. 1965. Effects of prolonged ethanol intake: Production of fatty liver despite adequate diets. J. Clin. Invest. **44:** 1009–1021.
2. LIEBER, C. S. 1977. Metabolism of Ethanol. *In* Metabolic Aspects of Alcoholism. C. S. Lieber, Ed.: (1) 1–29. University Park Press. Baltimore, Maryland.
3. LIEBER, C. S. & C. S. DAVIDSON. 1962. Some metabolic effects of ethyl alcohol. Am. J. Med. **33:**319–327.
4. LIEBER, C. S. & R. SCHMID. 1961. The effect of ethanol on fatty acid metabolism; stimulation of hepatic fatty acid synthesis *in vitro*. J. Clin. Invest. **40:** 394–399.
5. LIEBER, C. S., A. LEFEVRE, N. SPRITZ, L. FEINMAN & L. M. DECARLI. 1967. Difference in hepatic metabolism of long and medium-chain fatty acids: The role of fatty acid chain length in the production of the alcoholic fatty liver. J. Clin. Invest. **46:**1451–1460.
6. LIEBER, C. S., D. P. JONES, M. S. LOSOWSKY & C. S. DAVIDSON. 1962. Interrelation of uric acid and ethanol metabolism in man. J. Clin. Invest.**41:**1863–1870.
7. LIEBER, C. S. & L. M. DECARLI. 1970. Hepatic microsomal ethanol-oxidizing system: *in vitro* characteristics and adaptive properties *in vivo*. J. Biol. Chem. **245:**2505–2512.
8. MISRA, P. S., A. LEFEVRE, H. ISHII, E. RUBIN & C. S. LIEBER. 1971. Increase of ethanol, meprobamate and pentobarbital metabolism after chronic ethanol administration in man and in rats. Amer. J. Med. **51:**346–351.
9. BARAONA, E. & C. S. LIEBER. 1970. Effects of chronic ethanol feeding on serum lipoprotein metabolism in the rat. J. Clin. Invest. **49:**769–778.
10. HASUMURA, Y., R. TESCHKE & C. S. LIEBER. 1974. Increased carbon tetrachloride hepatotoxicity, and its mechanism, after chronic ethanol consumption. Gastroenterology **66:**415–422.
11. SEITZ, H. K., A. J. GARRO & C. S. LIEBER. 1978. Effect of chronic ethanol ingestion on intestinal metabolism and mutagenicity of benzo (α) pyrene. Biochem. Biophys. Res. Commun. **85:**1061–1066.
12. GORDON, G. C., K. ALTMAN, A. L. SOUTHREN, E. RUBIN & C. S. LIEBER. 1976. The effect of alcohol (ethanol) administration on sex hormones metabolism in normal men. New Eng. J. Med. **295:**793–797.
13. BARAONA, E., M. A. LEO, S. A. BOROWSKY & C. S. LIEBER. 1977. Pathogenesis of alcohol-induced accumulation of protein in the liver. J. Clin. Invest. **60:** 546–554.
14. HASUMURA, Y., R. TESCHKE & C. S. LIEBER. 1976. Characteristics of acetaldehyde oxidation in rat liver mitochondria. J. Biol. Chem. **251:**4908–4913.
15. KORSTEN, M. A., S. MATSUZAKI, L. FEINMAN & C. S. LIEBER. 1975. High blood acetaldehyde levels after ethanol administration. Differences between alcoholic and nonalcoholic subjects. New Eng. J. Med. **292:**386–389.
16. LIEBER, C. S. & L. M. DECARLI. 1974. An experimental model of alcohol feeding and liver injury in the baboon. J. Med. Primatology **3:**153–163.
17. VANWAES, L. & C. S. LIEBER. 1977. Early perivenular sclerosis in alcohol fatty liver: An index of progressive liver injury. Gastroenterology **73:**646–650.
18. SHAW, S., B. STIMMEL & C. S. LIEBER. 1976. Plasma alpha amino-n-butyric acid/leucine: An empirical biochemical marker of alcoholism. Science **194:** 1057–1058.
19. SHAW, S., T. M. WORNER, M. F. BORYSOW, R. E. SCHMITZ & C. S. LIEBER. 1979.

Detection of alcoholism relapse: Comparative diagnostic value of MCV, GGTP and AANB. Alcoholism: Clin. Exp. Res. **4:**297–301.

20. VanWaes, L. & C. S. Liever. 1977. Glutamate dehydrogenase, a reliable marker of liver cell necrosis in the alcoholic. Br. Med. J. **2:**1508–1510.
21. Baraona, E., R. D. Pirola & C. S. Lieber. 1974. Small intestinal damage and changes in cell population produced by ethanol ingestion in the rat. Gastroenterology **66:**226–234.
22. Friedman, H. S. & C. S. Lieber. 1977. Cardiotoxicity of alcohol. Cardiovasc. Med. **2:**111–112.
23. Gordon, G. G., A. L. Southren & C. S. Lieber. 1979. Hypogonadism and feminization in the male: a triple effect of alcohol. Alcoholism: Clinical and Experimental Research **3:**210–211.
24. Lindenbaum, J. & C. S. Lieber. 1969. Hematologic effects of alcohol in man in the absence of nutritional deficiency. New Eng. J. Med. **281:**333–338.
25. Saville, P. D. & C. S. Lieber. 1965. Effect of alcohol on growth, bone density and muscle magnesium in the rat. J. Nutr. **87:**477–484.

THE EFFECTS OF NARCOTICS AND ALCOHOL ON PREGNANCY AND THE NEWBORN

Loretta P. Finnegan

Departments of Pediatrics, Psychiatry and Human Behavior
Thomas Jefferson University Hospital
Philadelphia, Pennsylvania 19107

The effects of narcotics and alcohol on pregnancy and the newborn have been known for centuries, but only within the past decade have investigators been able to delineate them more specifically. The pregnant addicted woman and her unborn fetus have become an integral part of the special services provided in perinatal centers in many cities in our country. Although the exact magnitude of narcotic dependency in pregnant women is unknown, by way of "statistical gymnastics" it is currently possible to make estimates of the numbers of infants born to addicted mothers in the United States. The Services Research Branch of the National Institute on Drug Abuse recently reported that 5,000 infants were born to heroin and/or methadone maintained mothers in 1977. The incidence of fetal alcohol syndrome has been reported to be seen in one to two live births per 1,000 births with partial expressions seen in three to five live births per 1,000 births.[1]

Fortunately, with the assistance of investigators using animal models as well as the changing attitudes by medical professionals over the past decade concerning the problems of addiction and alcoholism, we have not only been able to help these individuals more, but have also been able to learn more about their disease entities. Physicians and other medical professionals have recognized that narcotic addiction and alcoholism are serious, chronic, relapsing diseases that need prompt diagnosis and long term treatment. Since pregnant drug dependent women are now welcomed into medical institutions for care during pregnancy, many perinatal centers have developed special programs for these women and have not only been providing service but also conducting research in regard to the effects of narcotics and alcohol upon the fetus and neonate.

This manuscript will review the current literature, as well as the experiences of the author, in regard to the pathophysiological and behavioral effects of the transplacental transfer of narcotic agents and alcohol upon pregnancy, the fetus, and the newborn.

The Effects of Narcotics

Social and Medical Characteristics of the Pregnant Drug-Dependent Woman Influencing the Intrauterine Milieu

The intrauterine milieu of the pregnant drug-dependent woman is greatly influenced by her social and medical characteristics. The pregnant narcotic addict is frequently depressed, lacks confidence and hope for the future, and has extreme difficulty in interpersonal relationships, especially heterosexual relationships. In order to meet her high cost of maintaining a heroin habit, she must often indulge in robbery, forgery, the sale of drugs, or prostitution. She therefore spends her day either in a euphoric state or a sick state during which time she is seeking drugs. She has little concern for a good diet, adequate sleep, or obtaining any prenatal care, the lack of which are known to seriously affect the outcome of pregnancy.[2]

Opiate dependence during pregnancy is not only overwhelming to the physical condition of the woman, but also to that of the fetus and eventually the newborn infant. The vast majority of these women neglect general health care and therefore are predisposed to a host of obstetrical and medical complications during pregnancy. These complications include abortion, abruptio placenta, amnionitis, breech presentation, increased need for Cesarean section, chorioamnionitis, eclampsia, intrauterine death, gestational diabetes, placental insufficiency, postpartum hemorrhage, pre-eclampsia, premature labor, premature rupture of the membranes, and septic thrombophlebitis.[3]

The decrease in birthweight in infants born to heroin addicted mothers has been reported by many investigators.[4–8] Although earlier reports did not differentiate between term infants who were small for gestational age and premature infants, it is evident that many of these low birth weight infants were, in fact, small for gestational age. It was long suspected that low birth weights were related to poor maternal nutrition and health. While these factors may be important, there is laboratory evidence that heroin itself may be a factor in growth retardation.[9–12] However, the mechanism for inhibition of growth by heroin is not known. Several investigators have noted that infants born to women who have used methadone have somewhat higher birth weights than infants born to women using heroin.[13–15]

More specifically, perinatal exposure to methadone has been found to retard the growth of young rats and affect brain development.[10] Studies in salamanders have shown that methadone prevents regeneration of the limbs and can cause taste bud degeneration.[11] Additional studies in rats have shown that methadone, particularly at higher dose levels, reduced maternal weight gain during pregnancy and increased both maternal mortality and total mortality among the young. This included resorptions as well as stillbirths.[12]

Effects of maternal morphine administration on maternal nutrition and on fetal growth in a rabbit model have shown significant inhibition of fetal growth which was not thought to be a result of alterations in maternal food intake, but did appear to be morphine dose dependent. Weight growth appeared to be most severely affected with relative sparing of brain growth. The investigators were not able to determine whether the growth inhibition resulted from a diminution in cell number, in cell size, or both. These investigators felt that the implications of the effects of these fetal growth restrictions on long term growth and development remain unclear. They concluded that narcotic associated fetal growth inhibition in the fetal rabbit does not prove that a similar mechanism is responsible for the observed growth restrictions noted in human offspring born to drug addicted mothers, since fetal narcotic metabolism and the effects of drugs or their metabolites on end organs might be markedly different in various species.[16]

Nearly 50% of women who are heroin dependent and have no prenatal care will deliver low birth weight infants.[17] In contrast, women who are maintained on methadone and who have adequate prenatal care have been reported to have an incidence of low birth weight infants of 20%.[17] These low birth weight infants may either be born prematurely and/or be of less than appropriate weight for their gestational age, even if they are of term gestation. Intrauterine growth retardation is frequently seen in association with not only opiates but also a variety of psychoactive agents including alcohol, amphetamines, barbiturates, and nicotine.[18]

Due to the obvious lack of quality control seen in street drugs, the pregnant woman frequently experiences repeated episodes of withdrawal and overdose. Since it appears that heroin has a direct effect on antenatal growth which cannot be explained on the basis of undernutrition in the mother, it was suggested that periodic episodes of heroin withdrawal during pregnancy might restrict fetal growth by reducing uterine or placental blood flow. However, it is unlikely that a uterine or placental disorder is responsible for the growth retardation since the organ and cellular growth pattern associated with fetal growth retardation in uteroplacental disorders is quite different from that observed in the offspring of heroin addicts. The smallness of organs of infants exposed to heroin in the third trimester was due mainly to a subnormal number of cells. In contrast, in nonaddicted women, undernutrition restricts both size and number of cells in many organs during the last trimester.[20, 21] Withdrawal prenatally, then, may be responsible for additional fetal morbidity. Severe withdrawal is associated with increased muscular activity, thereby increasing the metabolic rate and oxygen consumption in the pregnant woman and accompanied by a state of fetal distress in the unborn fetus. When the pregnant woman begins to withdraw, fetal activity increases, and the oxygen needs of the fetus increase as well. During labor, the fetus may be compromised if the mother is undergoing withdrawal. Severe hypoxia and possibly death may occur in the fetus if it is exposed to an environment of insufficient oxygen for any length of time.[19]

An analysis of birth weights of 337 neonates in relation to history of maternal narcotic usage was undertaken by Kandall and colleagues in 1976.[15] Mean birth weight of infants born to mothers abusing heroin during pregnancy was 2490 grams, an effect primarily of intrauterine growth retardation. Low mean birth weights were also seen in infants born to mothers who had abused heroin *only* prior to this pregnancy (2615 grams) and mothers who had used both heroin and methadone during the pregnancy (2535 grams). Infants born to mothers on methadone maintenance during the pregnancy had significantly higher mean birth weight of 2961 grams, but lower than the control group which was 3176 grams. A highly significant relationship was observed between maternal methadone dosage in the first trimester and birthweight; the higher the dosage, the larger the infant. In contrast to the fact that heroin has been found to cause fetal growth retardation which may persist beyond the period of addiction, this study has shown that *methadone* may promote fetal growth in a dose-related fashion *after* maternal use of heroin.

Similarly, in our own program in Philadelphia, 65 infants born to heroin dependent mothers had a mean birthweight of 2506 grams in contrast to a mean of 2678 grams for 104 infants whose mothers had used heroin and methadone and who had poor prenatal care. Infants whose mothers were maintained on methadone and who had adequate prenatal care had a mean birthweight of 2882 grams. The mean birthweight in any of the three addicted groups did not reach that of control infants born to nonaddicted mothers with or without prenatal care.[17]

If the woman decides to detoxify herself during pregnancy or insists that a physician detoxify her, the unborn fetus may be affected adversely. Detoxification of women during the mid-trimester of pregnancy has been monitored by serial amniotic fluid levels of epinephrine and norepinephrine. The detoxification of the mother showed a marked fetal response of the adrenal gland with an increase in epinephrine and of the sympathetic nervous system with an increase in norepinephrine which was blunted when the methadone dose was increased.[22] Fortunately, with the current advances in perinatology, fetal monitoring is available in such high-risk pregnancy situations and therefore detection of fetal distress would be possible. By intervention with rapid vaginal delivery or delivery by Cesarean section, fetal loss can be prevented.

The perinatologist has available a number of laboratory tests in order to evaluate the well-being and/or the maturity of the unborn fetus. Unfortunately, in the woman addicted to opiates, some of these tests are not useful. The estriol level will show a false negative in narcotic maintained women during their last trimester. Paradoxically, the urinary estriol concentrations rapidly increase toward or exceed the average values expected for their gestational time following withdrawal, a time during which the fetus should be stressed.[23]

Certain conditions associated with maternal hypertension and severe placental problems, including retroplacental bleeding and ruptured membranes, accelerate maturation of the lecithin/sphingomyelin (L/S) ratio. In contrast, other conditions, such as diabetes, delay the maturation of the L/S ratio. Narcotic addicted women have been shown to have accelerated L/S ratios, suggesting that an association exists between fetal major organ system maturation and the L/S ratio independent of gestational age or birthweight.[24]

In addition to the numerous obstetrical complications seen in pregnant narcotic dependent women, medical complications abound. The following are those most frequently encountered: anemia, cardiac disease (frequently secondary to subacute bacterial endocarditis), cellulitis, poor dental hygiene, diabetes mellitus, edema, hepatitis, hypertension, phlebitis, pneumonia, and tuberculosis. Urinary tract infection is common including cystitis, urethritis, and pyelonephritis. Due to the fact that a considerable number of women use prostitution as a means of supporting their drug habit, venereal disease is frequently seen. This includes condyloma acuminatum, gonorrhea, herpes simplex, and syphilis. In a series of several hundred narcotic dependent women in Philadelphia, medical complications were seen in nearly 40–50% of those observed in the prenatal period.[17]

The narcotic dependent pregnant woman often develops anemia due to iron and folic acid deficiency. Nutritional deficiencies in drug addiction are due largely to the lack of proper food intake because of inhibition of the central mechanism that controls appetite and hunger. Furthermore, toxic responses to narcotics may contribute to malnutrition by interfering with the absorption or utilization of ingested nutrients. Absorption abnormalities are common in drug addicts because of the high incidence of lesions of the intestine, liver and pancreas while malnutrition is common because of the frequent presence of liver disease. Sometimes, peripheral neuritis is seen in the chronic drug addict, usually due to thiamine depletion although a deficiency of Vitamin 6, panothenic acid or nicotinic acid may produce identical signs. Hypoglycemia, Vitamin B6 deficiency, thiamine depletion, or magnesium deficiency may cause seizures in both alcoholics and drug addicts. Hepatitis, a frequent complication of abuse of injectable drugs, is nutritionally depleting since it causes a loss of proteins, minerals, and trace elements. Intensive diet therapy is desirable in drug and alcohol addiction, and parenteral therapy may be necessary to correct fluid, mineral and vitamin deficits in acutely ill patients.[25]

The Teratogenicity of Narcotics

The teratogenicity of a pharmacologic agent involves the ability of that agent to cause a birth defect, either morphological, biochemical, or behavioral, which is induced at any stage of gestation and detected at birth or later. Investigators have found multifactoral causes for congenital malformations which generally result from an interaction between genetic and environmental factors. Twenty-five percent of human malformations can be attributed to genetic factors, 3% to chromosome aberrations, 3% to environmental factors such as maternal infection, radiation, and drug administration, and 69% are of unknown etiology.[26]

Teratogenic effects of opiates have been reported in hamsters after prenatal treatment with heroin[27] and morphine,[28] and in mice after treatment with morphine.[29, 30] The teratogenic effects were only produced when very high doses were used and the anomalies were usually anencephaly and axial-skeletal malformations.

Johanneson and Becker[31] evaluated the teratogenicity of opiates in Sprague-Dawley rats which they injected with 20 mg/kg of morphine sulfate. They found that the rat pups were essentially free of any observable teratogenic changes including bone defects and concluded that multiple administrations of morphine to pregnant rats during preimplantation, organogenesis or in late growth periods of pregnancy do not result in obvious teratogenic changes.

It appears that large doses of opiates are necessary to induce congenital abnormalities in animal models, although smaller doses that produce blood levels comparable to those observed in human users may be able to produce symptoms of fetal toxicity such as decreased birthweights and increased perinatal mortality.[27-31]

Recently, evaluation of 830 drug dependent mothers and their infants born at Hutzel Hospital in Detroit from 1973 to 1976 showed that there was an increase in congenital malformations. Sixty-nine percent of the women were clinic patients who used methadone and heroin during pregnancy; whereas 31% were non-clinic patients who were on heroin only. The incidence of congenital malformations was 2.4% which is within the national average although the control group in this study had an incidence of only 0.5%. The types of malformations were as varied as those seen in the control infants. Among the 37 infants of drug dependent mothers with malformations, 20 had significant defects including hydrocephalus, interrupted aortic arch, patent ductus arteriosus, ventricular septal defect, malrotation of the intestines, posterior urethral valves, multicystic kidney, hypospadias, hypoplastic lung, cleft lip, and inguinal hernias.[32]

In our evaluation of infants born in our program in Philadelphia, we have not seen a similar pattern of malformations except in the instance of inguinal hernias. This finding needs to be further delineated by evaluating appropriate control groups with clear specifications of gestational age and drug use.

Studies of Chromosomes in Infants Born to Narcotic Dependent Mothers

The cytogenetic risks to the offspring of the pregnant narcotic addict have been studied in peripheral lymphocytes of infants exposed *in utero* to heroin or methadone and of infants exposed to no drug at all. It was concluded that infants exposed predominantly to heroin *in utero* showed a significant increase in the frequency of chromosomal aberrations including dicentrics and rings in their peripheral blood compared to controls; whereas infants exposed predominantly to methadone *in utero* did not.[33]

In another study, chromosomal damage was assessed prenatally and at delivery from 99 addicted pregnant women (80 from a methadone maintenance program and 19 heroin addicts) and their 101 offspring at delivery. About 10% of the cells studied showed some type of chromosomal aberration. The chromosome damage was random, affected all chromosomes, and was mainly of the acentric fragment type. The dosage and duratioin of methadone treatment or years of heroin abuse did not affect chromosomal aberration rates in either the mother or the infant. In these patients, the drug addiction was compounded by the presence of poor nutrition, lack of rest, stress, increased incidence of tuberculosis, hepatitis, and syphilis, and a lack of early and consistent prenatal care. In this study as well as the previous study, the above compounding factors as well as simultaneous polydrug abuse make it impossible to isolate the narcotic agents as causative. Furthermore, the biological significance of opiate induced chromosome damage, if it does occur, is not really understood at this point in time.[34]

Morbidity of Infants Born to Narcotic Dependent Mothers

The pregnant narcotic-dependent woman frequently predisposes her infant to a host of neonatal complications due to the fact that she lacks prenatal care and, therefore, develops many serious obstetrical and medical complications. In heroin-dependent women, the majority of the medical complications seen in their neonates reflect the fact that they are prematurely born. These include such conditions as asphyxia neonatorum, intracranial hemorrhage, hyaline membrane disease, intrauterine growth retardation, hypoglycemia, hypocalcemia, septicemia, and hyperbilirubinemia which are seen in greater than 80% of the infants. Since infants born to women who receive methadone maintenance are more apt to have higher birthweights and a decreased incidence of premature birth, medical complications generally reflect: 1) the amount of prenatal care that the mother has had; 2) whether she has suffered any particular obstetrical or medical complications including toxemia of pregnancy, Rh hemolytic disease, hypertension, infection; and, most importantly, 3) multiple drug use which may have permitted an unstable intrauterine milieu complicated by withdrawal and overdose. The latter situation for the newborn is extremely hazardous in that it predisposes the infant to meconium staining and subsequent aspiration pneumonia which in itself causes a marked morbidity and increased mortality.[17]

Recent evidence shows that infants undergoing abstinence have an increased incidence of thrombocytosis and increased circulating platelet aggregates. Thirty-three neonates were studied respectively by Burstein and colleagues. The neonates were born to mothers using methadone plus other drugs. By the second week of life the infants had developed significant thrombocytosis. The increase persisted for over sixteen weeks with a significant peak at ten weeks of age. Platelet counts exceeding 1,000,000/mm^3 were found in seven infants. The thrombocytosis was not related to withdrawal symptoms or treatment with phenobarbital or paregoric. No thrombocytosis was found in 36 normal control infants up to eight weeks of life. Circulating platelet aggregates were also increased, and it was noted that the risk for this phenomenon correlated directly with an increase in platelet count.[35] These authors suggest that thrombocytosis and increased circulating platelet aggregates may be factors in the pathogenesis of focal infarcts, and subarachnoid and germinal plate hemorrhages, described at autopsy in infants of addicted mothers.[36]

The effects of maternal use of methadone during pregnancy on tests of thyroid function were studied in 14 women and their offspring, and in a control group of 12 normal nonaddicted women and their infants.[37] Concentrations of thyrotropin, thyroxine, and triiodothyronine were not significantly different in maternal and cord serum, and in infants' serum, at age 24 hours, but at two and seven days, triiodothyronine levels were significantly higher in the methadone than in the control group. Furthermore, at two, three, and seven days of life, the thyroxine levels in the methadone group of infants were significantly higher than those in the control group. The mechanisms responsible for the biochemical evidence of hyperthyroidism were not determined, but it was postulated that it may have been related to altered autonomic function and/or increased metabolic activity which occurs during neonatal narcotic abstinence.[37]

With more serious, or a greater number of, infant complications, the hospital stay is prolonged, producing maternal separation and the possibility of subsequent maternal detachment. In order to prevent future morbidity and possibly mortality, the addicted mother should be assessed for possible risk of child abuse and neglect. Certain dynamics of abuse which one should look for in the mother include: unrealistic expectations of children, history of abuse in her own childhood, severe criticism and absence of nurturing relationships in childhood, relationship stress, poor self concept and social isolation.

Neonatal Narcotic Abstinence Syndrome

Neonatal narcotic abstinence syndrome is described as a generalized disorder characterized by signs and symptoms of central nervous system hyperirritability, gastrointestinal dysfunction, respiratory distress, and vague autonomic symptoms which include yawning, sneezing, sweating, stuffy nose, mottling, increased lacrimation, and fever. Infants that are afflicted generally develop tremors which are initially mild and occur only when the infants are disturbed, but which progress to the point where they occur spontaneously without any stimulation of the infant. High pitched cry, increased muscle tone and irritability develop. The infants tend to have increased deep tendon reflexes and a hyperactive Moro reflex. The rooting reflex is exaggerated, and the infants are frequently seen sucking their fists or thumbs, yet when feedings are administered, they have extreme difficulty and regurgitate frequently. The feeding difficulty occurs because of an uncoordinated and ineffectual sucking reflex. The infants may develop loose stools, and therefore are susceptible to dehydration and electrolyte imbalance.[3]

The sucking reflex, noted to be ineffectual and uncoordinated from a clinical standpoint, was studied by objective measures. Of several sucking parameters studied, sucking rate appeared to be most sensitive in distinguishing infants undergoing narcotic abstinence from control infants, although pressure parameters also indicated significant differences. Differences were seen in infants undergoing heroin versus methadone withdrawal in that the latter infants had greater disturbances in sucking performance. In addition, when infants were studied in regard to treatment agents, it was noted that paregoric-treated infants tended to suck more vigorously than infants treated with sedatives such as phenobarbital and tranquilizers such as Valium®.[38–40]

At birth, most passively dependent infants, whether born to heroin or methadone dependent mothers, appear physically and behaviorally normal. The time of onset of withdrawal varies from shortly after birth to two weeks of age, but the majority appear within 72 hours after birth. If the mother has been on heroin alone, the majority of infants will develop clinical signs of withdrawal between four and 24 hours of age. If she has been on methadone alone, the baby's symptoms may not appear until the end of the first day. Several methadone babies have had their onset of withdrawal after the first or second week of life. The type of drug or drugs utilized by the mother, her dosage, timing of the dose before delivery, the character of labor, the type and amount of anesthesia and analgesia given during labor, the maturity, nutrition, and presence or absence of intrinsic disease in the infant may all play a role in determining the time of onset in the individual infant. The time of onset of abstinence may vary from a few hours to several days.[41]

More severe withdrawal seems to occur in infants whose mothers have taken large amounts of drugs for a long time. Usually, the closer to delivery a mother takes heroin, the greater the delay in onset of withdrawal and the more severe the symptoms in her baby. The maturity of the infant's own metabolic and excretory mechanisms play an important role after delivery. According to the severity of the withdrawal, the duration of symptoms is anywhere from six to eight weeks. Although the infants are discharged from the hospital after drug therapy is stopped, their symptoms of irritability may persist for three to four months or more. These infants have hyperphasia, increased oral drives, sweating, hyperacusis, irregular sleep patterns, poor tolerance to holding or to abrupt changes of position and space, and loose stools.[41] For further information on the intricacies of the symptomatology of the neonatal abstinence syndrome, the reader should consult additional references.[2, 9, 42–50]

The literature abounds with information concerning the comparative severity of neonatal abstinence from heroin and methadone.[13, 38, 39, 47, 51–54] Pitfalls in many of these studies include the fact that dosages were remarkably different in regard to heroin and methadone; parameters for the assessment of neonatal abstinence were different; the search for additional drugs by toxicology methods was not considered; and treatment regimens were variable.[17, 55, 56] In summarizing the many factors reported by various investigators, one might conclude that the severity of neonatal abstinence may be decreased if the maternal methadone dose is kept low and no additional opiate or other psychoactive drugs are used by the mother. In our own program we have observed, as others have, that the severity of the neonatal withdrawal increased as the average daily maternal dose of methadone and the duration of maintenance during pregnancy increased. There were no statistically significant differences in withdrawal severity between groups when the infants were defined as term appropriate for gestational age, premature, or intrauterine growth retarded.[57] From the available data of programs in several cities,[17, 55, 56] one could probably conclude that if the mother were provided with comprehensive prenatal care, and as low a dose of methadone as possible, preferably less than 30 mg., and she eliminated additional opiates and other psychoactive agents, the infant would be put at the best advantage for a mild to moderate abstinence syndrome. This does not mean that one should lower the dose of methadone so much that the pregnant woman will have abstinence in the last trimester with its concomitant hazards as previously described.

There still remain, though, many unanswered questions related to seizure activity, electroencephalogram status, and myoclonic movements observed during neonatal abstinence, especially in those infants born to methadone maintained mothers. In 1971, Zelson[4] reported that seizures were more frequent in infants with methadone dependent mothers. A low incidence of seizure activity in infants undergoing narcotic abstinence has been reported by Goddard and Wilson.[58] The most extensive report, and one which implicates seizures in infants born to narcotic addicted mothers, is that by Herzlinger in 1977 who reported that among 302 neonates passively exposed to narcotics during pregnancy, 18 had seizures that were attributed to withdrawal.[59] The mean day of seizure onset was 10.1 ± 8 days with a range of 3–34 days. Generalized motor seizures or rhythmic myoclonic jerks, each of which occurred in 7 infants, were the principal seizure manifestations. All infants with seizures manifested other withdrawal symptoms prior to the initial seizure.

In our own experience in Philadelphia with over 500 infants undergoing narcotic abstinence, we initially saw a very low incidence of seizure activity. Currently, though, nearly one-third of our infants exhibit myoclonic activity, usually within the first few weeks of the withdrawal syndrome and then again during the latent detoxification phase. In a small group of infants manifesting myoclonic activity, electroencephalograms have been done and have shown no abnormalities. In addition, those that have had abnormalities have converted to normal by the end of the detoxification.

In a small number of infants focal and generalized seizures were noted clinically, and electroencephalograms showed diffuse multi-focal discharges. These preliminary studies are not conclusive, and therefore, further information is necessary before the clinician will be able to know how aggressive one must be in the pharmacological treatment of these infants.

The behavioral effects of narcotic withdrawal in human infants have been studied by the Brazelton Neonatal Assessment Scale.[40, 60–62] Studies indicate the methadone baby's state of narcotic withdrawal. The infants were restive and tended to be in a neurologically irritable condition, cried more often and were state labile, were more tremulous, hypertonic, and manifested less motor maturity than the normal group. While quite available and responsive auditorially, the methadone subjects responded poorly to visual stimuli. These findings have substantial impact on the caregiver's perception of infants, and, depending on their extent and the duration of manifestation, may have long term consequences for the development of infant caregiver interaction patterns.

Lactation and Narcotic Use

Narcotics freely pass through into breast milk. The decision to permit a narcotic-addicted mother to breast feed must include not only a consideration of the amounts excreted in the breast milk, but, moreover, the social environment to which the child will go. Breastfeeding is a 24-hour a day, 7-day a week commitment by the mother which seems impossible for the heroin addict given her generally chaotic lifestyle. In those women who are carefully maintained on methadone and in whom no other drug use occurs, breastfeeding is possible, not only due to the fact that the mother may give the commitment, but also due to the fact that concentrations of methadone in milk in comparison to plasma have been found to be very low.[63] Less than 5% of our mothers have requested breastfeeding, but unfortunately, most of them do not continue for more than a few days or a few weeks due to their inability to persist with such a commitment.

Mortality

Mortality rates are generally higher in infants born to narcotic dependent mothers. The mortality rate depends on the amount of prenatal care that the mother has had as well as the gestational age and birthweight of the infant. The incidence of mortality in the drug dependent population in our program composed of heroin and methadone dependent mothers (the latter a stratified group of women having inadequate and adequate prenatal care) revealed an overall mortality incidence of 5% in contrast to controls in which it was 2%.[64] In low birth weight infants, mortality in the drug dependent population was 13% and in the controls it was 10%. In separating the overall addicted group into heroin addicted, methadone inadequate prenatal care, and methadone adequate prenatal care, the mortality rates were found to be 6%, 8%, and 3% respectively.

Specific neuropathological studies were done on 10 infants who died in our program.[36] Three types of lesions were noted to be associated with maternal drug dependence including gliosis, foci of old infarction, and developmental brain retardation.

There appears to be an association between alcohol, smoking and drug addiction and the incidence of sudden infant death syndrome or crib death, but whether the association is direct or indirect is undetermined.[65] There seem to be recurrent themes among these factors, though, which include prenatal and postnatal growth deficiency, vascular changes and hypoxic episodes. Hypoxia is caused by the interference with oxygen carrying capacity as with nicotine, or by episodes of depression or withdrawal as in opiates and alcohol. In regard to opiates, other hypotheses for the suddent infant death syndrome include the effects on the autonomic nervous system of the neonatal abstinence syndrome and its treatment, chronic fetal hypoxia, and chronic infection.[65]

Additionally, results of animal studies have suggested that the cerebral hypoperfusion which accompanies bradycardia may play a role in the sudden infant death syndrome.[66] Gliosis has been noted in areas crucial to respiratory control, very much as we have seen in infants born to opiate dependent mothers as previously described. Therefore, the mechanism may be perinatal asphyxia which disrupts the respiratory control center.

Behavioral, Neurological, and Developmental Effects on the Newborn, Infant, and Child of the Opiate Dependent Woman

In general, various investigators have agreed that no gross neurological abnormalities are generally seen in infants born to heroin or methadone maintained mothers unless perinatal events have caused severe asphyxia with subsequent brain damage. Growth and development evaluated by Wilson and colleagues [67] in 14 infants born to heroin-addicted women whose infants were placed in foster homes showed behavioral disturbances, predominantly hyperactivity, brief attention span, and temper outbursts. Two of these infants did have neurological abnormalities and growth impairment was seen in about a quarter of the infants. Subsequent studies by Wilson and colleagues [68] have shown disturbances of growth and behavior in infants and toddlers of women addicted to heroin during pregnancy. Wilson compared 22 3- to 6-year old children of heroin addicted mothers to three other groups including those with a drug environment (N = 20), those that were high risk infants (N = 15), and those that were normal and of the same socioeconomic class (N = 20). These groups were all matched for age, race, sex, birthweight, and socioeconomic status. Heroin exposed children weighed less and were shorter than those in the comparison groups, with 14% having a head circumference below the third percentile. Heroin exposed children were rated by parents as less well adjusted than control children and differed significantly in perceptual measures and on subtests of the Illinois Test of Psycholinguistic Abilities and McCarthy Scales of Children's Abilities relating to the process of organization. These findings suggest that chronic intrauterine exposure to heroin may affect growth and behavior as well as perceptual and learning processes in preschool children.[68]

Ramer and Lodge [69] studied 35 infants born to 32 mothers registered in the San Francisco city-operated methadone maintenance treatment program. The infants were studied by the Bayley Scale of Infant Mental and Motor Development which were given at three-month intervals during the first year and at six-month intervals during the second and third years. Results revealed that the older infants showed age appropriate development in the area of vocalization and language, but their performance on perceptual motor tasks was somewhat less adequate.

In 1976, Strauss and colleagues [70] reported evaluations on 60 infants born to women enrolled in the Hutzel Hospital's methadone treatment/perinatal care program. These infants were compared with 53 infants who were born to mothers who were not addicted. The psychological development of the infants was evaluated with the Bayley Scales of Infant Development at 3, 6 and 12 months of age. Anthropometric measurements were obtained at 12 months of age for about half of the study and control infants. These studies concluded that the average course of infants born to addicted mothers was well within the normal range throughout the first year of life, but they were significantly less likely to walk unaided at twelve months of age than the control population.

In our own follow-up studies in Philadelphia, which include 59 two-year old infants born to women maintained on methadone during pregnancy which were evaluated periodically in regard to development and physical growth, and compared with a control group of 42 infants, no correlation between maternal drug intake, degree of neonatal withdrawal, or Gesell Behavioral Profiles was seen. Data did indicate that children of mothers maintained on methadone during pregnancy were lighter in weight and shorter in stature from birth through 89 weeks of age when compared to the control group.[71]

An additional study of one and two year old infants born to women maintained on methadone in comparison to control infants has also been done in Family Center Program in Philadelphia. There were 45 infants exposed to methadone and 33 control infants who were assessed with the Bayley Mental Scale of Infant Development. No differences were found between infants exposed to methadone at birth and control infants at one and two years of age. These data support previous findings that *in utero* methadone exposure does not seem to have an adverse effect on mental development in infancy. However, the decrement in scores between the one and two year olds for both groups was significant, and suggests that environment may confound long-term infant outcome.[72]

Additional studies in progress in Philadelphia include assessments of 50 four-year old children. Twenty-five study children were born to women who received methadone maintenance during pregnancy as well as prenatal care. The 25 control children were randomly selected from a stratified population of comparable socioeconomic, racial, and medical backgrounds from a pediatric outpatient clinic. Children were assessed by way of a neurological examination, the Wechsler Preschool and Primary Scale of Intelligence and the Test of Language Development, Imitation of Gestures, and the Motor-Free Visual Perception Test. The differences between children born to women maintained on methadone and the controls were very small and not statistically significant for both subscales and the full-scale I.Q.s. Both groups performed better on the verbal scale than on the performance scale. All neurological findings were within the normal range and there was no relationship between the severity of neonatal withdrawal and the I.Q. scores.[73]

Although the above studies in infants of methadone maintained mothers seem somewhat encouraging, and those of heroin exposed infants appear somewhat ominous, they are plagued with several problems. The first is that of inadequate numbers, and the inability to eliminate confounding variables such as differences in social milieu, drugs used during pregnancy, neonatal conditions, and parenting skills. Furthermore, future evaluations will have to use testing materials that do not just develop summary scores, but, in fact, look at particular variables within the child's development. Children must be evaluated during the school years to determine the existence of minimal brain dysfunction.

In summary, illicit drugs taken individually, as well as in combination, are being excessively used by women in general as well as those that are pregnant. In the latter situation, the potential hazard to the fetus, neonate and child is overwhelming, not only due to the fact that the fetus has been exposed to an adverse physical and social milieu, but also because of the vast combination of drugs which may interact, compounding the total effect upon the fetus. Additional studies are still necessary to further define the physical, developmental, and social effects of these illicit drugs upon the neonate, infant and older child.

The Effects of Alcohol Use During Pregnancy upon the Fetus, Neonate and Child

Concern by physicians in the United States over the effects of alcohol on the unborn fetus and neonate has existed for only the past five to six years when our own literature came forth with such descriptions.[74] The effects of alcohol and certainly early descriptions of the fetal alcohol syndrome were known as early as Greek and Roman times; for example, in Carthage, the bridal couple was forbidden to drink wine on their wedding night in order that defective children might not be conceived. In 1720, in an effort to help the aristocratic farm interests by providing new markets for grain, the English government lifted the traditional restrictions on distilling and cheap, plentiful gin flooded the country. Between 1720 and 1750, the so-called "gin epidemic" occurred which created a social crisis in England. The epidemic did not end until 1751 when Parliament again controlled the manufacture of distilled spirits. From this period came the first surviving observations of the fetal alcohol syndrome since classical times.[75]

In 1834, a report to the House of Commons by a select committee investigating drunkenness indicated that infants born to alcoholic mothers sometimes had a starved, shriveled, and imperfect look. By 1900, Sullivan had reported increased abortion and stillbirth rates among chronic alcoholic women and an increased frequency of epilepsy in their surviving offspring. In 1942, in a book entitled *Alcohol Explored,* it was described that alcoholic mothers had two times the infant mortality and more miscarriages than nonalcoholic mothers.[75]

More currently, in 1967 in the French literature, Lemoine reported 127 cases of fetal alcohol syndrome. These infants had prenatal growth deficiency, malformations including cleft palate and cardiac malformations, psychomotor retardation with a mean I.Q. of 70, agitation, and character disturbances.[76]

Although the heroin addicted mother has contributed largely to the high risk pregnancy population of our country, the numbers of women in the childbearing age who are using alcohol to a moderate or a heavy amount far exceed, by manyfold, the numbers of women using opiates. For example, Youngs and colleagues[77] reported on experiences with 100 adolescents of low socioeconomic class at entry into prenatal care in Baltimore, Maryland. Of these, 3% were using heroin, 3% methadone, 8% barbiturates and other depressants, 10% marihuana, 50% cigarettes, and 25% alcohol.

It was not until 1973, when Jones and colleagues[74] reported on the fetal alcohol syndrome, that we became alerted to more specific effects of alcohol use during pregnancy. In this report, perinatal mortality was 17%; borderline moderate mental deficiency 44%; and abnormal features were seen in 32%. Similarities to other pediatric syndromes were noted in the evaluations of these infants such as the mental deficiency and abnormal facies in the Cornelia de Lange syndrome; facial, eye features and mental retardation in the Smith-Lemi-Opitz syndrome; growth retardation, facial, eye features, and ventricular septal defect in Trisomy 18; low birth weight, growth retardation, facial and eye features in Familial Blepharophimosis; growth deficiency, mental/motor deficiency, facial features, and cardiac defects in the Fetal Hydantoin Syndrome. Significant differences do exist so that differentiation is possible from fetal alcohol syndrome.

In his comparison of the 23 alcoholic mothers and 46 nonalcoholic control mothers, Jones found a marked increase in perinatal mortality, I.Q. less than 80, occurrence of microcephaly, length and weight below the third percentile, and adverse outcome in the infants born to alcoholic mothers. The mothers in his study had severe alcoholism, usually of 3 to 25 years duration, with delirium tremens, cirrhosis, nutritional anemia, and a mean age of 32 years and a gravity of greater than 4.[78]

Abnormalities described by Jones [78] included a large number of infants who had short palpebral fissures, strabismus, ptosis, and pale optic discs. They had a narrow vermillion border and a long convex upper lip ("fish mouth"), and cleft palate. Altered palmar creases included those that were rudimentary with aberrant alignment of palmar creases and those with a single upper palmar crease. Fine motor dysfunction included a weak grasp, poor eye-hand coordination, and tremulousness in the newborn period. Cardiac anomalies included ventricular and atrial septal defects, and patent ductus arteriosus. Joint anomalies included congenital hip dislocation, inability to completely extend the elbows, camptodactyly of the fingers, clinodactyly of the toes, and inability to completely flex the metacarpal phalangeal joints. The mean birthweight of the infants was 2034 grams, and the mean length 43.6 cm. Birth length was more severely decreased than birthweight and head circumference. Postnatal growth deficiency was severe in that linear growth was 65% of normal and weight gain 30% of normal. Mean intelligence quotients were found to be 63 at one year of age.

A subsequent study evaluated the adverse effects on offspring of maternal alcohol abuse during pregnancy. This study, by Ouelette and colleagues [79] in Boston, divided 633 women into three groups: Group 1 (N = 326), women who drank less than one time per month (abstinence/rare drinkers); Group 2 (N = 249), women who drank greater than one time per month but did not meet criteria for Group 3 (moderate drinkers); and Group 3 (N = 58), women who drank five or more drinks on occasion and also had a consistent daily average of greater than 45 ml. of absolute alcohol (heavy drinkers). The infants were evaluated by pediatric, neurologic, developmental, and Dubowitz evaluation for gestational age. Length, weight, and head circumference were plotted on the Lubchenco tables and minor and major congenital anomalies were recorded.

There were no differences in the mothers in Groups 1 and 2 in regard to age, gravity, cigarette smoking, and previous drug use, but in Group 3, the women were older, of higher gravity, and 60% smoked one pack of cigarettes or more per day and 36% had previous drug use. Significant increases were seen in Group 3 (heavy drinkers) in regard to abnormalities at the initial newborn exam, jitteriness and decreased sucking. In addition, Group 3 had a higher incidence of prematurity, intrauterine growth retardation, and microcephaly. Birthweight, birth length, and head circumference were significantly decreased in Group 3. Group 3 had a significantly greater number of congenital anomalies which included major and multiple anomalies. Ouelette concluded that heavy drinkers had twice the number of anomalies than moderate or abstinent drinkers. Nutritional intake, drug use, and sociologic factors in the three groups did not account for the differences. Although the presence of single, multiple, major and minor congenital anomalies was significantly increased, no specific pattern was noted. The investigators could not determine whether alcohol per se was acting as the direct toxin or whether its metabolites were. It was noted that in the first trimester the greatest effect of alcohol was on fetal maldevelopment whereas near term it had a greater effect on fetal nutrition and size.

A recent compilation of data concerning fetal alcohol syndrome has been reported by Clarren and Smith.[80] Principal features of the fetal alcohol syndrome as observed in 245 affected persons were reported. The three categories of malformations noted were central nervous system dysfunction, including intellectual, neurologic, and behavioral dysfunction; growth deficiency (prenatal and postnatal); and certain facial characteristics of the eyes, nose, maxilla, and mouth. More than 80% of patients had mild to moderate mental retardation, microcephaly, and irritability in infancy. More than 80% of patients were less than two standard deviations for length and height, prenatally as well as postnatally. Facial characteristics seen in more than 80% of patients included short palpebral fissures, hypoplastic philtrum, thin upper vermillion border, and retrognathia in infancy.

Associated features of the fetal alcohol syndrome observed in the same 245 persons affected included frequent occurrence of ptosis, strabismus, epicanthal folds, posterior rotation of the ears, prominent lateral palatine ridges, cardiac murmurs (usually due to atrial septal defect), renogenital anomalies including labial hypoplasia, cutaneous hemangiomas, aberrant palmar creases and pectus excavatum.[80]

Clarren [81] has also reported on brain malformations related to ethanol in four infants. For each infant the maternal alcohol consumption was very different and included only one woman who was a chronic alcoholic. The others' consumption included one who drank one gallon of wine biweekly, one who drank two to three times a month, and one who drank three to four times a week. Both of the latter mothers had occasional binge drinking. Features of the fetal alcohol syndrome were variable in the four infants in that one infant had no features, one infant had only short palpebral fissures and maxillary hypoplasia, and the other two infants had cerebral, facial and growth deficiency characteristics of the fetal alcohol syndrome. One infant had microcephaly and two had hydrocephaly. The neuropathological findings included either leptomeningeal neuroglial heterotopia, cerebral disorganization, or cerebellar and brainstem disorganization. These findings seem to have no correlation with those neuropathological findings of infants born to opiate-dependent mothers.

Maternal alcohol consumption resulting in fetal alcohol syndrome has been shown to affect infant behavior. Sucking studies have shown decreased sucking rate and pressure in infants born to alcoholic mothers. Brazelton studies on the first day show poor habituation, poor muscle tone, and decreased motor activity. Atypical movements, tremulousness, and increased hand-to-mouth activity have been noted. Fine motor problems include poor finger articulation, weak and primitive grasp, delayed gross motor development, severe feeding problems, self-stimulation such as rocking or head banging, hyperactivity, poor attentional skills and poor problem-solving ability.[82]

Minimal brain dysfunction which includes involuntary hyperactivity, short attention span, poor powers of concentration, impulsivity, inability to adjust to a change in the environment, poor school performance, and cognitive and perceptual problems, has been seen in a higher incidence of infants whose mothers, as well as fathers, have been alcoholic in contrast to those incidences seen in control children.[83, 84]

Streissguth and colleagues [85] studied the intelligence, behavior and dysmorphogenesis in fetal alcohol syndrome. Twenty subjects were studied from different socioeconomic strata. The average I.Q. was 65 with a range of 15 to 105. Dysmorphic features were directly related to mental deficiency; that is, the more severe the malformation, the greater the mental deficiency. With severe malformations, the mean I.Q. was 55. With lesser malformations, the mean I.Q. was 82. Heights appeared to correlate with intelligence. Recent studies by Hanson and others show that moderate alcohol consumption during pregnancy may also be hazardous to the developing infant.[86]

Infants born to alcoholic mothers who have the fetal alcohol syndrome have been shown to have withdrawal symptoms.[87] The initial symptoms occurred between 6 and 12 hours after delivery and included irritability, tremors, increased muscle tone, increased respiratory rate, hyperacusis, abdominal distention, seizures, opisthotonos, and vomiting. Seizures and opisthotonos seem to be more typical with the syndrome of alcohol abstinence than with the narcotic abstinence syndrome in that they occurred in all infants reported.

Other interesting features concerning the fetal alcohol syndrome have been reported. Hypothalamic pituitary function is normal.[88] Growth retardation has not been found to be caused by growth hormone deficiency. Fetal alcohol syndrome has been described in dizygotic twins. An altered sex ratio is suggested in that females are more often affected than males.

The effects of paternal alcoholism on the fetus and on human spermatogenesis are unknown. It is known that one-fourth of the heaviest drinking women have reported heavy drinking on the part of the baby's father. Thus, this factor may play an additive or compounding role in fetal alcohol syndrome.

In regard to the pathophysiology of fetal alcohol syndrome, we have evidence that ethanol rapidly crosses the placental and blood-brain barrier of the fetus and reaches approximately the same levels of concentration as those found in the mother. Alcohol has been detected on the baby's breath at birth, in the amniotic fluid, and in the cord blood. A direct toxicity may be likely, but toxicity is also possible by way of breakdown products, such as acidaldehyde, or unknown toxic agents. The amount of ethanol and the duration of fetal exposure is important. General maternal undernutrition is probably not the cause of fetal alcohol syndrome due to the fact that in other studies where there is general maternal undernutrition, a lesser degree of prenatal growth deficiency and no abnormalities are seen. As to the mechanisms of undergrowth and poor development, hypotheses suggest altered enzyme activity in the liver. Genetic polymorphism of enzymes for ethanol metabolism may alter fetal susceptibility. There may be poor microsomal or mitochondrial function or decreased ATP activity. The influence of folate deficiency, advanced maternal age, and multiparity; other drugs, especially CNS depressants, and cigarette smoking, as well as other substances in alcoholic beverages such as aldehydes and metals, has yet to be determined.

We do know that high concentrations of ethanol in the blood of the mother have caused severe fetal malformations in five species, including chicken, rat, mouse, sheep, and guinea pig. Proposed hypotheses by various investigators include: 1) Morphologic effects of fetal alcohol syndrome are caused by high concentration of alcohol in the blood at critical periods of fetal development.[89] 2) The pattern of malformations characteristic of fetal alcohol syndrome probably develops during the first eleven weeks of gestation.[90] 3) Lower concentrations of ethanol during the critical periods may result in functional disturbances of the developing nervous system and other organs.[89] Decrease in birthweight of the offspring of middle class women who consume moderate amounts of alcohol during pregnancy has been noted.[91]

Many women utilize alcohol socially in a small to moderate degree. What, then, can the physician tell a woman who is pregnant as to the possible consequences of this small or moderate amount of drinking? Several recommendations can be cited. In 1977, the National Institute on Alcohol Abuse and Alcoholism published the following recommendations: 1) Totally safe levels of drinking are unknown; 2) A risk is established with ingestion of the equivalent of three ounces of absolute alcohol or about six drinks per day; 3) The risk for lesser amounts is uncertain, but caution is advised; 4) Peak blood alcohol concentration is probably the most critical teratogenic factor; 5) A pregnant woman should not exceed two drinks per day even if she normally drinks alcoholic beverages only once per week, month or year.[92]

Hanson and others [86] describe that the risk of having a newborn with fetal alcohol syndrome increases proportionately with the average daily alcohol intake. With less than one ounce of absolute alcohol per day, the risk was low; with between one and two ounces of absolute alcohol per day, the risk was 10%; and with greater than two ounces per day, it was 19%.

The recommendations of Clarren and Smith include: 1) Chronic consumption of 89 ml. of absolute alcohol or more per day constitutes a major risk to fetus; 2) Lower levels of consumption or less frequent use of alcohol carries an unknown risk and may be shown to be associated with less seriously affected children; 3) No absolutely safe level of ethanol consumption has yet been established.[80]

The physician therefore is reduced to some common sense recommendations. In view of the fact that even the fetal alcohol syndrome does not occur in 100% of heavy drinkers, one should not recommend termination of pregnancy after just a few drinks by a social drinker who did not recognize that she was pregnant. Obviously further information is necessary in order to more clearly define the true incidence, not only of the severe form of the effects of alcohol, but also the effects upon behavior and learning in children.

In conclusion, the multitude of social and medical complications seen in the pregnant drug dependent woman seriously influence the intrauterine milieu and therefore contribute to the morbidity and mortality of infants born to these mothers. Clinicians in this field must continue to strive for excellence in the care of pregnant drug dependent women and their children. Government agencies must realize the responsibility to these women and children and to society, and provide adequate funding for comprehensive services. Appropriate education must be available for pregnant women in regard to alcohol consumption. Rehabilitation for the pregnant alcohol dependent woman is not as easily accomplished as that for the drug dependent woman who may be offered methadone maintenance. Irrevocable and severe damage to the fetus may have already occurred prior to the alcoholic woman's arrival at the treatment program. Perhaps the most effective treatment for alcohol dependent women is appropriate birth control measures until abstinence may be obtained. It is imperative that investigators continue to search within animal models as well as in humans for the more subtle effects of alcohol and narcotics on the fetus and newborn, as well as to further delineate better treatment regimens for both of these populations. Only if clinicians and our Government consider the appropriate care for pregnant drug and alcohol dependent women and their children as priorities will be able to cope with potential pathophysiological and behavioral effects of the transplacental transfer of narcotics and alcohol to the fetuses and newborns of these dependent women.

Acknowledgments

The author wishes to acknowledge the ongoing efforts of the clinical and research staff of Family Center Program without whom the many experiences with pregnant drug dependent women described in this manuscript could not have been made possible. Special gratitude is expressed to Dian S. Reeser, for her untiring efforts in editing and reference search, and to Kathleen Gibbons for her patience and diligence in the preparation of the manuscript.

Finally, in this, the International Year of the Child, the author wishes to acknowledge her own children: Mark, Matthew, Michael, Maureen, and Martin, whose tolerance, patience and love have permitted her to give so much of her professional time as well as her personal time to Family Center Program in an effort to prevent the potential hazards that befall those infants and children less fortunate than they.

References

1. Clarren, S. K., E. C. Alvord, Jr., S. M. Sumi, *et al.* 1978. Brain malformations related to prenatal exposure to ethanol. J. Pediatr. **92:**64–67.
2. Finnegan, L. P. & B. A. Mac New. 1974. Care of the addicted infant. Am. J. Nurs. **74:**685–693.
3. Finnegan, L. P. 1978. Drug Dependence in Pregnancy: Clinical Management of Mother and Child. A manual for medical professionals and paraprofessionals prepared for the National Institute on Drug Abuse, Services Research Branch. U.S. Government Printing Office. Washington, D.C.
4. Zelson, C., E. Rubio & E. Wasserman. 1971. Neonatal narcotic addiction: 10-year observation. Pediatrics **48:**178–189.
5. Glass, L. 1974. Narcotic withdrawal in the newborn infant. J. Natl. Med. Assoc. **66:**117–120.
6. Finnegan, L. P., J. F. Connaughton, J. P. Emich & W. F. Wieland. 1972. Comprehensive care of the pregnant addict and its effect on maternal and infant outcome. Contemp. Drug Problems **1:**795–809.
7. Sussman, S. 1963. Narcotic and methamphetamine use during pregnancy. Effect on newborn infants. Am. J. Dis. Child. **106:**325–330.
8. Newman, R. G. 1974. Pregnancies of methadone patients. N.Y. State J. Med. **1:**52–54.
9. Taeusch, H. W., Jr., S. H. Carson, N. S. Wang & M. E. Avery. 1973. Heroin induction of lung maturation and growth retardation in fetal rabbits. J. Pediatr. **82:**869–875.
10. Zagon, I. S. & P. J. McLaughlin. 1977. Effect of chronic maternal methadone exposure on perinatal development. Biol. Neonate **31:**271–282.
11. Smith, A. A., F. W. Hui & M. Crofford. 1974. Retardation of growth by opioids. *In* Perinatal Pharmacology: Problems and Priorities. J. Dancis & J. C. Hwang, Eds.: 195–201. Raven Press. New York, N.Y.
12. Hutchings, D. E., H. F. Hunt, J. P. Towey, T. S. Rosen & H. S. Gorinson. 1976. Methadone during pregnancy in the rat: Dose level effects on maternal and perinatal mortality and growth in the offspring. J. Pharmacol. Exp. Ther. **197:**171–179.
13. Zelson, C. 1973. Infant of the addicted mother. N. Engl. J. Med. **288:**1393–1395.
14. Connaughton, J. F., Jr., L. P. Finnegan, J. Schut & J. P. Emich. 1975. Current concepts in the management of the pregnant opiate addict. Addict. Dis. **2:**21–35.

15. KANDALL, S. R., S. ALBIN, J. LOWINSON, B. BERLE, A. I. EIDELMAN & L. M. GARTNER. 1976. Differential effects of maternal heroin and methadone use on birthweight. Pediatrics **58:**681–685.
16. RAYE, J. R., J. W. DUBIN & J. N. BLECHNER. 1977. Fetal growth retardation following maternal morphine administration: Nutritional or drug effect. Biol. Neonate **32:**222–228.
17. CONNAUGHTON, J. F., JR., D. REESER, J. SCHUT & L. P. FINNEGAN. 1977. Perinatal addiction: Outcome and management. Am. J. Obstet. Gynecol. **129:** 679–686.
18. JONES, K. L. & G. F. CHERNOFF. 1978. Drugs and chemicals associated with intrauterine growth deficiency. J. Reprod. Med. **21:**365–370.
19. REMENTERIA, J. L. & N. N. NUNAG. 1973. Narcotic withdrawal in pregnancy: Stillbirth incidence with a case report. Am. J. Obstet. Gynecol. **116:**152–156.
20. NAEYE, R. L. 1965. Malnutrition: Probable cause of fetal growth retardation. Arch. Pathol. **79:**284–291.
21. GRUENWALD, P. 1963. Chronic fetal distress and placental insufficiency. Biol. Neonate **5:**215–265.
22. ZUSPAN, F. P., J. A. GUMPEL, A. MEJIA-ZELAYA, J. MADDEN & R. DAVIS. 1975. Fetal stress from methadone withdrawal. Am. J. Obstet. Gynecol. **122:**43–46.
23. NORTHROP, G., J. DITZLER, W. G. RYAN & G. O. WILBANKS. 1972. Estriol excretion profiles in narcotic addicted women. Am. J. Obstet. Gynecol. **112:** 704–712.
24. GLUCK, R. & M. V. KULOVICH. 1973. Lecithin/sphingomyelin ratios in amniotic fluid in normal and abnormal pregnancy. Am. J. Obstet. Gynecol. **115:**539–546.
25. JONES, J. 1974. Nutrition, drugs and their interrelations. Penna. Health **35:**6–8.
26. YAFFE, S. J. 1974. Fetal and neonatal pharmacology. Clin. Perinatol. **1:**39–46.
27. GEBER, W. F. & L. C. SCHRAMM. 1969. Heroin teratogenic and behavioral activity in hamsters. Fed. Proc. **28:**262 (abstract).
28. GEBER, W. F. 1970. Blockade of teratogenic effect of morphine and dehydromorphinone by nalorphine and cyclazocine. Pharmacologist **12:**296 (abstract).
29. HARPEL, H. S., JR. & R. F. GAUTIERI. 1968. Morphine-induced fetal malformations. I: Exencephaly and axial skeletal fusions. J. Pharm. Sci. **57:**1590–1597.
30. IULIUCCI, J. D. & R. F. GAUTIERI. 1971. Morphine-induced fetal malformations. II: Influence of histamine and diphenhydramine. J. Pharm. Sci. **60:**420–425.
31. JOHANNESSON, T. & B. A. BECKER. 1972. The effects of maternally-administered morphine on rat foetal development and resultant tolerance to the analgesic effect of morphine. Acta Pharmacol. et Toxicol. **31:**305–313.
32. OSTREA, E. M., JR. & C. J. CHAVEZ. 1979. Perinatal problems (excluding neonatal withdrawal) in maternal drug addiction: A study of 830 cases. J. Pediatr. **94:**292–295.
33. ABRAMS, C. A. L. 1975. Cytogenetic risks to the offspring of pregnant addicts. Addict. Dis. **2:**63–77.
34. AMAROSE, A. P. & M. J. NORUSIS. 1976. Cytogenetics of methadone-managed and heroin-addicted pregnant women and their newborn infants. Am. J. Obstet. Gynecol. **124:**635–640.
35. BURSTEIN, Y., P. J. V. GIARDINA, A. R. RAUSEN, S. R. KANDALL, K. SILJESTROM & C. M. PETERSON. 1979. Thrombocytosis and increased circulating platelet aggregates in newborn infants of polydrug users. J. Pediatr. **94:**895–899.
36. RORKE, L. B., D. S. REESER & L. P. FINNEGAN. 1977. Nervous system lesions in infants of opiate dependent mothers. Pediatr. Res. **11:**565 (abstract).
37. JHAVERI, R., L. GLASS, H. E. EVANS, S. DUBE, W. ROSENFELD, F. KHAN, J. D. SALAZAR & O. CHANDAVASU. 1979. Effects of methadone on thyroid function in mother, fetus and newborn. Pediatr. Res. **13:**380 (abstract).
38. KRON, R. E., M. LITT & L. P. FINNEGAN. 1974. Effect of maternal narcotic addiction on sucking behavior of neonates. Pediatr. Res. **8:**346 (abstract).
39. KRON, R. E., M. LITT, M. D. PHOENIX & L. P. FINNEGAN. 1976. Neonatal nar-

cotic abstinence: Effects of pharmacotherapeutic agents and maternal drug usage on nutritive sucking behavior. J. Pediatr. **88:**637–641.

40. KRON, R. E., S. L. KAPLAN, L. P. FINNEGAN & M. LITT. 1975. The assessment of behavioral change in infants undergoing narcotic withdrawal: Comparative data from clinical and objective methods. Addict. Dis. **2:**257–272.
41. DESMOND, M. M. & G. S. WILSON. 1975. Neonatal abstinence syndrome: Recognition and diagnosis. Addict. Dis. **2:**113–121.
42. ROTHSTEIN, P. & J. B. GOULD. 1974. Born with a habit. Infants of drug-addicted mothers. Pediatr. Clin. North Am. **21:**307–321.
43. GLASS, L. & H. E. EVANS. 1972. Narcotic withdrawal in the newborn. Amer. Fam. Phys. **6:**75–78.
44. GLASS, L., B. K. RAJEGOWDA & H. E. EVANS. 1971. Absence of respiratory distress syndrome in premature infants of heroin-addicted mothers. Lancet **2:**685–686.
45. ROLOFF, D. W., W. F. HOWATT, W. P. KANTO, JR. & R. L. BORER, JR. 1975. The effect of long-term maternal morphine administration on the growth and lung development of fetal rabbits. *In* Basic and Therapeutic Aspects of Perinatal Pharmacology. P. L. Morselli, S. Garattini & F. Serini, Eds.: 121–129. Raven Press. New York, N.Y.
46. FINNEGAN, L. P., Z. SHOURAIE, J. P. EMICH, J. F. CONNAUGHTON, J. SCHUT & M. DELIVORIA-PAPADOPOULOS. 1974. Alterations of the oxygen hemoglobin equilibrium curve and red cell 2,3-diphosphoglycerate (2,3-DPG) in cord blood of infants born to narcotic addicted mothers. Pediatr. Res. **8:**344.
47. BLINICK, G. 1971. Fertility of narcotic addicts and effects of addiction on the offspring. Soc. Biol. **18:**S34–S39.
48. BEHRENDT, H. & M. GREEN. 1972. Nature of the sweating deficit of prematurely born neonates. N. Engl. J. Med. **286:**1376–1379.
49. FINNEGAN, L. P. 1979. Abstinence syndrome in the neonatal period: Diagnosis and ramifications. *In* Proceedings of the Conference on Genetic, Perinatal, and Developmental Effects of Abused Substances. Airlie, Virginia. March 20–22, 1979. In press.
50. FINNEGAN, L. P. & K. FEHR. 1980. The effects of psychoactive drugs (including opiates) on the fetus and newborn. *In* Research Advances. O. Kalant, Ed.: Plenum Publishing Company. New York, N.Y. 653–723.
51. NATHENSON, G., M. I. COHEN, I. F. LITT & H. MCNAMARA. 1972. The effect of maternal heroin addiction on neonatal jaundice. J. Pediatr. **81:**899–903.
52. REDDY, A. M., R. G. HARPER & G. STERN. 1971. Observation on heroin and methadone withdrawal in the newborn. Pediatrics **48:**353–358.
53. BLATMAN, S. 1971. Methadone and children. Pediatrics **48:**173–175.
54. RAJEGOWDA, B. K., L. GLASS, H. E. EVANS, G. MASO, D. P. SWARTZ & W. LEBLANC. 1972. Methadone withdrawal in newborn infants. J. Pediatr. **81:** 532–534.
55. OSTREA, E. M., C. J. CHAVEZ & M. E. STRAUSS. 1976. A study of factors that influence the severity of neonatal narcotic withdrawal. J. Pediatr. **88:**642–645.
56. HARPER, R. G., G. SOLISH, E. FEINGOLD, N. B. GERSTEN-WOOLF & M. M. SOKAL. 1977. Maternal ingested methadone, body fluid methadone, and the neonatal withdrawal syndrome. Am. J. Obstet. Gynecol. **129:**417–424.
57. REESER, D. & L. P. FINNEGAN. 1978. High versus low dose methadone and its effect on neonatal outcome. Presented at the National Drug Abuse Conference. Seattle, Washington. April 3–8, 1978.
58. GODDARD, J. & G. S. WILSON. 1977. Management of neonatal drug withdrawal. J. Pediatr. **92:**861.
59. HERZLINGER, R. A., S. R. KANDALL & H. G. VAUGHAN, JR. 1977. Neonatal seizures associated with narcotic withdrawal. J. Pediatr. **91:**638–641.
60. SOULE, A. B., III, K. STANDLEY, S. A. COPANS & M. DAVIS. 1974. Clinical uses of the Brazelton Neonatal Scale. Pediatrics **54:**583–586.

61. Strauss, M. E., J. K. Lessen-Firestone, R. H. Starr, Jr. & E. M. Ostrea. 1975. Behavior of narcotics-addicted newborns. Child Dev. **46:**887–893.
62. Lodge, A., M. M. Marcus & C. M. Ramer. 1975. Neonatal addiction: A two-year study. Part II. Behavioral and electrophysiological characteristics of the addicted neonate. Addict. Dis. **2:**235–255.
63. Kreek, M. J. 1981. Narcotic disposition and interactions during the perinatal period in humans. *In* Proceedings of the Conference on Genetic, Perinatal, and Developmental Effects of Abused Substances. Airlie, Virginia. March 20–22, 1979.
64. Finnegan, L. P., D. S. Reeser & J. F. Connaughton. 1977. The effects of maternal drug dependence on neonatal mortality. Drug Alcoh. Dep. **2:**131–140.
65. Finnegan, L. P. 1979. *In utero* opiate dependence and sudden infant death syndrome. Clin. Perinatol. **6:**163–180.
66. Takashima, S., D. Armstrong, L. Becker *et al.* 1978. Cerebral hypoperfusion in the sudden infant death syndrome? Brainstem gliosis and vasculature. Ann. Neurol. **4:**257–262.
67. Wilson, G. S., M. M. Desmond & W. M. Verniaud. 1973. Early development of infants of heroin-addicted mothers. Am. J. Dis. Child. **126:**457–462.
68. Wilson, G. S., R. McCreary, J. Kean & J. C. Baxter. 1979. The development of preschool children of heroin-addicted mothers: A controlled study. Pediatrics **63:**135–141.
69. Ramer, C. M. & A. Lodge. 1975. Clinical and developmental characteristics of infants of mothers on methadone maintenance. Addict. Dis. **2:**227–233.
70. Strauss, M. E., R. H. Starr, E. M. Ostrea, C. J. Chavez & J. C. Stryker. 1976. Behavioral concomitants of prenatal addiction to narcotics. J. Pediatr. **89:**842–846.
71. Finnegan, L. P., D. S. Reeser & R. Y. Ting. 1978. Methadone use during pregnancy: Effects on growth and development. *In* A Multicultural View of Drug Abuse. D. E. Smith, S. M. Anderson, M. Buxton, N. Gottlieb, W. Harvey & T. Chung, Eds.: 324–330. Schenkman Publishing. Cambridge, Massachusetts.
72. Kaltenbach, K., L. J. Graziani & L. P. Finnegan. 1979. Methadone exposure *in utero*: Developmental status at one and two years of age. Pharmacol. Biochem. Behav. Supplement **11:**15–17.
73. Kaltenbach, K., L. J. Graziani & L. P. Finnegan. 1978. Development of children born to women who received methadone during pregnancy. Pediatr. Res. **12:**372.
74. Jones, K. S. & D. W. Smith. 1973. Recognition of the fetal alcohol syndrome in early infancy. Lancet **2:**999–1001.
75. Warner, R. H. & H. L. Rosett. 1975. The effects of drinking on offspring. An historical survey of the American and British literature. J. Stud. Alcohol **36:**1395–1420.
76. Lemoine, P., H. Harousseau, J. P. Borteyru *et al.* 1968. Les enfants de parents alcooliques: Anomalies observées à propos de 127 cas. Ouest-Med. **25:**477–482.
77. Youngs, D. D., J. R. Niebyl, D. A. Blake, D. A. Shipp, J. Stanley & T. M. King. 1977. Experience with an adolescent pregnancy program: A preliminary report. Obstet. Gynecol. **50:**212–216.
78. Jones, K. L. & Smith, D. W. 1975. The fetal alcohol syndrome. Teratology **12:**1–10.
79. Ouellette, E. M., H. L. Rosett, N. P. Rosman & L. Weiner. 1977. Adverse effects on offspring of maternal alcohol abuse during pregnancy. N. Engl. J. Med. **297:**528–530.
80. Clarren, S. K. & D. W. Smith. 1978. The fetal alcohol syndrome. N. Engl. J. Med. **298:**1063–1067.
81. Clarren, S. K., E. C. Alvord, Jr., S. M. Sumi *et al.* 1978. Brain malformations related to prenatal exposure to ethanol. J. Pediatr. **92:**64–67.

82. STREISSGUTH, A. P. 1976. Psychologic handicaps in children with fetal alcohol syndrome. *In* Work in Progress in Alcoholism. Ann. NY Acad. Sci. **273:**140.
83. MORRISON, J. R. & M. A. STEWART. 1971. A family study of the hyperactive child syndrome. Biol. Psychiatry **3:**189–195.
84. CANTWELL, D. P. 1972. Psychiatric illnesses in the families of hyperactive children. Arch. Gen. Psychiatry **70:**414–417.
85. STREISSGUTH, A. P., C. S. HERMAN & D. W. SMITH. 1978. Intelligence, behavior, and dysmorphogenesis in the fetal alcohol syndrome: A report on 20 patients. J. Pediatr. **92:**363–367.
86. HANSON, J. W., A. P. STREISSGUTH & D. W. SMITH. 1978. The effects of moderate alcohol consumption during pregnancy on fetal growth and morphogenesis. J. Pediatr. **92:**457–460.
87. PIEROG, S., O. CHANDAVASU & I. WEXLER. 1977. Withdrawal symptoms in infants with the fetal alcohol syndrome. J. Pediatr. **90:**630–633.
88. ROOT, A. W., E. O. REITER, M. ANDRIOLA *et al.* 1975. Hypothalamic-pituitary function in the fetal alcohol syndrome. J. Pediatr. **87:**585–588.
89. ROSETT, H. L., E. OUELLETTE, L. WEINER & E. OWENS. 1977. The prenatal clinic: A site for alcoholism prevention/treatment. *In* Currents in Alcoholism. F. A. Seixas, Ed. **1:**419–430. Harcourt Brace, Jovanovich. New York, N.Y.
90. JONES, K. L., D. W. SMITH, C. W. ULLELAND *et al.* 1973. Pattern of malformation in offspring of chronic alcoholic mothers. Lancet **1:**1267–1271.
91. LITTLE, R. E. 1977. Moderate alcohol use during pregnancy and decreased infant birth weight. Am. J. Public Health **67:**1154–1156.
92. FDA DRUG BULLETIN. 1977. Fetal alcohol syndrome. September-October **7:**18.

GENERAL DISCUSSION

Norman Zinberg, *Session Chair*

Department of Psychiatry
Harvard Medical School
The Cambridge Hospital
Cambridge, Massachusetts 02139

NORMAN ZINBERG: I was quite impressed by how much emphasis was given by the panel toward laboratory studies or studies of very hard cases, and how little emphasis was placed on the psychosocial aspects of the use of a variety of substances and, particularly, on the subjective effects of the substances. It was almost not mentioned. In one sense, you could say Dr. Cohen did in his very painful description of the amotivational syndrome. I can't help but wonder how he would contrast his views of intoxication with the very hard-working heroin addicts described by Dr. Mendelson.

It is something of a trend in our field and I guess it's been necessary, certainly over the last fifteen years, to catch up with the fact that most of the previous work on these substances has not been careful and certainly left many gaps to be filled in. But to do these studies with so little consideration for how people feel about the substances, what they are doing with them, what they mean to them, and the entire social aspects of use, seems to me to be something of a loss.

Although I think the laboratories will produce innumerable psychoactive substances in the next few years, I doubt very much if the trend of psychosocial use will be toward these substances. We know exotic substances come and go. We all have cloudy crystal balls, but it would be very much to my surprise that exotic drugs, despite their high impact, will replace the so-called bread-and-butter drugs. The latter drugs have a certain level of impact and are flexible in psychosocial use. It will be interesting to see what happens.

ROSS FISHMAN: Dr. Luisada, regarding young people who have PCP-induced psychotic episodes, do you think they would have a greater likelihood of having a nondrug-induced psychotic episode at some future time than others? Dr. Cohen, there's been talk that alcohol is particularly bad for younger people because their bodies are changing and developing. I'm not quite clear what that means. You mentioned something about the residual psychological effects of marijuana on the developing brain of the young person. Could you elaborate what you mean by the developing brain and what there is about it that makes a young person more sensitive to the effects of marijuana?

PAUL LUISADA: I will reply regarding psychotic reactions and PCP, from the perspective of six years of working with these patients in a catchment admission ward. Anybody who lives in that catchment area comes to the same ward no matter how long a time has elapsed since their last admission. We've noted that around one-fifth of these people who came to us for the first time with psychotic reactions from PCP have come back again, sometimes as late as three to five years later, with schizophrenic episodes, without using other drugs. I think this is pretty strong evidence that the kind of psychotic reactions we were seeing are really schizophrenic-like ones. The people who are exquisitely sensitive to PCP are schizophrenics. Perhaps the people we've seen are somewhere on the borderline and may not have had a psychotic reaction had they not used PCP.

SIDNEY COHEN: Almost all young animals tested react more strongly to neurotoxins than fully grown adult animals. I extrapolate this to mean that it is possible that a substance like Delta-9 tetrahydrocannabinol may have a greater impact on the developing brain than on one which is completely grown, a no longer highly metabolically active brain.

JAMES HALIKAS (*Medical College of Wisconsin*): Dr. Luisada, I'd like to compliment you on the excellent clinical and treatment perspectives you provided for us. What I was hearing was a description of a fluctuating sensorium, confusion, disorientation-inappropriate affect, hallucinations, delusions, and paranoid ideation. These are the classic symptoms of toxic brain syndrome, described more than 40 years ago in a landmark article by Wolf and Curran. In over 110 cases from more than 40 causal agents, they pointed out that patients bring to the specific clinical episode their past physical and mental health. People with depressive episodes in the past look depressed. People who have had litigious or paranoid personalities look very paranoid during the acute brain syndrome. What you were describing is not a schizo-affective episode. It's not an acute schizophrenic reaction. We made that mistake 15 years ago with marijuana and LSD. And if we have to repeat that error, it will be tragic for the field to start calling these reactions psychotic episodes or start calling them by functional psychiatric terms rather than what they are, acute brain syndromes.

Those of us who are in public education, who are dealing with the public and trying to educate them, are still suffering the effects of clinicians who described what they saw, but mislabeled their findings. I caution us to be much more prudent this time around.

PAUL LUISADA: I have trouble with the notion that these reactions should be labeled organic mental syndromes. In fact, they present very much like schizophrenia; disorientation was not common. Disorientation and the other signs of an organic brain syndrome were much less prominent than the loosening of associations, the disturbance of affects, the autistic thinking, and the formal thought disorder that is much more in the direction of schizophrenia.

It would be very hard for an objective observer of one of the psychotic individuals to diagnose organic brain syndromes without knowing any other facts. It is clear that on the basis of etiology, we are dealing primarily with an organic problem. But on the basis of symptomatology and presenting circumstances, it looks like an acute schizophrenic episode.

ROBERT MILLMAN: I'd like to agree with both comments. Under PCP one can get acute delirium, an acute toxic state, but one also gets, I truly believe, an acute schizophrenic-form reaction.

TOM UNGERLEIDER (*UCLA*): People of widely differing viewpoints on marijuana testified recently before a House Subcommittee. They reached agreement on eight reasonable points. But I was struck by the lack of mention of the one point on which agreement could have made a real difference. It could have united the scientific community on marijuana, perhaps to end the bickering and disunity that is so prevalent. If health problems result from marijuana use in certain persons, should those problems be handled by health care facilities rather than by criminalizing the possessor or user? My question for Dr. Cohen or any of you is, why was there this omission?

SIDNEY COHEN: There certainly is a health aspect to our marijuana problem, but there's also a political one. This government does not consider it a socially acceptable, legal drug, and therefore, we do have a police system of control that I do not admire. Nevertheless, it is there, and we can't deny that sort of reality.

Gabriel Nahas: The main thrust of the Congressional statement which was hammered out after the House hearings was the concern of many towards the increasing use of marijuana among the young. Many 12- and 13-year-olds believe that it's an innocuous drug, and probably would benefit from information warning them that it is a dangerous substance when used in daily amounts, as many do.

Now, I'd like to ask Dr. Grinspoon these questions on cocaine. What is the half-life of cocaine and its primary metabolites? What is the mechanism of tolerance to this drug? Is it metabolic, functional, or cellular? Also, what is the effect of cocaine on the brain reward system?

Lester Grinspoon: Actually, as far as I know, the answers to your questions are pretty much unknown. The half-life of cocaine is relatively short. Within 48 hours, it's impossible to detect cocaine in the blood. It is broken down from methylbenzoethanine to ethanine, but I do not believe that its effect on the reward centers is known.

Charles Riordan: Dr. Grinspoon, you said that all the undesirable effects of cocaine are much more impressive after the intravenous route of consumption. The implication was that intravenous injections were rather unusual. In our work with methadone patients and active heroin addicts, the intravenous route is almost the universal route used for cocaine. Thus your description of the medical, psychological, and economic difficulties arising from cocaine use are familiar everyday events to us. It's probably important to study this subpopulation who uses cocaine in a different way and for whom it may have different significant effects.

Lester Grinspoon: The key to your question is your own note that this is a subpopulation. There's no doubt that the opioid-using population does use cocaine, as it has used amphetamines, in the "speedball" phenomenon, i.e., use of both opiates and amphetamines or cocaine simultaneously. My remarks were directed to a more general use of cocaine and not to that subgroup.

Part VI. Alternative Perspectives on the Drugs of Abuse

PATTERNS OF NARCOTIC DRUG USE IN A CANCER PAIN CLINIC *

Ronald M. Kanner and Kathleen M. Foley

Department of Neurology
Memorial Sloan-Kettering Cancer Center and
Cornell University Medical College
New York, New York 10021

Introduction

The treatment of pain caused by chronic disease presents several serious problems. Relief of moderate to severe pain often requires narcotic analgesics, yet physicians are often reluctant to use them because of their abuse potential.[1-3] This reluctance is further encouraged by the fact that these drugs are carefully monitored by federal and state governments and physicians in prescribing such drugs, and pharmacists in dispensing such prescriptions must follow strict regulations. In addition, the pharmacology of narcotic analgesics is poorly understood by many physicians and their patients, who believe that physical dependence and addiction are interchangeable terms. As a result, physicians generally tend to underuse narcotics in medically ill patients with severe pain[4, 5] and this issue has recently received much public attention.[6, 7] This article reviews the limited available data on the use of narcotics in patients with chronic medical illness and our own experience in treating patients with pain due to cancer, to determine the patterns of narcotic drug usage.

Materials and Methods

We undertook a retrospective analysis of all new patients seen in the Memorial Sloan-Kettering Cancer Center (MSKCC) Medical Pain Clinic from January 1, 1977 to December 31, 1978, allowing for a six-month follow-up. A total of 103 patient charts were available for review. We assessed age, sex, tumor type and stage of disease, referral diagnosis and source of referral, duration of pain symptoms, length and type of previous narcotic exposure (PNE), previous pain procedures and pain clinic diagnosis. We examined analgesic and other drug intake from the patient medication sheets or from the physicians' progress notes and expressed intake as morphine equivalent doses in mg per 24 hours (MS/24 hr), according to the relative potency estimates of Houde.[8] Since the clinic population included both cancer and noncancer patients, these patients were analyzed as two separate groups to determine any differences in the patterns of drug use. We used the following terms as defined by The World Health Organization[9]: *Tolerance* is that state in which an individual is less susceptible to the effect of a drug as a result of its prior administration. *Physical dependence* is present when an abstinence syndrome appears

* This work was supported, in part, by grants from the Rita Allen Foundation and the Patricia Drake Hemingway Fund. Dr. Kanner is the recipient of an American Cancer Society Fellowship.

TABLE 1

AGE AND SEX DISTRIBUTION OF 103 PATIENTS PRESENTING TO THE PAIN CLINIC
MSKCC Pain Clinic: January 1977–December 1978

	Number of Patients	Age Range	Sex	
			Male	Female
Total number of new patients	103		36	67
With malignant disease	86	23–80	26	60
With nonmalignant disease	17	17–75	10	7

upon withdrawal of the drug. *Substance abuse* is the use of a drug in a manner that deviates from accepted medical or social patterns. Addiction (now, preferably referred to as *psychological dependence*) is a behavioral pattern of compulsive drug use and preoccupation with securing its supply.

RESULTS

Precisely 119 patients visited the medical pain clinic for the first time between January 1, 1977 and December 31, 1978. TABLE 1 shows the age and sex distribution in the 103 patient charts that were available for review. Eighty-six patients had cancer and 17 did not. There were 67 women and 36 men in this study. There was a significant difference ($p < .05$ by chi^2) in the male:female ratios between the nonmalignant and malignant groups (10:7 vs 26:60, respectively). This was due to the large representation of breast tumors. There was no significant difference in age between the two groups, with the average age being 58 (range 17–75 years) in the non-tumor group and 55.4 years (range 23–80) for the tumor group. The types of tumor associated with the latter group are listed in TABLE 2. Carcinoma of the breast was the most common tumor, occurring in 34% of the patients, with carcinoma of the lung occurring in 20% and tumors of the genito-urinary system occurring in 14% of patients. The miscellaneous category included patients with neurofibromatosis, lipomatosis, epidermoid tumors of the mouth, submaxillary glands or palate, adenocarcinoma with an unknown primary and one case of chronic lymphatic leukemia. Using a previously described classification of pain in cancer patients (10), these patients could be categorized according to their specific pain problems (TABLE 3). Fifty-three patients (62%) had pain directly associated

TABLE 2

TYPES OF TUMOR IN 86 PAIN CLINIC PATIENTS

Tumor Type	Number	%
Breast	29	34
Lung	17	20
GU	12	14
GI	8	9
Sarcoma	5	6
Melanoma	3	3
Lymphoma	3	3
Miscellaneous	9	11

TABLE 3

PAIN SYNDROMES IN 86 PATIENTS WITH MALIGNANT DISEASE

	Number	Total Number	%
Pain related to tumor involvement		53	62
Cause: bone	18		
nerve	24		
hollow viscus	11		
Pain related to tumor therapy		24	28
Cause: surgery	20		
radiation therapy	4		
Pain unrelated to tumor		9	10
Cause: musculoskeletal	4		
postherpetic neuralgia	4		
psychogenic	1		

with tumor infiltration, 24 patients (28%) had pain resulting from cancer therapy and 9 patients (10%) had pain unrelated to cancer. The tumor-produced pain was further subdivided into metastatic bone involvement in 18 of 53 patients, hollow viscus or soft tissue compression in 11 of 53 patients, and nerve compression in 24 of 53 patients. The pattern of nervous system involvement is shown in TABLE 4. Brachial or lumbar plexopathy occurred in 15 patients. Epidural spinal cord compression occurred in 7 patients, and cranial nerve and leptomeningeal metastases occurred in one patient each. Five of the seven patients with epidural spinal cord compression had been referred to the clinic with a different and incorrect diagnosis. Pain in the nine patients with a history of cancer but unrelated pain included post-herpetic neuralgia in four, musculoskeletal pain in four, and an affective disorder (depression) in one.

Of the seventeen patients with chronic benign pain (TABLE 5), six patients had post-herpetic neuralgia, three had musculoskeletal pain and two had post-surgical pain. There was one case each of thalamic pain, trauma, trigeminal neuralgia, multiple sclerosis, pleurisy and an affective disorder (depression). The duration of symptoms in the tumor group with both tumor-related or unrelated pain was approximately the same, ranging from two weeks to six months in duration. In patients without an underlying tumor, the durations of symptoms was longer, ranging anywhere from four months to four years.

TABLE 4

NEUROLOGICAL PAIN SYNDROMES IN 24 PATIENTS WITH MALIGNANT TUMORS INVOLVING NERVOUS SYSTEM

Syndrome	Number of Patients
Brachial plexopathy	8
Lumbar plexopathy	7
Base of skull metastasis	1
Leptomeningeal metastasis	1
Epidural spinal cord compression	7

TABLE 5

PAIN SYNDROMES IN 17 PATIENTS WITH NONMALIGNANT DISEASE

Postherpetic neuralgia	6
Musculoskeletal pain	4
Postsurgical pain	2
Thalamic pain	1
Trigeminal neuralgia	1
Multiple sclerosis	1
Pleurisy	1
Depression	1

PATTERNS OF DRUG USE

At the time of their first evaluation in the Medical Pain Clinic (TABLE 6) 65 patients were receiving narcotic analgesics alone or in combination with other medications. Twenty-two patients were not taking any analgesic, five were taking only nonnarcotic analgesics, and eleven patients were taking either sedative, psychotropic or anticonvulsant drugs. Aspirin and acetaminophen were the most commonly used nonnarcotic analgesics, whereas Percocet® (oxycodone plus acetaminophen) and meperidine were the most commonly used narcotic analgesics. The other narcotic analgesics in use included: Percodan® (oxycodone + APC), codeine and levorphanol. All drugs were prescribed for oral use, and no patient was receiving drugs parenterally. The amount of drug intake ranged from the analgesic equivalent of 5 to 150 mg. of parenteral morphine sulfate per 24 hours (MS/24 hr), and varied with the nature of the pain. Patients with tumor-related pain were taking significantly higher doses of narcotic analgesics than were the patients with nontumor pain. Of the 38 patients not receiving any narcotic analgesic, narcotics were started in three following the initial clinic evaluation. These three patients had metastatic bone disease (carcinoma of the lung with back pain in 2 and carcinoma of the breast with chest wall pain in 1). At the end of three months, follow up data were available on 81 of the original 103 patients (TABLE 7). Forty-five patients were receiving narcotic drugs, 42 of whom had been taking narcotic analgesics at the initial evaluation. Within this group, three patterns of drug use were evident. Group I consisted of 14 patients who had increased or doubled their amount of narcotic analgesic in the three month period. Thirteen

TABLE 6

PATTERNS OF ANALGESIC DRUG USE

	Drug intake on presentation:			
Type of Pain	None	Non-Narcotic	Narcotic	Other *
Malignant	16	3	59	8
Nonmalignant	6	2	6	3
Totals:	22	5	65	11

* Includes antidepressants, anticonvulsants and anti-inflammatory medications.

TABLE 7

NARCOTIC DRUG INTAKE, THREE-MONTH FOLLOW-UP

Drug Intake	Number of Patients (81)	
Narcotic:	45	
increased		14 (12 dead 6 months)
decreased		11
stable		17
started		3
No narcotics:	36	
no PNE		33
PNE		3

of these patients had a malignant origin of their pain, and 12 of 13 were dead by the six month follow up. Escalation of their drug intake was associated with rapidly progressive disease. This contrasts sharply with only 11 deaths among 62 cancer patients who did not increase their drugs in that period. Group II patients included 14 patients who either reduced their drug intake (n = 11) or discontinued their drugs (n = 3). In this group, the reduction of drug intake was associated with concurrent anticancer therapy. In the 17 patients who maintained their stable drug intake, all had evidence of nonprogressive disease, or a nonmalignant pain syndrome; there were no available data on the degree of tolerance or physical dependence in this group, as this was a retrospective study. Thirty six patients were not receiving narcotic drugs at the end of three months (TABLE 8). Post-incisional, post-herpetic and musculoskeletal pain accounted for the majority of the syndromes in both the tumor and nontumor groups not receiving narcotic analgesics for pain. Six-month follow-up data were available on 76 patients of the 103 original patients (TABLE 9). Twenty three patients were dead and 53 were still alive. Twenty-eight (53%) were still taking narcotic analgesic drugs. Of the 28 patients

TABLE 8

PAIN SYNDROMES IN PATIENTS NOT TAKING NARCOTICS AT THREE MONTHS (N=36)

Tumor		Non-Tumor	
Post-mastectomy	8	Post-incisional	2
Musculoskeletal	4	Musculoskeletal	3
Post-herpetic	3	Post-herpetic	5
Post-thoracotomy	1	Multiple sclerosis	1
Post-laparotomy	1	Pleurisy	1
Bone	1		12
Depression	1		
Plexus tumor	1		
Meningeal carcinomatosis	1		
Epidural cord compression	1		
Local disease	1		
Totals:	24		

TABLE 9

NARCOTIC DRUG INTAKE

	1st Visit	3 Months	6 months
Narcotic drug	65/103 *	45/81 †	28/53
Non-narcotic drug	38/103	36/81	25/53

* Percodan,® Percocet,® Demerol.®
† Percocet,® levodromoran, methadone.

requiring narcotics, 25 had tumor-related pain and 3 benign pain. There was no evidence of drug abuse among the cancer patients receiving narcotic analgesics for pain relief. No patient overdosed with his/her medication, took more than was prescribed or illicitly tried to buy or sell their narcotic drugs. In contrast, 2/17 patients with chronic nonmalignant pain abused their drugs, continually took more than prescribed amounts and overdosed on the drugs prescribed, and both had a long history of drug abuse behavior.

Brief case histories on three pain patients are detailed below to exemplify our tabulated data.

1. T.W. (FIGURE 1) was a 57-year-old woman with metastatic melanoma, diagnosed in November of 1972, who did well until May of 1977, when she presented with mid-thoracic back pain. A bone scan and myelogram revealed metastatic lesions in the T2 and L4 vertebral bodies, with minor epidural defects. She was treated with radiation therapy to both involved areas and the

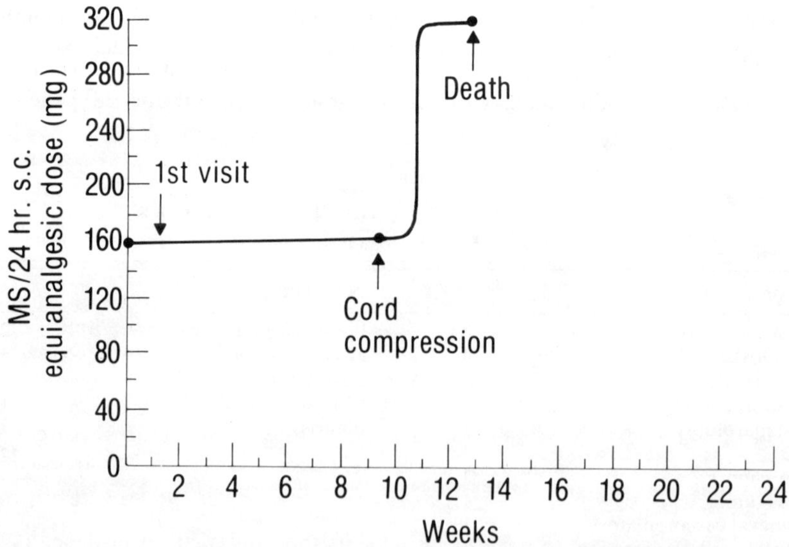

FIGURE 1. Pattern of narcotic intake in a 57-year-old female with malignant melanoma and bone metastases with narcotic intake expressed as morphine-equivalents per 24 hours (MS/24 hr) and plotted against time in weeks (see text).

pain was adequately controlled with levorphanol 4 mg p.o. q 4 hours (90 mg MS/24 hr). She remained on this dose for the next 8 months, at which time she developed a sudden exacerbation of pain, along with increasing shortness of breath, and a new pain in the right lower extremity. Levorphanol 12 mg p.o. every 3–4 hours with acetaminophen 600 mg and hydroxyzine 25 mg (total of 200–260 mg MS/24 hr) were required for adequate pain control. A myelogram now revealed progression of the bony vertebral disease with a complete epidural block in the thoracic region, and there were new metastatic lesions in several long bones and both lungs. Rapidly progressive metastatic disease had prompted the increase in her analgesic medication. The patient rapidly deteriorated and died within 4 weeks following the exacerbation of pain and the doubling of her narcotic intake.

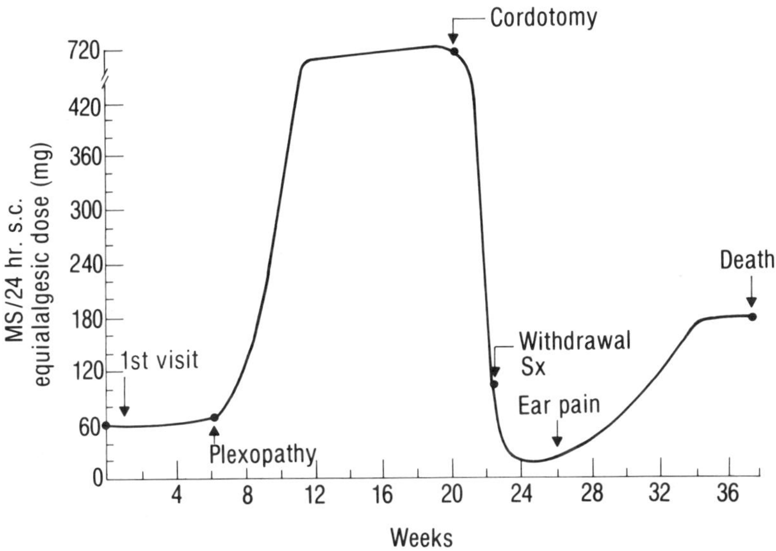

FIGURE 2. Pattern of narcotic intake in a 43-year-old female with carcinoma of the lung.

This patient illustrates a phenomenon often observed in patients with cancer: pain is controlled for long periods on a stable dose of narcotics, but progressive disease requires increasing doses of narcotic analgesic to effectively treat the pain. The onset of increased pain and increased drug intake heralded the worsening of the metastatic lesions and further progression of disease.

2. S.S (FIGURE 2) was a 43-year-old woman with the diagnosis of oat cell carcinoma of the lung, who first presented in August of 1977 with left scapular and neck pain. Three months later, she was noted to have a left Horner's syndrome with a chest x-ray revealing a tumor infiltrating the upper lobe of the left lung. An extent of disease work up at that time revealed no evidence of metastatic disease and the patient was started on chemotherapy and prophylactic whole brain radiation therapy. Her pain was initially controlled by small doses of codeine (10 mg MS/24 hr) but, by the time of diagnosis, the pain was so

severe that it required 4 mg of levorphanol by mouth every four hours (60 mg MS/24 hr). Radiation therapy to the lung apex was given, but in December 1977, she began to develop a C8 T1 radicular pain. Her doses of medication increased to 6 mg of levorphanol every 2 hours (180 mg MS/24 hr). By February of 1978, she had developed a brachial plexopathy with neurological deficits in the left upper extremity, unresponsive to radiation therapy and chemotherapy. Pain persisted but was partially controlled with 24 mg of levorphanol by mouth every 2 hours. By May of 1978, she required 30 mg of levorphanol, 60 mg of methotrimeprazine and 2 Percocet (oxycodone and acetaminophen) all p.o.q2h (nearly 1000 mg MS/24 hr) as well as amitriptyline 100 mg at bedtime. On this regimen she had partial relief of her pain, but her activities were limited by excessive sedation. She was then admitted to hospital for a high percutaneous cervical cordotomy. This procedure resulted in marked and dramatic pain relief. The patient discontinued her pain medications and, within a 24 hour period, developed a profound withdrawal syndrome characterized by yawning, lacrimation, diarrhea, diaphoresis and multifocal myoclonus. She did not request pain medication during this period of time and, in fact, refused narcotic drug because of the absence of pain. She was placed on a tapering dose of levorphanol (8 mg p.o. every 6 hours, 80 mg MS/24 hr) with complete resolution of her withdrawal signs. At the time of discharge, she was taking a total of 12 mg of levorphanol by mouth per day (30 mg MS/24 hr). Two weeks following cordotomy, she began to complain of pain in the left ear. This increased in severity and by July 1978, she required 6 mg of levorphanol p.o. every 2 hours (180 mg MS/24 hr). She developed further progression of disease with bronchial obstruction and died in August of 1978.

This particular patient exemplifies several points. She used narcotic analgesics for almost a year, with progressive escalation of dose always associated with objective evidence of progression of disease. Following the cordotomy, abrupt cessation of the drug precipitated a profound withdrawal syndrome without any drug seeking behavior. Withdrawal signs were controlled with reinstitution of low doses of narcotic analgesics. The surgical procedure was of limited value, with recurrence of pain requiring increasing doses of medication to treat the onset of the new pain. However, these doses of medication were significantly lower than those used in the patient prior to the cordotomy, suggesting that the relief of pain by cordotomy had allowed time for reduction of tolerance to medication and that lower doses of drug could be used effectively.

3. I.C. was a 60-year-old female with carcinoma of the breast widely metastatic to bone. Pain from her metastatic bone disease was well controlled on small doses of codeine (10 mg MS/24 hr), but progression of disease required increasing her drug intake to 2 Percocet p.o. q3h (20–30 mg MS/24). Further progression of disease, characterized by a left brachial plexopathy, required further analgesic medications, but with appropriate radiation therapy, she was able to return to baseline analgesic medications. Another increase in analgesic medications again heralded recurrence of disease and successful therapy was again able to return her to a low level of drug intake. She remained stabilized with adequate pain control on small doses of p.r.n. medications.

This particular patient demonstrates the long term (over two years) chronic use of analgesics in a patient with metastatic bone disease for which adequate pain relief is obtained by the use of such medications. Escalation of drug use in this patient was always associated with progression of disease, with rapid decrease in drug intake associated with appropriate radiation therapy.

Discussion

Chronic use of narcotic analgesics plays an important role in the management of acute and chronic cancer pain. From our study of the patterns of drug use in a cancer population, progression of metastatic disease with increasing severity of pain was the major factor in escalation of drug intake. Reduction of drug intake was associated with specific therapy directed at the cause of the pain for example, as in Figure 3, the use of radiation therapy in a patient with metastatic bone disease. Drug overdose, substance abuse and psychological dependence (addiction) did not occur in this population of patients with cancer. In contrast, 2 of 17 patients with nonmalignant pain syndromes abused narcotic drugs. Both patients had a prior history of narcotic abuse and had been specifically referred to the clinic as pain and drug management problems.

Since this study was a retrospective one, direct assessment of tolerance and

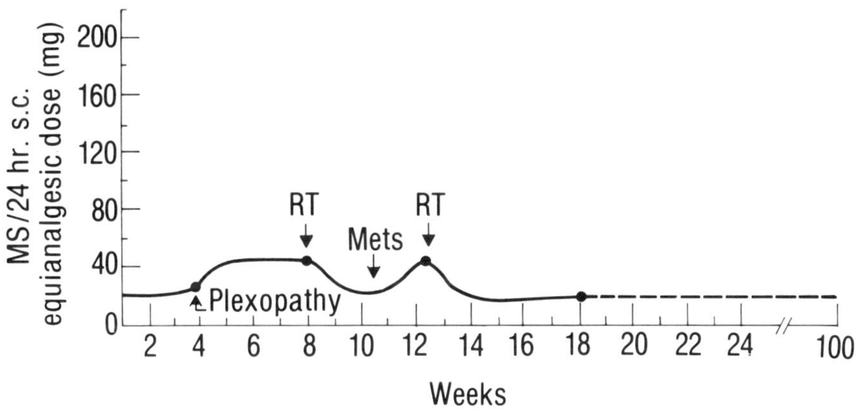

Figure 3. Pattern of narcotic intake in a 60-year-old female with carcinoma of the breast and bone metastases.

physical dependence could not be made. Previous studies by Houde *et al.* have demonstrated that tolerance occurs in cancer patients receiving narcotic analgesics for pain relief with a characteristic shift of the dose-response curve to the right.[8, 12]

The large amount of narcotic analgesics required by some patients who received narcotic analgesics for three months or longer suggests that tolerance did occur. The relationship of increasing pain severity and increasing requirements for narcotic drugs to the development of tolerance represents an important and unanswered question. Of particular interest is the group of patients without disease progression who stabilize on a set dose of narcotic drug with adequate pain control for three months or longer. Although Twycross has stated that tolerance is not a practical problem, tolerance is a practical clinical issue in patients with progressive disease and escalation of drug dose. In such patients, physicians are often reluctant to use sufficient doses of narcotic analgesics to overcome the existing tolerance.

Our experience with narcotic drug use in chronic pain is in sharp contrast to the anecdotal data suggesting that patients with chronic pain receiving narcotic analgesics are at high risk to become "addicted."[1, 3] As previously stated, it is this profound fear of addiction that plays a major role in physicians' underuse of narcotic analgesics in medical illness. In fact, there is little available published data to determine the degree of tolerance, physical dependence, substance abuse or addiction in patients receiving narcotic analgesics for chronic medical illness and pain. Many of the published studies do not adhere to strict definitions for drug use and abuse, making any review of such data practically impossible. However, in an attempt to review the available data on the subject of chronic pain and addiction, information on narcotic drug use can be obtained from several sources. Kolb, in a classic study in 1925,[13] described the personality types of 230 narcotic addicts and found 9% to be "persons of normal nervous constitution to whom an opiate had been prescribed to the point of addiction to relieve the suffering of some prolonged physical condition." Later studies by Pescor[14] reported that 3.8% of patients admitted to the Drug Addiction Center at Lexington, Kentucky, had become addicted to morphine given for "legitimate" reasons. In 1954, Rayport[15] used the term "medical addict" and defined such a patient as one who states that he first received narcotics from a physician to the point of addiction in the course of treatment of illness." Rayport divided medical addicts into three sub-classes based on the fate of their illness: Group 1 with self-limited illness; Group 2 with reversible illness; and Group 3 with irreversible illness. He studied a representative group of 1,020 male opiate addicts consecutively admitted to the Public Health Service Hospital in Lexington, Kentucky, and found the incidence of medical patients addicted to narcotics was 27% among whites and 1.2% among blacks. This high incidence figure is often quoted to support the anecdotal data that the use of narcotic analgesics in patients with chronic illness leads to narcotic addiction. However, these data present a very biased view of the subject. In a more recent prospective study, Porter and Jick[6] monitored the incidence of narcotic addiction in 39,946 hospitalized medical patients. Of 11,882 who received at least one narcotic preparation, there were only 4 cases of reasonably well documented addiction in patients who had no history of addiction. Their data, taken from a survey on a general population, suggest that medical use of narcotics is rarely, if ever, associated with the development of addiction. Further studies of prescription drug abuse provide other indirect data. In one study, Swanson *et al.*[16] looked at the patterns of abuse in a series of 225 patients hospitalized because of prescription drug abuse. Five of these patients had a history of past cancer, but no active disease. Sixty percent of patients abused more than one drug; 87 patients abused narcotic drugs as part of a multi-drug abuse pattern with meperidine and pentazocine the most common drugs abused among the narcotics. These patients all had long and complicated medical and psychiatric histories. In another study evaluating 500 veterans admitted to hospital for causes unrelated to drug use, Gault *et al.*[17] found that 32 or 6% fit the criteria for analgesic abuse. In that group, 18 of 32 patients complained of headache, 7 of 32 had arthritic complaints and only 1 of 32 had an underlying malignancy. Twenty-eight of the 32 patients took codeine in combination with non-narcotic analgesics, but the doses of codeine did not exceed 50 mg per day. Abuse of non-narcotic analgesics or combination drugs appeared to be a more common observation than the use of narcotic analgesics. This observation has been supported by two other studies by Bakewell and Wikler[18] and

Ewing and Bakewell[19] who found that approximately 7% of medically ill patients were dependent on non-narcotic rather than narcotic drugs. Further studies by Maruta *et al.*[20] described a group of 144 patients with chronic pain of nonmalignant cause referred to the Mayo Clinic. They classified 24% as drug dependent and 41% as abusers. However, their definitions left some boundaries rather unclear and the reason for referral to their pain clinic was often drug abuse.

Specific studies of narcotic use in specific medical pain syndromes are not available except from the data by Medina[21] who evaluated drug dependency in patients with chronic headache. Of 2,369 new patients, 62 patients had either taken a narcotic or a barbiturate during the six-month period prior to entry into the headache clinic. Of the 62 patients, 23 patients were taking narcotic drugs, but only 3 were abusing such drugs (2 were abusing codeine and 1 propoxyphene). These patients were in contrast to the 38 patients chronically taking Fiorinal®, a combination analgesic barbiturate, of whom 10 of 38 patients abused the medication.

The dearth of clinical studies therefore offer limited support to the belief that chronic narcotic use for analgesia is associated with a high risk of addiction. Analysis of the patterns of drug intake in our series of cancer patients suggests that drug abuse and drug addiction should not be the primary concern of the prescribing physician. Our data suggest that drug use alone is not the major factor in the development of addiction, but other medical, social and economic conditions seem to play an important role. This phenomenon has been well supported by studies of U.S. military personnel addicted to opiates in Viet Nam. From a random sample of 451 Army enlisted men who returned to the U.S. in September, 1971,[22] 44% indicated that they had used opiates in Viet Nam and 20% felt they were addicted. Eight to 12 months after their return, 10% reported some use of narcotics. Two percent indicated current use and 0.7% addiction. Only 5% of the sample received treatment after return to the U.S. and almost all of this was brief and occurred prior to discharge. This natural experiment demonstrated that drug-using behavior was strongly dependent on a series of factors including underlying personality and social, environmental and economic issues, all of which greatly influence and alter the risk of addiction.

There is no question that chronic painful medical illness represents a difficult clinical problem for both the patient and physician and a careful attempt to illuminate the usefulness, the appropriate role and the long-term effects of narcotic analgesics in this population may allow us to adequately treat patients with both acute and chronic pain on a more scientific and less anecdotal and fearful basis. It is only careful studies to clearly define the development of physical dependence and tolerance separate from psychological dependence that will allow us to use the drugs effectively and to advise their use in patients with specific pain problems.

References

1. Parkes, J. D. 1975. Diseases of the nervous system. Relief of pain: headache, facial neuralgia, migraine, and phantom limb. Br. Med. J. **4**:90–92.
2. Khatami, M. G. & C. O'Brien. 1979. Chronic pain and narcotic addiction: A multitherapeutic approach—A pilot study. Comprehensive Psychiatry **20**(1): 55–60.

3. LIPTON, S. 1980. Post Herpetic Neuralgia. *In* Relief of Pain in Clinical Practice. S. Liptson, Ed.: 240.
4. MARKS, R. M. & E. J. SACHER. 1973. Undertreatment of medical inpatients with narcotic analgesics. Ann. Int. Med. **78**:173.
5. GOODWIN, J. S. *et al.* 1979. Knowledge and use of placebos by house officers and nurses. Ann. Intern. Med. **91**(1):106–110.
6. PORTER, J. & H. JICK. 1980. Addiction rare in patients treated with narcotics. New Eng. J. Med. **302**(2):123.
7. MORGAN, J. P. 1977. Watching the monitors: "Paid" prescriptions, fiscal intermediaries and drug-utilization review. New Eng. J. Med. **296**(5):251–256.
8. HOUDE, R. W., S. L. WALLENSTEIN & T. W. BEAVER. 1966. Evaluation of analgesics in patients with cancer. *In* International Encyclopedia of Pharmacology and Therapeutics, Section 6, **1**: Clinical Pharmacology, L. Lasagna, Ed.: 59–70. Pergamon Press. Oxford, England.
9. MARTIN, W. R. 1977. Morphine Dependence. *In* Drug Addiction I. W. R. Martin, Ed.: 75–76. Springer-Verlag. Berlin, Germany.
10. FOLEY, K. M. 1979. The management of pain of malignant origin. *In* Current Neurology. H. R. Tyler & D. M. Dawson, Eds. **2**:279–302. Houghton Mifflin. Boston, Mass.
11. TWYCROSS, R. G. 1974. Clinical experience with diamorphine in advanced malignant disease. Int. J. Clin. Pharmacol. **9**:184–198.
12. HOUDE, R. W. 1979. Systemic analgesics and related drugs. *In* Advances in Pain Rescearch and Therapy. J. J. Bonica & V. Ventafridda, Eds.: **2**. Raven Press. New York, N.Y.
13. KOLB, L. 1925. Types and characteristics of drug addicts. Ment. Hyg. **9**:300.
14. PESCOR, M. J. 1939. The Kolb classification of drug addicts. Pub. Health Rep. Supp 155. United States Public Health Service. Division of Sanitary Reports and Statistics.
15. RAYPORT, M. 1954. Experience in the management of patients medically addicted to narcotics. J. Am. Med. Assoc. **156**(7):684–691.
16. SWANSON, D. W., R. L. WEDDIGE & R. M. MORSE. 1973. Abuse of prescription drugs. Mayo Clinic Proceedings. **48**:359–367.
17. GAULT, M. H., T. C. RUDWALL & N. I. REDMOND. 1968. Analgesic habits of 500 veterans: Incidence and complications of abuse. Canad. Med. Ass. J. **98**: 619–626.
18. BAKEWELL, W. E., Jr. & A. WIKLER. 1966. Incidence in a university hospital psychiatric ward. J. Am. Med. Assoc. **196**:710–713.
19. EWING, J. A. & W. E. BAKEWELL. Diagnosis and management of depressant drug dependence. Am. J. Psychiatry **123**:909–917.
20. MARUTA, T., D. W. SWANSON & R. E. FINLAYSON. 1979. Drug abuse and dependency in patients with chronic pain. Mayo Clinic Proceedings **54**:241–244.
21. MEDINA, J. L. & S. DIAMOND. 1977. Drug dependency in patients with chronic headaches. Headache **17**:12–14.
22. ROBINS, L. N. 1973. A Follow-up of Vietnam Drug Users. Spec. Action Office Monograph. Science A:1–23.

THERAPEUTIC USES OF THE DRUGS OF ABUSE

J. Thomas Ungerleider and Therese Andrysiak

Neuropsychiatric Institute
UCLA School of Medicine
Los Angeles, California 90024

Introduction

Any discussion of the therapeutic uses of the drugs of abuse requires careful attention both to definitions and to terminology. First of all, by therapeutic, we are here referring to a drug which is used in "modern" medicine rather than in folk medicine, and a drug which demonstrates more than a placebo effect. Time constraints preclude consideration of the therapeutic uses of all the drugs of abuse and even of all psychoactive drugs, those which affect the mind and behavior. Therefore, we will discuss selected drugs of abuse, particularly those drugs about which some controversy currently exists. We will make our selection from among those drugs which are in the Controlled Substances Act (C.S.A.), particularly in Schedule 1. The Controlled Substances Act of 1970, a Federal act which has been adopted by many states, imposes nine kinds of controls on scheduled or abusable substances. These drugs are here divided into five schedules according to the dual criteria of abuse potential and therapeutic usefulness. Severity of penalties for drug related offenses is partially related to these schedules. Those drugs which are in Schedule 1 have, by definition, a high drug abuse potential, are unsafe even when given under medical supervision, and have no therapeutic usefulness.

We will attempt to discuss only briefly policy and political issues, placing emphasis on scientific concerns. Thus, three of the four drugs selected for discussion are from Schedule 1. They include: LSD, marijuana, and heroin. Heroin has been covered in the previous presentation and so the material we will present about it will be somewhat abbreviated. We will also include, from Schedule 2, the amphetamines, currently the center of heated controversy in this country as far as the legal regulation of the indications for which they may be prescribed.

LSD

The prototype psychedelic drug LSD provides an excellent example of a situation in which promising research was being conducted for therapeutic uses when public hysteria forced discontinuation of this research. In the mid-1960s the number of projects dropped almost overnight from over seventy to half a dozen. This occurred following the adverse reactions which were being reported subsequent to widespread recreational use of LSD. This use was then being popularized by Timothy Leary's "Turn on, tune-in, drop-out" philosophy which featured alleged instant happiness, instant problem-solving ability and instant creativity in art and music by taking this compound.[1] There were over 1,000 clinical papers published and over 40,000 patients involved before this discontinuation of research with LSD.

The drug had early been studied as a simulator of schizophrenic psychosis, but the main source of psychotherapeutic interest was occasioned by the self reports of feelings of well being following use of the drug. In two studies, these self reports included decrease in depression, anxiety, guilt, and anger, as well as becoming more self-accepting, tolerant, religious, sensual, and introspective. Less materialism, greater calm, a tendency to not take themselves too seriously, and enhanced understanding both of self and others was also reported.[2, 3] In the area of psychodynamic psychotherapy LSD was used to recall early memories of childhood. A large LSD dose treatment regime, called psychedelic therapy, was employed to emphasize the mystical or conversion experience while the use of smaller doses, called psycholytic therapy, concentrated on exploring the unconscious via psychoanalytic techniques.[4] Some combined these techniques of LSD therapy.

Although the initial anecdotal reports were exciting and persons then treated with LSD claimed relief of symptoms and exhibited few adverse reactions, the work was preliminary, control groups were not used, nor were "double blind" techniques employed. This is especially important with LSD where set and setting are so crucial. Thus placebo effects had not been taken into account. Some work was also done with LSD in schizophrenic and autistic children, people with sexual problems, and with rehabilitation of criminals, but results again were also preliminary.

The second main research area in which LSD was used was in alcoholism where a number of studies were done, with some encouraging results and some controversy as to whether or not this condition would respond to LSD therapy.[5, 6] A third area of focus was in giving LSD to terminally-ill patients to help them face, approach and come to terms with dying and in needing less "narcotic" medication. This work had initially begun in an attempt to reduce pain in cancer patients. With LSD, morale was improved, less pain and depression were reported, and preparations for impending death were made.[7, 8]

Most potent drugs that are introduced are initially therapeutically embraced as cure-alls, followed by a time where disenchantment sets in, and eventually the drug takes its proper place in the therapeutic armamentarium. But with LSD, the therapeutic research was stopped by law and so no one knows just how effective it can be. This situation is significant because it illustrates how social policy and public hysteria can impede the scientific process, perhaps delaying it for decades. An excellent summary chapter on the therapeutic use of psychedelic drugs is provided by Lester Grinspoon and James Bakalar in their new book, *Psychedelic Drugs Reconsidered.*[9]

Marijuana

The retention of marijuana and its active ingredient, Δ-9-Tetrahydrocannabinol, in Schedule 1 of the C.S.A. has become controversial with the publication of double-blind studies confirming its therapeutic effectiveness, particularly as an antiemetic and antinauseant for cancer chemotherapy patients.[10, 11] In fact, the Food and Drug Administration (FDA), under legal constraint to reconsider the appropriate scheduling of marijuana and THC, found their own committee recommending removal of THC to Schedule 2, over one year ago. (This recommendation was ignored by both the Commissioner of the FDA and the Secretary of Health, Education and Welfare.)

At UCLA we have been administering THC in both oral and smoked form for almost nine years now in a variety of studies. Currently 24 states have passed marijuana therapeutic use bills, some also including its use for glaucoma, radiation sickness and a variety of other conditions. To receive approval for general use, a "C.S.A. drug" must be found to be *more* effective than other available drugs for a particular purpose, not just as effective or better than a placebo.

To digress for a moment, cannabis has been used since ancient times for a variety of conditions. In light of today's knowledge, the ancient uses of marijuana which seem promising include its use to stimulate appetite, alleviate pain and depression, and as a sedative. Until 1944, tincture of marijuana was listed in the U.S. Pharmacopoeia and The National Formulary, for use as an analgesic. Marijuana became more accessible to research with the synthesis of THC just a few years ago and provision of a stable supply by the government. This included grown cannabis with a standard THC content and the orally absorbable THC in sesame oil capsules.

The double-blind methodology is also important for this psychoactive drug. In our early marijuana research studies we originally found that some volunteers who were experienced marijuana smokers became "high" when smoking ordinary tobacco which they believed was marijuana. In the oncology research project, when giving oral THC, we have found that some patients had some extremely pleasant or unpleasant experiences which they attributed to marijuana. In fact, they had received the control drug prochlorperazine (Compazine®), which they had received many times previously, not THC. This should not surprise us if we recall past situations like the "mellow yellow" banana skin craze with persons having profound psychedelic experiences from smoking chemically inactive banana skins.

Before elaborating on THC in the nausea and vomiting of cancer chemotherapy, I would like to describe the serendipitious finding of the reduction of intraocular pressure which has led to the use of marijuana in glaucoma patients. At UCLA we were photographing the pupils of normal volunteers while they smoked the government-grown marijuana in a research setting. This experiment was designed to determine if cannabis dilated the subject's pupils, as was being claimed by Los Angeles Police Department's arresting officers when citing persons for marijuana intoxication, along with ataxia, dysarthria, circumoral pallor and a green coated tongue or palate. Doing a complete ophthalomologic work-up on these subjects at the time of photographing their pupils, Dr. Robert Hepler found that the pupils did not dilate, and also that the intraocular pressure was reduced significantly, in dose related fashion, by marijuana ingestion or inhalation in normal subjects. Following these preliminary findings, the study was extended to include glaucoma patients where the pressure reduction, particularly with wide angle glaucoma, was confirmed.[12]

Antiemetic and antinauseant effects of THC, particularly with cancer chemotherapy patients (and a few radiation therapy patients) have been described.[10] These may coexist with an increase in appetite, decrease in weight loss, reduction of anxiety and lessening of depression.[11] Both an increase and a decrease in the pain threshhold have been reported in different studies.

The UCLA cancer chemotherapy project over the past two and a half years has evaluated approximately 140 patients in a double blind THC vs. Compazine study with the patient serving as his own control. Approximately 20 of the patients have received multiple cycles of both drugs and an additional 90 patients have begun, but did not complete, the study for a variety of reasons. Preliminary findings on the first 66 evaluable patients indicate that the particular drug that each patient prefers is significantly related to a decrease in nausea, vomiting and relaxation but is not related to appetite, food intake, or mood. Contrary to what one might expect; all our marijuana *abusers* preferred Compazine, and of 31 marijuana users, only eight preferred THC. The age group 18 to 49 were divided equally in their drug preference; those aged 50–64 preferred Compazine and, surprisingly, those patients over 65 markedly preferred THC. In addition, patients for whom Compazine in previous cycles had helped *a lot* preferred Compazine, patients for whom Compazine had helped *a little* had a strong preference for THC, and patients for whom Compazine had not helped at all were equally divided in their preference for Compazine and THC (i.e., probably nothing helped these patients). These results have not yet been assessed as far as the amount of nausea reduction in proportion to the "high," as reported by Sallan and Zinberg,[10] the effect of mood elevation as reported by Regelson,[11] or to the specific chemotherapeutic regime.

Amphetamines

Amphetamines currently provide a particularly interesting area because the spotlight has been focused upon them by the Food and Drug Administration. The FDA claims that because they are "drugs of abuse" even if effective when taken as prescribed, their abuse potential justifies banning their use for obesity and allowing them only for hyperkinetic behavior and narcolepsy. There have been 100 therapeutic uses of amphetamines reported by a Medlars search. We will focus on its use in the conditions mentioned above as well as pain, depression, and epilepsy.

Obesity

A statement adopted by the American Medical Association's Council of Scientific Affairs in April of 1978 stated (regarding the medical use of amphetamines): "When used as anorexiants, these stimulants help some persons initially to curb their food intake. However, efficacy over a long period has not been demonstrated. Drugs should be prescribed for this purpose for a maximum of 4–6 weeks and then only as an adjunct to a comprehensive weight reduction program, including caloric restriction, appropriate exercise, and psychological support."[13]

Additionally, in the 1978–79 edition of the book, *Drugs of Choice,* dextroamphetamine is identified as the drug of choice as an anorexiant.[14]

Narcolepsy

The prevalence of narcolepsy is estimated to be between 40–70,000 persons in this country, effecting about as many men as it does women.[15] Amphetamines, introduced into clinical medicine in the 1930s, were first employed therapeutically in narcolepsy in 1935.[16] In 1957 the criteria now used for the diagnosis of narcolepsy were first presented by Yoss,[17] the main proponent of amphetamine as the conventional treatment of narcolepsy. He recommended that the dose of methamphetamine hydrochloride be increased until there is complete or nearly complete relief of symptoms and a move toward normal is demonstrated in the pupillogram.[17-19] Many narcoleptic patients report that the physicians to whom they have gone for help do not seem to understand the problem, have never heard of it, or have taken a moral stance with them, labeling them lazy, and unwilling to work. Lack of proper diagnosis and treatment may have serious psychological and social consequences.

While monoamine oxidase inhibitors also have a clearly confirmed therapeutic effect in narcolepsy their use is not recommended because of the severity of side effects, including hypotension, edema, and impotence.[20] Attempts to withdraw narcoleptics from MAO inhibitors have resulted in psychological effects ranging from hallucinations to suicidal thoughts. Tricyclic antidepressants are effective in relieving the cataplexy but are only minimally effective in decreasing the sleep attacks.

The long term use of amphetamines in the treatment of narcolepsy can be complicated by such side effects as irritability, paranoia, depression, and disturbance of nocturnal sleep. Although the REM-suppressing quality of amphetamines may be the mechanism of action, the beneficial effects are more likely related to their general stimulant properties.

Hyperkinesis

The use of stimulants in treating hyperkinesis, a condition characterized by overactive behavior, is indeed paradoxical.

Those who use stimulants for treatment of certain varieties of hyperkinetic behavior report definite improvement within a few days in those who will respond favorably.[21] Many physicians find the administration of stimulants a useful diagnostic as well as therapeutic tool.

Among the conclusions of the Conference on the Use of Stimulant Drugs in the Treatment of Behaviorally Disturbed Young School Children in 1971 were:

1. There is no evidence that the use of amphetamines in this age group leads to future "addiction" in later life.
2. No stigma should be attached to a child who has been prescribed medication for behavioral disorders.[22]

Pain

It was first known 30 years ago that amphetamines enhanced analgesics for post-operative pain. The use of amphetamines to reduce pain has received renewed attention with the discovery and publicity of the "Sunday Syndrome." This consists of high dose oral amphetamine use on game day among professional football players, particularly those playing in the defensive line, not only to increase alertness and induce a rage response but also to diminish pain and allow them to "play hurt."

Epilepsy

As recently as 1975 amphetamines have been described in the literature to play a role in the treatment of epileptic patients, particularly in diminishing the drowsiness induced by anti-convulsant drugs. In 1965 the HEW listed both dexedrine and metamphetamine under anti-convulsants currently available.

Depression

Psychiatrists have been using amphetamine preparations to treat depressed and anxious patients long before the tricyclic drugs were developed. Many affective disorder clinics carefully and judiciously will use amphetamines when there is no response to the tricyclics. Amphetamines have also been used as a predictor of tricyclic response.[23] An experimental oral methamphetamine derivative was given to 35 depressed patients, which resulted in significant improvement of mood, psychomotoricity, interest in work and environment, appetite and sleep.[24]

Heroin

The International Symposium on Pain of Advanced Cancer held in Venice, Italy, in May of 1978 stated as its primary goal, "to help rectify the serious deficiencies that exist in the current management of pain of advanced cancer." Among papers presented were those which focussed on trials of various opiates and derivatives thereof, and cautioned against unrealistic concern about tolerance and dependence. Frequent mention of the need for individual analgesic regimes was also noted. When asked to comment on the use of "addictive" drugs for the relief of pain in advanced cancer population Dr. Twycross, of Churchill Hospital in Oxford, England remarked, "I don't talk about addictive drugs; it's as alien to me as referring to, let's say, aspirin as a drug which induces deafness." [25]

A number of studies, particularly in England, have evaluated the efficacy of heroin as an analgesic and sedative, some with promising results. A randomized controlled trial of 146 patients with orally administered diacetylmorphine (heroin) and morphine given every four hours to an advanced cancer population at St. Christopher's Hospital, London, demonstrated heroin to be about 1.5 times more potent than morphine. The results also indicated (in a study of urinary excretion) that heroin is completely absorbed by the G.I. tract but that morphine is only two-thirds absorbed.[25]

In another study of 115 patients with advanced cancer, individually optimized doses of heroin were administered regularly for 12 weeks to relieve pain, coughing, and general distress. The data supported the hypothesis that generally increased doses are necessitated by pain rather than by tolerance.[26] And, a double blind comparison of intravenous morphine, heroin, methadone and pentazocine (Talwin®) in the relief of pain in suspected acute myocardial infarction (MI) was conducted at the Royal Victoria Hospital in Belfast (N = 118). This study concluded that all four drugs are effective analgesics and produce adequate sedation. However, heroin brought about rapid and complete pain relief in the highest proportion of patients, although a fall in systolic blood pressure with the heroin (which is known to be associated with increased mortality) did not make it the drug of choice following MI.[27]

Conclusions

Some of the promising and/or continued therapeutic uses of a selected list of drugs of abuse have been presented and discussed.

Social policy and political ramifications are difficult, but necessary, to separate from scientific pursuits with these compounds.

It is well to remember that no drug is good or evil; they are chemicals which have effects and side effects. It is how they are used, the context, that makes them useable/therapeutic or abusable.

References

1. Ungerleider, J. T., Ed. 1968. The Problems and Prospects of LSD. CC Thomas. Springfield, Illinois.
2. Savage, C., J. Fadiman, R. Mogar & M. H. L. Allen. 1966. The effects of psychedelic (LSD) therapy on values, personality, and behavior. Int. J. Neuropsychiatry **2**:241–254.
3. McGlothlin, W., S. Cohen & M. S. McGlothlin. 1970. Long lasting effects of LSD on normals. J. Psychedelic Drugs **3**(1):20–31.
4. Osmond, H. 1970. On being mad. *In* "Psychedelics: The Uses and Implications of Hallucinogenic Drugs." B. Aaronson & H. Osmond, Eds.: 21–28. Anchor Books. Garden City, N.Y.
5. Hoffer, A. 1967. A program for the treatment of alcoholism: LSD, malvaria and nicotine acid. *In* "The Use of LSD in Psychotherapy and Alcoholism." H. Abramson, Ed.: 353–402. Bobbs-Merrill. New York, N.Y.
6. Ludwig, A. M., J. Levine & L. H. Stark. 1970. LSD and Alcoholism: A Clinical Study of Treatment Efficacy. CC Thomas. Springfield, Illinois.
7. Kast, E. 1966. Pain and LSD-25. A theory of attenuation of anticipation. *In* LSD: The Consciousness Expanding Drug. D. Solomon, Ed.: 239–254. G. P. Putnam's. New York, N.Y.
8. Pahnke, W. N., A. A. Kurland, S. Unger, C. Savage, S. Wolf & L. E. Goodman. 1970. Psychedelic therapy (utilizing LSD) with cancer patients. J. Psychedelic Drugs **3**(1):63–75.
9. Grinspoon, L. & J. B. Bakalar. 1979. Psychedelic Drugs Reconsidered. Chap. 6: 192–238. Basic Books. New York, N.Y.
10. Sallan, S. E., N. E. Zinberg & E. Frei. 1975. Antiemetic effects of Δ 9 tetrahydrocannabinol in patients receiving cancer chemotherapy. N. Engl. J. Med. **293**(16):795–797.
11. Regelson, W., J. R. Butler, J. Schultz, T. Kirk, L. Peck, M. L. Green & O. Zakis. 1976. Δ 9 tetrahydrocannabinol as an effective antidepressant and appetite stimulating agent in advanced cancer patients. *In* Pharmacology of Marijuana. M. C. Braude & S. Szara, Eds.: 763–776. Raven Press. New York, N.Y.
12. Hepler, R. S. & I. M. Frank. 1971. Marihuana smoking and intraocular pressure. J. Am. Med. Ass. **217**:1392.
13. Council on Scientific Affairs. 1978. J. Am. Med. Ass. **240**(21):2317–2319.
14. Modell, W. 1978. Drugs for overeating. *In* 1978–1979 Drugs of Choice.: 312–322. Mosby Co. St. Louis, Mo.
15. Solidatos, C. 1978. Narcolepsy: Evaluation and treatment. J. Psychedelic Drugs. **10**(4):319–325.

16. Prinzmetal, M. & W. Bloomberg. 1935. The use of benzedrine for treatment of narcolepsy. J. Am. Med. Ass. **105:**2051–2054.
17. Yoss, R. E. & D. D. Daly. 1957. Criteria for the diagnosis of the narcoleptic syndrome. Proc. Staff Meeting Mayo Clinic. **32:**320–328.
18. Yoss, R. E. & D. D. Daly. 1968. On the treatment of narcolepsy. Med. Clin. North Am. **52:**781–787.
19. Yoss, R. E. 1969. Treatment of Narcolepsy. Mod. Treat. **6:**1263–1274.
20. Wytt, R. J., D. H. Fram & R. Buchbinder. 1971. Treatment of intractable narcolepsy with a monamine oxidase inhibitor. N. Engl. J. Med. **285:**987–991.
21. Cohen, S. 1972. Drug Abuse and Alcoholism Newsletter. Ritalin and Preludin. **1**(8).
22. Hearings: 1972. Subcommittee to Investigate Juvenile Delinquency. Amphetamine Legislation, July 15–16, 1971. U.S. Government Printing Office. Washington, D.C.
23. Fawcett, J. & V. Siomopoulos. 1971. Dextroamphetamine response as a possible predictor of improvement with tricyclic therapy in depression. Arch. Gen. Psychiatry **25:**247–255.
24. VanPraag, H. M. & J. Korf. 1973. 4-Chloramphetamines, chance and trend in the development of new antidepressants. J. Clin. Pharmacol. **13:**3–14.
25. Twycross, R. G. 1979. The Brompton Cocktail. *In* Advances in Pain Research and Therapy. J. . Bonica & V. Ventafridda, Eds. **2:**291–299. Raven Press. New York, N.Y.
26. Twycross, R. G. & J. Shari. 1976. Long term use of diamorphine in advanced cancer. Adv. Pain Res. Therapy. J. J. Bonica & D. Albe-Fessard, Eds. **1:** 653–661. Raven Press. New York, N.Y.
27. Scott, M. D. & R. Orr. 1969. Effects of diamorphine, methadone, morphine and pentazocine in patients with suspected acute myocardial infarction. Lancet **1:**1065.

GENERAL DISCUSSION

Roger Meyer, *Session Chair*

University of Connecticut Health Center
Farmington, Connecticut 06032

GABRIEL NAHAS: A comment concerning Dr. Ungerleider's comments about marijuana: Marijuana is a crude drug which contains about 400 chemicals, many of which have unknown and undesirable side effects. So the exploration of the possible therapeutic effects of marijuana should not be limited to that of a single compound, like THC. THC is a compound that we know a lot about. Dr. Foley, could we have your experience with the Brompton cocktail?

KATHLEEN FOLEY: The Brompton cocktail, a liquid mixture originally devised in the Brompton Hospital in England, includes heroin in varying doses, cocaine (up to 10 mg.), a phenothiazine, some type of cherry elixir, and alcohol. The Brompton mixture has come to this country in a series of abortive forms. It is used inappropriately and rather inexactly. At the present time, both Cecily Saunders and Robert Twycross, who have done most of the studies in this field, reported that they did not see the advantage of cocaine in the mixture and that the alcohol tended to burn the throats of patients, who usually did not like it unless they had previous interest in alcohol. Furthermore, they feel the phenothiazine was of questionable value. They now use either varying doses of heroin or morphine in tap water.

JOHN MORGAN (*New York City*): I agree with the remarks about the Brompton cocktail. Soon after reading about this cocktail, we made up a mixture using methadone. Methadone is the best-absorbed analgesic, although there are others that work as well. As you know, amphetamine is an adequate substitute for cocaine.

There are adequate data that amphetamine will lift the depression produced by the morphine-type drugs and that amphetamine seems to have an analgesic effect in combination with morphine.

KATHLEEN FOLEY: The problem with the studies on amphetamine is that they were all done on acute postoperative patients and not on patients with chronic pain. A comparable study of patients with chronic pain taking narcotics and amphetamines might be very interesting. Secondly, we cannot convince our patients to take dextroamphetamine because even on 10 mg. they complain bitterly of feeling too "zipped-up" on the drug. We've not had success in using it to overcome the sedative opiate effects.

IAN ZERKOFF (*Hershey, Pennsylvania*): Dr. Foley, in your studies of heroin and morphine as analgesics at Sloan Kettering, do they have the ability to extend the survival times of patients?

KATHLEEN FOLEY: The major therapeutic value has been to confirm the point made by the British that they can control pain in 97% of cancer patients when they use an adequate pain regimen which includes heroin. In this country, we at Memorial feel that we can control 95% of a patient's pain using any narcotic analgesic, and that the issue is not heroin versus morphine, but rather whether physicians have adequate information about the pharmacology of narcotic drugs and use them appropriately in patients. So, our particular thrust in looking at heroin was much more from the perspective of how heroin differs from other narcotic analgesics and also the pharmacokinetics of heroin. Looking at the cancer patient allowed us that experimental model.

IAN ZERKOFF: My question concerns a possible effect on the tumor itself.

KATHLEEN FOLEY: There is no evidence of an effect on tumors.

DONALD JASINSKI (*Addiction Research Center, Baltimore, Maryland*): Regarding abused drugs, it is useful to seek drugs which are effective therapeutic agents, but which do not have the abuse potential; also, to find ways to minimize their abuse and to seek new types of therapeutic uses. For example, the issue of heroin in analgesics is important, although most people who studied analgesics knew in advance what the results with heroin were going to be, similar to the situation with Dilaudid. Many years ago, we recognized that it was inappropriate to give someone with pain a multidose vial of morphine and a box of syringes. So we worked to develop other narcotic analgesics which we felt had lower abuse potential and which were orally effective.

The same thing can be said about THC. For example, in glaucoma management, it has too many side effects compared with other new types of agents. So the scientific community in its search for selective glaucoma agents has responded by making THC derivatives.

TOM UNGERLEIDER: I agree with Dr. Jasinski in one sense. When treating glaucoma with the new drug timolol, tolerance develops in some patients, and there is a real need for other drugs in certain other patients. But the problem is that some patients may get the wrong idea and go looking for marijuana first, before they've tried the other antiglaucoma drugs. One should recall that all these drugs may have severe side effects.

KARL VEREBEY: Dr. Jasinski just set the stage for my comment. The dilemma seems to be something that we met in drug metabolism way back in the 1950s, when Dr. Brody was looking for a typical animal model to study drug metabolism that will fit man. The problem and question were, which man? Perhaps there are individuals who will respond and some individuals who will not. Any drug in which only 25 percent of the population would respond would be discarded as a useful therapeutic agent. So I feel that individuality in response to certain medications or drug combinations is going to be a challenge of the future. Regarding Dr. Foley's presentation, don't patients who are treated for pain have very little likelihood of becoming dependent? I believe many cancer patients are undertreated with opioids because of fear of drug dependence. In terminal illness, it's totally absurd not to give patients the necessary pain relief. Physicians should be reeducated about the use of opiate therapy in cancer patients.

KATHLEEN FOLEY: Can I just comment on that last remark? This country has now moved dramatically toward treating the terminal patient better. But what about the burn patient? After they recover from their burns, they go back into normal society. That's the patient who is really undertreated. What about the patient with rheumatoid arthritis who is going to live 30 more years? How is that individual going to survive? Those are the patients for whose pain there's no headway being made at the present time. The cancer issue is before us all. If you're going to die, what does it matter? That's an easy way out.

I think the much harder issue to present to this group is the patient who is going to live for a long period of time. What are the risks, and the social issues in that population if chronic analgesics are given? There are just no data.

PART VII. ACUTE AND PROTRACTED ASPECTS OF THE ABSTINENCE SYNDROME

OPIATE WITHDRAWAL SYNDROME: ACUTE AND PROTRACTED ASPECTS

Donald R. Jasinski

National Institute on Drug Abuse
Addiction Research Center
Baltimore, Maryland 21224

For nearly 50 years, the focus of much therapeutic research at the Addiction Research Center (ARC) has been the opiate abstinence syndrome. Such research has been directed to treatment of acute abstinence, to detoxification and to understanding the role of physical dependence in compulsive narcotic use. The iatrogenic physical dependence of methadone maintenance and its negative impact on the rehabilitative process has intensified the need for continued therapeutically oriented studies of the abstinence syndrome. This presentation will summarize the highlight evolving concepts of the abstinence syndrome developed at the ARC.

In the 1920s efforts were made to detoxify addicted patients without suffering or discomfort since the therapeutic emphasis was on breaking the "habit." [1] Conceptually, the "narcotics habit" was equated to physical dependence; treatment of narcotic addiction was focussed on detoxifying patients.[1] In the 1930s and 1940s, Himmelsbach developed a sophisticated scoring system for abstinence based upon changes in physiologic parameters and behavior.[2] Using this scoring system, Himmelsbach rigidly assessed a number of treatment modalities, found their ineffectiveness and confirmed that morphine and codeine relieved abstinence, with gradual dose reduction the most efficacious means of detoxification.[2–4] Subsequently, Himmelsbach analyzed the time course of untreated acute abstinence,[2] showed that the intensity of abstinence was proportional to the maintenance dose,[5] established the principle of cross-dependence [6] and provided the classical description of the physiologic changes in the early or primary abstinence syndrome.[7]

During the 1940s, two other studies introduced new concepts regarding detoxification from morphine and the role of physical dependence in the addictive process. Intensive clinical studies of methadone by Isbell [8, 9] indicated that abstinence in methadone dependent patients had a longer latency, was milder and lasted longer than abstinence in morphine dependent patients. Isbell then introduced methadone as the agent for detoxifying addicts.[10] About the same time, Wikler made the observation that the abstinence syndrome could be conditioned and recognized the role of learning in the addictive process.[11] From a therapeutic viewpoint, it became apparent that the pharmacologic physical dependence was not by itself responsible for relapse.

In the early 1950s, clinical studies of the narcotic antagonist nalorphine resulted in the introduction of nalorphine precipitated abstinence as a diagnostic test for physical dependence and indicated the means for developing analgesics of lower abuse potential than morphine.[12]

Isbell recognized that addicts could distinguish morphine from other psychoactive drugs and that they reported stereotyped symptoms after morphine and pleasurable alterations in feeling states.[1] As a result, methodological studies were started to develop psychometric measures of the drug induced alterations in mood, feeling states, thinking and behavior (subjective effects).[1] Hill and Haertzen recognized that addicts shared personality characteristics with criminals and alcoholics characterized by an elevated psychopathic deviate scale score in the Minnesota Multiphasic Personality Inventory.[13] This observation led to studies defining the role of psychopathic feeling states in addiction.[14]

In the 1960s, Martin and his colleagues observed that the abstinence syndrome in rats had an early or primary phase and a longer lasting protracted (or secondary) abstinence syndrome.[15] A subsequent experimental direct addiction study was conducted in volunteers with morphine.[16-18] Chronic administration of morphine constricted pupils, elevated blood pressure and pulse rate, decreased respiratory rate, decreased the sensitivity of the respiratory center to CO_2 and increased urinary norepinephrine excretion. A two-phased abstinence syndrome was described. The early withdrawal phase, lasting 4 to 10 weeks, was characterized by increases in pupil size and elevation of blood pressure, pulse rate, body temperature and respiratory rate. The respiratory center was hypersensitive to CO_2 and urinary 17-hydroxycorticosteroids excretion were increased. This early phase gradually evolved into a secondary abstinence syndrome, lasting at least through 26 weeks of withdrawal, characterized by decreases in pupil size, blood pressure, pulse rate and body temperature to values below those observed in the pre-drug control. The respiratory center became hyposensitive to CO_2 and urinary epinephrine excretion increased.

Clinical studies of the narcotic antagonist cyclazocine[19] indicated that 1) physiologic changes of abstinence could be produced without the presence of subjective withdrawal discomfort or drug-seeking behavior and 2) that tolerance developed to the agonist but not the antagonist effects of cyclazocine. These two observations led to: 1) increased focus of clinical studies on the subjective effects of psychoactive drugs and their role in the addictive process and 2) the development of antagonists as treatment modalities in narcotic addiction which culminated in the development of naltrexone.[20]

The use of methadone as a treatment modality in addiction led to a reevaluation of its' clinical pharmacology with a direct addiction study in volunteer addicts.[21] Acute and protracted abstinence phases were observed which were similar to those observed for morphine. Two additional observations were made. Protracted abstinence was characterized by an increase of REM sleep and sleep time. More importantly, chronic administration of methadone was associated with increases in the negative feeling states associated with psychopathy. Withdrawal exacerbated these negative feeling states which then persisted into the protracted phase of abstinence.

A number of clinical studies[1] of the abuse liability of narcotic antagonists indicated that such compounds could produce little or no agonist effects (naloxone and naltrexone), agonist effects characterized by sedation and dysphoria (cyclazocine and nalorphine) and agonist effects similar to morphine (profadol and propiram). These studies, as well as those in the chronic spinal dog,[22] led to the introduction of the concepts of multiple receptors, receptor dualism and differences in intrinsic activity to explain the relationship of the morphine antagonist action of these drugs to their varied pattern of agonist effects. One class of such drugs are both morphine agonists and antagonists (partial agonists of the morphine type). One member of this class, buprenorphine, shares potential as a drug for treatment of narcotic addiction.[23] As a therapeutic agent for addiction, buprenorphine: 1) produces changes in feelings that are acceptable to addicts, 2) is long lasting and can be administered once daily or less frequently, 3) is significantly less toxic than methadone and 4) produces little, if any, physical dependence. Further, the drug is capable of blocking the toxic, euphorigenic and physical dependence producing properties of heroin or other narcotics through the mechanism of cross-tolerance and competitive antagonism. Buprenorphine appears to have the advantage of both methadone and naltrexone but without the major disadvantage of each.

In summary, 50 years of research has allowed us to potentially utilize narcotics therapeutically both to relieve pain as well as to treat addiction without the production of physical dependence.

References

1. Jasinski, D. R. 1977. Assessment of the abuse potentiality of morphinelike drugs (methods used in man). *In* Drug Addiction I: Morphine, sedative/hypnotic and alcohol dependence. W. R. Martin, Ed.: Handbook of Experimental Pharmacology **45:**197–258. Springer-Verlag. Heidelberg, West Germany.
2. Kolb, M. R., C. K. Himmelsbach. 1938. Clinical studies of drug addiction. III. A critical review of the withdrawal treatments with method of evaluating abstinence syndromes. Amer. J. Psychiat. **94:**759–797.
3. Himmelsbach, C. K. 1937. Clinical studies of drug addiction. I. The absence of addiction liability in "perparin." Public Health Reports Supp. 122.
4. Himmelsbach, C. K. 1937. Clinical studies of drug addiction. II. "Rosium" treatment of drug addiction. Public Health Reports Supp. 125.
5. Andrews, H. L. & C. K. Himmelsbach. 1944. Relation of the intensity of the morphine abstinence syndrome to dosage. J. Pharmacol. Exp. Therap. **81:**288–293.
6. Himmelsbach, C. K. 1934. Addiction liability of codeine. J. Amer. Med. Ass. **103:**1420.
7. Himmelsbach, C. K. 1941. The morphine abstinence syndrome, its nature and treatment. Ann. Int. Med. **15:**829–839.
8. Isbell, H., A. Wikler, N. B. Eddy, J. H. Wilson & C. F. Moran. 1947. Tolerance and addiction liability of 6-dimethylamino-4-4-diphenyl-heptanone-3 (methadone). J. Am. Med. Ass. **135:**888–894.
9. Isbell, H., A. Wikler, A. M. Eisenman, M. Daingerfield & K. Frank. 1948. Liability of addiction to 6-dimethylamino-4-4-diphenyl-3-heptanone (methadone, "amidone," or "10820") in man. Arch. Int. Med. **81:**362–392.
10. Isbell, H. & V. H. Vogel. 1949. The addiction liability of methadone (amidone, dolophine, 10820) and its use in the treatment of the morphine abstinence syndrome. Am. J. Psychiat. **105:**909–914.
11. Wikler, A. 1948. Recent progress in research on the neurophysiologic basis of morphine addiction. Am. J. Psychiat. **105:**329–338.
12. Isbell, H. & H. F. Fraser. 1950. Addiction to analgesics and barbiturates. J. Pharm. Exper. Therap. **99:**355–397.
13. Hill, H. E., C. A. Haertzen & R. Glaser. 1960. Personality characteristics of narcotic addicts as indicated by the MMPI. J. Gen. Psych. **62:**127–139.
14. Martin, W. R., B. B. Hewett, A. M. Baker & C. A. Haertzen. 1977. Aspects of the psychopathology and pathophysiology of addiction. Drug Alcoh. Dep. **2:**185–202.
15. Martin, W. R., A. Wikler, C. G. Eades & F. T. Pescor. 1963. Tolerance to and physical dependence on morphine in rats. Psychopharmacologia **4:**247–260.

16. MARTIN, W. R. & D. R. JASINSKI. 1969. Physiological parameters of morphine dependence in man—tolerance, early abstinence, protracted abstinence. J. Psychiat. Res. **7**:9–17.
17. MARTIN, W. R., D. R. JASINSKI, J. D. SAPIRA, H. G. FLANARY, O. A. KELLY, A. K. THOMPSON & C. R. LOGAN. 1968. The respiratory effects of morphine during a cycle of dependence. J. Pharm. Exp. Therap. **162**:182–189.
18. EISENMAN, A. J., J. W. SLOAN, W. R. MARTIN, D. R. JASINSKI & J. W. BROOKS. 1969. Catecholamine and 17-hydroxycorticosteroid excretion during a cycle of morphine dependence in man. J. Psychiat. Res. **7**:19–28.
19. MARTIN, W. R., H. F. FRASER, C. W. GORODETZKY & D. E. ROSENBERG. 1965. Studies of the dependence-producing potential of the narcotic antagonist 2-cyclopropylmethyl-2′-hydroxy-5, 9-dimethyl-6, 7-benzomorphan (cyclazocine, Win-20, 740; ARC II-C-3). J. Pharm. Exp. Therap. **150**:426–436.
20. MARTIN, W. R. 1977. Chemotherapy of narcotic addiction. *In* Drug Addiction I: Morphine, sedative/hypnotics and alcohol dependence. W. R. Martin, Ed.: Handbook of Experimental Pharmacology **45**:279–318. Springer-Verlag. Heidelberg, West Germany.
21. MARTIN, W. R., D. R. JASINSKI, C. A. HAERTZEN, D. C. KAY, B. E. JONES, P. A. MANSKY & R. W. CARPENTER. 1973. Methadone—a reevaluation. Arch. Gen. Psychiat. **28**:286–295.
22. MARTIN, W. R., C. G. EADES, J. A. THOMPSON, R. E. HUPPLER & P. E. GILBERT. 1976. The effects of morphine- and nalorphine-like drugs in the nondependent chronic spinal dog. J. Pharm. Exp. Therap. **197**:517–532.
23. JASINSKI, D. R., J. S. PEVNICK & J. D. GRIFFITH. 1978. Human pharmacology and abuse potential of the analgesic buprenorphine. Arch. Gen. Psychiat. **35**: 501–516.

GENERAL DISCUSSION

Vincent P. Dole, *Session Chair*

The Rockefeller University
New York, New York 10021

VINCENT DOLE: These are interesting and productive papers. Obviously, the hope for the future is to understand better the mechanism of relapse. Anecdotally, all of us who have treated patients have been struck by the triggering action of the environment on a particular relapse.

Whether it's possible in a more systematic way to desensitize, as the allergist tries to do with his mild injections of pollen, remains to be seen. We will be watching with the greatest interest what future developments come from this technique.

JOE LEVIN (*University of Illinois Medical Center*): In 1959, I had a heroin treatment group at Cook County Jail. I got into some trouble quite accidentally as part of an educational program. We showed them the film "Addiction in Monkeys" and then we discussed their withdrawal experiences. What I was interested in was how long does it take after an addict shoots up for the withdrawal to stop?

After this film session and our talk about withdrawal, they went back into their cells. The next day, the warden called me in to ask, "What's going on in your group? I don't think that you're pushing drugs, because seven of those guys got sick and I don't think they'd have gotten sick if you were pushing drugs." I assumed that talking about their own withdrawal might have actually triggered the withdrawal symptoms. Another interesting discovery in that session was that the withdrawal didn't stop when they "shot-up." Withdrawal stopped as soon as they made a buy even though sometimes it took them an hour or two before they found a place that was safe to "shoot-up." Yet, the withdrawal signs on the street stopped when they made the buy.

CHARLES O'BRIEN: If I could just comment on withdrawal. This is such a complicated phenomenon, but I do believe that there is an important anxiety component in withdrawal as it occurs naturally. The anxiety component is relieved when they've got the buy and they know that it's O.K., but the physiological part of it may still be there. Certainly interesting is the work that the Walter Reed group did in Viet Nam. During withdrawal without detoxification, the people just went "cold turkey" and had very few complaints because they knew they couldn't get anything. Yet, when the investigators examined the physiological data, the patients clearly had very heavy dependence, in fact, much worse physiological evidence of withdrawal than usually is seen in the States. Similarly, people in prisons often have less severe withdrawal when they know that there's no chance of getting anything.

In our studies, we are always trying to separate the anxiety components from the conditioned physiological components.

ROBERT MILLMAN: Meyer and Mirin report that the discriminative stimulus for heroin craving is heroin availability. Naltrexone protected patients, and those on Antabuse® often have little in the way of abstinence symptoms or drug craving. To look at these phenomena in another way, depression and anxiety may be an integral part of the opiate withdrawal syndrome. Some of the physical signs may be a reflection of the vegetative signs of these states. The meaning of the anxiety or depression in the individual may be critical in determining his subsequent behavior. Some may well integrate these affects and symptoms, particularly in supportive or highly structured environments; others perceive these feelings as life-threatening and may even attempt suicide.

PAUL CUSHMAN: I have a question for Dr. Jasinski. Buprenorphine has a biphasic dose response curve for analgesia. Do you know what the dose response curve with buprenorphine looks like for morphine-like subjective effects?

DONALD JASINSKI: We went up to two milligrams; the analgesic dose which was used about 0.2 mg. and, I think, equivalent to 10 mg. of morphine. We actually did three studies up to 2 mg., but then they took the prisoners away. So we never got to it. Our evidence suggests effects were beginning to plateau somewhere between 1 and 2 mg.

My guess is that the maximum degree of effects would be equivalent to 20 to 30 mg. of morphine, which puts it about 15 mg. of heroin. It's hefty from the viewpoint of the changes in feeling states in a nondependent, nontolerant subject. On the other hand, regarding apnea, it is not a very marked dose.

RICHARD RESNICK: Dr. O'Brien, the patient maintained on naltrexone, I assume, would have extinction of these conditioned responses in his natural environment. If that's true, what's the purpose of having this systematic extinction in the laboratory?

CHARLES O'BRIEN: Well, there we get into the cognitive phenomena as well as the autonomic sort of unconscious conditioning phenomena. There is a great deal of extinction that goes on in anybody that you keep on naltrexone for a long period of time. I totally agree with you there. We got good results with naltrexone patients who did not go through laboratory extinction. But naltrexone patients usually fail to extinguish the drug acquisition and self-injection effects, because they knew it would be pointless. Thus, they hardly ever tested.

So in order for us to get them to extinguish drug seeking and use, perhaps we have to do some sort of therapeutic intervention that gets them actively engaged; it's like cooking up behavior. But that's a hypothesis at this point, because there certainly can be good results without this if they stay on it long enough. We know from learning studies that just the mere passage of time is a pretty inefficient way for extinction to occur; active extinction is a much more efficient way. We found that the mass extinction seems to be the most efficient of all. Since it's done over a short period of time, it might really be a useful package to add to our treatment programs.

LAWRENCE HATTERER (*New York Hospital*): Dr. Jasinski, you delineated very excellently the history of the addictive process and its chronic or end stages. I'd like to know whether or not you studied the early or middle phases of the process outside of a hospital setting as a way of determining what these treatment processes would be.

DONALD JASINSKI: The answer to this is no. These were all done within the confines of the then U.S. Public Health Service Hospital at Lexington.

LAWRENCE HATTERER: The reason I asked that question is that it seems to me that so much of the work is done at the end stages of the addictive process and we know all too little about the psychological and chemical nature of the early and middle phases when the patient doesn't present himself as needing treatment. It distorts the complete picture.

DONALD JASINSKI: May I comment on this? The point which I hope came across was that merely passive physical dependence is not sufficient to make an addict.

Secondly, I would say that mere conditioning in combination with physical dependence is not sufficient to produce an addict. There has to be a third element, which is whatever these peculiar personality deficits are in the addict population. Many of these abnormalities we've looked at are great egocentricity and impulsivity. This particular will-state which these people have when they're not under narcotics is exacerbated by the narcotics and really goes out of kilter when the drug is withdrawn.

Is the hyperexcitability of the nervous system essentially a drug-induced disease or is there a preexisting diathesis? There is evidence that such people began having problems long before they started drugs. They had problems in school and problems with other drugs. It seems that the drugs which they are using may, in fact, exacerbate this natural process.

SIDNEY SCHNOLL (*Philadelphia*): In hearing about the protracted abstinence syndrome and the conditioned responses that we see in the people we are treating, I have to look at what's happening fiscally as the state agencies, PSRO's, and so forth, are cutting down on the time we have to treat people. This is especially important since we do have such high relapse rates.

ARNOLD SCHECTER (*Binghamton, New York*): Dr. Jasinski, in looking down the road perhaps two or three years to when buprenorphine is available in trial clinics, how will induction occur with buprenorphine?

DONALD JASINSKI: I can't answer that. They took the prisoners away. Extrapolating from animal pharmacology, especially in the chronic opioid-dependent dog, as in the studies of Bill Martin, depending upon the stage of the animal in terms of its level of morphine, one could either antagonize or suppress with buprenorphine. Very shortly after a stabilization dose of morphine is reached, buprenorphine would precipitate abstinence. However, if you allow the level of morphine to decrease, that is, let the animal start into a withdrawal syndrome, at this time buprenorphine would suppress withdrawal. Additionally, then it was also dependent upon size of the maintenance dose of morphine.

This phenomenon has been demonstrated in humans with other drugs in this class.

HERBERT KLEBER (*New Haven*): Dr. Jasinski stated that buprenorphine has a low abuse potential, and yet Dr. Mendelson indicated it had some objective effects very close to that of morphine.

DONALD JASINSKI: I often am asked what one means by abuse potential. One assumes that the prototypic narcotic drug for abuse potential is morphine or heroin. The fact that a substance can serve as a reinforcing substance in and of itself means very little. It is so nonspecific since monkeys can work their tails off to obtain raisins and chocolate bars. Secondly, if a substance is liable to cause pleasurable subjective changes, that doesn't mean it's a reinforcer or likely to be abused.

If you are a diabetic taking insulin, insulin is a very strong reinforcer with little abuse potential. The question of abuse potential also relates to its ability to produce physical dependence, its ability to cause death and other types of toxicity. The concept of relative abuse potential is one we've operated on in medicine for a long time. Certain drugs are safer than others.

If you're a doctor treating a patient with pain, you're going to get in less trouble treating him with oral aspirin and codeine than you are giving a bottle of morphine and a box of syringes. You're going to get into less trouble by prescribing buprenorphine than you would with morphine. That's what I mean by less abuse potential.

Our concepts of physical dependence are beginning to change. It's not solely the classical withdrawal syndrome. We're beginning to look at this problem as leading to what Abe Wikler used to call secondary pharmacological reinforcement of behavior. This includes ability to face behavior and subjective effects. We know that these are not necessarily related to the physical changes. Then this whole argument about physical dependence and psychological dependence is a meaningless semantic argument.

PETER GESSNER (*State University of New York at Buffalo*): Regarding relapse in alcoholics, at the University of Washington they are trying to educate their relapsed patients. Relapse is a help in learning not to do it again. They've also been teaching them to recognize prodromal symptoms.

They are finding that this training is facilitating greater ability to withstand relapses.

HENRI BEGLEITER: In human alcohol cases, the vermis of the cerebellum is a selective, vulnerable area. Have you had the opportunity to study this area?

DONALD JASINSKI: We have, in fact, looked at the acute effects of alcohol in animals, and the vermis is one of the areas which, of course, shows drastic effects. I am also conducting both electrophysiological, neuroradiological, and neuroatomical studies in alcoholics, looking at brains before and after death. There are changes, but most of the changes which occur in the brain as a consequence of alcohol abuse are primarily cortical.

The two areas which were described many, many years ago by Corveal, namely the frontal cortex and parietal cortex, are both drastically affected. There are now a number of CAT-scan studies, including our own, showing that these are the two areas which are primarily affected by long-term abuse of ethanol. But to be sure, these are not the only two areas. There have also been ventricular changes and changes in cerebellum and hippocampus.

HENRI BEGLEITER: And some vascular changes.

THE NEUROBIOLOGICAL IMPLICATIONS OF CLONIDINE HCl

Mark S. Gold and A. Carter Pottash

Fair Oaks Hospital and
Psychiatric Diagnostic Laboratories of America
Summit, New Jersey 07901

INTRODUCTION

We have previously reported that the imidazoline derivative, clonidine, is an effective nonopiate treatment for opiate withdrawal.[1-5] The alpha adrenergic agonist clonidine, in acute double-blind studies reversed the affective and physiological symptoms and signs of methadone[1, 2] and other opiate withdrawal.[5] In a 14-day study, clonidine was also demonstrated to be effective as a rapid nonopiate treatment for moderate dose methadone withdrawal which enabled patients to be opiate and clonidine-free in less than 14 days.[6, 7] These clinical data suggested that chronic opiate treatment could be abruptly discontinued with a nonopiate treatment without the expected affective or physiological consequences. We suggested that the opiate withdrawal syndrome itself might be better understood from the point of view of the critical (symptom-generating) neurobiological events. The critical neural events we were interested in were those which follow the discontinuation of chronic opiate administration and directly result in clinical signs and symptoms.[3, 4] In this paper, we review the rodent, primate, and human data which have supported an endorphin-locus coeruleus (LC) disinhibition hypothesis for opiate withdrawal.[1, 3, 5] This norepinephrine (NE) hyperactivity hypothesis can explain a large body of clinical and preclinical data and may be useful in predicting newer and more effective nonopiate treatments.[4] We will also briefly mention some of the clinical practice implications of clonidine treatment for drug rehabilitation programs and physicians. We will review the neuroanatomical and neurochemical implications of clonidine first, and in the most detail, because we believe that these implications of clonidine HCl may have more long range utility than clonidine HCl itself, as better nonopiate treatments became available. In other words, we predict that clonidine will be but the first in a series of noradrenergic-inhibitor medications which will become available for rapid and safe nonopiate detoxification.

Opiate—LC Connection

The effects of opiates on catecholamine neurons have been reported elsewhere[8-10] but have tended to show that opiates can decrease NE activity and turnover.[11, 12] Studies of the brain's major noradrenergic nucleus, nucleus locus coeruleus (LC), have clearly demonstrated that the prototype opiate, morphine, causes a marked reduction in the normal LC neuronal firing rate.[12] These LC neurons are known to respond to a painful stimulus with an increased firing rate and this pain-induced effect can be blocked by morphine.[12] These data demonstrated an important opiate-NE interaction and suggested the possibility that some of the effects of opiates might be mediated by opiate-induced decreases in LC activity and NE release.[12, 13] The discovery of specific opiate receptors in the brain,[14, 15] the data by Pert *et al.*[16] and Simon[17] demonstrating very dense opiate receptor accumulations in the LC and the use of naloxone reversal in electrophysiological studies as a means of identifying effects which could be attributable to opiate receptor stimulation[14, 18-20] allowed LC-endorphin, LC-enkephalin and LC-opiate interactions to be expanded and more clearly understood. Investigators using single neuronal recording techniques and microiontophoresis reported that endogenous opiates and exogenous opiates decreased LC firing rates and that this effect was specifically reversed by the opiate antagonist naloxone.[18-20] These data suggested that the specific opiate receptors on the LC which might normally utilize endorphins as a natural neurotransmitter inhibit LC firing rate and modulate ascending NE activity and release.[4, 18-20] Naloxone only antagonized opiate and enkephalin effects but did not, by itself, produce an increase in LC activity.[20] These data suggested that this LC-opiate interaction was not tonic; that is, endorphins do not tonically inhibit LC activity but rather endorphin is released in response to neural or environmental events. These data suggested to us that a critical endorphin-LC connection might exist and be related to some opiate effects and possibly play a critical role in opiate withdrawal[1, 4] as chronic exogenous opiate administration tonically inhibits the LC.

The existence of LC cell body receptors for norepinephrine (NE) and epinephrine (E) were also suggested by single neuronal electrophysiological and microiontophoretic studies by Aghajanian and coworkers[21, 23] and confirmed in binding–affinity studies.[24] LC neurons responded to the alpha-2 adrenergic agonist clonidine with a decrease in LC firing[21, 22] resulting in a marked decrease in NE release[25, 26] and turnover[27, 28] in whole brain, cortex, and more recently arteriovenous-difference studies.[29] This depressant effect of clonidine on LC neurons could be reversed by the alpha-2 adrenergic antagonist piperoxane but not other drugs (B-blockers, naloxone) without specificity for this alpha receptor.[21, 22] These data suggested that LC activity may be tonically modulated, under normal physiological conditions, by presynaptic NE or E release. These studies clearly demonstrated that in very low doses clonidine decreases LC activity and piperoxane increased LC activity and that these drugs influenced LC activity by their interaction with inhibitory alpha-2 adrenergic on the LC.[21, 22] In higher doses this specificity is lost and clonidine has effects on postsynaptic NE and other receptors.[30, 31]

LC: Pharmacological Activation Studies

Piperoxane was given to nonhuman primates[32] in doses (1 mg/kg; 2.5 mg/kg) which were previously shown to increase noradrenergic activity in rats[20] and turnover in these nonhuman primates.[32] Piperoxane produced a behavioral syndrome which resembled spontaneous opiate withdrawal.[32] A virtually identical primate "panic" syndrome was evoked by yohimbine, a drug similar in neurochemical action to piperoxane.[34] Piperoxane administration studies suggested that noradrenergic augmentation might be a model system for studying the neuroanatomy, neurophysiology, and neurochemistry of opiate withdrawal which related to specific physiological and affective parameters. We also demonstrated that piperoxane-induced increase in these specific monkey behaviors and physiological signs could be reversed by morphine through an opiate receptor-mediated mechanism, as assessed by naloxone reversal (see FIGURE 1). The synthetic M-Enkephalin FK 33–824 had a similar effect on this pharmacological NE-augmentation primate model system.[35] Clonidine was also demonstrated to block or reverse the effects of piperoxane.[32] This effect was not antagonized by naloxone. These behavioral data suggested that the noradrenergic LC is under the dual côntrol of inhibitory alpha-2 and opiate

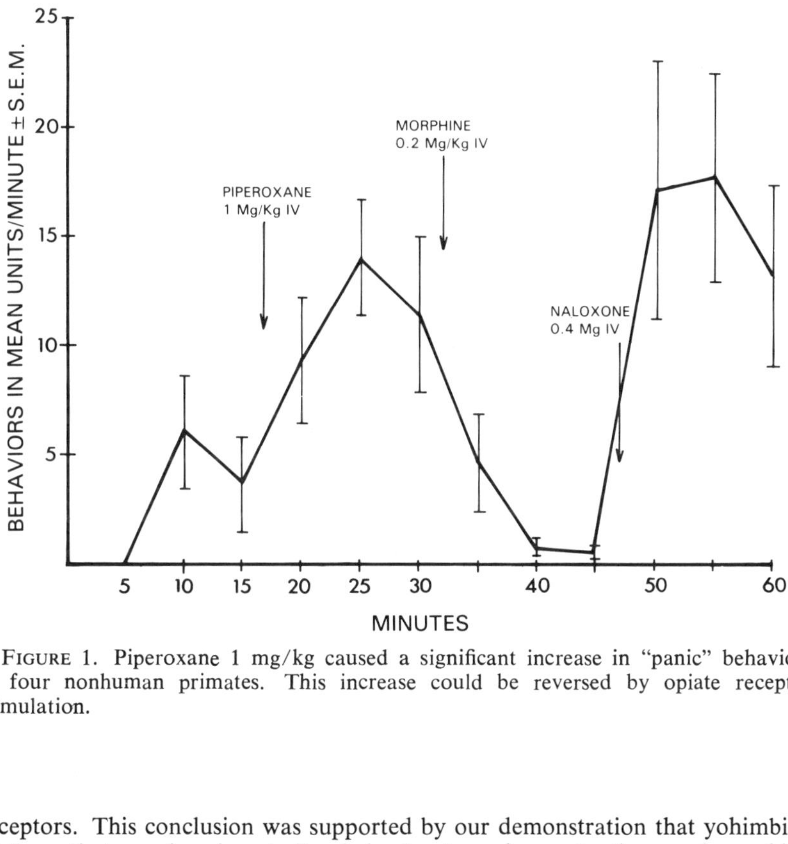

FIGURE 1. Piperoxane 1 mg/kg caused a significant increase in "panic" behaviors in four nonhuman primates. This increase could be reversed by opiate receptor stimulation.

receptors. This conclusion was supported by our demonstration that yohimbine (2.5 mg/kg) produced a similar behavioral syndrome in the monkey which could be blocked or reversed by morphine or clonidine.[36]

These primate drug studies led to the hypothesis that the effects of piperoxane and yohimbine mimicked the majority of opiate withdrawal signs and symptoms. We attributed the "panic syndrome" to NE effects and suggested that a common noradrenergic hyperactivity mediates the behaviors observed after piperoxane, yohimbine or discontinuation of chronic opiate administration (See FIGURE 2).[4, 32]

LC: Electrical Activation Studies

To test these hypotheses, we more specifically increased noradrenergic activity by electrical stimulation (biphasic, bipolar 0.2–0.4 MA, 0.5 mSec, 5–50 HZ) of the locus coeruleus. Electrical stimulation produced a behavioral syndrome with physiological changes which were very similar to that produced by piperoxane.[36, 37] Electrical stimulation-induced changes could be completely blocked or reversed by opiate receptor stimulation as assessed by naloxone reversal of the effects of morphine or FK 33–824.[35–37] These electrical stimulation changes could also be blocked or reversed by clonidine.[32, 37] These data again suggested to us that increases in NE release resulting from NE hyperactivity could be reversed by exogenous and endogenous opiates and clonidine.

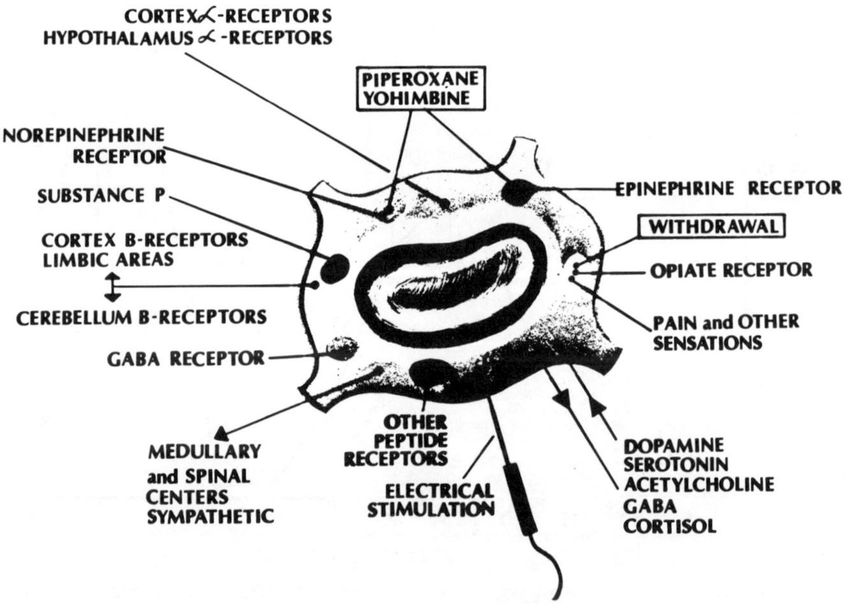

FIGURE 2. Receptors on the locus coeruleus: increasing activity and NE release produces monkey panic behaviors which are phenomenologically similar to opiate withdrawal behaviors. LC or NE augmentation may be a model for opiate withdrawal.

LC: Opiate Withdrawal Hypothesis

We hypothesized that chronic exogenous opiate administration might cause a decrease in endogenous opiate release and synthesis as well as a decrease in opiate receptor sensitivity.[1, 4] Abrupt discontinuation of chronic opiate administration would, according to our model system, result in the absence of exogenous opiate-mediated inhibition of ascending NE activity. As a result of this release from chronic exogenous inhibition and absence of adequate inhibitory neurotransmitters at the level of the NE nucleus,[4] there would be a resultant large increase in NE activity, release, and turnover.[1, 5] Attempts to use endorphin stores to autoregulate this profound LC firing increase would be too little too late, as the stores of available endogenous opiates would be of insufficient quantity and the receptor sensitivity would be too low to augment the available m-Enkephalin. In addition, it is likely that other available inhibitory presynaptic neurotransmitters such as E and NE would be of insufficient quantity and interact with receptors which are themselves abnormal to reverse the NE "rebound" release from opiate mediated inhibition.[4]

Tests of the Hypothesis in Man

We tested the efficacy of clonidine in opiate withdrawal not only to demonstrate that clonidine might be a new and important treatment for addicts but also to see which physiological and affective variables would be clonidine-reversible and thereby attributable to clonidine's agonistic effects on presynaptic alpha-2 receptors on the LC. We had speculated that clonidine would reverse in man the behaviors and affective state produced by electrical or pharmacological activation of the LC as we had demonstrated in primates. Our LC or NE hyperactivity hypothesis was supported by knowledge of LC neuroanatomy. The known anatomical connections of the LC suggested an important role for this structure in the wide variety of behaviors and physiological changes which accompany drug-withdrawal and spontaneous panic states. The LC also receives afferents from serotonergic, adrenergic, peptidergic and noradrenergic neurons, the hypothalamus, and may have transducer cells to receive and relay hormonal messages.[41, 42] This LC neuroanatomy supports an important neuromodulatory or "tone" role for the LC and does not necessitate the direct involvement of numerous brain systems in the feeling state, cardiovascular, sympathetic, parasympathetic, and many other manifestations of opiate withdrawal states.[1, 4]

After we administered 5 μg/kg of clonidine and placebo double-blind, orally in matching vehicles to 5 male opiate (methadone) addicts we recognized that clonidine was effective for the full spectrum of withdrawal signs, symptoms and affects. In a study of eleven methadone addicts[2] and a study of 5 male heroin and 5 male methadone addicts[5] we demonstrated that clonidine reversed the signs, symptoms and affects of opiate withdrawal. Clonidine effectively reversed withdrawal in patients addicted to high doses of methadone for many years.[2] Finally, in two well-controlled studies, one small[6] followed by another large[7] inpatient study we delineated a safe and 100% effective protocol for rapid nonopiate detoxification with clonidine which demonstrated that clonidine blocked and reversed acute withdrawal and continued (nearly completely) to suppress the reemergence of withdrawal symptoms after abrupt discontinuation of chronic opiate addiction. This series of studies demonstrated that clonidine could be substituted for opiates and discontinued without withdrawal signs of its own.

Support for the Hypothesis

All of this clinical data[1, 2, 5-7] served to offer strong support for an important Endorphin-LC interaction and NE hyperactivity as the most critical event in the generation of withdrawal symptoms on the basis of clonidine's known effects on the LC and NE activity when given in low doses. This NE hypothesis could only be directly investigated in animal studies. In rodent and primate studies it was demonstrated that clonidine decreased NE activity, release and turnover as assessed by changes in the brain's major NE metabolite MHPG.[29] Morphine and endogenous opiates were found to have a similar effect through interaction with LC opiate receptors as assessed by naloxone reversal. Finally, Aghajanian[43] demonstrated that chronic exogenous opiate administration produced tolerance of LC neurons to suppression. He also demonstrated that tolerance develops in the LC inhibition response to chronic opiates (in opiate addiction) and that naloxone-precipitated withdrawal was accompanied by the predicted[1, 2] noradrenergic hyperactivity.[43] He demonstrated in single neuronal electrophysiological and microiontophoresis that this NE hyperactivity could be reversed by clonidine.[43] This study confirmed the hypothesized LC activity in withdrawal and supported our notion that NE was the important neurotransmitter in the generation of withdrawal symptoms. Our studies and the studies in the literature[1, 2, 4, 44] did not exclude an important or at least significant role for other brain monoamine nuclei and neurotransmitters in opiate withdrawal. However, we did hypothesize that the NE hyperactivity could be demonstrated directly in studies of animals and man and that this hyperactivity was related to the signs and symptoms of withdrawal.[1, 2]

DA vs. NE Hyperactivity: DA

To investigate neurotransmitter changes in withdrawal we conducted indirect neuroendocrine and direct MHPG studies in methadone addicts. While we had proposed a NE hyperactivity hypothesis to explain the signs and symptoms of withdrawal, a dopaminergic (DA) hyperactivity hypothesis has also been proposed and supported in basic studies.[44, 45] Serum prolactin (PRL) is predominently controlled *in vivo* and *in vitro* by an inhibitory DA mechanism.[46] Consistent with this control mechanism, augmentation of DA function results in decreases in serum PRL and inhibition of DA function results in increases in serum PRL.[47, 48] To investigate the relation of opiate withdrawal symptoms to serum PRL and by inference to assess the role of DA in acute withdrawal symptom generation and relief, we measured serum PRL in duplicate by radioimmunoassay.[49] Fourteen days after being clonidine and opiate-free (drug-free baseline), during the peak of opiate withdrawal and after clonidine-induced suppression we collected samples for serum PRL. PRL was significantly reduced from a pre-clonidine mean ($\pm$SEM) of 10.8ng/ml $\pm$ 1.0 to 8.2 $\pm$ 0.8 at 60 minutes and 7.0 $\pm$ 0.8 at 120 minutes after clonidine administration (paired $t = 3.92$; $p < 0.02$). Serum PRL was significantly reduced during the peak of opiate withdrawal to a mean of 10.2 $\pm$ 0.7 ng/ml compared to a mean of 13.6 $\pm$ 0.9 ng/ml when the patient had been opiate and clonidine-free for 14 days ($t = 3.50$; $p < 0.02$).

Significant decreases in serum PRL are normally attributable to direct stimulation of DA receptors or increased DA release or neurotransmission.[46, 47] The decreased serum PRL for patients in withdrawal supports underlying DA hyperactivity in withdrawal.[45] These data were consistent with animal studies showing decreases in PRL in opiate withdrawal.[51] However, in our studies the serum PRL levels did not return to baseline after clonidine-induced amelioration of symptoms. This suggested that DA hyperactivity continues even though clonidine markedly relieves symptoms. Therefore we have suggested that DA hyperactivity is present but is not related to symptoms or symptom relief.

NE Hyperactivity Hypothesis

Direct testing of a NE hyperactivity hypothesis has been difficult due to the methodological problems in measuring plasma 3-methoxy-4-hydroxyphenyl glycol (MHPG). Our laboratory has recently developed a method for the rapid analysis of free MHPG levels. This method measures free MHPG levels after extraction of 5 ml of patient serum by a modification of Ross's extraction procedure. MHPG is separated from the extract mixture by a nonaqueous reverse phase procedure using an amino-propyl bonded phase and a acetonitrile-methanol mobile phase. Detection of separated MHPG is by flurometry with a Schoeffel Model 970 spectrofluro-monitor (280 Exc. 280 Em) set at the highest gain setting. Instrument baseline is stabilized with a proprietary electronic noise filter. Using this technique we have been able to reproducibly measure high picogram quantities of MHPG and related fluorescent compounds. In a pilot study of 3 patients in spontaneous withdrawal we have demonstrated increasing plasma-free MHPG levels which correlate with the increase in signs and symptoms with increasing time of abstinence. In addition, clonidine caused a significant decrease in withdrawal symptoms and plasma MHPG. These pilot data offer tentative support for the hypothesized NE hyperactivity and relationship of NE activity to symptom generation and relief. These data are supported by recent data in rodents and primates which demonstrate increases in MHPG in withdrawal and clonidine reversal of the MHPG increases.[52, 53]

Recent data reported in the literature also support a NE hypothesis. For example, clonidine withdrawal itself has significant phenomenological similarities to opiate withdrawal[54, 55] and would be expected to result, in part, from chronic exogenous inhibition of the LC through alpha-2 receptor stimulation. Clonidine withdrawal results in increases in MHPG and may be treatable with clonidine or opiates.[56] Clonidine while not an opiate drug and having no affinity for opiate receptors[57] has a number of opiate-like properties including analgesia, miosis, hypotension, sedation, antianxiety and decreased respiration.[58, 59] These data suggest that the effects of exogenous alpha-2 or opiate agonists which tonically inhibit brain areas like the LC may be responsible for tolerance and the development of withdrawal symptoms after abrupt discontinuation of chronic administration.

Implications of the Hypothesis and Clonidine

What would be important from the neurotransmitter hypothesis and clinical point of view, would be the development of an alpha-2 agonist like clonidine which decreases LC activity and NE release but which did not produce extreme sedation and severe hypotension. It may be that potent alpha-2 nonopiate drugs which reverse withdrawal from high doses of chronic opiate administration must produce sedation and decrease blood pressure because of other alpha-2 effects or that the LC is the common final neurotransmitter pathway in these phenomena. However, this remains to be demonstrated. While these clinical limitations exist, the main implication of clonidine's efficacy listed above will remain. The NE hyperactivity or LC hypothesis would predict that other drugs, which specifically inhibit the LC by an action at specific presynaptic LC receptors, will be found to have marked antiwithdrawal efficacy in man. Known drugs which we believe inhibit NE activity at the level of the LC and which may have antiwithdrawal efficacy are shown in FIGURE 3. Therefore, nonalpha adrenergic drugs and neural peptides may be found to be safe for use in humans, and to decrease LC activity. These medications may be safely developed for use in withdrawal. Nonaddicting opiate receptor agonists, vasopressin, or GABA agonists like baclofen may be found to have potent antiwithdrawal efficacy, but without hypotensive effects and with significantly less sedation than clonidine. These drugs would be without alpha-2 activity but might be expected to have antiwithdrawal activity by decreasing LC activity. These new possibilities would thus provide additional tests for the NE hyperactivity

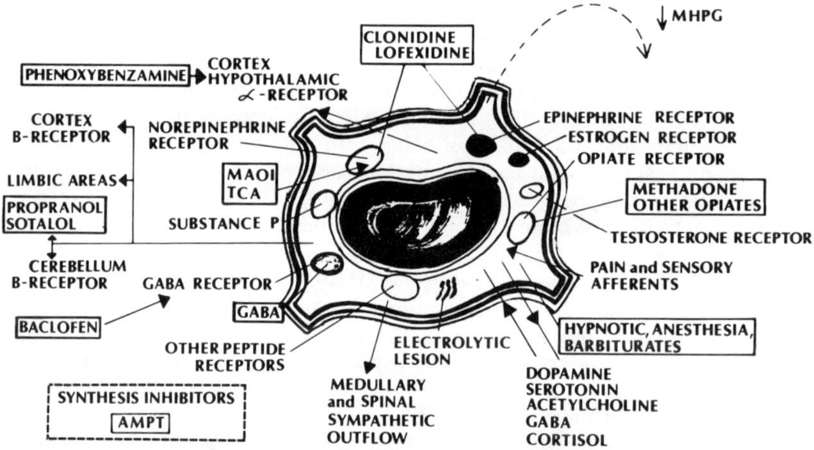

FIGURE 3. Strategies to use existing LC receptors to find new treatments. The main implication of clonidine is this model neuron. With the LC hyperactivity theory, presynaptic mechanisms which stimulate specific LC receptors to inhibit LC activity and NE release should have marked antiwithdrawal effects.

hypothesis for opiate withdrawal as well as possibly adding new, safe, and effective nonopiate treatments to the treatment armamentarium.

Finally, it should be mentioned that the discovery of opiate receptors, their density in the LC, the parallel function of alpha-2 and opiate receptor stimulation at the level of the LC have suggested the efficacy of clonidine in withdrawal and the possibility that NE hyperactivity may be responsible for the affects—anxiety and panic—as well as the physiological changes associated with withdrawal. This raises the question of naturally-occurring panic and anxiety states and whether these states share LC hyperactivity as a final common neurobiological pathway.[3] NE hyperactivity might then also provide a model for studying naturally and drug-related panic states and lead to a neural construct for these states which could predict new treatment possibilities including opiates, endorphins, and clonidine.[3, 5, 61]

Clinical Implications

Clonidine is by no means the most ideal drug for the rapid nonopiate treatment of withdrawal. Its sedative and hypotensive effects limit its usefulness in outpatient programs and make detoxification more difficult and potentially dangerous than methadone detoxification. In addition, clonidine's antiwithdrawal effects may be time-limited making its use in slow detoxifications difficult, if not impossible, for this reason and also because of the "rebound" effects reported after longer term clonidine administration.[54, 55] While these disadvantages are real and limit its general utility, clonidine has a number of distinct advantages as an antiwithdrawal agent. These advantages are the implications of clonidine for clinical use in drug abuse treatment:

1. Rapid detoxification without opiates
2. Abrupt discontinuation of opiates and treatment through nonopiate receptor system may allow normalization (more rapid) of opiate and alpha-2 receptors.
3. Detoxification from 15-50-70 or 100 mg of chronic methadone can be readily accomplished with equal ease in 8–14 days.
4. Detoxification can be readily linked to naltrexone induction and maintenance.
5. Enhancement of role of physician and physician-patient relationship which will relate to compliance in naltrexone maintenance.
6. Increase in treatment options available to patient and primary clinician.
7. Increase in ability of patients to use their methadone program to get out of street life, away from needles and drug friends, find a regular job and develop important relationships with friends and family by ensuring that the patient has a viable alternative to methadone and a chance at being drug-free or maintained on naltrexone in less than 14 days.
8. Possible treatment of choice for iatrogenic addictions.
9. Possible use in opiate holidays and reversal of tolerance in cancer or pain patients.

These clinical implications and the clinical utility of clonidine will become more evident and well studied as investigators with divergent patient groups begin to use clonidine as a nonopiate treatment. Results from others[62] and the results of our outcome studies suggest clonidine is well suited for working, middle, and upper class addicts and that clonidine is ideal for coupling with intensive drug-free or naltrexone treatment.

References

1. Gold, M. S., D. E. Redmond, Jr. & H. D. Kleber. 1978. Clonidine in opiate withdrawal. Lancet **1**:929–930.
2. Gold, M. S., D. E. Redmond, Jr. & H. D. Kleber. 1978. Clonidine blocks acute opiate-withdrawal symptoms. Lancet **2**:599–602.
3. Gold, M. S. & H. D. Kleber. 1979. A rationale for opiate withdrawal symptomatology. Drug Alcoh. Dep. **4**:419–424.
4. Gold, M. S., R. Byck, D. R. Sweeney & H. D. Kleber. 1979. Endorphinlocus coeruleus connection mediates opiate action and withdrawal. Biomedicine **30**:1–4.

5. GOLD, M. S., D. E. REDMOND, JR. & H. D. KLEBER. 1979. Noradrenergic hyperactivity in opiate withdrawal supported by clonidine reversal of opiate withdrawal. Am. J. Psychiat. **136:**100–102.
6. GOLD, M. S., A. L. C. POTTASH, D. R. SWEENEY & H. D. KLEBER. 1980. Clonidine: a safe, effective, and rapid nonopiate treatment for opiate withdrawal. J. Am. Med. Assoc. **243:**343–346.
7. GOLD, M. S., A. L. C. POTTASH, D. R. SWEENEY & H. D. KLEBER. 1979. Clonidine detoxification: a fourteen day protocol for rapid opiate withdrawal. NIDA Research Monograph. **27:**226–232.
8. EIDELBERG, E. 1976. Possible action of opiates upon synapses. Prog. Neurobiol. **6:**81–102.
9. LAL, H. 1975. Narcotic dependence, narcotic action and dopamine receptors. Life Sci. **17:**484–496.
10. ROBERTS, D. C. S., S. MASON & H. C. FIBIGER. 1978. 6-OHDA Lesions to the dorsal noradrenergic bundle alters morphine-induced locomotor activity and catalepsy. Eur. J. Pharmacol. **52:**209–214.
11. HERZ, A., J. BLASIG & R. PAPESCHI. 1974. Role of catecholaminergic mechanisms in the expression of the morphine abstinence syndrome in rats. Psychopharmacologia **39:**121–143.
12. KORF, J., B. S. BUNNEY & G. K. AGHAJANIAN. 1974. Noradrenergic neurons: morphine inhibition of spontaneous activity. Eur. J. Pharmacol. **25:**165–169.
13. BASBAUM, A. I. & H. L. FIELDS. 1978. Endogenous pain control mechanisms: review and hypothesis. Ann. Neurol. **4:**451–462.
14. GOLD, M. S. & R. BYCK. 1978. Endorphins, lithium, and naloxone: their relationship to pathological and drug-induced manic-euphoric states. NIDA Research Monograph No. 19.
15. HUGHES, J. 1975. Isolation of an endogenous compound in brain with pharmacological properties similar to morphine. Brain Res. **88:**295–308.
16. PERT, C. B., M. J. KUHAR & S. H. SNYDER. 1975. Autoradiographic localization of the opiate receptor in rat brain. Life Sci. **16:**1849–1854.
17. SIMON, E. J. 1975. Opiate receptor binding with 3H-etorphine. Neurosci. Res. Program Bull. **13:**43–50.
18. KLEBER, H. D. & M. S. GOLD. 1978. Use of psychotropic drugs in treatment of methadone maintained narcotic addicts. Ann. N.Y. Acad. Sci. **311:**81–98.
19. SVENSSON, T. H., B. S. BUNNEY & G. K. AGHAJANIAN. 1975. Inhibition of both noradrenergic and serotonergic neurons in brain by the alpha-adrenergic antagonist clonidine Brain Res. **92:**291–306.
20. KUHAR, M. J. 1978. Opiate receptors: some anatomical and physiological aspects. Ann. N. Y. Acad. Sci. **311:**35–48.
21. CEDARBAUM, J. M. & G. K. AGHAJANIAN. 1976. Noradrenergic neurons of the locus coeruleus: inhibition by epinephrine and activation by the alpha-antagonist piperoxane. Brain Res. **112:**413–419.
22. CEDARBAUM, J. M. & G. K. AGHAJANIAN. 1977. Catecholamine receptors on locus coeruleus neurons: pharmacological characteristics. Eur. J. Pharmacol. **44:**375–385.
23. CEDARBAUM, J. M. & G. K. AGHAJANIAN. 1976. Characterization of catecholamine receptors on noradrenergic neurons of the locus coeruleus. Neurosci. Abstr. **2:**683.
24. GREENBERG, D. A., D. C. U'PRICHARD & S. H. SNYDER. 1976. Alpha-noradrenergic receptor binding in mammalian brain. Life Sci. **19:**69–76.
25. SCHMITT, H., MME. H. SCHMITT & S. FENARD. 1971. Evidence for an alpha-sympathomimetic component in the effects of Catapresan on vasomotor centres: antagonism by piperoxane. Eur. J. Pharmacol. **14:**98–100.
26. STARKE, K. 1977. Regulation of noradrenaline release by presynaptic receptor systems. Rev. Physiol. Biochem. Pharmacol. **77:**7–124.
27. BERTILSSON, L., K. HAGLUND, J. OSTMAN, M. D. RAWLINS, V. A. RINGBERGER &

F. SJOQVIST. 1977. Monoamine metabolites in cerebrospinal fluid during treatment with clonidine or alprenolol. Eur. J. Clin. Pharmacol. **11:**125–128.

28. STROMBOM, U. 1975. On the functional role of pre- and postsynaptic catecholamine receptors in brain. Acta. Physiol. Scand. (Suppl.) **431:**1–43.
29. MAAS, J. W., N. M. GREENE, S. E. HATTOX & D. H. LANDIS. 1979. Neurotransmitter metabolite production by human brain. *In* Catecholamines: Basic and Clinical Frontiers. E. Usdin, I. J. Kopin & J. Barchas, Eds.: 1878–1880. Pergamon Press. Elmsford, N.Y.
30. ANDEN, N. E., H. CORRODI, K. FUXE, B. HOKFELT, T. HOKFELT, C. RYDIN & T. SVENSSON. 1970. Evidence for a central noradrenaline receptor stimulation by clonidine. Life Sci. **9:**513–523.
31. SASTUY, B. & J. PHILLIS. 1977. Evidence that clonidine can activate histamine H_2-receptors in rat cerebral cortex. Neuropharmacology **16:**223–225.
32. GOLD, M. S. & D. E. REDMOND, JR. 1977. Pharmacological activation and inhibition of noradrenergic activity alter specific behaviors in nonhuman primates. Neurosci. Abs. **3:**250.
33. MAAS, J. W., S. E. HATTOX, D. H. LANDIS & R. H. ROTH. 1976. The determination of a brain arteriovenous difference for 3-methoxy-4-hydroxyphenethylene glycol (MPHG). Brain Res. **118:**167–173.
34. GOLD, M. S., R. K. DONABEDIAN & D. E. REDMOND, JR. 1979. Further evidence for alpha-2 adrenergic receptor mediated inhibition of prolactin secretion: the effect of yohimbine. Psychoneuroendocrinology **3:**253–260.
35. EXTEIN, I., F. K. GOODWIN, A. J. LEWY, R. I. SCHOENFELD, L. FAKHURI, M. S. GOLD & D. E. REDMOND, JR. 1979. Behavioral and biochemical effects of FK 33–824, a parenterally and orally active enkephalin analogue. *In* Endorphins in Mental Health Research. E. Usdin, Ed.: 279–292. McMillan. London, England.
36. REDMOND, D. E., JR., Y. H. HUANG & M. S. GOLD. 1978. Evidence for the involvement of a brain norepinephrine (NE) system in anxiety. Proc. 4th Int. Catecholamine Symposium. Pacific Grove, Calif.
37. REDMOND, D. E., JR., Y. H. HUANG & M. S. GOLD. 1977. Anxiety: the locus coeruleus connection. Neurosci. Abstr. **3:**258.
38. DAHLSTROM, A. & K. FUXE. 1964. Evidence for the existence of monoamine containing neurons in the central nervous system. 1. Demonstration of monoamines in the cell bodies of brain stem neurons. Acta. Physiol. Scand. (Suppl.) **232:**1.
39. LOISOU, L. A. 1969. Projections of the nucleus locus coeruleus in the albino rat. Brain Res. **15:**563.
40. MORRISON, J. H., M. E. MOLLIVER & R. GRAZANNA. 1979. Noradrenergic innervation of cerebral cortex: widespread effects of local cortical lesions. Science **205:**313–316.
41. JONES, B. E., A. E. HALARIS, M. MCILHANY & R. Y. MOORE. 1977. Ascending projections of the locus coeruleus in the rat: I & II. Brain Res. **127:**1–21, 23–53.
42. SAKAI, K., M. TOURET, D. SALVERT, L. LEGER & M. JOUVET. 1977. Afferent projections to the cat locus coeruleus as visualized by the horseradish peroxidase technique. Brain Res. **119:**21–41.
43. AGHAJANIAN, G. K. 1978. Tolerance of locus coeruleus neurones to morphine and suppression of withdrawal response by clonidine. Nature **276:**186–188.
44. ARY, M., B. COX & P. LOMAX. 1977. Dopaminergic mechanisms in precipitated withdrawal in morphine-dependent rats. J. Pharmacol. Exp. Ther. **200:**271–276.
45. LAL, H. & M. D. HYNES. 1978. Effectiveness of butyrophenones and related drugs in narcotic withdrawal. *In* Neuropsychopharmacology. P. Deniker, C. R. Thomas, A. Villeneuve, D. Baronet-La Croix & F. Aarcin, Eds.: 289–295. Pergamon Press. Elmsford, N.Y.

46. CLEMENS, J. A., E. B. SMALSTIG & B. D. SAWYER. 1974. Antipsychotic drugs stimulate prolactin release. Psychopharmacologia **40:**123–127.
47. GOLD, M. S., D. E. REDMOND, JR. & R. K. DONABEDIAN. 1979. The effects of opiate agonist and antagonist on serum prolactin in primates: possible role for endorphins in prolactin regulation. Endocrinology: **105:**284–289.
48. GOLD, M. S., D. E. REDMOND, JR., R. K. DONABEDIAN, F. K. GOODWIN & I. EXTEIN. 1978. Increase in serum prolactin by exogenous and endogenous opiates: evidence for antidopamine and antipsychotic effects. Am. J. Psychiatry **135:**1415–1416.
49. GOLD, M. S., R. K. DONABEDIAN & D. E. REDMOND, JR. 1978. Effect of piperoxane on serum prolactin: possible role of epinephrine-mediated synapses in the inhibition of prolactin secretion. Endocrinology **102:**1183–1189.
50. GOLD, M. S., D. R. SWEENEY, A. L. C. POTTASH & H. D. KLEBER. 1979. Decreased serum prolactin in opiate withdrawal and dopaminergic hyperactivity. Am. J. Psychiatry **136:**849–850.
51. LAL, H., W. BROWN, R. DRAWBAUGH, M. HYNES & G. BROWN. 1977. Enhanced prolactin inhibition following chronic treatment with haloperidol and morphine. Life Sci. **20:**101–106.
52. CRAWLEY, J. N., R. LAVERTY & R. H. ROTH. 1979. Clonidine reversal of increased norepinephrine metabolite levels during morphine withdrawal. Eur. J. Pharmacol. **57:**2–3.
53. REDMOND, D. E., JR., R. H. ROTH, S. E. HATTOX, J. M. STOGIN & J. BAULU. 1979. 3-Methoxy-4-hydroxyphenethylene glycol (MHPG) in monkey brain, CSF, and plasma during naloxone precipitated morphine abstinence. Neurosci. Abstr. **5:**1160.
54. HANSSON, L., S. N. HUNYOR, S. JULIUS & S. W. HOOBLER. 1973. Blood pressure crisis following withdrawal of clonidine with special reference to arterial and urinary catecholamine levels, and suggestions for acute management. Am. Heart J. **85:**605–610.
55. HUNYOR, S. N., L. HANSSON, T. S. HARRISON & S. W. HOOBLER. 1973. Effects of clonidine withdrawal: possible mechanisms and suggestions for management. Br. Med. J. **2:**209–211.
56. TANG, S. W., D. M. HELMESTE & H. C. STAUCER. 1979. The effect of clonidine withdrawal on total 3-methoxy-4-hydroxyphenethylene glycol in the rat brain. Psychopharmacology **61:**11–12.
57. SIMON, E. 1979. Personal Communication. Brescia, Italy.
58. KOSS, M. C. 1979. Topical clonidine produces mydriasis by a central nervous system action. Eur. J. Pharmacol. **55:**305–310.
59. KOBINGER, W. 1975. Central cardiovascular actions of clonidine. *In* Central Action of Drugs in Blood Pressure Regulation. D. S. Davies & J. L. Reid, Eds.: 181. University Park Press. Baltimore, Maryland.
60. PAALZOW, L. 1974. Analgesia produced by clonidine in mice and rats. J. Pharm. Pharmacol. **26:**361–363.
61. GOLD, M. S., A. L. C. POTTASH, D. R. SWEENEY, H. D. KLEBER & D. E. REDMOND, JR. 1979. Rapid opiate detoxification: clinical evidence of antidepressant and antipanic effects of opiates. Am. J. Psychiatry **136:**982–983.
62. WASHTON, A. M., R. B. RESNICK & R. LA PLACA. 1978. Clonidine hydrochloride —a nonopiate treatment for opiate withdrawal. American College of Neuropsychopharmacology. Maui, Hawaii.

SHORT-TERM DETOXIFICATION WITH METHADONE *

Edward C. Senay
Walter Dorus

Substance Abuse Services
1439 South Michigan Avenue
Chicago, Illinois 60606

Craig V. Showalter

Department of Psychiatry
The University of Chicago
Chicago, Illinois 60637

Since the publication of the methadone regulations by the Food and Drug Administration,[1] patients with less than a two-year history of opiate addiction may receive methadone only for the purpose of detoxification for a maximum of 21 days. The intent of the 21-day medication limitation was to protect individuals only minimally addicted to opiates from continued dependence on methadone while allowing enough time for these individuals to be detoxified. The regulations state that during detoxification the dose of methadone "shall always be sufficient to keep withdrawal symptoms at a tolerable level."

Many studies have raised questions about the effectiveness of rapid detoxification from opiates.[2-7] These studies criticized rapid detoxification because 1. Dropout rates are high; 2. Success in achieving abstinence is low; and 3. Success in maintaining abstinence is almost zero. Tennant *et al.*[8] reported that among 25 of 36 methadone patients who completed a 21-day detoxification schedule, only 25% exhibited urines negative for morphine during their third week of detoxification. At one month follow-up, 47% were using heroin, 42% had entered maintenance and none were drug-free in the community. Canada[9] conducted a study of 157 subjects who were admitted to a short-term (30–60 days) methadone detoxification program. At six-month follow-up, 80% of the subjects were using illicit narcotics or had enrolled in methadone maintenance; and only 7% of entire sample completed the course of treatment and were drug-free.

Patients on a rapid detoxification schedule do experience severe withdrawal symptoms,[10] and their discomfort may complicate therapeutic intervention. It takes time to change behavior and to adjust to a lifestyle free of illicit drug use. It is difficult enough for patients to begin to take advantage of available counseling and rehabilitative services within three weeks without the complication of experiencing withdrawal symptoms. Although patients are encouraged to continue treatment after their 21-day detoxification, it is our clinical impression that most of these patients leave treatment because they are no longer receiving pharmacologic support and there has not been enough time to establish the strong therapeutic relationship to keep them in treatment.

In this study we assessed rapid detoxification for short-term addicts. We

* This research was supported by Grant H81 DA-01827 from the National Institute on Drug Abuse.

randomly assigned recently addicted patients to either a 21-day (FDA detoxification) schedule or an 84-day schedule under double-blind conditions. The objectives were to describe the drug use patterns of patients receiving 21-day detoxification and to determine the relative efficacy of 21 and 84-day detoxification schedules on the following treatment outcomes: length of treatment, use of heroin, discomfort experienced during withdrawal, and ability to reach and maintain abstinence.

Method

Experimental Procedures

Subjects were recruited according to Department of Health, Education, and Welfare guidelines for informed consent from the Illinois Dangerous Drugs Commission Central Intake facility. Subjects had to meet the following criteria: 18 years of age or older; good general health; ineligible for methadone maintenance because of a less than two-year addiction history; at least six months' experience with intravenous heroin use, including a period of daily use for three or more months prior to treatment; objective clinical evidence of intravenous heroin use as evidenced by needle marks, old and new; and a history of withdrawal symptoms. The FDA extended the 21-day detoxification time limit in our clinic in order to implement the 84-day withdrawal schedule.

The duration of the double-blind period of the study was 90 days. Upon admission to the clinic a research physician randomly assigned patients to one of two study groups. Seventy-two patients participated: 35 in the 21-day group and 37 in the 84-day group. Patients assigned to the 21-day detoxification schedule received decreasing doses of methadone according to a predetermined schedule for 21 days followed by placebo for the remaining 69 days. Patients assigned to the 84-day schedule received methadone for 84 days and placebo for the final week. Dose decrements were larger in the early stages of the detoxification and more gradual near the completion of the detoxification period. These schedules reflect our clinical impression and that of others [11] that methadone dose decreases are less well tolerated at low levels.

On the first day of treatment, each patient met with a staff physician who completed the necessary enrollment procedures after explaining the study protocol and obtaining informed consent. The physician recorded the patient's drug-use history, completed a brief medical and psychiatric evaluation, and assigned a starting dose of methadone.

For the first three weeks of the study, patients had weekly appointments with a clinic physician; thereafter, appointments with the physician were twice monthly. All subjects participated in the same treatment program which included intensive individual and group counseling.

An increase or decrease in methadone dose was permitted during the first seven days of treatment if the patient experienced moderate or marked discomfort. In these cases, the nonblind physician made the appropriate adjustment in dose and placed the patient on the detoxification schedule appropriate for his new dose level.

Patients who dropped from the study before 90 days had elapsed but who wished to continue treatment were treated according to FDA regulations. If they had not completed detoxification, they were required to do so within 21 days.

Research Instruments and Measures

Data concerning specific physical symptoms related to withdrawal, general health status, psychological status, drug and alcohol use, and narcotic craving were obtained weekly using a structured questionnaire, the Weekly Research Interview (WRI). The WRI was administered by trained research assistants who were blind to the status of patients; interrater reliability was .85. The symptom section of the WRI consists of 50 items from which we generated a WRI index of frequency and severity of symptoms for each subject and for each study group. A summary score was calculated on the basis of a 3-point rating scale: 0, symptom not present; 1, mild or moderate symptom; and 2, severe symptom. A subject's weekly symptom score could range, then, from 0 to 100.

Each subject submitted two urine specimens on a random schedule each week for determination of the presence of morphine (the principal metabolite of heroin) and quinine using thin layer chromatography.[12] We considered the presence of morphine or quinine evidence of heroin use and scored it as positive. These urine specimens were obtained under direct observation to prevent substitution.

At the end of 90 days or at early termination, before the blind was broken, a research technician obtained a global evaluation of each patient's response to treatment. At a clinic meeting the staff evaluated the degree of difficulty of withdrawal, the presence of withdrawal symptoms, and degree and type of licit and illicit drug use during detoxification.

Results

Table 1 shows the demographic characteristics for each experimental group and for the total sample. There are no statistically significant differences between the two experimental groups.

The mean starting dose for the study patients was 20.6 mg. methadone (±5.6). The mean dose for the 21-day schedule group was 20.1 mg. (±4.8) and the 84-day group 21.0 mg. (±6.3). The difference in starting dose between experimental groups was not statistically significant. The mean dose for methadone maintenance patients admitted during the same period of time was, by contrast, 27 mg. These data reflect the low level of addiction among patients participating in the study. They also reflect the program's general policy of alleviating withdrawal symptoms with the lowest methadone dose possible.

Drug Use Histories

Table 2 lists the substances used by patients during the month prior to entering treatment. Eighteen percent of the subjects reported only heroin use. Marijuana was used by 54% of the subjects, alcohol by 42%, benzodiazepines by 35%, and pentazocine-tripelennamine by 24%. Of the 81.7% of the subjects reporting multiple substance use, 24% reported use of 2 substances; 21%, 3 substances; and 37%, 4 or more substances.

The mean time elapsed between first heroin use and entering treatment was 23 months (S.D. ± 14.8 months). The mean length of addiction or "run" of

TABLE 1

DEMOGRAPHIC CHARACTERISTICS OF PATIENTS BY WITHDRAWAL GROUP

	21-Day Group N=35		84-Day Group N=37		Total Sample N=72	
	N	(%)	N	(%)	N	(%)
Sex						
Male	21	(60.0)	19	(51.4)	40	(55.6)
Female	14	(40.0)	18	(48.6)	32	(44.4)
Race						
Black	25	(71.4)	28	(75.7)	53	(73.6)
White	8	(22.9)	6	(16.2)	14	(19.4)
Other	2	(5.7)	3	(8.1)	5	(6.9)
Marital Status						
Single	16	(45.7)	19	(51.4)	35	(48.6)
Married/common law	15	(42.9)	8	(21.6)	23	(32.0)
Divorced/separated/ widowed	4	(11.4)	10	(27.0)	14	(19.4)
Occupational Status						
Employed	11	(31.4)	12	(32.4)	23	(31.9)
Unemployed	23	(65.7)	20	(54.1)	43	(59.7)
Student/homemaker	1	(2.9)	5	(13.5)	6	(8.3)
Education (Mean, S.D.)	11.5 ± 1.7 years		11.4 ± 1.9 years		11.4 ± 1.7 years	
Age (Mean, S.D.)	24.6 ± 4.5 years		24.8 ± 4.2 years		24.7 ± 4.3 years	

TABLE 2

SELF-REPORTED SUBSTANCE USE DURING MONTH PRIOR TO TREATMENT (N=71)

Substance	Total Sample Number of Patients Reporting Use		Withdrawal Regimen 21-Day N=34		Withdrawal Regimen 84-Day N=37	
	N	% *	N	%	N	%
Heroin only	13	18.3	6	17.6	7	18.9
Multiple substance use	58	81.7	28	82.4	30	81.1
Other Opiates	9	12.7	4	11.8	5	13.5
Alcohol	30	42.3	15	44.1	15	40.5
Amphetamines	11	15.5	4	11.8	7	18.9
Antidepressants	6	8.5	2	5.9	4	10.8
Barbiturates	13	18.3	6	17.6	7	18.9
Benzodiazepines	25	35.2	12	35.3	13	35.1
Cocaine	17	23.9	9	26.5	8	21.6
Marijuana	38	53.5	21	61.8	17	45.9
Pentazocine/tripelennamine	17	23.9	6	17.6	11	29.7
Phencyclidine (PCP)	6	8.5	4	11.8	2	5.4
Propoxyphene	2	2.8	1	2.9	1	2.7

* Exceeds 100% due to multiple substance use.

drug use prior to entering treatment was 11.6 months (S.D. ± 5.6; range, 2 to 23 months).

Length of Treatment

The mean number of days in treatment for the 21-day detoxification group was 23.2; for the 84-day group the mean length of treatment was 42.6. This difference between groups is significant ($p < .001$).

FIGURE 1 shows the cumulative percent of study dropout by week for each experimental group for the first 90 days of the study. After the first week there

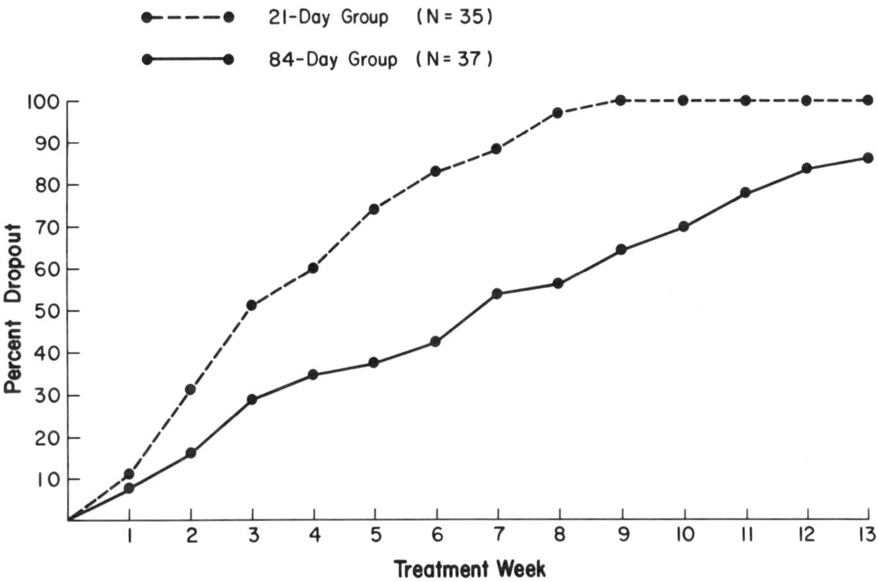

FIGURE 1. Cumulative percent of study dropout.

are substantial differences between groups in the proportions of patients who have dropped from the study. For weeks 6 and 8 there is approximately a 40% difference. All 21-day detoxification patients had dropped out of treatment by the end of week 9, at which time, 13 (35%) of the 84-day patients remained in treatment. Five patients (13.5%) in the 84-day group were in treatment at least until the end of the experimental period.

Urinalysis Report

During the first 8 weeks of the study 39 (28%) of the 139 urine specimens in the 21-day group were positive compared to 44 (21%) of the 214 specimens in the 84-day group. TABLE 3 shows the number and percent of urines positive

TABLE 3

PERCENT OF URINES POSITIVE FOR MORPHINE OR QUININE IN TREATMENT REMAINDERS

Treatment Week	21-Day Group N in Treatment	N	%	84-Day Group N in Treatment	N	%
1	35	9	25.7	37	11	29.7
2	31	4	12.9	34	5	14.7
3	24	6	25.0	31	3	9.7
4	17	8	47.1	26	7	26.7
5	13	4	30.8	24	4	16.7
6	9	3	33.3	23	4	17.4
7	6	3	50.0	21	4	19.0
8	4	2	50.0	18	6	33.3

by experimental group for the first 8 weeks of the study. The percentages are based on the number of patients remaining in treatment at each week. Beginning in week three there is a higher percentage of positive urines in the 21-day group than in the 84-day group. For the 84-day group the percentages of urines positive during weeks 9 through 13 were 23, 9, 44, 17, and 0%. Since all 21-day group patients had dropped out by week 9, there were no urinalysis results for these patients during last five weeks of the study.

Symptomatology

We utilized three measures of symptomatology in this study: 1. The total symptom score which is the sum of individual symptoms reported by patients in each experimental group; 2. The frequency of report of individual symptoms; and 3. The average severity of individual symptoms reported. Symptom reports are presented at three-week intervals beginning with the third week of treatment. Because of the high attrition rate we maintained sample size for this analysis by using the symptom report from the previous week for patients on whom no report was available on the week selected for analysis. For example, if a patient's symptom report for week six was missing, his symptomatology score for week five was utilized.

The average symptomatology score for each group is illustrated in FIGURE 2. For the 21-day detoxification group, data are presented for weeks three, six and nine only since no patients were available for study beyond week nine. Since the total score is the sum of all symptoms on the WRI, it does not discriminate between symptoms of withdrawal and other physical symptoms. Of the 50 symptoms comprising the total score, 35 are opioid withdrawal symptoms. The 84-day group complains of typical opiate agonist symptoms such as constipation and drowsiness at a higher frequency than the 21-day detoxification group. Therefore, the scores do not represent pure withdrawal symptomatology but rather indicate total level of discomfort experienced by patients.

The most frequently reported symptoms at weeks three and six are presented in TABLES 4 and 5. At week three the frequency of reports for each symptom is similar in each group. However, by week six (TABLE 5) there is a clearly higher frequency of symptoms for the 21-day group. Nine of the 11 symptoms listed occurred with a higher frequency in the 21-day group.

The severity of individual symptoms was also calculated. As with frequency, the greatest difference between groups occurred in week six, after the detoxification of the 21-day group had been completed. The difference between groups in severity reached statistical significance ($p < .05$) on 11 of the 50 symptoms.

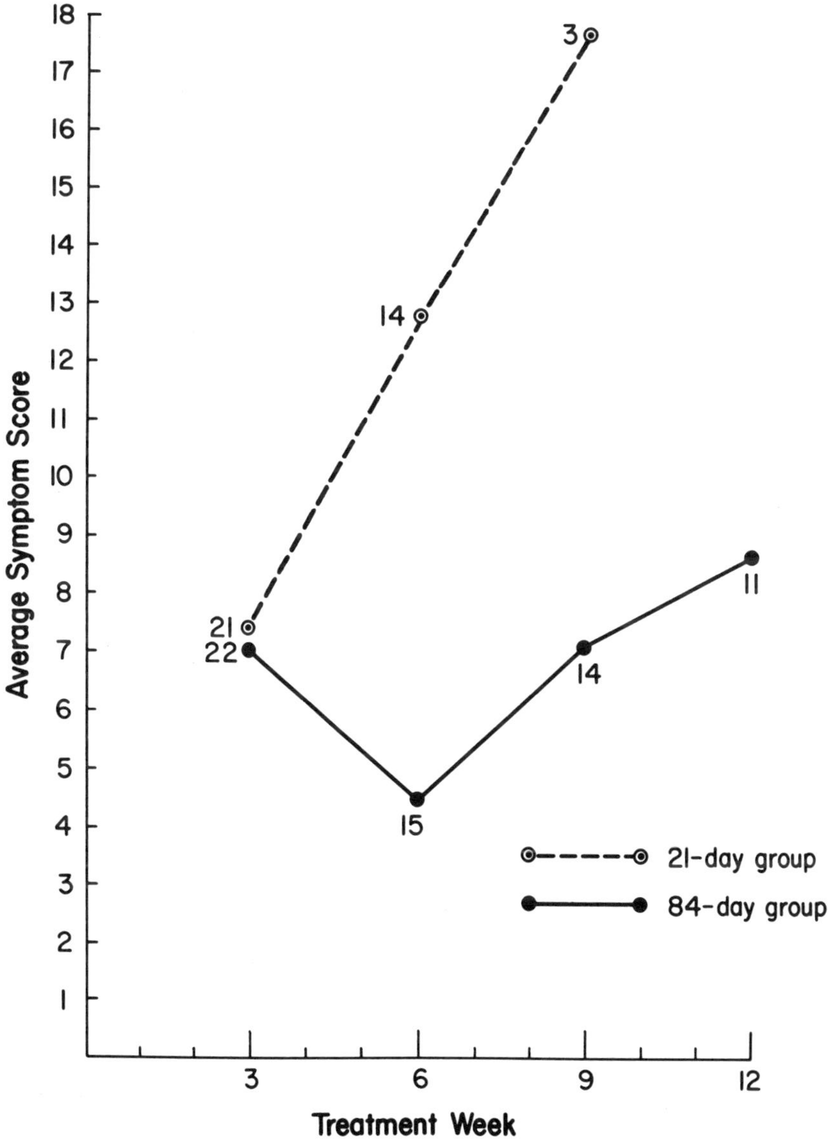

FIGURE 2. Average symptom score by experimental group.

TABLE 4

FREQUENCY OF REPORTED SYMPTOMS BY WITHDRAWAL GROUP AT THREE WEEKS, N=43

Symptom	21-Day Group N=21 N	%	84-Day Group N=22 N	%	Total Sample N	%
Urge to get high	12	66.7	14	54.5	26	60.5
Too much sweating	8	38.1	7	31.9	15	34.9
Constipation	6	28.6	9	40.9	15	34.9
Waking up at night	7	33.3	8	36.4	15	34.9
Irritability	7	33.3	8	36.4	15	34.9
Anxiety (tense/nervous)	8	38.1	7	31.8	15	34.9
Feeling depressed or blue	9	42.9	6	27.3	15	34.9
Runny nose	6	28.6	7	31.8	13	30.2
Drowsiness	5	23.8	8	36.4	13	30.2
Feeling cold or chills	6	28.6	6	27.3	12	27.9
Loss or appetite	6	28.6	6	27.3	12	27.9
Nausea or vomiting	6	28.6	6	27.3	12	27.9

These results are presented in TABLE 6. These eleven symptoms are all typical of opioid abstinence. In every case the symptom severity was greater in the 21-day group, and the difference in severity between groups for several of the symptoms (abdominal cramps, chills, early insomnia) was large.

Counselor Evaluations

The staff evaluation of the severity of withdrawal symptoms is presented in TABLE 7. Fifty percent of the patients in the 21-day detoxification group were

TABLE 5

FREQUENCY OF REPORTED SYMPTOMS BY WITHDRAWAL GROUP AT SIX WEEKS, N=32

Symptom	21-Day Group N=16 N	%	84-Day Group N	%	Total Sample N	%
Urge to get high	12	75.0	7	43.8	19	59.4
Yawning	9	56.3	6	37.5	15	46.9
Anxiety (tense/nervous)	7	43.8	7	43.8	14	43.8
Watery eyes	7	43.8	6	37.5	13	40.6
Feeling cold or chills	9	56.3	3	18.8	12	37.5
Abdominal cramps	8	50.0	3	18.8	11	34.4
Irritability	8	50.0	3	18.8	11	34.4
Feeling depressed or blue	8	50.0	3	18.8	11	34.4
Constipation	5	31.3	5	31.3	10	31.3
Trouble getting to sleep	8	50.0	2	12.5	10	31.3
Lack of pep, no energy	7	43.8	3	18.8	10	31.3

TABLE 6

SYMPTOMS WHICH SIGNIFICANTLY DIFFER IN SEVERITY BETWEEN GROUPS AT STUDY WEEK SIX *

	Mean Severity 21-Day Group	Mean Severity 84-Day Group	p
Abdominal cramps	.6	.1	<.05
Chills	.7	.1	<.02
Excessive perspiration	.7	.2	.05
Nausea	.4	0	<.05
Heartburn	.6	.1	<.05
Early insomnia	.7	.1	<.01
Middle insomnia	.6	.1	.02
Morning drowsiness	.5	.1	.02
Sneezing	.3	0	<.05
Irritability	.6	.1	<.05
Depression	.6	.1	.05

* Range: 0=no symptom, 1=mild symptom, 2=severe symptom.

rated as having experienced moderate to severe symptoms during their participation in the study compared to 16.7% of the patients in the 84-day withdrawal group ($p < .05$). The counselors' perception of patients' attitude toward the treatment program is presented in TABLE 8. Only three (9.4%) of 32 patients evaluated in the 21-day detoxification group were thought to have had a favorable treatment experience; 19 (59.4%) of the patients had an unfavorable experience ($p < .05$). In marked contrast eight patients (22%) regarded the 84-day withdrawal attempt as a positive experience and 11 (31%) rated the experience unfavorably.

Abstinence and Follow-Up

There were no patients in the 21-day detoxification group who detoxified successfully and remained in treatment during the 90-day study period. Thus, if one considers rapid 21-day detoxification followed by abstinence treatment as a successful outcome, there were no successes in the 90-day experimental

TABLE 7

COUNSELOR EVALUATION OF PATIENTS' SYMPTOMS DURING WITHDRAWAL *

Severity of Withdrawal Symptoms	21-Day Group N=34		84-Day Group N=36		Total Sample N=70	
	N	%	N	%	N	%
None	13	38.2	23	63.9	36	51.4
Mild	4	11.8	7	19.4	11	15.7
Moderate/severe	17	50.0	6	16.7	23	32.9

* $\chi^2=8.81$, $p <.05$.

TABLE 8

COUNSELOR EVALUATION OF PATIENT ATTITUDE TOWARDS WITHDRAWAL *

	Withdrawal Schedule					
	21-Day Group N=32		84-Day Group N=36		Total Sample N=68	
	N	%	N	%	N	%
Favorable	3	9.4	8	22.2	11	16.2
Unfavorable	19	59.4	11	30.6	30	44.1
No Opinion	10	31.2	17	47.2	27	39.7

* $\chi^2=6.01$, $p<.05$.

period for this group. However, four patients in the 21-day group completed the detoxification without evidence of return to heroin use. All four patients dropped out of treatment during the experimental period while still receiving placebo. One dropped out in week four, two in week six, and one in week seven (mean 2.75 weeks post-detoxification).

Five patients successfully completed withdrawal in the 84-day group and were abstinent at the end of the experimental period. These five patients have remained in treatment for periods ranging from 0 to 12 months (mean 4.1 months) following the end of the experimental phase and have remained abstinent. Two additional patients in the 84-day group dropped out of treatment shortly before the end of the study and remained abstinent.

TABLE 9 shows the treatment histories for the study subjects in the year following the study. All patients have completed at least three months of follow-up; 28 patients in the 21-day group and 21 patients in the 84-day group have been followed more than one year. There was no difference between groups in the percent of patients receiving treatment during this year. The patients who received uninterrupted maintenance were those for whom exceptions to the detoxification rule were obtained from the regulatory agencies.

Two of the four 21-day patients who reached abstinence returned to methadone maintenance treatment more than one year after dropout. The third patient is reported to be drug free 17 weeks after dropping out; the last patient has not returned to treatment and is lost to follow-up. Of the seven patients in the 84-day group who reached abstinence, one returned to methadone main-

TABLE 9

PATIENTS IN TREATMENT DURING YEAR FOLLOWING STUDY

	21-Day Group N=35		84-Day Group N=37		Total Sample N=72	
Status	N	%	N	%	N	%
Total Receiving Treatment	22	62.9	24	64.9	46	63.9
Uninterrupted Treatment						
Maintenance	6	17.1	5	13.5	11	15.3
Drug-Free	0	—	4	10.8	4	5.6
Returned to Treatment	16	45.7	15	40.5	31	43.0

tenance 26 weeks after completing withdrawal. None of the six remaining patients returned to treatment. Three patients completed one year of follow-up. Of these, two are drug-free and not in treatment; and one, abstinent upon leaving the clinic, has been lost to follow-up. Of the three patients who have not completed one year follow-up period; one is drug-free at three months; one patient is drug-free at nine months; and one patient is known to be occasionally using heroin but had not returned to treatment at three months.

Discussion

This study represents the first attempt to evaluate experimentally the 21-day detoxification time limit imposed by the FDA on opioid addicts with short addiction histories. Our results indicate that the 21-day group dropped out of treatment earlier, had a higher percent of urines positive for morphine, reported higher levels of symptomatology, was less likely to remain drug-free, and expressed more negative feelings about the treatment experience than did patients on the 84-day schedule. On the other hand, the percentage of patients reaching abstinence and remaining drug-free was not large in either group.

Treatment Impact

None of the 21-day patients was able to utilize the detoxification experience to become drug-free and to remain in treatment long enough to allow for individual change. We believe that 21-day detoxification perpetuates the notion among addicts that detoxification from methadone is difficult or impossible and contributes to the bad reputation which methadone has developed among many active heroin addicts and the lay public. Patients may generalize their negative treatment experience making them less likely to return to any form of treatment. They may be left with the sense of personal failure and assume that they, rather than the treatment, are responsible for their continued drug use. The negative experience of detoxification confronts the addict again with failure associated with his attempt at a socially acceptable pursuit.

One argument used to justify the 21-day detoxification time limit is that it reduces the potential for minimally addicted individuals to become more severely dependent on methadone than they had been on heroin. The follow-up results of this study demonstrate that the gradual schedule does not result in a greater number of patients continuing or returning to methadone treatment.

Limitations of the Study

We had hoped to study a larger number of patients but were unable to do so despite an active recruitment program. One reason for the difficulty in obtaining subjects is undoubtedly the general decline in new cases of heroin addiction during the past two years. We believe a more important reason is the unpopularity of detoxification treatment among eligible addicts. All but the most naive heroin addicts know the important points of the FDA regulations. Recently addicted persons either tend to avoid treatment altogether, knowing that 21-day detoxification is all that is available to them, or misrepresent the length of their addiction and claim to have been addicted for two years. Data from other clinics indicate that although many patients will initially enroll as 21-day detoxification patients, they will be early treatment dropouts or will produce "evidence" that they have actually been addicted for two years and switch to a maintenance program. Thus, a well-intentioned rule has the effect of placing knowledgeable patients in the situation of either rejecting treatment or lying about their medical history in order to obtain adequate treatment. The 21-day detoxification rule requires clinicians to offer treatment to patients which the clinicians know will most likely be unsuccessful.

Despite a very high attrition rate, the differences between groups on several outcome measures reached statistical significance. In a sense, since treatment length may be the single most important outcome variable, the analysis of other outcome measures should not be criticized because of the high dropout rate in one study group. It is difficult to compare groups on other outcome measures when one of the experimental treatment conditions is so adverse that it is impossible to keep the patient in treatment.

The urinalysis results are particularly difficult to assess because of study attrition. Although there was a difference of 7% in the total number of positive results between groups, there are unmistakably lower rates of positive results in the 84-day group as the study progressed. However, the large dropout, particularly in the 21-day group, made statistical comparisons of the differences impossible.

Multiple Substance Abuse in Heroin Addicts

This study documents our clinical observation of increased multiple substance abuse in heroin addicts. Among other benefits, gradual detoxification from opioids in multiple substance abusers permits diagnosis of withdrawal symptoms from nonopioid drugs while rapid detoxification may temporarily mask the withdrawal symptoms from sedative-hypnotics or alcohol. These withdrawal syndromes are potentially more serious than the opioid withdrawal syndrome. Gradual detoxification increases the probability that patients will remain in treatment and experience fewer opioid withdrawal symptoms, which also increases the chances for other withdrawal syndromes to be diagnosed and adequately treated.[13]

What Is Rapid and What Is Gradual

It is important to maintain a perspective about what is rapid and what is gradual narcotic withdrawal. In a previous report [2] we compared 10-week and 30-week withdrawal schedules in methadone-maintained patients. This study demonstrated the superiority of the 30-week schedule over the 10-week schedule. The rapid schedule in our previous study was very similar to the gradual 84-day schedule used in our present work. There is every reason to believe that what we found with our methadone-maintained patients would also be true of our recently addicted detoxification patients: treatment results are better with gradual withdrawal schedules.

It is our clinical impression that if a study were conducted comparing three-week, 12-week, and 30-week withdrawal schedules in recently addicted people, the 30-week group would do better during detoxification followed by the 12-week group, and the three-week group.

Medical Detoxification vs. Comprehensive Addiction Treatment

At the time the 21-day detoxification time limit was established, methadone-based comprehensive drug abuse treatment was just beginning to develop. In many clinics treatment consisted of little more than the dispensation of methadone. Over the past seven years, prompted in part by FDA and National Institute on Drug Abuse policy, methadone treatment has become one aspect of a comprehensive approach which also includes counseling, legal assistance, family therapy, and employment training or placement. In order for any of these treatment components to occur, the patient must cease heroin use and be relatively free from withdrawal symptoms.[14] Our study indicates that to a certain extent this is possible with patients detoxified on an 84-day schedule; clearly, patients treated with methadone for 21-days missed the opportunity for the social and interpersonal aspects of treatment to occur.

Benefits of the 21-day detoxification regulation have not been observed. On the other hand, reports of high failure rates for this technique in out-patient settings have been frequently published. For example, on the basis of a large follow-up study, Sells *et al.*[15] have concluded that detoxification was not an effective treatment. Our data support this conclusion. Furthermore, our data indicate that the 21-day detoxification time limit is too short to enable the physician to keep withdrawal symptoms at a tolerable level. Finally, our results indicate that the more gradual 84-day schedule did not result in an increase in the number of patients who would require long-term maintenance. We believe that the data presented in this paper should stimulate a review of current detoxification policies.

Acknowledgments

We thank Mark Joseph for the data analysis; Karen Sobieraj, Marsha Baumgardner, and John Krystal assisted in the preparation of the manuscript. The Illinois Dangerous Drugs Commission provided data for the follow-up.

References

1. Methadone listing as a new drug with special requirements. December 15, 1972. Federal Register, Part III. **37**(242):26790–26807.
2. Senay, E. C., W. Dorus, F. Goldberg & W. Thornton. 1977. Withdrawal from methadone maintenance. Arch. Gen. Psychiatry **34:**361–367.
3. Silsby, H. & F. S. Tennant, Jr. 1974. Short-term ambulatory detoxification of opiate addicts using methadone. Int. J. Addict. **9:**167–170.
4. Werner, D., R. G. Newman, C. Hooper & R. Craig. 1973. Experience of large-scale ambulatory detoxification program. Proceedings, Fifth National Conference on Methadone Treatment. NAPAN. New York.
5. Wilson, B. K., R. R. Elms & C. P. Thomson. 1975. Outpatients vs. hospital methadone detoxification: an experimental comparison. Int. J. Addict. **1:** 13–21.

6. DEANGELIS, G. G. & W. X. LEHMANN. 1973. Adolescents and short-term low dose methadone maintenance. Int. J. Addict. **8:**853–863.
7. PAULUS, I. & R. HALLIDAY. 1967. Rehabilitation and the narcotic addict: results of a comparative methadone withdrawal program. Can. Med. Assoc. J. **96:**655–659.
8. TENNANT, F. S., JR., B. A. RUSSELL, S. K. CASS & R. N. BLEICH. 1975. Heroin detoxification: a comparison of propoxyphene and methadone. J. Am. Med. Assoc. **232:**1019–1022.
9. CANADA, A. T., JR. 1972. Methadone in a 30-day detoxification program: a critical review. Int. J. Addict. **7:**613–617.
10. GOLDSTEIN, A. 1972. Heroin addiction and the role of methadone in its treatment. Arch. Gen. Psychiatry **26:**291–297.
11. GOLDSTEIN, A. 1972. The pharmacologic basis of methadone treatment. Presented at the Fourth National Conference on Methadone Treatment. San Francisco.
12. KAISTHA, K. K., R. TADRUG & R. JANDA. 1975. Simultaneous detection of commonly abused drugs in a urine screening program using thin-layer identification techniques. J. Chromatography **107:**359–379.
13. SMITH, D. E. & D. R. WESSON. 1970. A new method for treatment of barbiturate dependence. J. Am. Med. Assoc. **213:**294–295.
14. BOURNE, P. G. & J. D. SLADE. 1974. Methadone: the mechanism of its success. J. Nerv. Ment. Disorders **159**(5):371–375.
15. SELLS, S. B., R. A. DEMARIE & C. W. MORNICK. 1978. The comparative effectiveness of methadone maintenance, therapeutic community, outpatient drug-free, and outpatient detoxification treatments for drug users in the DARP. IBR Technical Report. 78–4. Texas Christian University. Fort Worth, Texas.

DETOXIFICATION AFTER METHADONE MAINTENANCE TREATMENT

Paul Cushman, Jr.

Department of Pharmacology, Medicine and Psychiatry
Medical College of Wisconsin and DePaul Rehabilitation Hospital
Milwaukee, Wisconsin 53221

Methadone has been administered to thousands of opiate dependent persons since its acceptance as a standard maintenance treatment for opiate addiction in the 1960s. Extensive studies have recorded the impact of methadone maintenance on the drug use[1–3] reduction in criminal activities,[4] improvement in the adverse health consequences, including lowered mortality rates of the methadone recipients compared to the untreated opiate addict controls.[5] Few medical efforts have been so amply documented regarding the effectiveness of treatment in health, behavioral and pharmacological terms.

Nevertheless, controversy continues to rage over this not-well-understood treatment process. Much concern centers around the concept that drug dependent persons should be supplied a substitute drug for extensive periods of time. Most accept the pragmatic aspects of opioid maintenance treatment but greatly prefer its cessation after a term of treatment to the concept of indefinite maintenance.

Thus patients' desires to detoxify are augmented by ubiquitous external pressures. Pressures come from the local and national regulatory bodies, which have set up regulatory requirements periodically to justify continuation of methadone treatment for each individual patient. In addition other pressures come from treatment persons themselves.[6]

Now 15 years later it is instructive to examine what happens to methadone treated narcotic addicts. How often do spontaneous remissions occur? Are those in treatment better or worse than those who left? What problems do the methadone treated patients experience during and after detoxification? What factors, if any, can be identified as predictors of the capability to refrain from extensive opiates after detoxification?

By mid-1979 in New York City, which has had the largest treatment experiences with addicts, about 27,000 persons were actively taking methadone according to the methadone maintenance registry of the Community Treatment Foundation (CTF).[7] Yet another 58,000 individuals or 68.2% of all those who had ever been registered as methadone maintenance recipients in greater New York area were no longer in active treatment. Thus the majority of 85,000 methadone recipients had received methadone temporarily. The CTF records showed readmissions outnumbered the new admissions to treatment by 2:1. Since the incidence of narcotic addiction had dropped recently,[8] the high rates of readmissions indicated that former methadone recipients did not always do well.

Spontaneous Recovery after Opiate Use

Although many are exposed to opiates, only some use them often enough to become addicted. A sizeable number of opiate dependent persons are able to discontinue their use spontaneously. This may apply especially to young recently addicted persons, who may be more experimenting with drugs than chronically addicted to them.[9] The epidemiological studies of Robins *et al.*[10, 11] of the Vietnam veteran, who had used opiates in Vietnam, revealed low rates of continuing opiate use after return to the United States, suggesting that cultural and environmental factors are of great importance.

Of course, methadone maintenance is offered only to those who are beyond the experimentation stage. This population is generally believed to have high relapse rates. Yet data exist to support the view that some chronic addicts will achieve stable abstinence from opiates.[12–15] Perhaps 3% of the hard core chronic urban heroin addicts will stop using heroin, apparently permanently, each year.[14, 15] Recently, Robbins has argued that termination of narcotic addiction often occurs after a mean of about 8–9 years of addiction.[9] Therefore, it would be expected that some methadone maintained patients would be able to detoxify and remain abstinent from narcotics. Whether they are permanently abstinent or in remission cannot be accurately predicted until their full life span is completed.

Detoxification Categories

In the first category are patients who abscond or who voluntarily decide to stop treatment against the advice of their treatment center. Then there are those who detoxify in confinement, as in jail or other institutions. Thirdly, there are others who are administratively discharged after violation of some important rule. Finally there are those who underwent a supported detoxification in their clinic with both the staff and patient in agreement. This group can be termed therapeutic detoxificated persons (TD).

Patients undergoing TD are usually those with few recent drug abuses, with stable residences and occupations, who display responsible behavior regarding methadone and other aspects of life. This regimen includes a psychologically supported detoxification with weekly decrements of about 5 mg or less until the dose is about 20 mg/day, whereupon the decrements are decreased to no more than 2.5 mg weekly, a process that can be slowed or discontinued depending upon the individual patient. A careful study by Senay *et al.*[16] showed a 30 week regimen with average weekly decrements of 3 mg to be much superior to a 10 week rapid detoxification schedule amongst methadone maintenance patients. Other alternatives, as the use of repeated injections of naloxone until the symptoms of opiate abstinence are no longer evident, have not had adequate study or wide acceptance.[17] The use of other opiate agonists, as propoxyphene, a weak oral analogue of methadone, has not had adequate study for its efficacy in opiate detoxification.[18]

Recently, the oral alpha adrenergic agonist, clonidine, has been reported to be very effective in alleviating the symptoms of opiate withdrawal and craving for narcotics.[19] This drug is thought to inhibit sympathetic outflow emanating from the locus cereuleus, a central nervous system center which may serve as a final pathway for the symptoms of opiate abstinence. Any nonopioid which can ameliorate the symptoms of opiate withdrawal would represent a major aid in detoxification. However, the long term fate of patients whose detoxification include clonidine-like drugs are needed before it will be possible to conclude what role this treatment may play in detoxification. Over the years, getting the addict to stop heroin has been relatively easy. The big problem is to prevent relapse.

Some Factors in Detoxification Outcomes

It is difficult to quantify the relative importance of each variable in the detoxification process, but opiate withdrawal symptoms are clearly important. As detoxification proceeds, symptoms associated with opiate abstinence frequently appear, i.e., anxiety, hyposomnia, restlessness, difficulty in concentrating, yawning, gastrointestinal hyperactivity and disturbed sexual activity. Diagnosed by the narcotic patients as withdrawal and usually interpreted as a cue for additional narcotics, these symptoms most frequently occur when the methadone dose is below 20 mg/day. Methadone treatment centers are well aware that patients who are not detoxifying may complain of these symptoms also. These pseudo-withdrawal features may relate to methadone dosage negotiation by the patients, or from past conditioned responses to various stimuli, or from the patient's difficulties in distinguishing between opiate abstinence and anxiety. These symptoms may slow down or even abort detoxification. For example, in an early study at St. Luke's of a group of persons trying to detoxify, about one-fourth did not succeed in stopping methadone within one year because of the symptoms associated with opiate abstinence.[20] Some of these subjects were later able to detoxify in a very slow process.

Patients undergoing detoxification need considerable special attention, often more than prior to their detoxification. They should have the opportunity to discuss their symptoms, and problems on all return visits to their clinics. After the last methadone dose has been dispensed, the treatment centers should offer aftercare, especially to help with narcotic related problems which may become evident by self report or by urinalysis in which drug excretion may be detected. Those who drop out unexpectedly warrant vigorous efforts to locate by various means, since they may need help. Retreatment should be offered readily when clinically warranted.

Results of Detoxification

Present status after detoxification was studied in a sample derived from a composite registry of all the New York City methadone programs.[21] Vincent P. Dole and Herman Joseph constructed a random stratified sample of 897 out of 17,000 persons listed as being in methadone maintenance treatment in 1972 in the New York City methadone registry. A second cohort of all 647 persons in treatment in 1964–65 was included, although the latter group differed notably from the former group in their higher retention rates in treatment and may have been more highly motivated for methadone treatment than the later cohorts. Data pertaining to their present status were obtained from personal interviews and from institutional records, including those of their treatment centers (TABLE 1).

Opiate users were classified as opiate^{++}, when the patients admitted weekly use at least 3 times, or who had entered an opiate detoxification program, or whose death included opiates at autopsy. Opiate^{+} included those whose admitted opiate use was less than three times weekly. Opiate 0 were those whose records

TABLE 1

STATUS IN TREATMENT COMPARED TO STATUS AFTER DISCHARGE

	Active Continuously in Treatment N	(%)	Readmitted N	(%)	Discharged N	(%)
Opiate ++	5	(1)	8	(3)	540	(64)
Opiate +	12	(2)	16	(7)	50	(6)
Opiate 0						
Other Problems *	195	(34)	97	(40)	184	(22)
Apparently Well	355	(63)	120	(50)	72	
Total	567		241 †		846	

* Problems: alcoholism, nonopiate drugs, criminal activity with arrest, death not caused by opiate abuse.

† The group of 241 subjects listed as "Readmitted" is a subgroup of the total number discharged (846). None of the readmitted subjects had qualified for "Apparently Well" status while discharged. Therefore all of the 120 persons classified as "Apparently Well" while in readmitted status had previously been in "Opiate, ++" "Opiate +" or "Opiate 0 with Problems" status prior to readmission. The remainder of the discharged persons (605) had not been readmitted to any maintenance program or had been readmitted for too short a period for evaluation (less than 3 months).

and histories did not disclose opiate use. Opiate 0 was subdivided into those who were apparently well from those who had problems: i.e., alcohol, or other drug abuse, criminal activities including arrests, and deaths not due to opioids.

In a remarkable feat of follow-up, reaching 92% of the target groups, these investigators found that the patients who had remained continually in treatment had much higher rates of opiate 0 apparently well-compared to those who left treatment. Those who left treatment had high rates of admitted opiate use (70%) and amongst the others without opiate use there were high frequencies of problems. In the entire series only about 8% were judged to be well, free of problems and nonusers of opiates. The sizeable and important group of persons who had received methadone treatment, became detoxified, and returned to treatment tended to have much lesser opiate use, and much fewer problems than the discharged and not readmitted group. This retreated group resembled the group who had remained in continuous treatment.

There was no relationship between ethnic grouping, gender, or educational achievements and the more favorable outcomes. Nor were the age of first use of heroin, age on admission to methadone (which is usually set above 18 years), number of arrests, number of years of addiction prior to entry into methadone treatment associated with favorable outcomes (TABLE 2). On the other hand, methadone treatment of at least three years was associated with more favorable outcomes than shorter treatments. Records in the treatment centers showing no problems in the clinic and steady employment were all separately identified as strong variables associated with favorable outcomes.

Prospective Studies of Detoxification

Detoxification was studied in three New York City clinics which tried to keep track of all patients who had been treated. Fortunately, the treatment methods, data collection and, for the most part, treatment philosophies were sufficiently similar to allow pooling of data. The Cornell-New York Hospital methadone clinic started in 1968 [22] and has treated 158 adolescent patients in 10 years. This treatment unit aimed for ultimate detoxification after many months of methadone maintenance treatment. The Mt. Sinai Methadone Maintenance and After Care Treatment Program [23] began in 1969 and treated 1220 adults with the aim of indefinite methadone maintenance. St. Luke's Hospital methadone treatment program began in 1966 and treated 646 adults with indefinite maintenance.[24] In TABLE 3 are listed the numbers in treatment, the discharges related to transfers and deaths, or administrative, or confinement, or absconders (with voluntary detoxification, not assented in by staff at Mt. Sinai only) therapeutic detoxifications (TD) and those remaining in treatment.

TABLE 2

STATUS IN POST-TREATMENT PERIOD RELATED TO STATUS IN TREATMENT

					Opiate 0			
	Opiate ++ (N=540)		Opiate + (N=50)		Other Problems (N=184)		Apparently Well (N=72)	
	(Mos.)		(Mos.)		(Mos.)		(Mos.)	
Mean Time in Treatment	16.64		23.07		32.52		46.62	
Distribution (Mos.)	(%)		(%)		(%)		(%)	
0–12	57	(87%)	58		44		22	
13–36	30		22		18		25	
37–60	9		6		16		22	(53%)
61–84	3		6		12		10	
85–108	1		8		8		18	
> 108	0		0		2		3	
	N	(%)	N	(%)	N	(%)	N	(%)
Problems in Clinic *								
None	127	(12)	17	(37)	35	(19)	63	(88)
Illicit Opiates	68	(13)	5	(10)	5	(3)	1	(1)
Nonopiates	115	(21)	9	(18)	20	(11)	3	(4)
Alcohol	127	(24)	9	(18)	59	(32)	3	(4)
Arrests	71	(13)	7	(14)	23	(13)	1	(1)
Behavior, Psychological	85	(16)	6	(12)	15	(8)	0	(0)
Unknown	45	(8)	4	(8)	27	(15)	1	(1)
Employment								
Steady	87	(16)	16	(32)	53	(29)	45	(63)
Occasional	93	(17)	10	(20)	26	(14)	11	(15)
None	272	(50)	23	(46)	60	(33)	14	(19)
Unknown	88	(16)	1	(2)	45	(24)	2	(3)

* Some patients had multiple problems. Therefore, the sum is greater than 100%.

TABLE 3

TEN YEAR EXPERIENCE IN METHADONE TREATMENT IN THREE LARGE N.Y.C. CENTERS' CATEGORIES OF DISCHARGE

Series	Total in Treatment	Remaining in Treatment	Deaths and Transfers	Voluntary Absconders	Confinement	Therapeutic Detoxification	Administrative
Cornell–N.Y. Hospital	153	49 (32%)	23 (15.0%)	15 (9.8%)	4 (2.9%)	45 (29.4%)	17 (11.1%)
Mt. Sinai	1220	559 (45.8%)	123 (10.1%)	225 (18.4%)	89 (7.3%)	88 (7.2%)	136 (11.1%)
St. Luke's	646	288 (44.5%)	133 (20.5%)	42 (6.5%)	28 (4.3%)	89 (13.8%)	66 (10.2%)
TOTAL	2019	896 (44.3%)	279 (13.8%)	282 (13.9%)	121 (6.0%)	222 (11.0%)	219 (10.8%)

It is notable that 44.3% of the aggregate 2019 individuals are still in methadone treatment and that the rates of discharge in the various categories were similar in all three treatment groups. About 11% had undergone TD, but the individual clinics ranged from 7.2–29.4% for discharge in the TD category.

Criteria for relapse to opiate use included: readmission into methadone or other opiate treatment programs, admission of opiate use, and/or detection of opioids in the urine at any time since discharge. Apparently abstinent persons were those who were not known to have relapsed. For Cornell-New York Hospital only, patients judged drug abusers included those who are compulsively or heavily using drugs or alcohol. Therefore, in the Cornell-New York Hospital group, occasional drug abusers were grouped within the apparently abstinent.

Abstinence after Detoxification

The numbers of patients classified as abstinent from narcotics are listed in Table 4 for the three New York City clinics, in four discharge categories. The results show that about 25% were judged abstinent. Compared to all patients entering treatment (2019) or those remaining after deaths and transfers are subtracted (1740) 9 or 11%, respectively, were judged abstinent for narcotics. In the follow-up which accounted for 83% of the patients, most of the abstinent patients (70.8%) had become so as a result of the TD process, while those who became abstinent after voluntary detoxification or absconding were only about 2% of the total under consideration but amounted to 16.6% of the total judged to be abstinent. Very few were classified as abstinent after confinement or administrative discharge.

These data show that the better rehabilitated patients who agreed to a prolonged detoxification in the clinic had a much greater chance of apparently maintaining abstinence from narcotics than those who were jailed, administratively discharged, or who detoxified without the assent of the clinic's staff.

Variables Associated with Sustained Abstinence from Narcotics

In the outcome data of the three New York City clinics, the length of addiction prior to entry into methadone treatment was not a variable at St. Luke's or Mt. Sinai. More abstinence was found in the more recently addicted persons over those youths with longer addiction histories in the Cornell-New York clinic. Perhaps the short periods of addiction amongst young methadone treated patients were associated with a lesser commitment to the life styles of the urban addict and greater potential for change.

The age at completion of detoxification was not a factor in outcome. In the St. Luke's series somewhat more persons over age 40 attempted detoxification than those under 40 years, but the rates of abstinence from narcotics in follow-up were not age related. At St. Luke's, highest educational achievements were not a factor in detoxification nor outcome of detoxification, nor was marital status nor manifest alcoholism.[25] Alcoholism, defined as daily use of four ounces of ethanol, is a large problem amongst methadone treated narcotic addicts.[26–27] What role alcohol abuse plays in methadone patients' outcome during and after detoxification from narcotics is not clear at this point.

The longest voluntary period of abstinence from narcotics prior to entry

TABLE 4

NARCOTIC STATUS AT TIME OF LAST FOLLOWUP BY CATEGORY OF DISCHARGE IN THREE LARGE N.Y.C. METHADONE CLINICS

Category of Discharge	Series	Number	Apparently Abstinent from Narcotics	Relapsed to any Narcotic Use	Dead or in Jail	Inadequate Followup
1—Absconders,	NY/C †	42	0	17 *	5	16
Voluntary	Mt. S.	116	26	63	10	17
Detoxified	St. L.	15	6	3	2	10
Total		173	32 (18.5%)	83 (48%)	17 (9.8%)	43 (24.9%)
2—Administrative	NY/C	66	2	28 *	11	27
	Mt. S.	136	18	95	6	17
	St. L.	17	1	11	2	2
Total		219	21 (9.6%)	134 (61.2%)	19 (8.6%)	46 (21%)
3—Therapeutic	NY/C	59	41	15 *	2	1
Detoxification	Mt. S.	88	50	22	7	9
	St. L.	89	41	27	6	15
Total		236	132 (55.9%)	64 (27.1%)	15 (6.3%)	25 (10.4%)
4—Confinement	NY/C	–	–	–	–	–
	Mt. S.	89	4	66	10	9
	St. L.	28	0	11	10	7
Total		117	4 (3.4%)	77 (65.8%)	20 (17.4%)	16 (13.7%)

* Includes those whose narcotic or alcohol use was judged to be excessive. Distinction between narcotics only or alcohol plus narcotics or alcohol abuse only was not made.

† NY/C is New York Hospital/Cornell methadone program. Mt. S. is Mount Sinai Medical Center Methadone Maintenance and After Care Program. St. L. is St. Luke's Hospital Center methadone program.

into methadone treatment was not a significant variable in remaining abstinent from narcotics after a TD (less than 2 years vs. more than 2 years, chi square 1.2; $p < 0.30$).[20]

On the other hand, occupational status was a significant variable in both St. Luke's and Mt. Sinai. Full time employed persons did much better than those who were unemployed. However, this variable was an important part of the criteria for inclusion in the TD category and may not have been a separately acting variable.

The social milieu of the detoxified patients was a variable in that those whose social life was almost exclusively outside the drug world, except for their methadone clinic. had much greater probabilities of remaining abstinent than those whose social life was extensively in the drug subculture in the St. Luke's study.[25] These data are similar to those of Oppenheimer *et al.*[28] who found in a seven-year follow-up of English addicts that those who had a steady job, less contact with addicts, and in good health were more likely to have stopped using narcotics, although youth and recent onset of heroin use were also associated with high rates of abstinence from opioids.

Length of methadone treatment was a major factor in being classified as abstinent with longer treatment, (>3 years much better than shorter ones, <3 years). But long treatment was included in the TD procedures which usually was carried out over many months. (In the Mt. Sinai group after the components of the TD group were factored out, there was a slightly increased rate of return to addiction in those who had been treated for 24 and 36 months versus 12 months when duration of treatment was considered separately). During the lengthy detoxification process many patient-clinic contacts may have helped whatever psychological, social or pharmacological problems that may have arisen. Furthermore, patients receiving a slow, unpressured, open ended detoxification would have plenty of time to develop and employ coping skills without using narcotics which may have been useful after completing detoxification.

Therapeutic Detoxified Patients

Since the TD patients had the best outcomes, it is instructive to examine TABLES 3–4 together with some data from the New Haven Methadone Center, which seemed to have a comparable experience.[29] The frequencies with which TD was undertaken was low in all four centers, a mean of 12.6% (range of 7–39%, TABLE 5). The TD process was very long requiring 14–36 months (means). The follow-up was 1.6–2.8 years after last methadone, with acceptable accountability in three N.Y.C. clinics (83–98%). At the time of the outcome classification 55.1% (range of 46–69%) was apparently abstinent from narcotics.

Relapses in Relation to Time Since Last Methadone in the TD Group

The percentage of the known relapses and narcotics are plotted in FIGURE 1 as a function of time in the St. Luke's series. The solid line represents those known to relapse and the dotted line represents the relapse rate if all those who were no longer in contact with the clinics had relapsed immediately after their

TABLE 5

THERAPEUTIC DETOXIFICATION IN FOUR METHADONE CLINICS

Treatment Center	Total Ever Treated	Completed Therapeutic Detoxification	Duration Therapeutic Detoxification (months)	Duration of Followup (years)	Abstinent from Narcotics	Known Relapse to Narcotics	Not Adequately Followed
Cornell–N.Y.	151	59 (39%)	36	2.9 ± 1.9	69%	25%	2%
Mt. Sinai	1220	88 (7%)	22	2.3	57%	25%	10.3%
New Haven	242	49 (20%)	19.5	1.6	53%	24.5%	22.4%
St. Luke's	646	89 (14%)	14.5	2.4 ± 1.4	46%	30%	17%
Total	2259	285 (12.6%)			55.1%	26.7%	12.6%

last contact. It is evident that the frequency of relapse after last methadone was greatest immediately after the last methadone and that the likelihood of relapse was considerably less after 3 years of apparent abstinence.

These data differ impressively from the usual published experiences with chronic addicts where 80–90% of patients generally relapsed to opiates within six months.[9, 30]

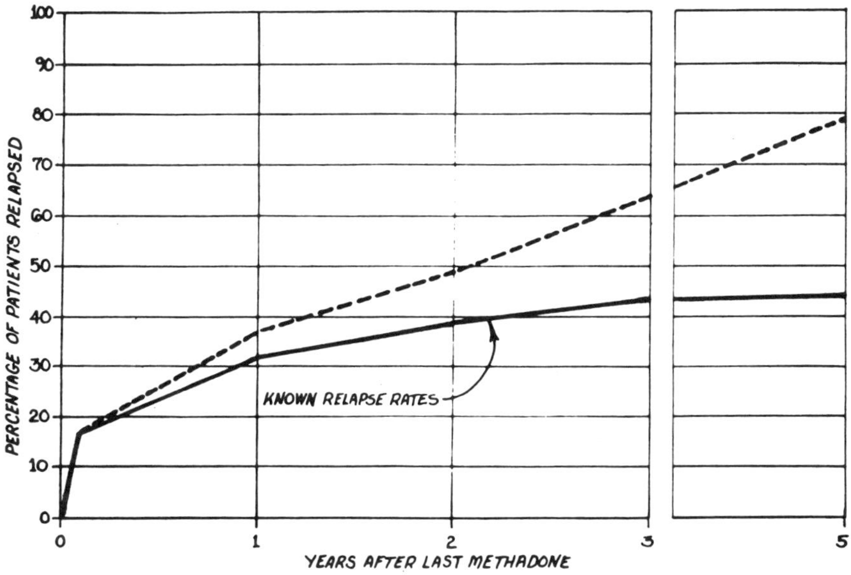

FIGURE 1. Relapses in 106 therapeutic detoxified patients.

DISCUSSION

Despite the pressures of various sorts to end methadone treatment, it appears that the great majority of patients did best if they stayed in treatment, better than those who left and returned to treatment and far better than those who were detoxified. To what extent these favorable outcomes were due to continuous availability of methadone as a substitute for other opioids cannot be determined. What part the continuing exposure of the patients to the clinics' rehabilitation services and referral mechanisms, or other factors cannot be evaluated.

Do methadone clinics hold patients unduly long? No. The small number of patients who seek detoxification against the advice of the clinics' staff can accomplish their ends. A few actually do achieve a sustained abstinence from narcotics. Could the process be accelerated? Based on past data, the answer would appear to be no. On the other hand, if the mechanics of detoxification are significantly changed and shortened with alpha adrenergic agonist treatment, the severity of the the primary narcotic withdrawal syndrome may be minimized. Thus, clonidine or other effective non-narcotic treatment would be worthwhile.

If the detoxification process requires time for supportive care to solidify rehabilitation achievements, and time to develop nondrug coping mechanisms, then shortening of the process might have drawbacks.

Patients seeking detoxification from methadone often are impetuous, requesting to be off methadone in an unrealistically short time. With only some justification, many tend to blame the methadone and their treatment centers for some of their problems. The data show that notions that they would be better off without methadone are often wishful thinking. Other patients use methadone for several months and seem to make many improvements in their adjustments to society, secure employment, reduce their illicit drug use sharply, and then decide that they do not need the drug anymore. If their rehabilitation has come about as a result of their being supplied with a low cost, orally effective long acting opiate agonist, then its discontinuation may jeopardize their rehabilitation and bring back some of their old problems, held in abeyance by the pharmacological effects of the methadone. Both the impetuous and the rapid initial responders should be discouraged from premature cessation of methadone treatment.

There is considerable evidence to support the view that narcotic addiction is a chronic relapsing condition. Cycles of addiction, remission and readdiction are well known. Methadone recipients also undergo cycles of addiction, treatment, detoxification and readdiction.[27] Accordingly, it makes sense to treat the exacerbations and to detoxify the patients when remission has occurred. The usage of active treatment capability would be especially efficiently deployed under such circumstances. Continue patients in treatment indefinitely, both those on methadone and those who completed detoxification. The long term goal of sustained abstinence is too infrequently achieved. Certainly outcome criteria of treatment might be employed to include some more global measures of function rather than whether or not narcotics are used: i.e., stability of family, residence, employment, degree of physical wellness, and lack of other drug abuse.

There are considerable variabilities amongst methadone treatment centers, despite their common basis of providing methadone to eligible recipients. Patients vary extensively; the degree to which patient-staff involvement occurs and is meaningful varies widely; some centers were little more than methadone filling stations[31] while others employed extensive supportive care. The expectations for patient improvement varies widely from center to center. Therefore, the results of treatment in the three to four centers in this study may not be generalizeable. One important variable, retention in treatment, was 44 percent over ten years in the present study, while a pool of centers in a study comparing LAAM and methadone had 50 percent drop out rates in only 40 weeks.[32]

Most addicts with sufficiently long history of narcotic addiction to receive methadone treatment will relapse after its discontinuation. The major exception seems to be the most rehabilitated patient, i.e., those with stable residences, jobs, no drug abuse, with the ability to plan ahead, and to derive satisfaction from life without the use of drugs. This group appears to need a long time for detoxification and many years in methadone treatment to achieve sustained abstinence from narcotics. The relapse rates of all the other groups are enormous. Even amongst those who did not appear to relapse to narcotics, there was heavy involvement with alcohol, other drug abuse, criminal activities and adverse health events which far exceeded these undersirable outcomes amongst patients who remained continually in treatment or those who had returned to methadone treatment.

REFERENCES

1. GEARING, F. R. 1971. Evaluation of Methadone maintenance treatment program. Methadone maintenance. S. Einstein, Ed.: 171–197. Marcel Dekker. New York, N.Y.
2. SELLS, S. B., R. G. DEMAREE, D. D. SIMPSON & G. W. JOE. 1971. Evaluation of present treatment modalities: Research with DARP admissions 1909–1973. Ann. N.Y. Acad. Sci. **311**:270–284.
3. GOLDSTEIN, A. 1972. Heroin addiction and the role of methadone in its treatment. Arch. Gen. Psychiatry **26**:291–301.
4. CUSHMAN, P. 1972. Methadone Maintenance Treatment of Narcotic Addiction. N.Y. State J. Med. **72**:1752–1756.
5. GEARING, F. G. & M. D. SCHWEITZER. 1974. An epidemiologic evaluation of long term methadone maintenance treatment. Am. J. Epidomiol. **100**:101–112.
6. BROWN, B. S., D. R. JANSEN & G. J. BERM. 1975. Changes in attitude toward methadone. Arch. Gen. Psychiat. **32**:214–218.
7. KONIGSBERG, L. Personal communication.
8. PAVELCIK, D. 1979. Many reasons for decline heroin abuse.: 5. U.S. J. Drug Alc. Dep.
9. ROBINS, L. N. 1799. Addict Careers. *In* Handbook on Drug Abuse. R. I. DuPont, A. Goldstein & J. O'Donnell, Eds.: 325–336. National Institute of Drug Abuse. Washington, D.C.
10. ROBINS, L. N., J. E. HELZER & D. H. DAVIS. 1975. Narcotic use in Southeast Asia and Afterward. Arch. Gen. Psychiat. **32**:955–972.
11. ROBINS, L. N., J. E. HELZER & M. HESSELBROCK *et al.* 1977. Vietnam veterans 3 years after Vietnam: how our study changed our views of heroin addiction. Problems of Drug Dependence. Proceedings of Committee on Drug Dependence. Richmond, Va.
12. NURCO, D. M., A. J. BONITO & M. LERNER. 1975. Studying Addicts over time: methodology and preliminary findings. Am. J. Drug Alc. Abuse **2**:183–188.
13. Burt Associates. 1977. Drug Treatment in Washington, D.C. and New York City: followup studies. National Institute of Drug Abuse. Service Research Monograph. DHEW publication No. 77-506. Washington, D.C.
14. VAILLANT, G. E. 1973. A 20-year followup of New York narcotic addicts. Arch. Gen. Psychiat. **29**:237–241.
15. RICHMOND, A. & E. V. BOWLES. 1975. Recent status of New York City narcotics addicts detoxified, 1961–3. Proceedings. National Drug Abuse Conference. New York City.
16. SENAY, E. C., W. DORUS & F. GOLDBERG *et al.* 1977. Withdrawal from methadone maintenance. Arch. Gen. Psychiat. **34**:361–369.
17. RESNICK, R. B., R. S. KESTENBAUM & A. WASHTON *et al.* 1977. Naloxone precipitated withdrawal: a method for rapid induction onto naltrexone. Clin. Pharm. Therap. **21**:409–416.
18. JASINSKI, D. R., J. S. PEVNICK & S. C. CLARK *et al.* 1977. Therapeutic usefulness of propoxyphene napsylate in narcotic addiction. Arch. Gen. Psychiatry **34**: 227–237.
19. GOLD, M. S. & H. D. KLEBER. 1979. A rational for opiate withdrawal symptomatology. Drug Alc. Dep. **4**:419–430.
20. CUSHMAN, P. & V. P. DOLE. 1973. Detoxification of rehabilitation methadone maintenance patients. J. Am. Med. Assoc. **226**:747–751.
21. DOLE, V. P. & H. JOSEPH. 1978. Long-term outcome of patients treated with methadone maintenance. Ann. N.Y. Acad. Sci. **311**:181–190.

22. MILLMAN, R. B., S. T. KHURI & M. E. NYSWANDER. 1978. Therapeutic detoxification of adolescent heroin addicts. Ann. N.Y. Acad. Sci. **311:**153–164.
23. STIMMEL B., J. GOLDBERG & M. COHEN *et al.* 1978. Detoxification from methadone maintenance risk factors associated with relapse to narcotic use. Ann. N.Y. Acad. Sci. **311:**173–184.
24. CUSHMAN, P. 1978. Methadone maintenance: long-term followup of detoxified patients. Ann. N.Y. Acad. Sci. **311:**165–172.
25. CUSHMAN, P. 1978. 10 years of methadone maintenance treatment. Am. J. Drug Alc. Abuse **4:**581–585.
26. STIMMEL, B., M. COHEN & R. HANBURY. 1979. Alcoholism and poly drug abuse in persons on methadone maintenance. Ann. N.Y. Acad. Sci. **311:**99–109.
27. SHUT, J., T. FILE & T. WOHLMUTH. 1973. Alcohol use by narcotic addicts in methadone maintenance treatment. Quant. J. Stud. Alc. **34:**1356–1367.
28. OPPENHEIMER, E., G. V. STIMSON & A. THORLEY. 1979. Seven-year followup of heroin addicts: abstinence and continued use compared. Br. Med. J. **2:**627–632.
29. RIORDAN, C. E., M. MEZRITZ & S. SLOBITZ *et al.* 1976. Successful detoxification from methadone maintenance. J. Am. Med. Assoc. **235:**2604–2608.
30. STEPHENS, R. & E. COTTRELL. 1972. A followup study of 200 narcotic addicts committed for treatment under Narcotic Addict Rehabilitation Act (NARA). Br. J. Addict **67:**45–48.
31. MANDEL, T. W., P. G. GOLDSCHMIDT & P. GROVER. 1973. Evaluation of treatment programs for drug abuse. Johns Hopkins School of Hygiene and Public Health. Baltimore, Md.
32. BLAINE, J. D., H. P. RENA & G. L. LEVINS *et al.* 1979. Clinical use of LAAM. Ann. N.Y. Acad. Sci. **311:**214–231.

LONG-TERM OUTCOMES AFTER TERMINATION FROM METHADONE MAINTENANCE TREATMENT *

Don C. Des Jarlais and Herman Joseph

New York State Division of Substance Abuse Services
Two World Trade Center
New York, New York 10047

Vincent P. Dole

The Community Treatment Foundation
New York, New York 10021

The methadone maintenance treatment program began as a research study of six patients in 1964 at Rockefeller University Hospital under the sponsorship of the Health Research Council of New York City. Following the success of this small pilot program, a structured treatment program was developed, combining pharmacological support and rehabilitative services. During the next ten years, with funding from the New York State Division of Substance Abuse Services and its predecessor agencies, the number of patients in treatment in the New York City area grew to a peak of 37,000.

From the beginning of this work and continuing until the fall of 1979, every patient admitted to maintenance treatment in the New York City area was listed in a common registry. This data service was administered during the first nine years by the research unit at Rockefeller University, and then was transferred to a not-for-profit corporation, The Community Treatment Foundation. It provided a continuous record of admissions, discharges and readmissions of methadone patients over a period of fifteen years. This historical registry was terminated in September 1979, when the Community Treatment Foundation ceased to operate, and identifying information was purged to protect patient confidentiality. Thus, the present study is in some respects unique; it cannot be continued and is unlikely to be repeated on such a large scale.

The central focus of this study was the long-term outcome of patients discharged from maintenance treatment. Some outcomes were known, as the registry did provide return to treatment data, but there was no information for those discharged patients who did not return to treatment. This study should not be considered an evaluation of methadone *maintenance* treatment, since, by definition, the benefits of a maintenance treatment will be largely confined to the during treatment period.

Sample

A sample of 1545 subjects was selected from the total listing of names in the registry—a pool of approximately 80,000 when the study was begun in 1975.

* Supported in part by Contract No. 5 H81-DA-01778-02 from the National Institute on Drug Abuse. Opinions expressed in this paper do not necessarily reflect official policy of the Division of Substance Abuse Services.

To permit analyses of historical changes in methadone maintenance treatment, subsamples were selected from two different time periods: 648 of the 661 † patients who entered treatment in 1965–66; and a stratified random sample of 897 from the 19,004 who first entered treatment in 1972. Nine hundred fifty-six patients had been discharged at least once by the time of data collection, and form the subsample for post-treatment outcomes.

Data Collection

The interviews were administered by trained ex-addicts, using a detailed summary form as a guide, but conducted in semi-structured manner, without a fixed order of questions or particular wordings of specific questions. It was found that this style of interviewing, and the use of peer group interviewers established a rapport with the subjects and led to more reliable data than could be obtained with more structured interviews and with interviewers who did not share the same cultural backgrounds as the subjects.

The interviews were usually conducted at the subject's place of residence, or in public places such as restaurants and bars. After completion, each interview was reviewed by the project director for completeness and consistency. If the interview appeared to be incomplete or inconsistent, or if the project director suspected that the subject had not been fully candid, the subject was reinterviewed by another interviewer.

Data were obtained from various correctional, health and other agencies, including registries of vital statistics, hospitals, criminal justice agencies and social service bureaus. The data were used for location of subjects prior to the personal interviews, for corroborating the statements made in the interviews and as a partial definition of outcome when a personal interview could not be obtained.

Interviews were conducted with 528 of the 956 discharged subjects (55%). For the 428 discharged subjects who were not interviewed, usable agency information was obtained for 357 (83%). As one would expect given the nature of agency records, this information uniformly indicated difficulties in post-treatment rehabilitation. It does not appear that there was a large number of subjects who "did well" after discharge and for whom follow-up information was not obtained.

Results

The post-treatment drug use must be considered in relation to the relatively long periods of intensive drug use prior to the first entry into methadone treatment. Table 1 presents the demographics, pretreatment histories, and duration of treatment for the 528 interviewed subjects. These subjects fit the description of the chronically addicted patients for whom methadone maintenance was originally designed. They averaged 11 years between their first use of heroin and their first entry into methadone maintenance treatment.

Figure 1 summarizes the post-treatment drug use for the 528 interviewed

† There were thirteen methadone patients who were admitted to a state hospital program, which subsequently closed. No records were available for these patients.

TABLE 1

DEMOGRAPHICS AND TREATMENT HISTORIES FOR 528 INTERVIEWED SUBJECTS

Sex	
Male	81%
Female	19%
Ethnicity	
Black	47%
Hispanic	29%
White	23%
Pretreatment arrests	
None	14%
One	11%
Two or more	75%
Mean age of first heroin use	17.7
Mean age at first entry into methadone treatment	28.6 yrs.
Mean time in first methadone treatment	2.1 yrs.
Mean time in follow-up period	1.9 yrs.
Percentage returning for additional treatment	52%

subjects. "Drug use" was defined as the most intense use of a particular drug class that was maintained for a period of at least one month. The "illicit narcotics" category was primarily heroin and nonprescribed methadone; the nonopiate category was primarily tranquilizers, sedatives, amphetamines and cocaine; and "heavy" alcohol use was defined as an average daily consumption

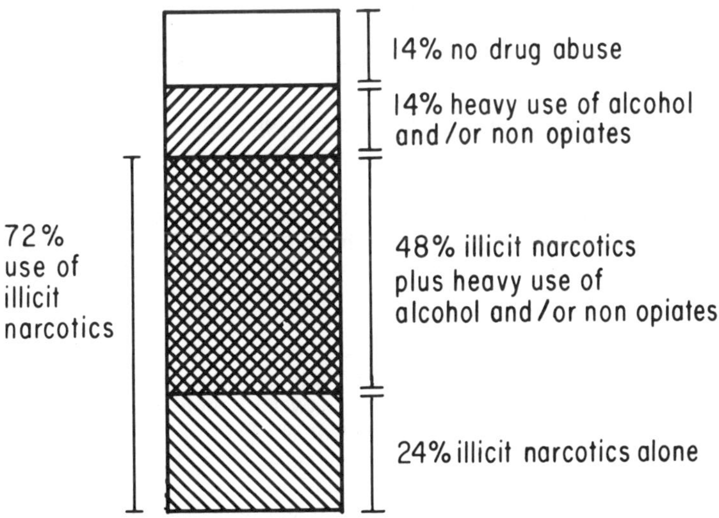

FIGURE 1. Incidence of drug abuse after discharge from methadone maintenance programs that included 528 interviewed subjects.

of four or more ounces of ethanol, however consumed. Marijuana use is not included in this report.

It should be noted that one seventh of the subjects in the drug-free category and in the nonopiate/heavy alcohol only category subsequently returned to maintenance treatment because they felt threatened with returning to narcotic use.

FIGURE 2 analyzes the use of illicit narcotic drugs at time of entry into treatment, during, and after treatment. Both the therapeutic effect of the treatment programs in suppressing use of illicit narcotics and the failure of this treatment to eliminate the underlying causes of narcotic abuse are clearly shown. While there is an important reduction in illicit narcotic use from time of entry to the post-treatment period, the majority of these subjects did return to illicit narcotics use in the post-treatment period.

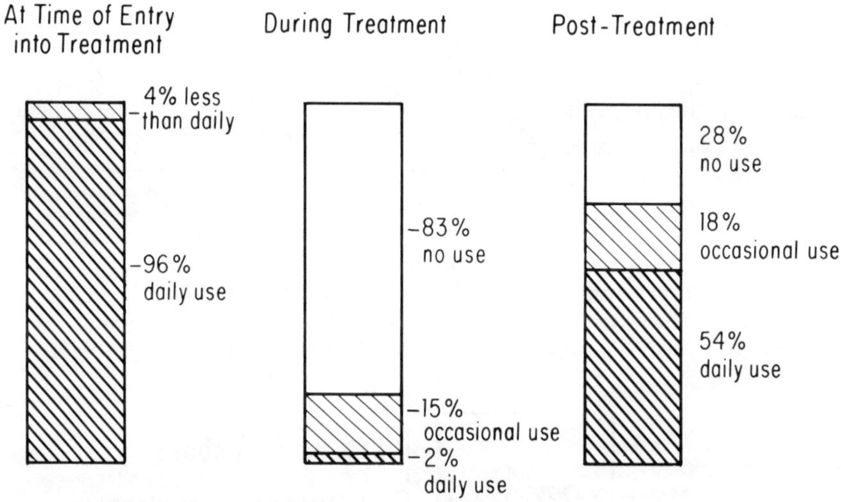

FIGURE 2. Incidence of illicit narcotic use before, during and after methadone maintenance treatment (528 subjects).

FIGURE 3 presents nonopiate use (sedatives, tranquilizers and stimulants) for the three time periods. Presumably the reduction in this type of drug abuse reflects the nonspecific effects of social rehabilitation in the programs, since methadone maintenance has no known pharmacological action against nonopiates.

Subjects who abused nonopiates in the post-treatment period tended to be those who had abused nonopiates at the time of entry and during treatment. There were relatively strong correlations between nonopiate abuse at the time of entry into treatment and during treatment ($r = .38$, $p < .001$), and between abuse during treatment and post-treatment ($r = .44$, $p < .001$). During treatment nonopiate abuse was only weakly linked to during treatment use of illicit narcotics ($r = .15$, $p < .001$), and post-treatment nonopiate use was moderately related to post-treatment illicit narcotic use ($r = .26$, $p < .001$)

FIGURE 4 shows the incidence of heavy alcohol use, defined as an average-

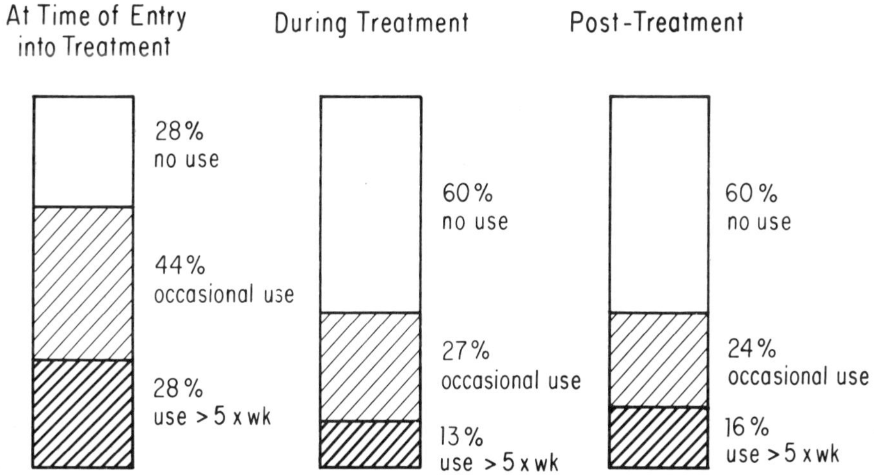

FIGURE 3. Incidence of nonopiate abuse before, during and after methadone maintenance treatment (528 subjects).

daily consumption of four or more ounces of ethanol per day. In general the subjects who drank heavily during and after methadone maintenance were those who had drunk heavily prior to treatment. The correlation between alcohol use at the time of entry and the during treatment period was 0.60, and between the during treatment and discharged periods was 0.49, both $p < .001$. Alcohol use was not related to nonopiate use or illicit narcotic use for any of the time periods.

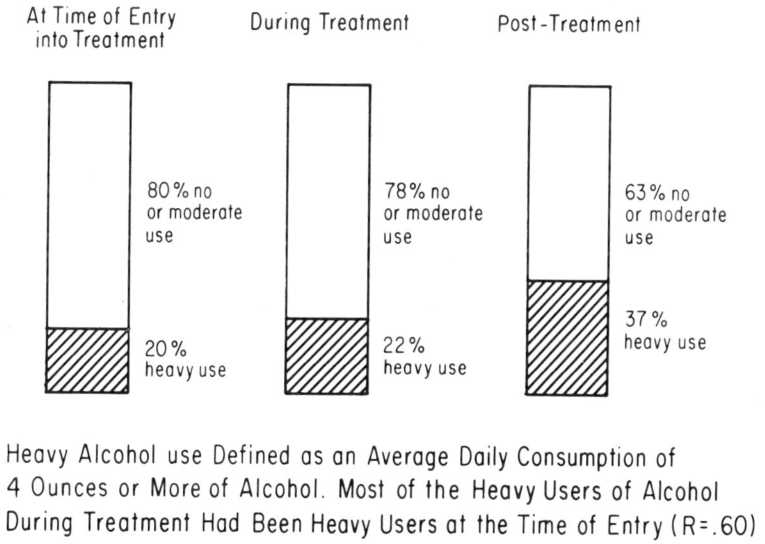

FIGURE 4. Incidence of alcohol abuse before, during and after methadone maintenance treatment (528 subjects).

TABLE 2 shows the association between the status of the subjects at termination and drug use in the post-treatment period. (Subjects who used both illicit narcotics and non-opiates/alcohol are included in the illicit narcotic use category.) The "good standing" discharge category includes those subjects who left treatment with the approval of the staff. They were the subjects who had completed their social rehabilitation within the program. While the precise criteria for this category varied from program to program, they generally included having a legitimate means of support, lack of alcohol and nonopiate abuse, and stable interpersonal relationships. The "premature" category includes those subjects who left without staff approval, but were not expelled from the programs (the "rule violation" category).

As one would expect, the patients who left the program in the good standing category had significantly less post-treatment drug abuse than those in the other two categories (chi square = 47.2, $p < .001$). Still, only one quarter of the subjects in this good discharge category did not abuse drugs, and more than half did return to illicit narcotics use.

TABLE 2

RELATION BETWEEN DISCHARGE CATEGORY AND OUTCOME AFTER DISCHARGE

	Drug Free (%)	Illicit Narcotics (%)	Alcoholism and/or Nonopiate Abuse (%)	(%)
"Good Standing"	10	22	7	39
"Premature"	1	13	3	17
"Rule Violation"	3	37	4	44
	14	72	14	(N=516)

DISCUSSION

First, we must emphasize that the subjects in this study had histories of intense and prolonged illicit narcotic use prior to their entry into methadone maintenance. Recall that these subjects averaged 11 years from their first use of heroin until they first entered methadone treatment. For subjects with lesser pre-treatment involvement in narcotic addiction, less post-treatment drug use is likely.[1, 2]

Second, there seem to be relatively distinct patterns of use for the different drug classes. Nonopiate use was only weakly or moderately correlated with illicit narcotic use; and heavy alcohol use was not correlated with either nonopiate or illicit narcotic use. The three types of drug use also showed marked differences in response to treatment and through time. There is a clear need for improving the treatment of nonopiate and alcohol abuse among methadone patients.

Finally, the present data are consistent with the reports of many previous investigators who have observed high rates of post-treatment drug abuse for persons chronically addicted to narcotics.[1-8] Indeed, we are not aware of any large sample follow-up study that has shown drug-free post-treatment outcomes for the majority of subjects with pretreatment histories comparable to those in the present group. Given present treatment methods, significant reductions in drug abuse can be achieved, but a permanent drug-free status does not appear to be a realistic goal for the majority of persons with a long pretreatment history of intensive heroin use, nor is social rehabilitation while in treatment an assurance of a drug-free status after treatment.

Other studies have also found that the probability of avoiding drug use in the post-treatment period increases with the extent of social rehabilitation accomplished while in the program.[4, 5] While it is difficult to compare data across studies, it appears that the stricter the criteria for "completed treatment/graduation" discharge, the greater the probability of remaining drug free after discharge. More research is clearly needed to determine the relative importance of the various criteria.

The expectation of leaving treatment appears to be very common among methadone maintenance patients. One study in New York City found that 100% of a sample of 115 methadone patients held detoxification and leaving maintenance treatment as a personal treatment goal.[9] The present data indicate that this may be an unrealistic goal for many patients. Given the relatively high probability that discharged patients will encounter drug abuse problems, further treatment needs to be made readily available. This further treatment should specifically include techniques for treating chronic nonopiate and alcohol abuse as well as treatment for chronic narcotic abuse.

Acknowledgments

We wish to express our gratitude for the invaluable assistance of James Schmeidler in the analysis of the data, and to Douglas S. Lipton for his thoughtful comments on an earlier draft.

References

1. Simpson, D., L. Savage, M. Lloyd & S. Sells. 1978. Evaluation of Drug Abuse Treatments Based on First Year Follow-up. National Institute on Drug Abuse Services Research Monograph. U.S. Department of Health, Education and Welfare. Public Health Service, publication ADM 78-701.
2. Panepinto, W., F. Silver, G. Ottomanelli & B. Kissin. 1976. A two year follow-up on patients therapeutically detoxified from methadone maintenance. Paper presented at the Fifth National Drug Abuse Conference. New York, N.Y.
3. Simpson, D., L. Savage & B. Sells. 1978. Data Book on Drug Treatment Outcomes. IBR Report 78-10. Institute for Behavioral Research. Texas Christian University. Fort Worth, Texas.
4. Cushman, P. & V. Dole. 1973. Detoxification of rehabilitated methadone-maintained patients. J. Am. Med. Assoc. **226:**747–752.
5. Stimmel, B., J. Goldberg, E. Rotkopf & M. Cohen. 1977. Ability to remain abstinent after methadone detoxification: A six year study. J. Am. Med. Assoc. **237:**1216–1220.
6. Kremen, E. & R. Bayer. 1973. New choices for methadone maintenance patients-planned, voluntary, long term detoxification. *In* Proceedings of the Fifth National Conference on Methadone. NAPAN: 667–674. New York, N.Y.
7. Lowinson, J. & J. Langrod. 1973. Detoxification of long term methadone

patients. *In* Proceedings of the Fifth National Conference on Methadone Treatment. NAPAN: 256–261. New York, N.Y.

8. RIORDAN, C., M. MEZRITZ, F. SOLBERT & H. KLEBER. 1976. Successful detoxification from methadone maintenance: Follow-up study of 38 patients. J. Am. Med. Assoc. **235**:2604–2607.
9. LANGROD, J., D. DES JARLAIS & J. LOWINSON. 1978. Locus of control and initiation of detoxification among male methadone maintenance patients. Paper presented at the National Drug Abuse Conference. Seattle, Washington.

GENERAL DISCUSSION

Joyce H. Lowinson, *Session Chair*

Albert Einstein School of Medicine
Bronx, New York 10461

KARL VEREBEY: Dr. Gold and colleagues did an excellent piece of work that allows us to look at the withdrawal syndrome, which has been a mystery for a long, long time to pharmacologists and people who are involved in the area of opiate dependence. I'd like to ask Dr. Gold how he envisions the temporal implementation of these new discoveries.

MARK GOLD: My own personal opinion about the use of clonidine would be as follows: That clonidine has the distinct advantage of being a nonopiate. So, one could take someone who had used the methadone program to get off the street, get away from needles, get a job, change friends, and so forth. Then while stable on a particular dose, the patient could be switched off methadone with clonidine and into the next phase, or "step," of treatment, which might include naltrexone. One could readily perform this switch on an inpatient basis within seven to ten days.

Also, in iatrogenic addictions there's always a question as to how they should be treated. Clonidine is apparently useful in reversing withdrawal symptoms in a wide variety of opioid drugs.

Clonidine's use in protracted abstinence is very interesting and encouraging and will require much additional work.

RICHARD RESNICK: Clonidine would also have use for people who don't want, or are not eligible, to receive methadone.

PAUL CUSHMAN: Concerning your theoretical formulations, wouldn't the failure of naloxone to increase spontaneous locus ceruleus electrical activities speak against the notion of its inhibition at the locus ceruleus?

MARK GOLD: That's an excellent question. Endogenous enkephalin produces tolerance at the level of the locus ceruleus, either through electrical or other stimulation. Enkephalins are probably not released continuously throughout the day, but rather are released after a stimulus, i.e., pain or other environmental event or something else. It's like a long neuroendocrine loop where arterial norepinephrine modulates the activity of the locus ceruleus through a feedback mechanism that involves the receptor that clonidine stimulates. Under normal physiological conditions, there's an ongoing inhibition of adrenergic activity through this system. Therefore, one can block the system, produce a loss of inhibition with piperoxane, or one can stimulate the system as if to imitate the endogenous norepinephrine, and turn the system off.

Although it hasn't been demonstrated that naloxone will increase locus ceruleus firing rate, what it does under conditions with increased firing rate, as pain, is to block the feedback through the opiate receptor, and thus inhibit the continued excitation of the locus ceruleus.

ARNOLD WASHTON: We've been doing some clinical work with clonidine during the past year. Our interest in clonidine was not from the standpoint of getting more information on neurobiological mechanisms, but in an attempt to try to facilitate the detoxification of patients who had made previous attempts to get off opiates, particularly methadone, and had been unsuccessful.

After treating approximately 150 patients, we found that clonidine can be used as a safe, acceptable, and an effective method of detoxifying opiate-dependent outpatients in a clinical setting. The most effective procedure that we have found after trying out several methods, was an abrupt switch from 25 mg or less daily methadone to clonidine. Individuals dependent upon much higher doses of methadone don't do as well. By successfully detoxified, we mean ten days opiate free and induced onto naltrexone.

If one is careful about adjusting the clonidine dose on a day-to-day basis according to the patient's symptomatology and blood pressure, the negative side effects can be avoided. Clonidine's efficacy relative to traditional methadone detoxification has not yet been established because we have done only open clinical trials at this time. I think it's safe to say that clonidine does offer a potentially useful treatment modality in cases where methadone is either inappropriate or unavailable.

HAROLD BLUMBERG (*New York Medical College*): Dr. Gold, if a patient injects heroin while on clonidine, can he become readdicted?

MARK GOLD: Although we have not carried out any experiments on that, I think the answer is definitely yes.

SIDNEY SCHNOLL (*Philadelphia*): Dr. Gold, is there a rebound when people come off clonidine, as in hypertension?

MARK GOLD: That was not a problem in the protocol that we use. I'd like to add that clonidine withdrawal itself also supports this neuradrenergic locus ceruleus hypothesis, i.e., chronic inhibition of locus ceruleus activity probably induces a tolerance to clonidine administration. On abrupt discontinuation, a "clonidine rebound" occurs, which, interestingly enough, includes anxiety and panic as well as hypertension.

Also, this rebound is associated with increased norepinephrine metabolites and MHPG excretion and probably could be treated with an opiate.

KIM KEELEY: The idea that a person should stay on methadone or in treatment for a long time is a very difficult concept for the public as well as my bureaucratic colleagues to accept. It strikes me that we should be able to say for drug abuse, just as we say for alcoholism, that treatment does help. We ought to do more. Especially, we should continue to provide treatment to patients during and after cessation of pharmacotherapy. I think we should never discharge them from treatment. We should allow them to remain in a treatment setting to explore abstinence, if that's what they desire, without having to say that treatment is over, no more methadone, and we're not going to see you unless you come back to us again. It would allow us to make a much more positive description of the results of treatment, whether it involves methadone or not.

DONALD DES JARLAIS: I would second your point that continuation of treatment does not necessarily mean continuation of methadone for all persons. In these outcome data, 28 percent did not go back to illicit narcotics after discharge. Although approximately 40 percent of them were having alcohol or other drug use, the treatment should provide for some treatment continuation for other drug problems beyond the end of methadone maintenance. Also, the simple provision of resuming methadone maintenance should be readily available.

Robert Millman: A major problem with continuing rehabilitative contacts with patients after they have completed detoxification is that patients don't want to come back to clinics. The facilities are generally unattractive, overcrowded, and fraught with bad associations. If the therapeutic milieu of programs were more positive, the staff-patient ratios better, and more useful services available, patients might continue to attend programs after they are drug free.

Chairman Lowinson: We must educate the bureaucrats, legislators, and other policy makers so that they understand better the phenomenon of a chronic relapsing disease where treatments might be tailored to the situation.

Charles Riordan: Dr. Senay, you talked about 21- and 84-day detoxifications. We know from some of the studies that Don Jasinski did that even a single dose of methadone followed by naloxone can produce symptoms of withdrawal. Is it wise to try to do a 21- or 84-day detox? You'd probably be giving people more opioids than they would have received on the street given the low level of purity of street samples.

Might we not really be creating a much greater dependence in some individuals in our attempt to detox than they would have if they were just continuing to use street drugs?

Edward Senay: We're in a position of having to respond to patient requests and patient needs. The amount of methadone we gave, 20 mg in both of these groups, was probably roughly comparable to what they were getting on the street. I don't think we worsened things for them. The position you're adopting ignores the fact of psychosocial crisis, which we know surrounds people when they come into treatment.

Paul Cushman, Jr.: Dr. Washton, you have had 75 patients detoxified with clonidine and have them off clonidine for various periods of time. How many of them have gone back on narcotics?

Arnold Washton: We haven't really done any kind of formal outcome study.

Duke Stanton (*University of Pennsylvania*): We recently looked at 16 demographic variables prior to treatment in methadone patients, and treatment outcomes. Eleven of the variables were similar to those on Dr. Cushman's charts. Six of them did emerge with such correlations. One was employment, as so many studies have shown. Also, family parameters, as living with parents, frequency of contact with family of origin, whether the parent had a spouse-type person in the house.

We agree that outcome is not related to sex and education levels. Also, a fairly strong predictor was type of discharge. We also did a factor analysis of many pretreatment narcotic variables such as arrests, time from first use to entry into treatment, time spent in institutions, time spent on the street using, and time spent on the street not using. All these collapsed to a single factor, which was fairly strongly related to post-treatment outcomes. The longer the time from first use until entry into treatment, the more likely the person was to return to narcotic use.

Index of Contributors

(Italicized page numbers refer to comments in Discussions)